S0-BYG-990

1295

Public Administration: Government in Action

Ivan L. Richardson

Sidney Baldwin

Both, California State University at Fullerton

Charles E. Merrill Publishing Company
A Bell & Howell Company
Columbus, Ohio 43126

MERRILL POLITICAL SCIENCE SERIES

Under the editorship of

John C. Wahlke

Department of Political Science
The University of Iowa

Published by
Charles E. Merrill Publishing Company
A Bell & Howell Company
Columbus, Ohio 43126

This book was set in Melior.
The production editor was Linda Gambaiani.
The cover was designed by Will Chenoweth.

Copyright © 1976 by Bell & Howell Company. All rights reserved. No part of this book may be reproduced in any form, electronic or mechanical, including photocopy, recording, or any information storage and retrieval system, without permission in writing from the publisher.

ISBN: 0-675-08605-1

Library of Congress Catalog Card Number: 75-36883

2 3 4 5 6 7 8 — 83 82 81 80 79 78 77 76

Printed in the United States of America

To our wives, Jane Richardson and Diana Baldwin, and to our families — Robert, Ann, and John Richardson, Susan and Jane Baldwin

Preface

From its very beginning, public administration has been burdened with a philo-sophical dualism in which there is a pairing of opposites, such as mind and body, thinking and doing, policy and administration, fact and value, effi-ciency and equity, organization and individual. As a result of such dualism, the house of public administration has been compartmentalized into different schools of thought, perspectives, paradigms, and approaches. This book rep-resents an attempt to introduce the subject of public administration to the new student, and to map some of the terrain of public administration in a more ecumenical spirit. The central organizing principle underlying this book is that while govenment is many things, it is intended to act, and that the pivot on which government turns is public administration. The book's point of view, then, is not that of a separate academic discipline, but rather a recogni-tion that the tasks of government must be performed.

A second ecumenical feature of this book is an attempt to find a balance between theory and practice, between the concerns of the scholar and those of the practitioner. Admittedly, there is tension between the academic world and the world of practice, but that tension is viewed in this book as an op-portunity rather than a calamity.

A third ecumenical element is the attempt to pursue a balance between levels of government — national, state, regional, and local. In other words, the authors find significance for public administration in the work of governments in Washington, D.C., state capitals, regional centers, and local jurisdictions.

The book consists of twenty-one chapters, organized into five parts dealing with the following: the study of public administration, public administration in the web of government, the task of public administration, public administration as management, and the challenge of change.

No attempt is made to be totally comprehensive; the authors do not tell the reader everything they know or think they know about the subject of public administration. This field is evolving in a world of great and rapid change. Much is tentative. But every effort is made in this book to identify those ideas, practices, institutions, and problems that are pertinent to governance during the 1970s.

I. L. R.

S. B.

Contents

Figures
and
Tables

The
Study
of
Public
Administration

Introduction

1

Over the ages, certain social roles have emerged as paramount in society — priests, warriors, master builders, law-givers, philosopher-kings, and merchants. With the rise of the "administrative state" in the twentieth century, such a role is now played by the government bureaucrat, the public executive, or the public administrator, as he or she is variously called. Public administration — the study and practice of the tasks associated with the conduct of the administrative state — is now recognized as a central concern in the art and science of governance. The purpose of this book is to present some of the leading ideas, institutions, practices, and issues involved in modern American public administration.

Definition of Public Administration

For more than three quarters of a century, public administration in the United States has eluded an authoritative definition that could win and hold the acceptance of most scholars and practitioners. Political scientists, for instance, have generally regarded public administration as a political process and as an academic subdivision of their discipline. Some scholars in the field of management, such as Peter F. Drucker, have viewed public administration as concerned primarily with work processes included in the scope of general management. People with a strong legalistic perspective have preferred to treat public administration as an extension of lawmaking and the adjudication of disputes. And those who are concerned primarily with the making and evaluation of public policy have regarded public administration as a stage in the cycle of public policy making, administration, review, and revision.[1]

The complex character of public administration reflected in such views was further illustrated at the 1973 National Conference of the American Society for Public Administration — the major professional association of public administrators in the United States. For five days, participants explored the problems of crime prevention, mass transportation, health care delivery, welfare administration, tax administration, environmental protection, human resources development, voluntary armed forces, management of social change, labor-management negotiation, and federal revenue sharing. There was also a panel discussion on "Future Shock: How To Succeed At Insanity Without Really Trying," and one on "What Every Public Administrator Can Learn From the Jesus Freak Movement." The ambitious theme of the conference was declared to be, "Putting It All Together."[2]

During the past few years, however, progress has been made in at least identifying some of the key attributes of modern public administration. For instance, Stephen K. Bailey, in examining the purposes of public administration theory, has implicitly posited three basic qualities or concerns in public administration: (1) a striving toward achievement of the public interest in the making of public choices; (2) a concern with management technology; and (3) an interest in organizational behavior and the behavior of individuals and groups within organizations. This perception of public administration also underlies the approach of Lewis C. Mainzer who, in 1973, suggested that the following three kinds of criticism to which administrative agencies are subjected should be the focus of concern in the field of public administration: technical competence, sensitivity to humane values within the government as well as in relations between the agency and the citizens, and responsiveness to the will of the people.[3]

A similar statement of the attributes of public administration has been offered by the National Association of Schools of Public Affairs and Administration (NASPAA), based in Washington, D.C. Emphasizing a professional rather than a liberal arts approach, NASPAA has developed a useful "Matrix of Professional Competencies" that addresses *system-related* variables — such as the institutional context — and *personal* or *affective* variables — such as human values and skills.[4] A matrix of the NASPAA model is shown in figure 1. According to the NASPAA approach, for each of the system-related subject-matter areas listed in the vertical column, there are four important subject-matter categories related to the student's personal development. Although the NASPAA guidelines were designed especially for graduate-level instruction, they contribute to a more operational definition of public administration.

Although there may be no single acceptable definition of public administration, there is growing consensus about the subject matter, the criteria and norms, and the problems involved in the development of a more professionalized public service. How this evolving field is perceived and what is

	Knowledge	Skills	Public-interest Values	Behavior
A. Political, social and economic context				
B. Analytical tools: quantitative and non-quantitative				
C. Individual/group/organizational dynamics				
D. Policy analysis				
E. Administrative/management process				

Source: National Association of Schools of Public Affairs and Administration, *Guidelines and Standards for Professional Masters Degree Programs in Public Affairs/Public Administration* (Washington, D.C.: NASPAA, 1974), p. 7. Used by permission.

Figure 1   Matrix of Professional Competencies

emphasized in it are properly related to the *purposes* to be served by such study. It is appropriate, for instance, for the student of political science to perceive public administration primarily as conflict resolution and public policy making. It is also appropriate for the "public administrationist" concerned primarily with education and training for careers in the public service to perceive public administration as a body of practical knowledge and technical skills. Further, it is appropriate for those with more philosophical orientations to perceive public administration as the pursuit of particular values. It would be a mistake to impose boundaries prematurely on this fertile field.

Importance of Public Administration

A pervasive definition of public administration describes public administration as *instrumental* work, work intended to accomplish legitimate public purposes rather than work that is an end in itself. This association of public administration with means instead of ends is often linked with the pejorative view of public administration as "tinkering with machinery," "nuts and bolts," "nitty gritty," and "how-to" minutiae. In contrast to this view, a perceptive reading of history would suggest that the rise and fall of governments depend significantly on the performance of public administrators.

On the eve of World War I, Brooks Adams, a member of the celebrated Massachusetts family and a critic of his times, linked the survival of civilization to public administration. Similarly, in the 1960s, S. N. Eisenstadt argued in his study of the decline of empires that the declines of the ancient Egyptian, Roman, Chinese, and Byzantine empires were significantly related to such *administrative* factors as weaknesses in civil service systems, fiscal administration, inadequate communications, and capriciousness in decision making.

In 1974, Vincent Ostrom, a political scientist who has attempted to build a more meaningful theory of public administration, added that there might be a link between public administration and the health of society.[5]

Such examples as these confirm the appropriateness of considering the social importance of public administration and the significant role that public administration plays in the larger system of politics and government. Moses' leadership of the Israelites in the Sinai wilderness, the exploration and colonization of the New World, the building of great cities, the waging of war and peace, and the landing of men on the moon — there was an administrative dimension in each such historic event. There was in each the necessity of dealing with the fundamental elements of public administration — activity, task, problem resolution, decision making, work process, competency, product or outcome, and consequences of actions.

Public administration within the web of government is part of an "if-then" relationship. *If* public policy intentions are to be converted into public policy accomplishments, *then* certain administrative and political structures may either have to exist or be created, certain functional needs may have to be fulfilled, certain actions may have to be taken, and certain consequences of those actions may have to result. To be more specific, *if* public aspirations are to be converted into public achievements, *then* the following kinds of activities must be considered:

1. Translating policy intentions into feasible action programs
2. Defining specific purposes, goals, and objectives of administrative agencies
3. Assigning and scheduling day-to-day work
4. Providing for control over the direction, speed, and quality of governmental services
5. Reconciling or mediating certain competing or clashing ideas, interests, and activities
6. Motivating people
7. Mobilizing and maintaining public understanding and support
8. Securing and managing financial and other resources

If governments are to be more than debating societies, *then* there must be substantial concern for the administrative dimension.

Our Approach

This book is intended to introduce the reader to the field of public administration as both academic study and professional practice. That is, the history, trends, values, traditions, institutions, practices, and issues of this field will be discussed, along with the realities faced by practicing public administrators in contemporary America. It is also the purpose of this book to whet the reader's interest in career opportunities in the public service.

These purposes are based on an "action approach" to public administration in which the following terms best convey our interests: activity, task, problem solving, decision making, process, work, competency, output, and consequence. This does not mean that there is a concentration here on low-level, detailed, routine work procedures and techniques, but rather that considerable attention is devoted to the tasks, problems, decisions, and choices imposed on public administrators today. Increasingly, governments are being challenged to justify themselves, not in terms of ideological purity but in terms of practical performance. It is the contemporary emphasis on governmental performance that furnishes some of the thrust of the "action approach" to public administration pursued in this book.

Part One presents the study of public administration in its context. More specifically, the focus is on the following: various perspectives from which one might view public administration; the relationship of public administration to related academic disciplines; the historical, intellectual, social, and material environment of American public administration; the comparative study of public administration across the boundaries of nation and culture; and the role of public administration in the development and modernization of the "developing nations." The purpose of this introduction is to show that while public administration has a relatively distinct identity, it is also highly interdisciplinary in character.

In Part Two, public administration is treated as part of the all-embracing web of government. The chapters in this part discuss such important matters as the special nature of urban administration and the needs encountered in administering the modern city; the complexities and innumerable difficulties of public administration within the federal system along with some of the ways in which public administration helps the nation to escape some of those difficulties; and the legal powers granted to and legal constraints imposed upon the modern American public administrator.

In Part Three, there is an examination of the four fundamental tasks imposed upon the public administrator: policy making and analysis, decision making, leadership, and communication. The chapters in this part consider the requisite knowledge, skills, behavior styles, and public-interest values for effective, humane, and responsible public administration.

In Part Four, public administration is treated as management. The focus is on work processes and techniques through which the basic tasks are accomplished. Those chapters examine attributes of public administration that have historically been accepted as lying at the heart of the field of management — the development and management of organizations, personnel management and manpower planning, and financial management.

Part Five is concerned with the challenges and changes that will confront public administration during the remainder of the 1970s and beyond. The last two chapters of this book are therefore devoted to such matters as values, ethics, responsibility, and change in American public administration as we begin the third century of national life.

NOTES

1. Peter F. Drucker, *Management: Tasks, Responsibilities, Practices* (New York: Harper & Row, 1973).

2. American Society for Public Administration, *Putting It All Together,* The National Conference on Public Administration, 1973 (Washington, D.C.: ASPA, 1973).

3. Stephen K. Bailey, "Objectives of the Theory of Public Administration," *Theory and Practice of Public Administration: Scope, Objectives, and Methods,* Monograph 8 (Philadelphia: American Academy of Political and Social Science, 1968), pp. 128–39; Lewis C. Mainzer, *Political Bureaucracy* (Glenview, Ill.: Scott, Foresman, 1973), pp. 1–3.

4. National Association of Schools of Public Affairs and Administration, *Guidelines and Standards for Professional Masters Degree Programs in Public Affairs/Public Administration* (Washington, D.C.: NASPAA, 1974), p. 7.

5. Brooks Adams, *The Theory of Social Revolutions* (New York: Macmillan, 1913); S.N. Eisenstadt, ed., *The Decline of Empires* (New York: Prentice-Hall, 1967); Vincent Ostrom, *The Intellectual Crisis in American Public Administration,* rev. ed. (University: University of Alabama Press, 1974), p. 4.

Perspectives on Public Administration

A key proposition in our introductory chapter is that the way one perceives public administration should be closely related to the *purposes* to be served in examining the field. A corollary proposition, which serves as the focus of this chapter, is that the "action approach" to public administration which we have adopted in this book can be strengthened by some of the insights, values, and emphases embraced by various "perspectives" on this complex and dynamic field. In this chapter, we delineate what we believe are seven fruitful perspectives or frames of reference. They are useful because they *slant* our view of the subject matter. The value of these different perspectives lies in the fact that they focus our attention on alternative and complementary conceptions of public administration and the values that result from these conceptions. They tell us: *this* may be more (or equally) important or useful to us than *that;* or we should search *here,* instead of (or as well as) *there.*

These various perspectives provide keys to understanding exceedingly complex phenomena. They raise significant questions about our data and thus help us avoid becoming shackled to a narrow and dogmatic conception of public administration. When we adopt a particular perspective, we make many additional judgments about what is real and what is illusory, what is important and what is trivial, what is cause and what is effect.

Knowledge is partly a function of experience; therefore, it can be assumed that our perspectives on public administration are, to a significant degree, the product of our interactions with our environment. The rise of big government, the increase in the power and importance of the executive in government, the growth of science and technology, the shift from *laissez faire* to the politicization of government, the professionalization of the public service, the discovery of human behavior as a social force within organizations, and the expanded role in international affairs — these are only some of the environmental forces that have been involved in the structuring of knowledge about public administration.[1]

At the individual level, environmental factors also affect perceptions of reality and the prescriptions and principles that we derive from those perceptions. The need to attract or deflect attention, to win recognition or security for ourselves or our point of view, to criticize or rebut criticism, or to find a particular perspective that fits our personal intellectual style are also influences that help determine our perspective or combination of perspectives on public administration.

The central idea of this chapter is that while no single perspective is sufficient, a perspective — or better still, a combination of perspectives — is necessary in the pursuit of wisdom. There is truth in the observation of the philosopher Morris Rafael Cohen that "wisdom does not come to him who gapes at nature with an empty head." This chapter will introduce the reader to various ways of seeing public administration to help guide future study.

The Perspective of History

Neglect of History

Public administration, like the social sciences generally, suffers from what has been called the *ostrich approach,* a state of mind that focuses only on current problems or future problems, while actively avoiding a backward look toward what is assumed to be the ignorance and errors of the past. For example, governmental efforts to combat poverty during the 1960s were remarkably unenlightened by the experiences of the 1930s, and public administrators responsible for regulating the national economy in the 1970s have not been sensitive to the experience of the post-World War II years. Meyer H. Fishbein, of the National Archives in Washington, D.C., has reminisced about the unwillingness of federal public administrators in Washington, D.C., to explore the records of the past in coping with the problems of today. He recalls, for instance, how a staff member of the Office of Price Administration during World War II requested anonymity because he feared that his superiors at OPA would criticize him for wasting his time at the National Archives.[2]

The *ostrich approach* is reflected in one of the most celebrated social inventions of modern public administration — PPBS (Planning, Programming, Budgeting System). Designed to improve governmental decision making by furnishing decision makers with systematic and comprehensive comparisons of costs and benefits of alternative programs for accomplishing particular policy goals, PPBS was promoted at all levels of government as something new. Frederick C. Mosher, who had participated in an earlier stage of the movement, was moved to criticize PPBS for its "ignorance or deliberate rejection of historical precedents. . . . The majority would have us believe that PPBS has come to us as Aphrodite from the sea, fullblown, fresh, beautiful, and top-less."[3]

Scholars of public administration and the social sciences have not entirely neglected the potential uses of historical precedents. Since World War II especially, there have been frequent reminders and some useful practical examples of the lessons that history can tell us. In 1971, a report of a survey under the auspices of the National Academy of Sciences and the Social Science Research Council declared:

> . . . the growing sophistication of social-scientific techniques makes it all the more important for practitioners of these techniques to know and appreciate the humanistic approach to historical knowledge. We cannot afford to gain a world of numbers and models and lose our historical souls in the process.[4]

Five Thousand Years of Public Administration

Public administration existed long before the term "public administration" came into use. Some of the oldest records of public administration are the clay tablets on which the Sumerians, in what is now Iraq, recorded their public affairs. As long ago as 5,000 years, Sumerian priests were occupied in equipping and feeding a standing army, administering temples and storehouses, collecting and accounting for taxes, recording financial transactions, administering courts of justice, assuring the integrity of public officials, and preparing and distributing the clay tablets on which these affairs were recorded. Similarly, in ancient Egypt under the Pharaohs, young men were instructed in statecraft—leadership training, communications planning, rulemaking and enforcement. In ancient China, during the sixth and seventh centuries B.C., Lao-Tzu, Confucius, and others emphasized in their teachings the importance of system, planning, control, coordination, impartiality, consistency, and hard work in the affairs of state. Ramses, David, Isaiah, Pericles, Julius Caesar, Elizabeth I, Napoleon, Jefferson — there has hardly been a prince, prophet, potentate, or president who has not had to wrestle with what we call the administrative dimensions of statecraft.[5]

Uses of the Past

The perspective of history is based on the idea of continuity in the study of man. Our lives are bound up with the lives of all people — past, present, and future. Sensitivity to the stream of history increases our analytical power: it helps us to distinguish between the eddy and the current; it furnishes solid data for making comparisons and testing theoretical propositions; it provides a time dimension which is lacking from contemporary behavioral studies of administration; it offers a cultural context for understanding administrative practices in different nations and societies; and it helps to stimulate our creative imaginations toward solutions of current problems. To study and practice public administration without reference to the past would be a form of amnesia. Without memory we operate in the dark, repeating the errors of the past.

In exploiting the lessons of history, some caution is necessary. First, we should try to avoid applying our own or current values and perceptions to past events. Such misperceptions may result in inappropriate comparisons. Second, our contemporary problems in public administration exist in the present; therefore, our salvation may lie not in searching the past to reconstruct a similar problem in the past nor in merely searching ancient motives, but rather in trying to understand the past in order to better understand how we came to be where we are. Third, we should be sensitive to the danger of exaggerating the power of human rationality; we should not be blind to the meaninglessness and madness in human history. Fourth, random search of the past may swamp us with more information than we can handle, and also may uncover more contradictory lessons than we, who are not historians, can sort out. Finally, we should avoid the temptation to employ history and tradition to reinforce the *status quo* and obstruct change.

If we exercise caution, then, the perspective of history in public administration will lead us not to a trash heap of irrelevance, as some "practical-minded" people would have us believe, but rather to a potentially rich and fresh source of data, imagination, and creative insight.

The Perspective of Law

Rise of the Administrative State and the
Problem of Discretion

A second perspective on public administration, suggested by a definition presented in chapter 1, is the view of this field of activity as a consequence or extension of law. That is, it is through the administrative process of government that the provisions of constitutions and statutes are particularized — made specific with reference to time, place, person, and circumstance. It was this legal perspective through which the early founders of public administration in the United States approached the subject. In 1887, for instance, Woodrow Wilson, who is generally credited with doing much to introduce the idea of administration to the United States, saw administrative work in government as the execution of law. It is, however, the definition of public administration as the delegation of responsibility in the work of government that introduces the idea of the administrative state and the concomitant problem of *administrative discretion* which is at the heart of the legal perspective.

In ancient times, the governing of society was relatively simple and consisted primarily of two types of "governors": warriors who settled problems and disputes among the people on the battlefield and recordkeepers who performed the "housekeeping chores" of state. As statecraft became more complex, the recordkeepers evolved and became lawyers, whose tasks included the drafting and execution of the crown's laws and decrees. Over time, law and the lawyers came to dominate the public service. By the middle of the eighteenth century, for instance, the systematic study of public administration in Prussia under Frederick William I was thoroughly in the control of professors of law, the cameralists. Later in that century, in America, Thomas Jefferson viewed the study of law as the main gateway to a career in the public service.[6]

During the century and a half following the founding of the American republic, national industry grew, and to control that industry new regulatory institutions were created, accompanied by the development of a bureaucracy to manage the new regulatory programs. The nature of the state consequently shifted. From a concern primarily with such *political* issues as the representative quality of the government, rules governing eligibility for public office, the powers of the separate branches of government, relationships between national and state levels of government, and control of governmental power generally, the focus of attention moved to a preoccupation with technical expertise and operational efficiency. In other words, there arose what has come to be called the *administrative state*.

"The essence of the administrative state," Emmette S. Redford has written, "is that men are born and live not merely . . . in subordination to power, but under a regime in which they are both served and controlled by an institutional complex composed of organizations."[7] The distinguishing features of this administrative state include the delegation of responsibility for exercise of these various service and regulatory tasks to a variety of specialized administrative agencies and officials who operate, not necessarily in accordance with fixed rules and customary standards of right and wrong, but rather with a measure of discretion — freedom of choice — that is sometimes unpredictable. The prison warden who enforces cruel and unusual punishment, the welfare administrator who discriminates against Spanish-speaking recipient families, the Internal Revenue Service official who bases his judgment on shadowy hearsay evidence, the police officer who lectures the son of the rich family and arrests the son of the poor — these are some examples of the actions that make administrative discretion a problem, especially in a time of turbulent social change.

Administrative Law

To cope with the rise of the administrative state, a body of law called "administrative law" has developed to provide a balance between the democratic responsiveness of the bureaucracy and its commitment to constitutional, or limited, government. Especially influential in England and America in the development of this administrative law was the formulation of a "rule of law" by A.V. Dicey. This formulation provided that, first, punishments and convictions for offenses must be determined only through the ordinary courts and, second, that public officials possess only limited power and are subject to the same ordinary law and ordinary courts as private citizens. The central concerns of administrative law have therefore been the following: the legal powers of public servants, remedies available against official determinations, the powers of administrators to make binding rules and enforce and arbitrate these rules, the power of officials to investigate alleged offenses and make findings and judgments, and the immunity of officials from court review and action.[8]

From this legal perspective, public administration consists of a complex body of legal norms — rights, obligations, and standards of performance — that are supposed to be observed by officials of government. In other words, if the public administrator must exercise discretion, because of the magnitude and complexity of modern government, let him or her operate within the law as commonly understood. Where other perspectives on public administration are concerned with such concepts as effectiveness and efficiency, the perspective of the law focuses our attention on the concept of *justice*.

Rediscovery of the Law in Public Administration

During the first half of this century, the legal perspective in public administration was widely employed. Textbooks usually included substantial discussions of administrative law topics, and public administration curricula in colleges and universities usually included coursework in administrative law. However, in recent years, with the growth of the behavioral persuasion in the study of political science and public administration, reinforced by the systems approach, the normative orientation of the legal perspective has been supplanted by a concern with the *is* rather than the *ought*. Administrative law has been eclipsed in the study of public administration.

The decade of the 1970s, however, is seeing a rediscovery of insights that are available through the perspective of law. The turbulent environment in which public administration must now operate is focusing attention again upon administrative law themes: the powers of public officials, administrative "due process," grievance procedures and remedies, unpredictability in the exercise of administrative discretion, and the like. Unionization of public employees, determination of eligibility for welfare benefits, policing the streets, affirmative action in hiring of minorities in the public services, and — of course — the offenses associated with the "Watergate Affair" and with such federal agencies as the Central Intelligence Agency and the Federal Bureau of Investigation are reminders that public administration in a democratic system is supposed to operate within and not above the law. In chapter 7 of this book, these issues are examined further.

The Perspective of Management-Process

Administration and Management

The terms "administration" and "management" are frequently used as synonyms to signify the people and the activities associated with the apex of bureaucracies in both public and private sectors of society. There is no consistent usage, but "management" seems to be more commonly used in reference to business affairs generally, and in connection with that part of public administration dealing with budget management, personnel management, program management, data processing, systems and procedures, supervision, and the like. Also, when the user wishes to focus attention on efficiency, economy, and technical expertise, the term "management" seems to be preferred. For instance, *The Municipal Year Book* of 1974, authoritative source book of urban data and affairs published annually by the International City Management Association, has distinguished between "management" matters (personnel management, general revenue sharing, public relations, and the like) and "administrative" matters (home rule, metropolitan reorganization, city-county consolidation, intergovernmental relations, and the like).[9]

In this book, the term *management* is employed to denote the classical conception of public administration which stresses work tasks, the search for general "principles" or criteria of efficiency, and the machine model of organization. It was this conception of administration which Luther Gulick and Lyndall Urwick, two of the founders of public administration, had in mind when they coined the acronym of POSDCORB in 1937 to represent the ideas and practices embraced by the term *management*. That is, management is sequential activity consisting of the following specific tasks: planning, organizing, staffing, directing, coordinating, reporting, and budgeting. Today, when POSDCORB is employed, it is intended to convey the narrow concern in public administration with work tasks, technical efficiency, and the like.[10]

Genesis of the Management-Process Perspective

It was from the same intellectual and historical taproot that nourished the growth of public administration itself in the United States early in this century that the management-process perspective grew. After nearly half a century of intense continental expansion, industrial growth, and political conservatism and corruption following the Civil War, a spirit of reform — manifested by the Populist and Progressive movements — spurred significant changes in the public institutions of the United States. Reformers sought, in particular, to combat such "evils" as railroad influence in Congress and the state legislatures, machine politics and "bossism" in the cities, "spoils" in public employment, exploitation of the small farmer and the urban laborer, and concentration of economic and political power in the hands of the "trusts." The reformers, of course, did not accomplish all of their goals, but one of their achievements, central to our purposes here, was the separation of administration from politics. Actively involved in both the reform movement of the time and in the development of the field of study of public administration were such men as Woodrow Wilson, Frank J. Goodnow, and Richard S. Childs (regarded as the father of the city management movement).

For instance, in 1900, Woodrow Wilson's friend and fellow political scientist, Frank J. Goodnow, then president of Johns Hopkins University, called for separation of administration from politics:

> . . . there is a large part of administration which is unconnected with politics, which should therefore be relieved very largely, if not altogether, from the control of political bodies. It is unconnected with politics because it embraces fields of semi-scientific, quasi-judicial and quasi-business or commercial activity — work which has little if any influence on the expression of the true state will.[11]

On the basis of this principle of separatism, a number of reforms were carried out during the years that followed: establishment of the so-called independent regulatory commissions to regulate business enterprise; promotion of the city manager-council system, presumably to take municipal government out of politics; assignment of responsibility for municipal fire and police protection to special lay commissions; creation of special-purpose districts to take school administration out of politics; and the establishment of politically neutral civil service systems, bolstered by laws and regulations forbidding partisan political activity by civil servants.

Meanwhile, the management-process perspective was being strengthened by the work of Frederick W. Taylor and the Scientific Management Movement. Possessed of a puritanical and aristocratic orientation and a stern Calvinist morality of self-discipline and good works, Taylor dedicated his life to the application of rational principles to human endeavor in business and government. The canons of the new secular religion, called "Scientific Management," were the following: escape from disorder and rule-of-thumb work methods; efficiency in the use of time, energy, and resources; the combining of human intelligence with machine power; search for the "one best way" to solve problems and perform work tasks; employment of mathematical work standards wherever possible; application of universal principles to business and governmental administration; and scientific selection and training of workers for particular jobs.

In the words of Leonard D. White, author of the first textbook in public administration in the United States, "scientific management joined hands with the moral reformers to demand responsibility in government . . . and generally to improve operating methods." White acknowledged "the very great influence of the scientific management movement in government" and found a major reason for that influence to lie in the movement's idea "that some ways of organizing and operating are better than others, and it is the duty of top management to find the best way for a given staff under given conditions of operation." The study of public administration, White suggested, should be based more on management than on law, and it was "more absorbed in the affairs of the American Management Association than in the decisions of the courts."[12] During the late 1920s and the decade of the 1930s, the ideas and practices of scientific management greatly influenced the study and practice of public administration.

Focus of the Management-Process Perspective

While the perspective of law is based on the search for justice, the management-process perspective is built on the model of work. Here we turn away from the lawyers and their concern with legalistic and philosophic "oughts." This perspective attracts not legal philosophers, but "practical, hard-headed realists."

In approaching public administration from the perspective of management-process, we go not to the work of courts, tribunals, and regulatory agencies, but to the tasks and problems of bureaucrats. We become involved not with philosophical commentaries, constitutional powers, and legal issues, but rather with technical work procedures, bureaucratic rules and regulations, and tangible technology. The law is concerned with ideas and ideals; management process is concerned with work and action. The metaphors and analogies employed in management process are mechanical and sometimes anatomical — the machinery of government, the tools of administration, the wheels of progress, organizational friction, the levers of power, the head of government, old hands in the established organizations, the heart of a problem, and staff people who serve as an organization's eyes and ears.

Underlying the management-process perspective are the principles of *universality* and *rationality* — the twin belief, first, that there is a universal process involved in all large-scale human enterprises, and that through careful detailed analysis, guiding principles can be extrapolated; and, second, that human rationality can and should be applied in the operation of complex orgnizations. Things and people must be manipulated—that is, *managed*. Goals and objectives must be determined, methods of work devised, tasks assigned, resources secured and allocated, control exercised, and review and evaluation provided. The emphasis of this perspective is upon rational action, upon relating means to ends, upon technique, and upon the tools and instruments of task accomplishment. Unlike the model of law, the management model is highly empirical, hostile to philosophical speculation, and more concerned with what *is* than with what *ought to be*.

Furthermore, when we employ the management-process perspective, we focus not on the *"public"* but on the *"administration"* in public administration. We tend to be less concerned with the political, moral, ethical, and ideological nature of administrative work in government. It was not an accident of history that the attempt to separate municipal government from politics produced the city *management* movement. Nor is it surprising to see that the movement to apply "sound business methods" to all kinds of organizations — public and private — led to the development of the *management* consulting business. And, still further, President Nixon's Executive Order in 1970, which aimed "to bring about more efficient and economical conduct of Government service," converted the federal Bureau of the Budget into the Office of *Management* and Budget. When we employ the management-process perspective, we tend to follow the counsel of the eighteenth-century British poet and satirist, Alexander Pope, who declared: "For forms of government let fools contest/Whate'er is best administered is best." In other words, whether a system of public administration is more or less democratic, more or less representative, or more or less responsive to the wishes of the people is less important than whether it is more or less well managed.

Limitations of the Management-Process Perspective

In a sense, a perspective is a set of blinders. In the use of the management-process perspective we should be sensitive to the limitations involved. First, there is the danger of becoming so preoccupied with minute, analytical details that we become blinded to the larger purposes of public administration. Second, this perspective has tended to be overcommitted to a faith in human rationality and has paid insufficient attention to nonrationality and irrationality in human behavior. Third, the importance assigned to the principles of hierarchy and command have conferred upon the management-process perspective an authoritarian slant, not always the best approach to administration. Fourth, the strong belief in a generic conception of administration, cutting across public and private institutional boundaries, has led to principles that may have little relevance to *public* administration. Fifth, those who approach public administration from the management-process perspective are often criticized, and justifiably so, for insufficient sensitivity to their values and assumptions, and to the political consequences of what they do. They tend to forget, for instance, that the rational contribution of certain management processes and techniques may decline over time, as those processes and techniques become the vested interests of their specialists, and there is potent political power in certain administrative procedures. Finally, the highly determined thrust toward professionalization among disciples of this perspective has led to their being criticized for an excessively narrow definition of the scope of this field and to a strong elitist tendency.[13]

The Behavioral Perspective

Genesis of the Movement

Intellectual and social movements do not appear suddenly. The behavioral perspective in the study of public administration is part of the long historical evolution of the social sciences from classical Greek philosophy, to the eighteenth-century Enlightenment, to the nineteenth-century concern with social relationships, to the twentieth-century effort to build a unified theory of man in society under the name of the "behavioral sciences." Aristotle, Condorcet, Saint-Simon, Comte, Marx, Weber, Freud, and Lewin — these are some of the people who are part of the lineage.

The historical context within which the behavioral perspective on public administration developed included the convergence of several trends following the end of World War II. First, the increasing bureaucratization of modern life was accompanied by growing anxieties about the human costs of that trend: loneliness, meaninglessness in life, alienation. Second, conventional wisdom in public administration, which was found undependable in many respects as a guide to action during World War II, came increasingly under challenge. Third, there was an explosion in social science knowledge resulting especially from the work of sociologists, industrial psychologists, social psychologists, labor economists, and psychiatric analysts. Fourth, there was a dramatic increase in the prestige and resources of scientific inquiry in the United States, and this carried over to the behavioral "sciences." Finally, the development of cybernetics and computer science provided powerful new research instruments for the behavioral sciences.

As behavioralism grew in political science, it reinforced the behavioral influences on public administration coming from other related social science disciplines. The behavioral perspective in public administration was therefore both a response to changes in the world as well as a challenge to established thinking and practice within public administration.

Herbert Simon: The Behavioral Challenge

The battering ram that breached the walls of self-confidence in classical public administration was Herbert A. Simon's book, *Administrative Behavior,* published in 1946. According to Simon, the hallowed "principles" long expounded in classical management thinking, such as those concerning efficiency, work specialization, hierarchy, authority, and control, were merely "proverbs," untrustworthy guides for action applicable only under certain specified circumstances, if at all. His focus of attention in this and later books was on the psychology of human choice.[14]

Simon conceived of organizations not as work machines, but rather as problem-solving and choice-making instruments. Public administration, he argued, is "purposive" — that is, it is concerned with problem-solving. The essential task of public administrators is to make decisions: perceive the problem, apply information bearing on the problem, take account of the personal and other "extraneous" factors that may influence the satisfactory resolution of the problem, and make the choice. Decision, according to Simon, is the moment of truth for an organization.

This challenge from Simon did not revolutionize the study and practice of public administration, but it did leave this legacy: (1) it helped to sensitize the field of public administration to the value-content of its earlier prescriptions; (2) it helped to promote a research tradition in public administration based on the generation and testing of hypotheses; and (3) it helped to promote a crisis of identity in public administration which has not yet been resolved.

Focus of the Behavioral Perspective

There is no one accepted behavioral perspective on politics, government, and public administration, but a common thread in the complex fabric of this approach is the attempt to become more "scientific." More specifically, behavioral scholars emphasize such assumptions and objectives as the following: (1) the search for pattern and regularity in politics and government; (2) concern with the need for verification of theoretical generalizations on the basis of empirical data; (3) self-conscious concern about analytical techniques; (4) greater appreciation of the importance of quantification in research method; (5) acceptance of the assumption that research must be systematic, that is, that there is an intimate interconnection among various phenomena; and (6) belief that theoretical knowledge should come before practical application.

Where the perspective of history focuses on the past, the behavioral perspective tends to be hostile to or oblivious of that which has gone before, as it directs our attention to the here and now. Where the perspective of law is heavily normative and value-laden, the behavioral perspective attempts to distinguish between ethical evaluation and empirical explanation. Where the management-process perspective leads to a concern with technical details and formal organizational structures, the behavioral perspective concentrates on people interacting in organizational settings.

From the perspective of management-process, there is special attention to such concepts as the following: accountability, authority, command and control, costs, efficiency, hierarchy, productivity, utility, and work. But when one approaches public administration from the perspective of behavior, there is emphasis on such concepts as these: anxiety, attitude, communication, conflict, human needs, influence, interaction, motivation, and perception.

Limitations of the Behavioral Perspective

Like the other ways of viewing public administration, the behavioral perspective also has limitations. First, the thrust toward theory and abstraction often leads toward more academic questions, to the neglect of the practical applications of theory. Second, behavioralists in public administration tend to focus their attention on private organizations to the neglect of the administrative agencies of government. Third, the selection of research problems in the behavioral perspective may be more greatly influenced by methodological interest than by social importance. Finally, research and reform efforts that emphasize such behavioral methods as survey research, behavior modification, organizational development, and the like tend to raise people's fears about individual freedom and the right to privacy.

The Perspective of Politics

The Idea of Politics

Just as there is no one best way to define public administration, so is there no one best way to define *politics*. Few words in the dictionary have been more elusive than *politics* and *political*. They have been used to refer to the workings of such diverse institutions as the United Nations, congresses and parliaments, presidents and prime ministers, state legislatures and city councils, state governors and city mayors, bureaucratic agencies at all levels, political parties, special-interest groups, and public relations firms. The activities customarily embraced by *politics* have ranged from the bombing of an enemy people abroad to the repairing of potholes in the streets at home. In attempts to define *politics* and *political*, emphasis in the literature has been focused on such matters as the following: the making of binding public decisions for society; the exercise of power; the art of compromise; determination of "who gets what, when, how" as suggested by Lasswell; the contesting for control of government; and the process of coping with human problems for the people as a whole.

In this book, politics is conceived as essentially concerned with conflict and its resolution. This view has been well stated by Edward C. Banfield.

> . . . the laying of a sewer pipe by a "public body" may involve the same kinds of behavior as the manufacture of the pipe by a "private" one. Difficulties that are "political" arise . . . only insofar as there is conflict . . . over what the common good requires or between what it requires and what private interests want.[15]

Planning for suburban subdivisions; regulating prices and wages; raising and lowering taxes; regulating pension funds of labor unions and other organizations; protecting the environment; routing of streets and highways; locating shopping centers, airports, and civic malls; granting and withholding welfare benefits; licensing motor vehicles, businesses, and professions—these are the kinds of public activities in which conflicts arise "over what the common good requires or between what it requires and what private interests want." Therein lies some of the meaning of the political perspective on public administration.

Public Administration as Conflict Resolution

The essence of public administration as politics lies in the resolution of conflict. For instance, routine removal of garbage may not be a political matter;

that is, it may involve no conflict over interpretations of the common good. Garbage removal becomes political when such questions as these arise: Should the city council defer to one faction in the city which wants the city itself to provide the service, financed by property tax revenues, or to the opposing faction which wants commercial garbage removal on the basis of individual contracting by householders? If the city performs the service itself, should garbage collectors be allowed to organize and bargain collectively? If the schedule of collections, devised by the commercial collecting company, displeases part of the community, what should the schedule be and who should determine it? Irrespective of whether the collecting is done by the city or by a contracting company, should the city insist on a more effective affirmative action program in the hiring of garbage collectors, to assure greater employment opportunities to minority people? In making authoritative decisions on such questions as these, the public administrator is involved in the resolution of political conflict.

The resolution of political conflict is not limited to an administrative agency's relationships with its public or with other elements of its environment. A network of internal relationships may also be involved. Party control of administration in many jurisdictions of government requires careful attention to relationships with the political parties. The role of administration in legislative policy making emphasizes the importance of the public administrator's relationships with the legislative body, whether it is the Congress, state legislature, county board, or city council. With administrative agencies becoming committed to the interests of particular interests in society, agencies may clash with each other in fulfilling their advocacy roles. An administrative agency might engage in "empire building," that is, attempting to enhance its jurisdiction and authority at the expense of another agency. Or there might be conflict between two administrative agencies because of different backgrounds of the members of the groups — such as police officers versus social workers, or urban planners versus public works engineers. Furthermore, there might be internal conflict due primarily to different group identifications — such as social-workers who are client-oriented against budget analysts and cost accountants who are taxpayer-oriented. When such conflicts threaten the decision-making structure of an administrative agency or seriously hamper the agency's ability to perform its tasks, there is a particularly serious political problem that must be resolved if the agency's mission is to be accomplished.[16]

The political perspective directs attention not to the work processes of administration, but rather to the crucial question of institutional survival. This survival, whether it involves the fate of a city government, a state regulatory agency, or a national bureau, depends upon two sets of relationships for the public administrator — *externally* with elements of the environment, and *internally* with other agencies and institutions that are also part of the political system.

The Remarriage of Politics and Administration

With the coming of the Great Depression and World War II in the 1930s and 1940s, there was an enormous politicization of government. That is, governments were called upon to become more deeply involved in exercising power; in determining who got what, when, how; in mediating disputes among conflicting interests; in coping with a great variety of human problems; in engaging in what has since come to be called the dispensation of distributive justice. As agencies of government intruded ever more deeply and intimately into the affairs of the people, the dichotomy between politics and administration became increasingly less realistic.

Reflecting the changes that were occurring around them, some scholars in political science and public administration started in the 1930s and 1940s to call for a remarriage of politics and administration.[17] By the 1960s the intellectual remarriage was still not fully consummated. Textbooks in public administration, for instance, contained a few more chapters on political themes, and academic curricula included more courses with political content, but the hiatus between political scientists and public administrationists widened. The celebrated war on poverty, launched by the administration of President Lyndon Johnson in the mid-1960s, was based heavily on assumptions about the importance of proper administrative organization and management procedure, but the problem of the political viability of the Office of Economic Opportunity and its subsidiary organizations was neglected. Similarly, PPBS (Planning, Programming, Budgeting System) was essentially a management-process solution to a deeply political problem of power and the allocation of resources and values for society. Under the Nixon administration, the political problem of improving intergovernmental fiscal relationships, including especially the political problem of strengthening the governments of cities, was treated with a basically structural and managerial remedy — revenue sharing.

In an earlier and simpler time, when the pace was slower and the scope of social change was less broad than today, and when governments were expected to do little, there may have been some validity to the notion that public administrators and their work were not political. The turbulence and challenge of the 1970s, however, appear to be pushing politics and administration to a remarriage in practice as well as in theory. Ralph Nader and other leaders of the consumer movement are challenging the resistance of independent regulatory commissions to new social needs and demands. The city management movement is being challenged from several directions — environmental protection, citizen participation, law and order, delivery of services, housing, transportation, labor relations, equal job opportunity, rising costs of government, and taxpayers' rebellions. At all levels of government, demands for greater citizen participation in government, greater decentralization of decision making, greater unionization of public employees, and greater equity in the provision of public services will further politicize public administration.

This trend was reflected in a report in 1973 by the National Academy of Public Administration, based on an attitude survey of eighty leaders in academic and practical public administration throughout the United States. The report included the following portrait of the future public administrator:

> The administrator of the future will be more of a moral leader, broker, and coordinator than he [or she] will be a boss or issuer of orders . . . .

[He or she will need] a thorough understanding of the administrative The public administrator and his [or her] management team must have the capacity to adopt bargaining and political roles if they are to deal success-fully with the variety of competing interests which may face them . . . . [He or she will need] a thorough understanding of the administrative process. This must include the political process in which it is imbedded.[18]

Limitations of the Political Perspective

Criticism of the political perspective comes especially from those students and practitioners of public administration who are nostalgic for the greater order, simplicity, and self-confidence of the earlier scientific management movement. In general, "public administrationists" yearn for harmony, order, and predictability. Politics, on the other hand, means conflict, ambiguity, and uncertainty.

Interest in the art of conflict resolution, like attraction to strong drink, may become addictive. Therefore, in the fascination with conflict it should be remembered that there is also much consensus and reconciliation in politics and government. In devotion to the crucial values of democracy, equity, and a humanistic regard for the rights of the individual, we should not lose sight of the values of simplicity, symmetry, neatness, efficiency, and productivity.

The Perspective of Ecology

Genesis

The ecological perspective on public administration did not have a precisely definable beginning, but like the political perspective with which it is theo-retically associated, it reflects the post-World War II attempt by scholars to escape from a narrow management-process conception of public admin-istration and from the cultural bondage of conventional thinking and practice. The concept of ecology had been fruitfully applied in the science of biology to describe the interdependence between an animal species and its natural environment. Urban sociologists had adopted the term *ecology* to help explain spatial relations in communities.

Starting about 1945, social science scholars, drawing on earlier work in their field, began to focus more attention on the interactive relationships between the individual, human institutions, and the physical and social environment. In 1946, for instance, Alexander H. Leighton demonstrated how a particular administrative body was part of the social organization of the community in which it operated. Similarly in 1947, John M. Gaus pub-lished a provocative book whose introductory chapter was prophetically entitled "The Ecology of Government." In that chapter, Gaus offered a set of environmental factors that he called "the raw materials of politics": *people, area, social structure, technology, ideology,* and *catastrophe.* The following year, Chester I. Barnard, in a particularly influential book, viewed administrative organizations in terms of systems, and he argued that the function of organizational decision making was to maintain balance between the purposes of the organization and the external physical and social world.[19]

Focus of the Ecological Perspective

This perspective is based on the idea that public administrators operate within an environment which *constrains* them, but that what the public administrators do may, in turn, affect the environment. Population change, for instance, influences the behavior of public administrators, but public administration decisions, in turn, may influence future population change. In other words, human beings, human institutions, and the social and physical environment are in continual transaction. The balance of that transaction may lead to human adaptation to the environment, to the adaptation of the environment to human beings, or to both results. The term "transaction" emphasizes the absence of a clear distinction between human beings and their environment. We must think of public administration *in* its environment.

The environment does not *determine* structure, process, behavior, and performance in public administration; it *constrains* them. It is from the environment that the public administrator perceives the problems to be resolved, the alternative possibilities between choices to be made, the resources to be employed, and the support and opposition to policies and programs. Further, *within* the environment are found the clients to be served or regulated, the market forces which establish the costs for the goods and services "produced" by government, special-interest groups that have particular concern about what the public administrator does, and other public and private institutions that may offer support or opposition. Finally, it is *within* the environment that the consequences of public administration are judged to be "right" or "wrong."

Public administrators are not passive straws in the wind, although in reality some may behave as if they were. Rather, public administrators have varying degrees of freedom and discretion. However, in public administration, as in biology, if disruptive changes in the environment are allowed to go too fast and too far, they may become irreversible and thus destroy the dynamic ecological balance. In such a catastrophe, the public administrator has no freedom nor discretion.

When one approaches public administration through the perspective of ecology, one's attention is directed to *change* rather than to stability, to macro- and micro-analytical *relationships,* and to the *product, output,* and *consequences* of public administration rather than the instrumental means and methods. For purposes of illustration, consider the complex environment of a municipal government department, such as a police department, a public works department, or a department of parks and recreation. The *physical* environment might include the facilities of the department's offices, the size of the city's territorial jurisdiction, the availability of transportation and communication, and the adequacy of health and safety. The department's *economic* environment might include such factors as the income level of the people in the community, the level and causes of chronic poverty and unemployment, the economic base and growth rate of the community, and the cost levels of goods and services "consumed" by the municipal government in "producing" the goods and services for the public. The *political environment* would probably include relations with other governmental agencies, party politics, special-interest group politics, the influence of the communications media, attitudes of the people toward their government and toward politics generally, the constitutional powers of the city government within the larger intergovernmental system, and the relative "liberal" or "conservative" political climate of the community. The *social* environment of the department might include the character, density, and distribution of the population in the community, race relations, and the pattern of group relations. The *psychological* environment might include the intelligence, emotional stability, and personality structure of both the people of the community generally as well as the employees of city hall. The *ideological* and *philosophical* environment of the municipal department might include such factors as the attitude and belief systems of the people toward change, political stability, civic responsibility, personal independence and interdependence, democracy, participation, and other similar ideological and philosophical attributes. This, then, is the complex world of the urban public administrator.

Limitations of the Ecological Perspective

To employ the perspective of ecology fruitfully, some cautions are in order. First, ecology, like history and politics, may diffuse the attention of public administration too widely. Care should be taken not to undertake more than what can be accomplished. Second, adequate tools and measures must be developed for isolating and weighing the impact of ecological factors upon public administration, lest one is carried into a bottomless pit of undependable, irrelevant, and contradictory data. Third, to employ successfully the ecological approach, it may be necessary to develop considerable skill in the methods and insights of all the social sciences. Finally, the highly theoretical quality of the ecological approach renders it vulnerable to impracticality and excessive abstraction.

The modern student and practitioner of public administration can and should develop some facility in the ecological perspective. Failure to do so might lead to an "ecological crisis" — that is, the viability of public administrators and their agencies may be endangered in two ways: (1) by the inability or refusal of public bureaucrats to exercise their discretion and to accommodate their behavior to changing environmental requirements; and (2) by the imprudent actions of public bureaucrats (probably aided and abetted by politicians and the public) causing disruptive or irreversible alterations in their environment.

For example, the following train of events might lead to an "ecological crisis" in public administration. The governmental leaders of a small peaceful city, which has few people but much growth potential, decide that there would be economic and social benefits in the promotion of growth in the city. The administration of their developmental policies promotes urbanization, which in turn leads to the generation of acute problems — congestion, inadequacy of municipal services, diversity in the demographic character of the city, crime, grime, and tension. The creation of these problems generates more self-conscious efforts of the city government to find solutions, which in turn undermines the *status quo* in city hall and leads to serious conflict and disagreement. The increasing turbulence in the city jeopardizes the capacity of the city's political system to meet the challenge, and the city arrives at the brink of political and administrative chaos.

The Comparative Perspective

In the study and practice of public administration, we inevitably make comparisons. The organizational structure in Springfield, Massachusetts, let us say, may be better than it is in Springfield, Illinois; the government of the state of California may include a more efficient civil service system than does the government of the state of New York; President Lyndon Johnson's White House staff may have been more responsible than President Richard Nixon's; or the government of the Soviet Union may be more bureaucratic than the government of the United States. When practitioners borrow and adapt administrative methods and techniques from other agencies and jurisdictions and apply them in their own, they implicitly make comparisons.

The thrust of the argument in this section is that in making generalizations about public administration, in making analytical and normative comparisons, and in transferring administrative practices and innovations across boundaries, one must be sensitive not only to the ecological transaction discussed earlier but also to the crucial differences and similarities between nations, between societies, and between subnational jurisdictions. For purposes of discussion, the ecological and comparative perspectives are treated separately, but in reality they are intertwined.

Development of the Comparative Perspective

Since World War II, the classical theory of public administration, as reflected in scientific management and the machine model of organization, has been subjected to profound challenge. In chapter 12, the challenge to classical theory of organization will be examined in some detail. The development of the comparative perspective in public administration was such a challenge.

First, one of the impacts of World War II on public administration was the discovery, as will be discussed more fully in chapter 12, that many of the so-called principles of sound public administration were not relevant to the problem-solving demands of the times. Academics who worked in military and war-related civilian agencies found that the conventional wisdom that they had professed in their textbooks and classrooms was wanting. Second, highly critical literature, such as the studies by Simon and others, persuasively argued that the early scholars of public administration had been unaware or had failed to examine critically their own premises. This was more than the issue of organizational theory, as developed in chapter 12. Further, the growth of behavioralism and comparative studies in political science influenced some public administration scholars. In addition, the growth of the "development movement" — rendering technical assistance to the so-called underdeveloped nations by the United Nations, the government of the United States, and by American universities and business firms — mobilized an army of specialists in public administration and other fields who applied their expertise in strange and diverse cultures. Finally, at home in the United States, a renaissance began to develop in the research on policy making and administration at the state and local levels of government, and new and more sophisticated insights were gained concerning the significance of economic, political, geographic, and historical variables in government and administration at the subnational level.

The Comparative Method of Analysis

The comparative perspective in public administration is primarily a *mode of analysis* — that is, a way of studying the field. Making comparisons is more than adding up the similarities and differences; it demands the development of an explanatory frame of reference that might help in understanding the reasons for the similarities and differences. For example, suppose that one wanted to make a comparative analysis of personnel administration in the city governments of St. Paul and Minneapolis. It would be necessary to go beyond merely cataloging the similarities and differences and to try to develop an overall theory of municipal personnel administration that might *explain*.

The development of such explanatory theory requires (1) *abstract concepts* that permit the formulation of generalizations and hypotheses about public personnel administration in the two cities — such as classification of positions, personnel selection, service ratings, and training; and (2) *criteria of relevance* — that is, propositions that describe patterns in the relationships between two or more observable phenomena, such as the proposition that the more innovative and "developmental" the training program, the better the performance rating of the personnel.

The essential task is to develop an exploratory frame of reference. In earlier years, at a precomparative stage, scholars and analysts usually did not seek such a frame of reference. Instead, they concentrated on cataloging formal structural characteristics. For instance, in 1953 a textbook on the governments of Latin America included what was supposedly a comparative analysis of the presidencies of the twenty Latin American nations; in reality, attention was limited to electoral procedures, terms of office, powers of appointment, and the like.[20]

In contrast, a 1965 study by John A. Armstrong on administrative behavior in the Soviet Union and Western Europe employed abstract concepts of bureaucracy, behavior, organizational structure, communications, and informal relationships. The purpose was not to catalogue structural and procedural details, but rather to identify the similarities and differences in administrative behavior and to understand the underlying causes.[21]

In summary, then, the comparative perspective in public administration is characterized by the following:

1. A shift from prescribing what *ought* to be to a greater concern with what *is* and *why it is*
2. A shift from what Riggs has called "ideographic" studies to "nomothetic" studies — that is, less emphasis on the study of unique cases and situations, and more emphasis on the search for testable generalizations

3. A shift from a nonecological to a more ecological approach, with greater attention to the interaction between public administrative systems and their environments.

The purposes of the comparative perspective in public administration have been well summarized by Nimrod Raphaeli as follows:

> ... to find out what makes certain administrative features work well in one country or era while they fail dismally in another; to identify the factors — cultural, political, and social — that are involved in success or failure; to explain the differences in behavior of bureaucrats and bureaucracies in different countries and cultures; and, finally, to discern what changes, if any, ought to be introduced and how they can be introduced, to improve the performance of a bureaucracy. Above all, we compare to arrive at a conceptual knowledge rather than a knowledge of details.[22]

Conclusions

At the beginning of this chapter, it was argued that different perspectives on public administration focus attention on different facets of reality, and that the choice of perspective should be related to the purposes being pursued. There was next an examination of the origins, uses, and limitations of seven perspectives — history, law, management-process, behavior, politics, ecology, and comparison. One conclusion is that these perspectives are not sharply compartmentalized and that some of them are closely related. The management-process and behavioral perspectives, for instance, both were reactions to the heavily legalistic and formalistic character of early public administration in the United States. Also, both the behavioral and political perspectives are particularly concerned with conflict in human relations, and with the search for theoretical propositions. And both the ecological and comparative perspectives are especially concerned with significant environmental and cultural conditions.

A second conclusion is that an "action approach" to public administration, which attempts to enlarge students' knowledge and skill areas in this field, should devote considerable attention to a management-process perspective, but not at the price of neglect of outputs and consequences. Contemporary concern with the quality of governmental performance, with governmental productivity, and with the delivery of public services is fundamentally a concern with outputs — with who gets what, when, and how.

Third, eclectic use of the various perspectives discussed in this chapter should be closely related to the particular problems to be resolved and tasks to be performed. For instance, in coping with the problem of arbitrary and irresponsible exercise of administrative discretion, there is special value in the legal perspective. In attempting to enlarge the knowledge and skill areas in planning and controlling the use of money and other resources, the management-process perspective is especially fruitful. And in seeking greater knowledge and skill in relating to the public, there is special value in the perspective of politics.

Finally, it should be emphasized that from its early beginnings as a field of study and practice in the United States, public administration has been intimately entwined with the changing environment in this country. Public administrative doctrine, standards of sound administrative practice, value commitments, patterns of organizational structure, styles of administrative behavior — all reflect the changing world in which they evolved. In the following chapter, therefore, the focus is on the environment of contemporary public administration in the United States.

NOTES

1. For literature on the sociology of knowledge, see the following: Martin Landau, *Political Theory and Political Science* (New York: Macmillan, 1972), pp. 34–39; Karl Mannheim, *Ideology and Utopia: An Introduction to the Sociology of Knowledge* (New York: Harcourt Brace Jovanovich, 1936); Talcott Parsons, *The Structure of Social Action* (New York: McGraw-Hill, 1937); and Herbert A. Simon, *Administrative Behavior* (New York: Free Press, 1945).

2. Meyer H. Fishbein, "A Viewpoint on Appraisal of National Records," *The American Archivist* 33 (April 1970): 176.

3. Frederick C. Mosher, "Letter to Editor-in-Chief," *Public Administration Review* 27, no. 1 (March 1967): 70.

4. David S. Landes and Charles Tilly, eds., *History as Social Science* (Englewood Cliffs, N.J.: Prentice-Hall, 1971), p. 2. Used by permission. See also the article by Landes and Tilly, "History as Social Science: Excerpts From the Report of the History Panel of the Behavioral and Social Sciences Survey," in the publication of the Social Science Research Council, *ITEMS* 25 (March 1971): 1–6.

5. Two useful historical surveys of administration are the following: Claude S. George, Jr., *The History of Management Thought*, rev. ed. (Englewood Cliffs, N.J.: Prentice-Hall, 1972); and Gerald D. Nash, *Perspectives on Administration: The Vistas of History* (Berkeley: Institute of Governmental Studies, University of California, 1969).

6. A. Dunsire, *Administration: The Word and the Science* (New York: John Wiley, 1973), p. 54.

7. Emmette S. Redford, *Democracy in the Administrative State* (New York: Oxford University Press, 1969), pp. 38–39, used by permission; Allen Schick, "Toward the Cybernetic State," in Dwight Waldo, ed., *Public Administration in a Time of Turbulence* (Scranton, Pa.: Chandler, 1971), pp. 216–22.

8. Kenneth Culp Davis, *Administrative Law and Government* (St. Paul: West Publishing Co., 1965), pp. 1–28; and his book, *Discretionary Justice: A Preliminary Inquiry* (Baton Rouge, La.: Louisiana State University Press, 1969. See also the following: Walter Gellhorn, *When Americans Complain: Governmental Grievance Procedures* (Cambridge, Mass.: Harvard University Press, 1966); and Joel F. Handler, *The Coercive Social Worker: British Lessons for American Social Services* (Chicago: Rand McNally, 1973).

9. *The Municipal Year Book, 1974*, Vol. 41 (Washington, D.C.: International City Management Association, 1974). For discussion of the distinction between *management* and *administration*, especially in business, see Lyndall F. Urwick, *The Meaning of Rationalisation* (London: Nisbet & Co., 1929), pp. 115–16.

10. Luther Gulick and Lyndall F. Urwick, eds., *Papers on the Science of Administration* (New York: Institute of Public Administration, 1937), pp. 13–14.

11. Frank J. Goodnow, *Politics and Administration: A Study in Government* (New York: Macmillan, 1900), p. 85.

12. Leonard D. White, *Introduction to the Study of Public Administration*, 4th ed. (New York: Free Press, 1974), pp. xvi, 20–21. Copyright © 1974 by the Free Press. Used by permission.

13. For provocative discussion of the limitations of modern management science, see the following: Robert Boguslaw, *The New Utopians* (Englewood Cliffs, N.J.: Prentice-Hall, 1965); Ida R. Hoos, *Systems Analysis in Public Policy: A Critique* (Berkeley: University of California Press, 1972); and Victor A. Thompson, *Bureaucracy and Innovation* (University: University of Alabama Press, 1969), especially chapter 3.

14. Herbert A. Simon, *Administrative Behavior*, 2d ed. (New York: Free Press, 1965), p. 1. See also Simon's other works: "The Proverbs of Administration," *Public Administration Review* 6 (Winter 1946): 53–67; *Public Administration*, with Donald W. Smithburg and Victor A. Thompson (New York: Alfred A. Knopf, 1954); *Models of Man* (New York: John Wiley, 1957); *The New Science of Management Decision* (New York: Harper & Row, 1960); and *Organizations* with James G. March (New York: John Wiley, 1967).

15. Edward C. Banfield, "The Political Implications of Metropolitan Growth, *Daedalus* 90 (Winter 1961): 61. Used by permission.

16. Paul Diesing, *Reason in Society* (Urbana, Ill.: University of Illinois Press, 1962), p. 278.

17. E. Pendleton Herring, *Public Administration and the Public Interest* (New York: McGraw-Hill, 1936); Marshall E. Dimock, "The Meaning and Scope of Public Administration," in John M. Gaus et al., eds, *The Frontiers of Public Administration* (Chicago: University of Chicago Press, 1936), pp. 3–4; Paul H. Appleby, *Big Democracy* (New York: Alfred A. Knopf, 1945), and *Policy and Administration* (University: University of Alabama Press, 1949); and V.O. Key, Jr., *Politics, Parties, and Pressure Groups*, 3rd ed. (New York: Thomas Y. Crowell, 1952), pp. 720–41.

18. Richard L. Chapman and Frederick N. Cleaveland, *Meeting the Needs of Tomorrow's Public Service: Guidelines for Professional Education in Public Administration* (Washington, D.C.: National Academy of Public Administration, 1973), pp. 17–19. Used by permission.

19. Alexander H. Leighton, *The Governing of Men* (Princeton, N.J.: Princeton University Press, 1946); John M. Gaus, *Reflections on Public Administration* (University: University of Alabama Press, 1947), pp. 1–19; and Chester I. Barnard, *The Functions of the Executive* (Cambridge, Mass.: Harvard University Press, 1948).

20. Miguel Jorrín, *Governments in Latin America* (New York: Van Nostrand, 1953).

21. John A. Armstrong, "Sources of Administrative Behavior: Some Soviet and Western European Comparisons," *American Political Science Review* 59, no. 3 (September 1965): 643–55.

22. Nimrod Raphaeli, "Comparative Public Administration: An Overview," in Nimrod Raphaeli, ed., *Readings in Comparative Administration* (Boston, Mass.: Allyn & Bacon, 1967), p. 4. Used by permission. For the contribution of Fred W. Riggs, the most prolific theorist in comparative analysis of public administration, see the following: *The Ecology of Public Administration* (New York: Asia Publishing House, 1961); and *Administration in Developing Countries* (Boston: Mass.: Houghton Mifflin, 1964).

The Environment of Public Administration

3

As suggested in the preceding chapter, the public administrator does not work in a vacuum. The parameters within which she or he operates are rooted in the environment. The purpose of this chapter is to identify and to discuss briefly those sensitive environmental variables that have some correlation with public administration.

People

Growth, Change, and Movement

One of the significant environmental variables for public administration is population — its growth, change, and movement. From a nation of 3.9 million people in 1790, of whom more than 95 percent lived on farms and in rural areas, the United States has grown to a population of over 205 million, of whom approximately 73 percent live in cities and urban areas.[1] Despite inhibitors of population growth — such as increased use of contraceptives, the tendency to marry later, more lenient abortion statutes, financial anxieties caused by economic instability — it is estimated that the population of the United States will continue to rise, by more than 25 percent by the year 2000.

Data on the composition, geographical distribution, education, employment, and income levels of the American people represent much change. The proportions in relation to the total population of younger people, fourteen to twenty-four years of age, and of people over sixty-five years of age are increasing. Blacks are increasing slightly in their proportion to the total population. During recent decades, there has been a steady increase in the number of young adults with college degrees, climbing from 6 percent in 1940 to 16 percent in 1970. The gap in educational achievement between young black adults and their white counterparts continues. With regard to employment patterns, the proportion of working women continues to grow, white-collar workers are expected soon to outnumber blue-collar workers by more than 50 percent, and the rate of unemployment among blacks continues to be much higher than among whites. Poverty continues to be concentrated among blacks, people of Spanish-speaking heritage, and native Americans, with an increasing gap between those at the bottom of the economic pyramid and the rest of society. Urban areas continue to have the greatest concentration of poverty, and at an increasing rate of growth.[2]

With respect to the spatial distribution of people, there is also much change. The two most significant trends of the twentieth century — urbanization and suburbanization — continue unabated. More than 44 percent of the people now reside in urban communities with at least 25,000 people. Southern blacks continue their exodus to northern cities, and the white exodus from central cities to suburbs has also continued. Almost half of the black people in the United States now live in fifty cities. Also, there is a continued movement of farm people to the cities and urban areas.

There has been great disparity in the geographical impact of such change. For instance, the Census of 1970 reported that population density varied from a high of 700 persons per square mile in the District of Columbia, New Jersey, Rhode Island, and Massachusetts, to less than fifty persons per square mile in twenty-one states located primarily in the Mountain region, the Plains, Northern New England, and the South. Approximately 52 percent of the nation's people were concentrated in nine states (California, New York, Pennsylvania, Texas, Illinois, Ohio, Michigan, New Jersey, and Florida). California, with 9.8 percent of the nation's people in 1970, felt the brunt of this great movement.[3]

Impacts and Implications

Since public administration means coping with human problems, and since these problems tend to concentrate where people congregate, it becomes apparent that population changes have important immediate impacts upon and longer range implications for those who conduct public affairs. For instance, it is estimated that the equivalent of a city the size of Philadelphia (approximately 2,000,000 people) must be built every twelve months to accommodate the additional population. Mayors and city managers, police and fire officials, public works and recreation administrators, social-welfare administrators, public school administrators — there is hardly a public official or agency that does not watch the tide of population growth and change with nervous anxiety.

Less easy to anticipate and to gauge are the more subtle and long-run implications flowing from changes in population. For instance, dramatic and sometimes quite unexpected short-run changes in age structure have profound future effects on public schools. Similarly, the ebb and flow in the number of marriages and new households, and in the size of families, have important implications for the structure of the labor market, school enrollments, tax base, crime rates, housing demand, and the like. Some municipal officials may brag about the growth of their cities in traditional "booster" spirit, but urbanization and suburbanization mean "people problems" for the public administrator.

The variable of population in the environment of public administration is deeply implicated in the issue which seems to be of increasing concern to public policy makers — the shortage of energy. Historically, the influences governing population growth and change in the United States included availability of land, opportunities for jobs and business, the search for freedom of worship and other civil liberties, and flight from oppression. The availability of energy sources, including water, power, wood, coal, gas, and oil, has been significant in the pattern of population growth and change in this country, but these sources have been regarded as abundant. It is likely that for at least the remainder of the twentieth century, the shortage of energy will be a significant influence in population growth and change.

Place

The Kaleidoscope of Human Settlement

An airplane flight across modern America can produce a shock of discovery. Massive urban agglomerations of single-family dwellings, high-rise apartments and business towers, factories, railyards, fuel tank farms, old downtown business districts, suburban shopping malls, an occasional urban park; fingers of urban growth extending out into farming lands; smaller cities, towns, and villages nestled in mountains and valleys or dotting open plains and deserts; vast open spaces seemingly untouched by man except for occasional ribbons of transcontinental highways and rail and power lines — this is the range of human settlement within which public administration must perform. At whatever level of government, and in whatever functional area of activity, the modern public administrator has transactions with that environment. An important element of that environment is *place*.

Spatial Relations

What difference does it make how closely a person is located to his or her neighbor? Does it matter whether a country is situated in the center of a huge continent, surrounded by other countries, or is an island open to the sea? What difference does it make whether we can walk to our city hall or must travel there over a long distance? Does the administration of government in a small state, such as Rhode Island, differ significantly from that in a large state, like California or Texas? Can we expect the same kind of citizen participation in public affairs in a tiny village of one square mile as in a megalopolis like metropolitan Chicago or Los Angeles? What are the effects of location on public institutions, such as state capitals, county seats, city halls, universities, prisons, and places of public assembly? Can we have as meaningful a sense of "community" in governmental jurisdictions that embrace vast territories as we can in small concentrated jurisdictions? These are the kinds of questions that must be addressed when we consider *place* in the environment of public administration. Many of the central concerns of public administration are intimately intertwined with issues of place: federalism, regionalism, neighborhood control, centralization and decentralization, intergovernmental relations, citizen participation, public trust, the exercise of leadership.

The Politics of Place

Questions of place are political questions. If, as reasoned in the preceding chapter, politics is essentially the resolution of conflict in terms of decisions that affect society, then location of people, institutions, enterprises, and resources may become a fighting matter. Some of the issues of the 1970s — such as the "bussing" of school children to achieve racial balance, securing of fresh water for thirsty metropolitan areas, the locating of prisons, efforts to preserve open spaces, and programs to combat pollution — are examples of such conflict issues.

The politics of place was clearly reflected in the findings of the National Commission on Urban Problems in 1969 concerning restrictive zoning practices: large-lot zoning, which attempts to limit development to single-family residences on very large lots; exclusion of multiple dwellings, which limits residential development to single-family houses; minimum house-size requirements, which exclude housing which fails to contain a minimum floor area as determined in the zoning ordinances; and various administrative practices which can impose rigid restrictions on who builds where or can lead to long delays which frustrate plans.[4] Such practices, which are widespread, become especially controversial politically at a time of concern about urban blight; emphasis on equal opportunity in housing; diminishing availability of urban land; rising construction costs; and white reaction against remedial public policies designed to improve the position of urban black people. It is often the public administrator who stands between the contending parties; and sometimes he or she is one of them.

The politics of place has become particularly heated with the realization of the fragility of our natural environment. Pell-mell urban development of precious agricultural lands, the pouring of city sewage into nearby rivers, and reckless building of freeways without regard to ecological consequences have become highly political issues. The *1974 Municipal Yearbook,* for instance, highlighted such problems and developments as the following: increasing public demands for responsible governmental action, appearance of serious environmental management problems, increasing numbers of citizen-initiated suits against polluters, trial-and-error remedial strategies, and increasing restlessness of the American people about the deterioration of the quality of their lives.[5]

In relation to the variable of *place,* the energy shortage punctuates the need for more careful coherence in formulation and administration of public policies. The recent "discovery" that the United States, like most industrialized nations, does not have sufficient energy to satisfy current needs, not to mention expanding requirements, is already compelling Americans to change substantially the ways in which they use their land and resources and locate their people and institutions. How far an American may be willing to travel to and from work and how much he or she may be willing to pay for that journey is no longer the overriding question underlying suburban growth in this country. Rather, it is realistic to expect that energy scarcity will become an ever-greater *intervening* variable in the impact of place on public administration.

The traditional *laissez-faire* philosophy, sometimes disguised as freedom, is being modified or perhaps even replaced, by a sober realization that *place*, like time and gravity, cannot be safely ignored. This new awareness has even been given a name. Bertram M. Gross, calling for greater attention in public administration to the processes of coping with space and location, has applied the term "mobiletics" to the cluster of interrelated phenomena concerning the movement of people and their things, and intercommunication among people.[6]

Groups

The Instinct for Combination

One of the most significant environmental variables influencing public administration is what has variously been called the "passion for belonging," the "herd instinct," or the "instinct for combination." It was this tendency for people to group together that De Tocqueville referred to after visiting the United States a century ago. But this is not uniquely American. Sociologists have observed that the essence of human existence lies in human organizational tendencies, which are reflected in a variety of social organization.

Some of the different forms which these human groupings take are *collectivities,* such as publics, crowds, and audiences; communities, such as villages, towns, cities, and metropolises; *associations,* such as clubs, pressure groups, and sects; and *institutions,* such as large corporations, schools, universities and colleges, and church establishments. They all influence and are influenced by public administration, especially in urban communities. To understand government at work one must move beyond the immediate bureaucratic habitat of the public administrator into the multitude of groups created to advance or protect special interests, and therefore to influence the administrator.

Special-Interest Groups

Interest groups differ in many ways, such as size, resources, organizational cohesiveness, intensity of commitment, strategy and tactics, political skill, and proximity to the handles of power. Some are transitory, tenuous, and not taken seriously by people in government. Others are politically muscular and deeply rooted in American society, enjoying virtually a veto power over certain public proposals and decisions. Some are sources of crucial support for public agencies; others are bitterly hostile. A crucial requirement for the public administrator is to know the difference between the helping hand and the collar of constraint.

The organizational germ is contagious. The public administrator must deal not only with such "external" groups as the American Medical Association, the AFL-CIO, the National Rifle Association, or the National Association for the Advancement of Colored People; he or she must also cope with the spread of special-interest groups *within* the public services. The ICMA, for instance, lists a bewildering variety of groups that provide service and guidance to state and local governments in the United States, including:

American Association of Airport Executives
American Institute of Planners
American Public Welfare Association
American Public Works Association
American Society for Public Administration
International Association of Assessing Officers
International City Management Association
International Institute of Municipal Clerks
National Institute of Governmental Purchasing
National Municipal League
U.S. Conference of Mayors[7]

They make important contributions to a more professional public service through membership requirements, recommendation or prescription of educational and training standards, promotion of certain programs and priorities, the contracting of consultant services, and the conduct of research. But, at the same time and often by means of these very contributions, they exercise influence over what governments do and how they do it.

Interest Politics and the Public Administrator

One of the most important facts of life for the public administrator is *group politics*. One school of thought views such politics as a necessary and legitimate aspect of democracy. According to Robert Dahl, the essence of democracy lies in the search for policy consensus among special-interest groups. Groups, it is reasoned, do not necessarily obstruct or subvert the proper working of government. Rather, they serve such functional purposes as transferring citizens' interests and demands to remote legislatures and bureaucracies, providing for two-way communication between constituents and governments, helping in the process of negotiation and reconciliation among conflicting interests in the community, helping to clarify issues, and helping to legitimize public policies and programs.[8]

On the other hand, there is a school of thought which believes that interest-group politics are leading to irresponsible government. For instance, Grant McConnell, after a thorough study, concluded that "a substantial part of government in the United States has come under the influence or control of narrowly based and largely autonomous elites." More recently, Theodore J. Lowi found that interest-group politics have led to the serious weakening of the capacity of governments in this country to govern. And, of course, the studies of Ralph Nader and his associates point to the conclusion that interest-group politics leads to placing the sheep in the care of the wolf.[9]

The group structure of the environment thus presents the modern public administrator with a dilemma. How does one maintain cordial and constructive relationships with the leaders of interest groups without endangering personal freedom of decision and ethical standards? While there is no simple and easy answer to this crucial question, education and training in public administration is now much more concerned with promoting an understanding of the repertoire of strategies and tactics by which organizations respond to different environmental circumstances. That repertoire is an important item on the agenda of modern public administration.

Technology

Technological Development

No feature of the environment has exerted greater influence on government and its administration than has technology. Today it is a commonplace for the president of the United States to begin his day with a breakfast meeting at the White House in Washington, address a luncheon gathering in California or Oregon, and be back at the White House for dinner. But for the first president of the United States a journey of 200 miles could be a difficult undertaking. President George Washington, in returning from Bedford, Pennsylvania, to the seat of government in Philadelphia, was once marooned in the middle of the Susquehanna River when his coach became lodged between boulders, and he had to sit there and wait while help was sought in extricating him.[10]

The shift, in less than two centuries, from the presidential coach to the presidential jet is symbolic of the enormous influence that technology has had not only on public administration, but also on many aspects of American life. It was for good reason that President Richard M. Nixon, in a message to the Congress in 1972, declared:

> The ability of the American people to harness the discoveries of science in the service of man has always been an important element in our national progress. . . . Americans have long been known all over the world for their technology ingenuity — for being able to "build a better mousetrap" — and this capacity has undergirded both our domestic prosperity and our international strength.[11]

The tangible manifestations of technology in our environment are abundant. The automobile, the airplane, television, the copying machine, the jumbo oil transport, the communications satellite, the computer, the transistor radio, the tape recorder and other monitoring devices, and new fertilizers and insecticides have radically altered our institutions and our lives. More subtly, perhaps, but not less significantly, technology has transformed the social environment of America. The business corporation, the labor union, special-interest groups, citizen action bodies, grievance mechanisms, behavior modification, and what B. F. Skinner has called "operant conditioning" — these are only some of the social inventions and discoveries that have transformed the environment of the American people.

Technology as Problem-Solving Knowledge

Technology is not the artifacts of mankind, but rather the *problem-solving knowledge* that is accumulated in human experience and recorded in human memory, books, other records, and recorded in the artifacts themselves. The technologist is fascinated with finding means to ends, with results, with efficiency and effectiveness. It should not be surprising, therefore, to find that students and practitioners of public administration have historically been technologically oriented.

Technology — problem-solving knowledge — has had special impact on public administration. Most of the significant innovations in public administration in the twentieth century have been technological: the *merit system,* based on a particular set of personnel management techniques; *human relations* methods, rooted in certain behavioral techniques; *PPBS* (Planning Programming, Budgeting System), built on knowledge about the relationship between work, time, money, and procedure; and *organizational development* which is indebted to new knowledge about human behavior in complex organizational systems.

The Price of Technological Development

It is ironical, perhaps, that despite the enormous accomplishments of science and industry, or perhaps because of these accomplishments, the technological environment is not regarded as entirely benign. The automobile has helped to weld this nation into one, but at the price of mass murder on the highways, smog, and dependence on foreign sources of energy. The airplane has helped to minimize the elements of space and time in everyday life, but the price of these gains is hijacking, noise, air pollution, and jet lag. Technological improvements in nutrition and health care have extended the human life span, along with the horror of nursing homes, old-age homes, loneliness, and sometimes mere physical existence. Electronic inventions have given us the power to communicate across continents and oceans and to the moon and the planets, but we have paid for this with loss of privacy and the threat of unauthorized surveillance of our lives.

Technology, at an increasing rate, is coming to be regarded as a threat to mankind. In 1954, for instance, the French sociologist Jacques Ellul found technology to be best illustrated by totalitarianism and the concentration camp. In 1970, Lewis Mumford warned that humanity was in danger of being "cannibalized" by what he called the "megamachine." And in 1972, the polling firm of Louis Harris and Associates found that science and technology enjoyed about half as much public confidence as they did five years earlier. Much of the heat of the challenge from the counter culture of the 1960s was directed at scientists and technologists who were regarded as anti-humanists. If technology presents a threat to mankind, the threat lies not in the new knowledge itself, but rather in the immoral purposes to which some technology is applied.[12]

Much attention is being paid during the 1970s to what has been called variously the "knowledge explosion" or the "learning revolution." Also, there is a great interest in "technology assessment" — the evaluation of both adverse and beneficial effects of technological innovations. Students and practitioners of public administration will continue to serve in the mainstream of these movements.

Ideology

"Ideology" is one of the most common and slippery terms in the lexicon of public affairs. In this book, the term is employed to mean a "world view" of reality and of how to deal with that reality. The ideological environment of American public administration is a system of ideas, assumptions, beliefs, value propositions, and norms. Not a closed or consistent system, it contains contradictions and illusions. The ideological environment offers rationales regarding the nature of human beings, the role of government, the nature of change, the appropriate use of human energy, rights and obligations of citizens, relations among citizens, relations between ruler and ruled, and so on.

Americans are distinctly nontheoretical in their approach to public affairs, and they tend not to be "ideological" in the sense of a rigid commitment to doctrine. Furthermore, "practical" people in public administration, as in some other fields of work and study, may protest that they are not bound or even influenced by any ideological forces in the environment. Yet, evidence seems to support the argument made many years ago by the British economist, John Maynard Keynes, that even the supposedly most practical-minded people were subject to intellectual influences.[13] In the following paragraphs, we introduce briefly some of the major features of the ideological environment within which American public administration takes place.

Individualism

The Preamble to the Constitution of the United States begins, "We the People of the United States," but the political institutions and ideology of this country are based on the singular pronouns I, you, he, and she. There is a strong belief in this country in the importance and supreme worth of each person. We tend to be hostile toward collective identities, such as classes, even though we are quick to join forces in a variety of special-purpose groups. The prevailing orientation in the United States is toward the conviction that the individual is capable of being self-sufficient and of participating meaningfully in self-government.

The Frontier Tradition

Although the physical frontier disappeared years ago, its concepts, values, and ethics remain alive in the United States. Americans have not forgotten the forest primeval, the settling of a continent, and the building of a nation. It may seem incongruous for some Americans in the 1970s to behave as their grandparents or great grandparents did in the wild and woolly west, but frontier attitudes toward use of land and water, local enforcement of law, neighborhood relations, and the legal powers and rights of private enterprise have not disappeared.

An important part of the frontier tradition is the continuing reverence for land. This reverence was an important influence on the settling of the North American continent. Land has historically been a root cause of much conflict and struggle in American history. Men and women faced torture, starvation, and death to secure land. An enduring consequence of the worship of land is the historical commitment in the United States to territorial representation. A great many Americans are still as much Virginians, Texans, and Californians as were their pioneer forebears.

Optimism

One of the reasons why the social upheavals, economic instability, ecological imbalance, and energy shortages of recent years have been traumatic for the American people is that these disturbances have challenged this country's historic sense of optimism. Americans have long believed that progress and enlightenment are inevitable. Neither the Great Depression of the 1930s nor the shock of World War II were able to quench the indomitable American conviction that tomorrow will be better than today.

The American people, Arnold Kaufman has observed, have been particularly susceptible to promises. Presidents, state governors, mayors, congressmen, state legislators, and other political people have long known that the American people are basically optimistic and want to believe the promises that are made to them. Public administrators, as the instruments through which promises are fulfilled, are highly dependent on this force of optimism in the national environment.[14]

Pragmatism and Activism

"Democratic government does something," declared Henry James, "and waits to see who hollers." It was that sense of pragmatism that has characterized much of American politics and government. Complementing the individualism, optimism, and frontier tradition is a strong experimental orientation, a willingness to innovate, an emphasis on practicality and feasibility. The American tends to ask not, "Is it right?" but rather, "Will it work?" The worst offense that the American can commit, according to this philosophy, is to try to re-invent the wheel.

Americans are pragmatic activists. At the depth of the Great Depression in 1932, Franklin D. Roosevelt, running for president for the first time, expressed the mood in classic terms: "The country needs and, unless I mistake its temper, the country demands bold, persistent experimentation . . . . take a method and try it: If it fails, admit it frankly and try another. But above all, try something."[15] The key words in the American lexicon are progress, change, innovation, experimentation, development, and growth. It may seem contradictory, but it can truly be said that this commitment to pragmatism and activism is an American doctrine.

The American Business Creed

In many ways, the United States is a business society. Virtue lies in values that are basically business values — competition, mechanical efficiency, productivity, the sanctity of private property, the freedom to contract and the binding quality of the contract, and the administration of affairs on the basis of personal advantage and gain. The market mechanism has influenced the structure of many public services. The corporate form of organization has influenced the organizational structure of many agencies of government — federal, state, and local. That frequent question, "Why can't government be more businesslike?" is symptomatic. Finally, the tendency to glorify bigness is an important element in the creed of American business. As already seen, it was not an accident of history that the principles of scientific management, which have been influential in the development of American public administration, found their first fulfillment in American commerce and industry.

Democracy

Here again is a most influential but slippery idea in the ideological environment of public administration. By "democracy" is meant a system which emphasizes certain substantive guarantees, such as freedom of assembly and speech, and certain procedural guarantees, such as limited government, popular control of policy makers, the individual citizen's equality and freedom in the political arena, majority rule when the people's representatives disagree, and due process in law and administration.

Closely associated with democracy in this ideology are the ideas of constitutionalism and the rule of law. Government, it is believed, should be controlled and power limited through enforcement of a system of restraints which are, in a sense, "rules of the game." They are rules that are supposed to assure fair play in politics and government. And it is through the instrument of a constitution that these rules are formulated and set down for posterity.

Constitutionalism provides for making changes in the rules themselves, such as through constitutional conventions and the amending process. In other words, no person, village dogcatcher or president of the United States, is above the law as formulated in the Constitution and interpreted by the courts. If one wants to change the system, one must do so through the system. Of the offenses committed by the offenders in the Watergate Affair, perhaps the most serious is that they set themselves above the law. Here, for instance, are the words of the House Judiciary Committee in a report on the impeachment of President Richard M. Nixon in August of 1974:

> The conduct of Richard M. Nixon has constituted a repeated and continuing abuse of the powers of the Presidency in disregard of the fundamental principle of the rule of law in our system of government . . . . Reverence for the laws, said Abraham Lincoln, should "become the political religion of the nation." Said Theodore Roosevelt, "No man is above the law and no man is below it; nor do we ask any man's permission when we require him to obey it." . . . Our nation owes its strength, its stability, and its endurance to this principle.[16]

Catastrophe

Finally, in delineating the environment of public administration, some attention should be devoted to catastrophe as a variable. As a nation, the United

States of America has never experienced anything comparable to such catastrophic events as the destruction of the holy Jewish Temple in ancient
Jerusalem, the Mongol invasion of central Asia by Genghis Khan, the Communist Revolutions in Russia and China, or the Black Plague of the Middle
Ages. Perhaps the closest the American people have come to such catastrophes were the Civil War of the 1860s and the Great Depression of the 1930s.
Both have left indelible marks on American politics, government, and world
view.

At the subnational level, minor catastrophes have been influential — for
example, the Chicago fire and the San Francisco earthquake. The tidal wave
and hurricane that wrecked the city of Galveston, Texas, in 1900 led to the
invention of the commission form of government. The great drought of the
1930s in the Great Plains caused fundamental changes in population patterns,
agricultural methods, politics, public policies, and workways in the area.

The effects of catastrophe on humanity and on human institutions have
been neglected by students of public administration, but not by scholars
generally. In 1942, for instance, Pitirim Sorokin, the anthropologist, studied
the effects of war, revolution, and pestilence upon various aspects of civilization, including politics and government. In 1952, the Committee on Disaster
Studies, sponsored by the National Academy of Sciences and the National
Research Council, was created for the purpose of studying the behavior of
people under the stress of catastrophes, such as modern war. Their findings
were published in subsequent years, shedding much light on how catastrophes affect the structure and workings of institutions. In 1970, Russell
Dynes inaugurated the publication of various studies by the Disaster Research Center at Ohio State University. An excellent case study of community behavior under the stress of catastrophe, having relevance to public
administration and government, was published in 1970, concerning the tornado that struck Topeka, Kansas, on June 8, 1966.[17]

While the literature of the so-called "New Public Administration Movement" in the late 1960s and early 1970s implied that turbulence was something new in the environment of public administration, the fact is that
political and administrative leaders in the United States have succeeded in
coping with catastrophes surprisingly well. Dahl has summed it up eloquently:

> It [the American political system] is not a static system . . . . It has evolved
> and survived from aristocracy to mass democracy, through slavery, civil
> war, the tentative uneasy reconciliation of North and South, the repression
> of Negroes and their halting liberation; through two great wars of world-
> wide scope, mobilization, far-flung military enterprise, and return to haz-
> ardous peace; through numerous periods of economic instability and one
> prolonged depression with mass unemployment, farm "holidays," veterans
> marches, tear gas, and even bullets; through two periods of postwar
> cynicism, demagogic excesses, invasions of traditional liberties, and the
> groping, awkward, often savage, attempt to cope with problems of sub-
> version, fear, and civil tension.[18]

Written in 1956, the above interpretation has not been rendered invalid by
the tumultuous events of the years since.

Conclusions

In delineating the environment of public administration there is the danger of sketching a still life. This should be avoided. Population, location, social organization, technology, ideology, and catastrophe are in constant flux. The world of public administration is a world of fluidity and change. Perhaps, in an earlier and simpler time, it was sufficient for the public administrator to persist in theories and practices that were rooted in times of stability. But the modern student and practitioner must be a student of change if he or she is to serve as a change-agent.

Progress has already been made in developing instruments for detecting environmental changes and for projecting their likely impacts on society, government, and public administration. Social indicators, for instance, which are based on *social* accounting, are being developed to measure the social dimensions of environmental change. Similarly, during the 1960s, an "Urban Observatory" program was conceived and developed to provide for working partnership between universities and municipal governments, not only to observe changes in the urban environment, but also to help to design and implement appropriate public programs. Further, a new profession of "futurists" is emerging in which systematic analysis of environmental change is developing considerable technical sophistication. These developments present public administration with opportunities and challenges.

In this chapter, discussion has been limited to *American* public administration; but, in reality, many of the important environmental forces are global in origin and impact. The "brain drain" and the rise of the international corporation are only two of the trends in the world today that are presenting challenges to public administration and are requiring that public administrators cope with problems that cut across the boundaries of nations and cultures. In the next chapter, public administration beyond the boundaries of American experience is discussed.

NOTES

1. Bureau of the Census, Census of Population: 1970, Vol. 1, *Characteristics of the Population* (Washington, D.C.: Government Printing Office, 1973), Vol. I, Part I, Sec. I, pp. 37, 42.

2. U. S. Department of Labor, *U.S. Manpower in the 1970's, Opportunity & Challenge* (Washington, D.C.: Government Printing Office, 1970); *The Job Crisis for Black Youth* (New York: Twentieth Century Fund, 1971); 1970 Census of Population, *General Social and Economic Characteristics*, pp. 434–35.

3. 1970 Census of Population, *Characteristics of the Population*, Part I, Sec. 1, pp. 21, 24, 43, 58–59; E. Arriaga et al., *The Magnitude and Character of California's Population Growth* (Berkeley, Calif.: Institute of Population and Urban Research, 1971).

4. National Commission on Urban Problems, *Building the American City* (Washington, D.C.: Government Printing Office, 1969), pp. 211–17.

5. *The Municipal Year Book, 1974*, Vol. 41, No. 3 (Washington, D.C.: International City Management Association, 1974), pp. 255–94.

6. Bertram M. Gross, "Planning in an Era of Social Revolution," *Public Administration Review* 31 (May-June 1971): 259–97.

7. *Municipal Yearbook: 1974*, pp. 393–97.

8. Robert A. Dahl, *A Preface to Democratic Theory* (Chicago: University of Chicago Press, 1956).

9. Grant McConnell, *Private Power & American Democracy* (New York: Alfred A. Knopf, 1966), p. 339; Theodore J. Lowi, *The End of Liberalism* (New York: W.W. Norton, 1969); and Robert C. Felmeth, *The Interstate Commerce Commission: The Public Interest and the ICC* (New York: Grossman, 1970).

10. Leonard D. White, *The Federalists: A Study in Administrative History* (New York: Macmillan, 1948), p. 1.

11. Richard M. Nixon, "Science and Technology," *The President's Message to the Congress*, 16 March 1972 (Washington, D.C.: Government Printing Office, 1972).

12. Jacques Ellul, *The Technological Society* (New York: Alfred A. Knopf, 1964); Lewis Mumford, *The Pentagon of Power*, Vol. II, "The Myth of the Machine" (New York: Harcourt Brace Jovanovich, 1970), p. 435.

13. John Maynard Keynes, *The General Theory of Employment, Interest and Money* (New York: Harcourt Brace Jovanovich, 1936), p. 383.

14. Arnold S. Kaufman, *The Radical Liberal* (New York: Simon & Schuster, 1968).

15. Franklin D. Roosevelt, *Public Papers and Addresses*, Samuel I. Rosenman, comp. (New York: Random House, 1933), I, 646.

16. Report of the House Judiciary Committee, quoted in *Los Angeles Times*, 23 August 1974.

17. Pitirim A. Sorokin, *Man and Society in Calamity* (New York: E.P. Dutton, 1942); George W. Baker and Dwight W. Chapman, eds., *Man and Society in Disaster* (New York: Basic Books, 1962); Allen H. Barton, *Communities in Disaster, A Sociological Analysis of Collective Stress Situations* (Garden City, N.Y.: Doubleday, 1969); Russell R. Dynes, *Organized Behavior in Disaster* (Lexington, Mass.: Heath Lexington Books, 1970); and James B. Taylor et al., *Tornado, A Community Responds to Disaster* (Seattle, Wash.: University of Washington Press, 1970).

18. Dahl, *Preface to Democratic Theory*, pp. 150–51. © 1956 by The University of Chicago. Used by permission.

4

The Study of Comparative and Development Administration

American public administration, both in its study and practice, has been ethnocentric. In his often cited essay in 1887, Woodrow Wilson called for a uniquely American field of administration, free of irrelevant foreign ideas and influences. To a considerable extent, scholars and practitioners have followed his counsel. The early textbooks and other literature in public administration in the United States concentrated on formulating principles of practice that were especially related to the historical, constitutional, technological, and social circumstances of the American people in a developing continent. Scholars and practitioners of public administration in this country have tended not to be familiar with nor concerned about the administrative experience of foreign countries, with the exception of Great Britain. While other countries have freely borrowed from each other and from American administrative ideas and practices, Americans have tended not to reciprocate.[1]

Much of the importance of the study of comparative and development administration is that it has helped to reduce significantly this ethnocentric myopia toward the values, ideas, and experiences of other people and other lands. Under the leadership of the Comparative Administration Group (CAG) within the American Society for Public Administration (ASPA), now called the Section on International and Comparative Administration (SICA), American public administration has opened its doors to foreign influences. An impressive body of theoretical and empirical literature has been produced. Closer intellectual links between scholars working in comparative administration and practitioners working in development administration in foreign countries have been forged. American public administrators have discovered their counterparts in other lands, through working abroad and through such professional bodies as the International Institute of Administrative Sciences. Through this linkage of academic comparative administration and practical development administration, there has been gain for all parties. In this chapter, some of that experience is examined, for in such an examination it becomes clear that the administrator of an American city may have as much in common with his or her foreign counterpart as with an administrator in a distant state capital or in Washington, D.C.

Models of Analysis

The introductory discussion of the comparative perspective (chapter 2) emphasized that merely identifying and adding up the surface similarities and differences among national systems of public administration does not constitute comparative study. Needed, it will be recalled, are concepts that "permit us to formulate generalizations and hypotheses." Since the 1950s, a number of different analytical models have been employed in an effort to develop theoretical frameworks for understanding, to organize complex data, to provide bases for meaningful comparisons, and to capture the realities of public administration in different countries and cultures.

Academicians have concentrated on models, such as *bureaucracy, administrative culture*, and *political change*, which strive toward a high theoretical level and toward convergence with political science and the other social sciences. Other scholars, impatient with the highly speculative character and the lack of empirical support in much comparative public administration, have pursued the search for measurable data. Also, scholars having a strong practical orientation have studied comparative public administration through the analysis of particular administrative institutions and practices, such as civil service systems, local governments, financial administration systems, and systems of social services. And those who have strong reformist tendencies have devoted their attention to the administrative issues and problems involved in the development of countries in Asia, Africa, and Latin America.

Bureaucracy

An analytical model that has interested the more academic students of comparative public administration is *bureaucracy*, based on the ideal-type construct of Max Weber (discussed in chapter 12), which focuses attention on certain structural and functional characteristics of public administration within the cultural milieu. The use of various bureaucratic models has shed light on such important matters as the political roles of public administrators, the social composition of the public service, the nature and sources of bureaucratic power, the different types of authority enjoyed by public officials, the processes of decision making, and interactions of governments with their environments.

An early attempt to employ a bureaucratic model in the comparative study of public administration was Walter R. Sharp's study of administration in Egypt.[2] His work shed light on such matters as the political context of the

Egyptian bureaucracy, its ethnic and social composition, the administrative structure of the Egyptian government, the level of professionalism in the public service, the influence and prestige enjoyed by bureaucrats in Egypt, and the Egyptian system of internal sanctions and rewards in controlling the bureaucracy.

A landmark study is the work of Michael Crozier, originally published in France in 1963. Comparing public and private bureaucracy in France, he shed light on some of the mysteries of bureaucratic life, such as the bases of power and exercise of power in bureaucratic organizations, intergroup relations and the struggle for institutional survival of groups and other entities within bureaucracies, bureaucratic bargaining strategies, problems of coping with change, the bureaucratic personality, and the dilemma of democratic social action versus bureaucratic organization.[3]

In a provocative and disturbing study originally published in Germany in 1969, Henry Jacoby effectively employs the bureaucracy model in analyzing the benefits and costs of the bureaucratic form of government, which he believes has prevailed in history.[4] Students and practitioners who rejoice in the rise of the administrative state and in the growth of public administration are reminded by this book that dangers to civilization as we have known it lie along the way.

A popular definition of the expert—and the professional public administrator is an expert — is a person who knows all there is to know about her or his work but does not have even the slightest notion of what that work has to do with the universe. One of the virtues of the bureaucracy model is that it helps to remove the blinders from the public administrator and to show that there may be profound connections between what happens in the bowels of governments and what happens to the universe.

Administrative Culture

Similar to the use of the bureaucracy model is the employment of the administrative culture model. A comparison of public administration in different countries and cultures involves much more than a choice of analytical methods. Comparisons involve an encounter with different, competing, and sometimes clashing cultures, for it is in the context of a particular culture that public administration occurs, as we have already seen in our discussion of the environment of public administration.

From generally accepted definitions of the term "culture" there can be derived a definition of "administrative culture": *the cluster of beliefs, attitudes, values, institutions, and methods which are socially learned and which influence and constrain public administration in a particular country or society.* Although administrative culture as a model for the study of the realities of public administration in different countries has not been *explicitly* employed as widely as has the bureaucratic model, it does offer valuable insights.[5]

For instance, although the countries of Latin America differ in important ways, empirical literature suggests that there is an identifiably Latin American administrative culture, generally composed of such attributes as the following:

1. The influence of the Spanish colonial tradition, including inherited attitudes toward certain administrative procedures
2. Strong social-class patterns, defense habits, and tendencies toward conflict in intergroup relations
3. Attitudes and practices regarding the issues of administrative hierarchy and authority, including especially what has been called the "cult of the caudillo" or the tradition of the man on horseback
4. Emphasis on personal and partisan loyalty
5. The tendency for public bureaucrats, compelled to operate in a highly unstable political system, to develop a preoccupation with their own survival
6. A tradition of cultural dependency, or what has been called "administrative mimicry," manifested by the readiness with which Latin American countries have borrowed from other nations, especially from the United States
7. Reluctance to delegate administrative authority to subordinates, a tendency which is related to such cultural patterns as the authoritarian political environment, political regime instability, class consciousness and deference, the unitary pattern of government prevailing in Latin American countries, and the widespread and long-standing lack of adequately trained personnel

An insightful application of the model of administrative culture is the 1970 study of Israeli public administration by Gerald E. Caiden.[6] Although not carefully supported empirically, the study does argue persuasively that public administration in that tiny country is shaped and conditioned by a complex cultural milieu. That milieu includes linguistic diversity (Hebrew, Arabic, English, and Yiddish); continual war and threats of war; a mixed legal tradition (Biblical, Ottoman, British, and European); Zionism and the pioneering ideology of the early immigrants; and the tide of immigrants coming from many corners of the globe.

The administrative culture that has developed within that milieu is a crucial factor in the survival of the Israeli state and in the successes and failures of the Israeli government. Caiden has found a strong tendency toward self-government, high sensitivity toward anything affecting the national security, a crisis atmosphere pervading all governmental institutions, personalistic rather than bureaucratic patterns of behavior, a tendency toward administrative improvisation rather than detailed planning, popular disdain for public officials generally but high regard for military leaders, and extensive politicization of administrative institutions.

An especially creative use of the cultural model in comparing systems of public administration is that of Fred W. Riggs, the most prolific scholar in comparative studies.[7] Dissatisfied with the catalogue approach of many earlier comparative work and with the imprecise concepts and terminology employed, he created what he regarded as simplified pictures of two basically different cultural milieus within which systems of public administration operate.

One image he called "Agraria," the other "Industria." Agraria was characterized by a self-contained economy, strong in-group attitudes and hostility toward outsiders, tendencies toward governmental decentralization, relatively little mobility across class lines, aristocratic rule in government, emphasis upon accepted or proper behavior rather than on the search for "truth," and communally oriented values which emphasize the group rather than the individual. The consequences of Agrarian cultural characteristics for public administration were important. There were, for instance, greater opportunities for individual administrators to enjoy freedom from restraint and engage in empire building. Personnel recruitment was constrained by class lines. The Agrarian bureaucrat was relatively more resistant to pressures. Nepotism abounds in Agraria. In Agraria, taxes are collected locally and sent up to the central government. And in Agraria, the public official avoids any intimacy that might threaten stable working relationships. Communications systems are weak and public officials tend to depend heavily on their own sources of information. Agraria, according to Riggs, was an ideal-type construct, and not an attempt to describe a particular country, but many of the "undeveloped" nations of Africa and Asia have administrative systems that include such "Agrarian" features.

"Industria," on the other hand, according to the Riggs image, is characterized by features that also have consequences for public administration. For instance, the Industrian economy is more interdependent, thus requiring planning and coordination. Many "secondary" associations, such as universities, trade unions, business firms, and professional groups cut across the old traditional in-group boundaries of family, clan, and village. Government in Industria tends to be more centralized. With greater social mobility in Industria than in Agraria, the public personnel systems are less constrained by aristocratic influences. The Industrian public administrator is more concerned with science and technology as a guide to behavior, than with etiquette and chivalry. The administrator is more sensitive to popular pressures. The merit principle replaces nepotism. In Industria, administrative communications are highly developed and complex, with information flowing through a variety of institutionalized channels, horizontally and vertically.

Again, it should be remembered that this is a simplified image of reality and not a description of a particular country. Western nations, such as those of Europe and North America, tend best to illustrate Industria. Some developing countries, such as Thailand, Iran, and Nigeria, have features of both Agraria and Industria.

The busy public administration practitioner might be moved, in the face of all this, to ask, "So what? What does all this have to do with the problems that I face on my job here and now?" One answer is this: the kind of analysis that Riggs has made, and the use of the administrative culture model remind the public administrator that his or her work is part of a larger universe and the model offers a key which helps to unlock what might otherwise be dark and mysterious governmental ways in different countries.

Specific Administrative Institutions, Policies, and Practices

Less theoretical than the models of bureaucracy and administrative culture and more concerned with practical problem-solving and administrative improvement is the analytical approach that focuses on particular administrative institutions, policies, and practices. This is an *analogical* method in which two or more entities are selected for detailed comparison, in the belief that general "principles" or "laws" might be extrapolated for wider applications and evaluations.

For instance, an early use of this method was the study by Brian Chapman, published in London in 1959.[8] Tracing the history of administrative institutions from ancient Rome to twentieth-century Europe, he compared European public service institutions on the basis of composition of the civil services, methods of recruitment and training, systems of rewards and penalties, training institutions, control and oversight of public administrators, public service trade unions, and the ombudsman. Permeating the Chapman study are important themes, such as the rise of the administrative state, the relations between politics and administration, the professionalization of the public service, and the diverse public attitudes of the European people toward their public servants. The generalizations that he extrapolates from the comparisons include: (1) greater efforts should be made to absorb the newer public services into the regular structure of the government; (2) a more sharp distinction should be made between public officials and administrators in the private sector; and (3) there is a need for improved public relations in government which seeks more vigorously and creatively to develop a truly informed public.

Extensive application of this method has been made by Harold F. Alderfer in two detailed studies of public administration and local government in the developing nations.[9] Less theoretical than the studies that employ the models of bureaucracy and administrative culture, they emphasize the more practical work-related tasks and procedures associated with the management-process perspective in public administration. Anyone interested in learning how local revenues are distributed in India, how the French maintained law and order in their African colonies, how village elders in Turkey make decisions, how the civil service operates in Egypt, and how the Brazilians prepare their government budgets would find the Alderfer studies enlightening.

A more recent interest in comparative studies has been the systematic analysis of particular public policy areas in different countries. For instance, in 1968, Barbara N. Rodgers and her associates examined the social security policies and related administrative problems in France, Norway, and Canada.[10] The study offers insights on the need for planners to be sensitive to the economic consequences of their decisions, the central importance of priorities, and the importance of assuring that program data are made understandable and acceptable to the people. The Rodgers study emphasizes that regardless of the particular country, level of government, or sector of the economy involved, or the service to be performed, the issue of effective communications in the public policy process is of critical importance.

A symposium on "Policy Studies Around the World," published in 1973, offers a balanced discussion of substantive policies, theoretical framework for such analysis, and methodological problems.[11] The symposium examines some of the practical and theoretical problems and possibilities in transnational research on public policies in the areas of crime control, education, poverty and welfare, and resource allocation.

An especially productive vehicle for the comparative study of particular institutions, policies, and practices has been the International Institute of Administrative Sciences, with headquarters in Brussels. For many years, its publication, the *International Review of Administrative Sciences*, has published comparative studies of budget and financial administration, personnel development, administrative law, environmental protection, economic and social planning, automation and other aspects of what the institute calls "Informatics."

During July, 1974, the institute conducted its sixteenth triennial International Congress of Administrative Sciences in Mexico City. Over 1500 delegates from more than eighty countries participated.[12] The agenda included administrative problems of regionalization within nations, public administration education and training, manpower planning and development, public information, public works administration, and the like. The conference served as an arena within which some of the conceptual difficulties, terminological ambiguities, and doctrinal conflicts embodied in the comparative study of public administration were aired.

Development Administration

History of the Development Movement

As we have already pointed out, the "development movement" contributed to the growth of the comparative perspective in the study of public administration. Following the end of World War II, a variety of motives led to increased interest in the "underdeveloped nations." These motives included cold-war competition between East and West; the admission of many former British, French, Belgian, and Italian colonies, mostly in Africa, to membership in the United Nations; and commercial motives, such as the industrialized countries' search for new markets. A dramatic early landmark event in the United States was President Truman's announcement of his "bold new program," the Point Four of his inaugural address in 1949, in which the United States committed itself to an ambitious program of technical assistance to the underdeveloped nations.[13]

During the years that followed, there were many important events in the development movement in the United States and abroad. In 1954, Soviet Russia started granting trade and aid to certain countries, such as Argentina and Afghanistan. During the 1950s, the British provided development assistance to their colonies, some of which were to become independent by the end of the decade. In 1953, the United States initiated its "Food for Peace" program. In 1961, most nonmilitary United States assistance to developing countries was reorganized under the Agency for International Development (AID). During the 1960s, President John F. Kennedy's "Alliance for Progress" was promoted in Latin America; and in the United Nations several specialized bodies for the promotion of economic and social development were created, such as the International Bank for Reconstruction and Development, the International Development Association, the United Nations Special Fund, the United Nations Technical Assistance Board, and the United Nations Expanded Programme for Technical Assistance.

The early emphasis in the movement was on problems of "underdevelopment," especially on chronic disease and hunger, poverty, and unemployment. The term "development" was viewed primarily and simplistically as an economic process in which the remedy was an infusion of capital and technical expertise as a means of reviving sick economies.

As time passed, the conception of "development" was broadened to include more than economic growth and vitality. What was perceived to be wrong with certain underdeveloped countries was a lack of adequate institutions and workways for economic, social, and political well-being. There was concern about more than disease and hunger. Attention came to be focused also on disparities and inequities between the "haves" and the "have-nots," between the rulers and the ruled. It was now seen that there was a lack of modern communications, transportation, and other elements of infrastructure through which the people of these countries might be absorbed or incorporated into the stream of modern culture. Development also now meant trying to remedy the lack of political institutions which might help to promote meaningful citizen participation, responsible political leadership, and legitimate transition from one political regime to another. Attention was also devoted now to the lack of a sense of national identity in many of these countries, and to the failure of these countries to exploit fully their natural economic and physical potentialities. Around the movement, there developed an ideology whose slogans were "progress," "modernization," "growth," "development," and "planning."

But it did not take many years of the development movement to discover that between the dream and the reality there falls the shadow of administrative feasibility. Officials in the developing countries were often unable to do the necessary planning for the proper investment of foreign development aid. Adequate planning and administrative institutions did not exist, and proper methods were not practiced. Also, there was a bias, among both the recipients and donors, toward favoring dramatic and more easily planned infrastructural projects—such as highways, airports, dams, and public buildings—but with little regard for these less visible and more difficult projects: civil service reform, modernization of the budgeting and accounting systems; improvement of public information programs and other bridges to the people; and the promotion of appreciation for important administrative values, such as promptness, exactness, a sense of organizational relations, and continuity and coherence between separate tasks and activities.

Public administration began to be taken more seriously as an important aspect of development in 1951, when H. L. Keenleyside, director-general of the United Nations' Technical Assistance Administration, appointed a Special Committee on Public Administration Problems. Two members of the committee were American professors who had contributed to the development of public administration studies in the United States, Rowland Egger of the University of Virginia, and Albert Lepawsky of the University of California at Berkeley. The committee's report became a basic document for United Nations experts working in development administration.[14]

In the United States, during the years of the Eisenhower administration, development continued to be conceived primarily as a relatively simple economic process. This was a climate that was hostile to any attempt to give greater attention to public administration in the development movement.

But from the beginning of the Kennedy presidency in 1961, development was more clearly understood as a complex process requiring a more comprehensive cultural and institutional framework. This broader approach placed more emphasis on wide-reaching national planning, improvement of educational opportunities in the developing countries, promotion of social justice, and the strengthening of public administration. This was partly the result of thinking by a group of professors in the Cambridge, Massachusetts, area, dubbed by Arthur M. Schlesinger, Jr., the "Charles River Group." The group included a number of men who were destined to become powerful during the presidencies of John Kennedy and Lyndon Johnson—John Galbraith, Walt Rostow, David Bell, and Harlan Cleveland.

The emphases of the Charles River Group's approach were articulated in some detail in a 1959 study for the Committee on Foreign Relations of the United States Senate by the Maxwell School of Syracuse University, under the direction of the School's Dean, Harlan Cleveland.[15] The report had much to say about the institutional inadequacies of the newly independent nations, the need for promotion of democracy as it is practiced in the United States and Western Europe, the importance of national identity and consensus in combatting poverty and disease, the inevitability of political conflict resulting in the developing countries as a consequence of some development programs, and the importance of paying attention to the operational or administrative requisites of development.

Prophetically, the Cleveland report reminded the Senate Committee of what scholars in comparative and development administration had been contending for some time: success in attempts to promote the development of certain countries depends as much on the behavior of the donors as on that of the recipients. Americans working in development programs abroad, the report declared, should possess five attributes:

1. *Technical skill:* The versatility and willingness to improvise that requires both a thorough knowledge of a specialized field, but the attitude toward it of a general practitioner rather than a narrow specialist.
2. *Belief in mission:* A dedication to his work regardless of geography that enables a man to survive repeated frustrations and still retain a zest for the job.
3. *Cultural empathy:* The curiosity to study and the skill to perceive the inner logic and coherence of the other fellow's way of thinking; and the restraint not to judge it as bad just because it is different from the American way.
4. *A sense for politics:* The sensitivity to see oneself as a "political man" whose action (or inaction) affects the power structure around him . . . .
5. *Organization ability:* A tolerance for large-scale organization and an understanding of complicated headquarters-field relationships; and a special talent for building social institutions and teaching others to manage them.[16]

Cleveland and his colleagues perceived development administration as a challenge, not only to the developing countries, but to the donors as well.

Lessons From American Experience in Development Assistance

From 1953 to 1961, American programs to promote the development of the less developed countries were administered under the Mutual Security Act by a succession of federal agencies—Mutual Security Agency, Foreign Operations Administration, and International Cooperation Administration. During this period, the total nonmilitary American expenditure for the development of the less developed countries was $24 billion. In addition, during that period, $10.3 billion were provided to these countries for military assistance.

In 1961, the Foreign Assistance Act, emphasizing nonmilitary support and the self-help of the people in the less developed countries, replaced the old Mutual Security Act as the legislative basis for the development efforts. All programs were reorganized and combined under a new agency called the Agency for International Development (AID). The total nonmilitary American expenditure for development assistance to the less developed countries, from 1946 to 1968, was $31.7 billion. Assistance for military purposes during the same period totaled $20.7 billion.

The bulk of this assistance went to a relatively few countries. Robert E. Asher, in his authoritative study of development assistance, has shown that almost 90 percent of development assistance given by AID in fiscal year 1968 was received by fifteen countries: Vietnam, India, Brazil, Pakistan, Colombia, Korea, Turkey, Laos, Chile, Thailand, the Dominican Republic, Indonesia, Nicaragua, Nigeria, and Panama.[17]

American support for these development programs reached a peak about the mid-1960s and then began to decline sharply. Each year budgets were cut more drastically, as congressional scrutiny and public criticism grew. During the late 1960s, several blue-ribbon commissions, such as the President's General Advisory Committee on Foreign Assistance Programs, which reported in 1968, and the Task Force on International Development, which made its report in 1970, challenged many features of the program, including those in public administration.

The reasons for the decline in support are many: accumulating evidence of some failures and mistakes; preoccupation of the American people and their government with the war in Indochina and with the related peace movement at home; worldwide problems of inflation, energy shortages, unemployment, and pollution; a warming in the relationships between the United States and the Communist world; and growing American fatigue with overseas commitments generally.

In a study by Milton J. Esman and John D. Montgomery, sponsored and financed by AID and published by the American Society for Public Administration, a candid evaluation of American development administration was made.[18] The authors acknowledged that there had been some accomplishments, such as promotion of rice production in the Philippines, rural reform in Taiwan, malaria eradication, and tsetse fly elimination. However, they also recognized that American development administration had been too narrowly confined to the concern with practical and specialized work-related tasks of administrative management — concerns usually associated with the so-called POSDCORB approach to public administration.

Esman and Montgomery called for a new doctrine of development administration for the 1970s that would embrace the new currents in the field, such as abandonment of the "simplistic 'economy and efficiency' models of the 1930s," greater sensitivity to connections between politics and administration, a stronger behavioral perspective, a more sophisticated conception of public administration which gives a larger place to quantitative and analytical techniques, and a truly comparative approach that is more sensitive to social and cultural constraints in the environments of the developing countries.

The limits of conventional theory and practice in public administration, in their application to developing countries, were demonstrated by Gilbert B. Siegel in his study of the experience of the University of Southern California in working with the Administrative Department of the Public Service of Brazil in the 1960s. "It was the selection of a strategy of control and centralization," Siegel has reported, "that led to the failure of administrative reforms."[19] In other words, some of the classical ideas and practices of public administration collided with the Brazilian administrative culture.

During the 1970s, criticism of American experience in development administration has increased. Development programs, it is argued, are predicated upon excessive faith in the capacity of American capital, energy, goodwill, and technical competence to accomplish miracles. Development, as promoted by AID and other American institutions, tends to bureaucratize simpler systems of government, fastening a set of "technocrats" on the backs of people only recently liberated from colonialism. Some of the objectives embraced by the development programs, the critics go on, are beyond the moral and intellectual resources of foreign developers. The developmental emphasis upon order and stability tends to maintain unpopular and undemocratic regimes in power and to perpetuate social injustices—witness Greece under the colonels, Pakistan under the generals, and Brazil under the junta. There has been too much reliance on professional intermediaries who are not sufficiently knowledgeable about the countries in which they work. There has been neglect of the human problems that commonly occur in the less developed countries. There has been insufficient collaboration among the various national and international bodies that render technical assistance to the developing countries. And, finally, it is charged that there has been insufficient commitment in the United States to the need for international technical assistance for its intrinsic worth and not as a weapon in the Cold War against Communism.

With the crescendo of criticism rising, the American development programs have continued to decline during the 1970s. The AID, which has been the major federal agency in planning and carrying out projects in development administration, has been sharply curtailed. For instance, the total number of direct-hire personnel in AID declined from 17,569 in 1968 to approximately 9,900 in 1974.[20]

Lessons From United Nations Experience in Development

Another chapter in the story of development administration is the work of the United Nations Public Administration Division in the Department of Economic and Social Affairs. At least on paper, the objectives of the United Nations Development Programme (UNDP) are ambitious and provocative:

1. Effective exploitation of the vast opportunities offered by scientific and technological innovations
2. Reduction of unjustified privileges, extremes of wealth, and social injustices
3. Maintenance of an average annual growth of the economies of the developing countries at a level of at least 6 percent.
4. Holding the annual rate of population increase at no more than 2.5 percent
5. Significant reduction of unemployment and underemployment, with rapid increase of the work force and greater income security
6. Expansion and improvement of the countries' facilities for education, health, nutrition, housing, and social welfare
7. Protection of the natural environment
8. Improvement of the well-being of children
9. Meaningful participation of youth and full integration of women and minority groups in the developmental process

Within these larger objectives, the United Nations' public administration program has been dedicated to the following repertoire:

1. Assignment of experts to developing countries, and provision of appropriate support, equipment, and materials for those experts to serve their missions
2. The granting of fellowships to promising persons from developing countries
3. The requirement that "country programmes" be developed—that is, granting United Nations approval for projects only if the requesting government has demonstrated appropriate political and administrative capability, high-level interest and commitment, and planning for necessary training and related essentials
4. A set of instruments designed to serve clusters of developing countries that share common needs and capabilities. Included are the preparation of training materials, development of a worldwide system of public administration information gathering and dissemination, and the convening of regional and interregional meetings and conferences
5. Appropriate criteria and the provision of assistance in evaluating the administrative capabilities of developing countries
6. An interdisciplinary process involving all sectors and levels of government, and also involving private organizations and individuals
7. The reform and improvement of the administrative structures and systems that are essential for the acceleration of social and economic progress
8. Improvement of public personnel administration, including especially the promotion of the capabilities of executive managers and the knowledge, skills, motivation, and productivity of the entire work force
9. Improvement of financial administration, including governmental budgeting and financial management, taxation, local government finance, and financial institutions. Special emphasis is placed on accuracy in financial reporting, close linkage between financial administration and develop-

ment planning and administration, managerial accounting and reporting procedures, enforcement of procedures that assure full value received for money spent, and vigorous and impartial collection of revenues
10. Application of computer technology
11. Encouragement of employee participation in official organizations and citizen participation in government
12. Comprehensive reform of local governments, including especially their structural simplification, strengthening of their role in national development planning and administration, and the strengthening and improvement of national agencies for assisting local governments in public administration

This repertoire generally reflects the conventional public administrative wisdom as developed and practiced in the United States since World War II.

In January, 1971, the "Second Meeting of Experts on the United Nations Programme in Public Administration" was held at the United Nations Headquarters in New York.[21] The purpose of the conference was to review past accomplishments and failures, and to plan for the decade of the 1970s. Specialists attended from seventeen countries — including the United States, Soviet Russia, highly developed countries of Europe, and developing countries of Africa and Asia. There was agreement among them on some of the accomplishments of the United Nations program: greater attention in the developing countries to country-wide programming; advancement of knowledge through the conduct of various interregional meetings and the publication of useful materials; closer collaboration with other national, international, professional, and educational organizations; some strengthening of regional and subregional institutions and activities; and improvement of the methods of recruiting experts by the United Nations Public Administration Division.

Measured against the need and the bold declarations of intent, these were modest accomplishments, indeed! The reasons for such disappointing performance are many. First, there were financial constraints, caused by inadequate funding and by inflation. Second, there were difficulties in recruiting competent specialists for service in developing countries. Third, recipient countries failed to follow up adequately on regional and interregional conferences. Fourth, the Public Administration Division at New York Headquarters failed to make a significant start in building a worldwide information system. Finally, underlying these failures was the acknowledged low status of public administration in world councils generally. The participants at the "Second Meeting of Experts" concluded their report pessimistically:

> In assessing those achievements and shortcomings . . . the Meeting regretted the fact that the role of public administration in development was still not well appreciated. It received much lip service everywhere, but little in the way of tangible support. The implications for the future of such a situation were largely self-evident.[22]

Constraints Upon Development Administration

One of the pervasive attitudes among those who promoted and conducted development administration, in the United States as well as in the United

Nations and other donor countries, was an excessive and unjustified optimism that envisaged a world of the future wrapped in a benign blanket
of industrialization, urbanization, and technologization. To the surprise of
many developers — even those who were intellectually aware of the complexities and difficulties of the development process — political, social,
psychological, and other constraints frustrated their utopian dreams.

One of the discoveries that was painfully made by Americans promoting
modern systems of public administration in the developing countries was
this: there are reciprocal political impacts between the environment of the
nation and formal administrative institutions. For instance, in 1964, Edward
Weidner, who had been deeply involved in technical assistance to the
developing countries, offered what he believed were the crucial political
factors that affect the promotion of modern public administration in such
countries:

1. Influences from the colonial past, such as rigid administrative centralization, lack of self-government, and governmental orientation toward
   inaction
2. Differences among the countries in level, intensity, quality, and extent
   of their public administration systems
3. Variable degrees of political freedom within the countries which affect
   technical assistance efforts, including such factors as the role of the
   military, sensitivity to revolutionary forces, openness of the political
   party system, level of democracy, and readiness of the country to place
   power in the hands of politically neutral administrative technicians
4. Quality and stability of political leadership in the country
5. Pluralist factors of interest representation, including especially the degree
   to which labor, farm, and business groups are effectively organized to
   promote their special interests
6. The relationship between the bureaucracy and other political institutions,
   including especially the electorate, the political party system, and the
   legislature.[23]

Weidner saw no possibility of developing universal or standardized strategies or formulas with which to escape such constraints. What was needed
was not *adoption* of innovations, but rather *adaptation.*

Another constraint on development administration is the tendency for
the people of developing countries to resist, reject, or be resentful of innovations that come from abroad. This is especially true of those innovations
that have profound implications for a country's way of life or which may
challenge the established political system. This point was made by Preston
James, a geographer at the Maxwell School of Syracuse University and a
member of the working group that helped to prepare the Cleveland Report
to the Senate in 1959. The following poignant story as told by James has
pertinence to anyone who has ever tried to promote modern public administration in a developing country:

> Two men were standing on a tropical hillside overlooking the Caribbean
> Sea. One was an engineer from the United States, the other was a Latin
> American. The engineer was pointing out some of the recent develop-

ments made under his direction. A formerly uninhabited swamp had been cleared and drained; rows of flourishing trees marked the newly created plantation; in the distance were the neat, white houses of a workers' village, built in accordance with the most modern plans for tropical housing. The engineer was justified in the pride he showed, for the development had required a large capital investment in previously unproductive land, and could not have been carried out without a high degree of technical skill. But the reaction of the Latin American left the engineer baffled. After some hesitation the Latin American replied slowly and thoughtfully: "*Si, es bueno—pero no es nuestro.*" (Yes, it is good, but it is not ours.)[24]

This is the same message conveyed by the United Nations' *Handbook of Public Administration* in 1961: "In the long run, every country has to solve its administrative problems in its own way, since administration is part of the national culture."[25]

Another cultural constraint in some developing countries is the tenacious belief in fatalism, especially among the more traditionalist people. For instance, Joseph L. Sutton has observed that the bureaucrat of Thailand, although exposed to influences other than Buddhism, remains a firm believer that affairs of this world do not matter. And, according to Sutton, the Thai bureaucrat sometimes employs that philosophy to justify bureaucratic inaction.[26]

Various studies of development in Arab and Moslem countries have cited the tenacity of traditional beliefs against change and personal activism. Daniel Lerner, for instance, has shed some light on the impact of this influence of fatalism in Turkey, Syria, and other Middle Eastern countries where the Koran ascribes to supernatural authority the source of all power and direction.[27]

Throughout Latin America, the belief in fatalism has obstructed and deflected the more ambitious plans of developers. Joseph A. Kahl, in his study of modernism in Brazil and Mexico, has cited *activism* (the opposite of fatalism) as the distinctive variable in comparing the modern man and his traditional brother.[28] For the modern technical specialist attempting to promote profound change in traditional countries, the force of fatalism is particularly frustrating.

Finally, those in development administration must accept some of the blame for failure. For years, the literature of development administration has reiterated the long list of complaints about the obstacles to development that lie in the people, the culture, and the governments of recipient nations. Not until the past few years, however, has there been open acknowledgment of the constraints on development administration that lie in the people, the culture, and the governments of the donors of such assistance.

For instance, Garth Jones, who spent thirteen years promoting technical assistance in public administration in Pakistan and other countries in Southeast and Southern Asia for the United States Agency for International Development, is highly critical of the developers themselves. His indictment includes the following: lack of an appropriate and clear conceptual framework; overemphasis on macro-analytical schemes, such as long-range development plans; neglect of practical and operational problems of development; lack of understanding among the American people of what successful technical assistance to developing countries requires of them; and excessive expediency and pragmatism among the American developers abroad.[29]

Conclusions

Considering the profound implications of comparative and development administration, the modest state of the art, and the highly complex and unstable nature of the world with which we must deal, it is premature and probably impossible to formulate at this time a firm verdict on the successes and failures of this aspect of the study of public administration. But there have been some accomplishments.

For the world at large, regimes enjoying the support of the people have been assisted in surviving partly because of improved administrative knowledge and competence. Newly independent nations, partly because of the insights and information resulting from comparative and development administration studies, have succeeded in making the perilous passage from colonial dependency to responsible self-government. Also, in particular substantive areas, such as agriculture, education, and community development, the study of comparative and development administration has made distinguished contributions.

More narrowly, for the discipline and profession of public administration, there have also been some accomplishments. Since the 1950s, the overconfidence and excessive abstractness of comparative study has been partially balanced by greater appreciation of the need for communication with practitioners and the need for testing of theory in actual practice. On the other hand, there is a greater respect among development administration practitioners for the importance of theory building.

Such progress is reflected in two handbooks for practitioners. One was the United Nations *Handbook* cited above. It declared that there was "strong evidence that there exists a common body of principles and techniques in the field of public administration which has some degree of worldwide and general validity." Eight years later, a handbook by Hiram S. Phillips appeared. It was based on the author's fifteen years of experience with AID and predecessor agencies.[30] Both manuals strove to serve the practitioner, but where the United Nations volume concentrated on the conventional rubrics — such as organizational structure, personnel administration, and budget and financial administration — the Phillips book was heavily based on the institution-building theories and concepts of scholars in comparative and development administration.

The relationship between comparative and development administration has had a symbiotic quality. In overseas development programs, scholars have found supportive research funds, access to empirical data, and laboratories for the testing of some of their theories. At universities and other places of academic study, practitioners have found challenging questions, useful insights, and places to work after retirement from government. But the relationship has been threatened over the years by tension between academicians and practitioners.

This tension was expressed a few years ago by a man who had worked in both areas. Herbert Emmerich was one of the founders of modern public administration in the United States earlier in this century. He held important positions in the federal government during the 1930s and 1940s and directed the prestigious Public Administration Clearing House in Chicago. He was also intimately involved in many other professional public administration organizations. He served as a senior consultant to the United Nations Development Program, for which he edited the United Nations *Handbook* referred to above. He was the author of many books and scholarly articles and received honorary doctorates from major universities. In 1963, at the age of sixty-six, he became a full-time professor of government and foreign affairs at the University of Virginia, where he led in the establishment of a graduate degree in public administration.

Yet, just before his death in 1970, in an essay heralding the United Nation's "Second Development Decade," he lamented the tendency of scholars in comparative and development administration to become preoccupied with theoretical studies, to neglect the practical details of implementing grand designs, and to devote too much of their energies to such academic frivolities as seminars and meetings that lead to academic publications.[31] In other words, too many professors in comparative and development administration were behaving like professors.

Such tension, however, is not a catastrophe. As Stephen Bailey, another activist scholar has written, it may be a source of great strength:

> There is an inherent tension between public administration as a self-discipline and institutional discipline on the one hand, and as an intellectual discipline on the other. This tension is not unique to public administration. In any endeavor encompassing both practical action and academic theory, such as medicine or law, the knowledge possessed at a given time frequently is inadequate to guide the action required by the pressure of the events.
>
> Properly directed, this tension can be a creative one. It can stimulate a continuing effort to improve knowledge and practice as mutually reinforcing processes. Improperly directed, this tension can degenerate into hostility, futility, and indifference.[32]

Under the guidance of such groups as the Section on International and Comparative Administration of the American Society for Public Administration, the symbiotic relationship between scholarship and overseasmanship shows promise of bearing more robust fruit.

With this discussion of the study of comparative and development administration concluded, attention will now be directed to an examination of public administration within the web of government in the United States. In the chapters that follow, there will be discussion of the impacts of three important influences upon American public administration, and the implications of those influences: urbanization, intergovernmental relations, and law.

NOTES

1. The report of the "Brownlow Committee" to President Franklin D. Roosevelt in 1937 has been long recognized as one of the documents marking the high-water point of orthodox public administration thinking in the United States. Its analyses and prescriptions are steeped in special references to American history, American experience, and American values. There is no evidence or suggestion in the document that the United States might learn from foreign experience. See President's Committee on Administrative Management, *Administrative Management in the Government of the United States* (Washington, D.C.: Government Printing Office, 1937).

2. Walter R. Sharp, "Bureaucracy and Politics — Egyptian Model," in William J. Siffin, ed., *Toward the Comparative Study of Public Administration* (Bloomington: Indiana University Press, 1959), pp. 145–81. See also his chapter, "International Bureaucracies and Political Development," in Joseph LaPalombara, ed., *Bureaucracy and Political Development* (Princeton, N.J.: Princeton University Press, 1963), pp. 441–74. For an early attempt to treat the study of comparative public administration through the model of bureaucracy, see Ferrel Heady, *Public Administration: A Comparative Perspective* (Englewood Cliffs, N.J.: Prentice-Hall, 1966).

3. Michel Crozier, *The Bureaucratic Phenomenon* (Chicago: University of Chicago Press, 1964).

4. Henry Jacoby, *The Bureaucratization of the World,* Eveline L. Kanes, trans. (Berkeley: University of California Press, 1973).

5. For conceptions of political culture, see: Gabriel A. Almond and James S. Coleman, *The Politics of the Developing Areas* (Princeton, N.J.: Princeton University Press, 1960); George M. Foster, *Traditional Cultures and the Impact of Technological Change* (New York: Harper & Brothers, 1962); Lucian W. Pye, *Politics, Personality, and Nation-Building* (New Haven, Conn.: Yale University Press, 1962); and E. B. Tylor, *Primitive Culture* (London: John Murray, Ltd., 1871).

6. Gerald E. Caiden, *Israel's Administrative Culture* (Berkeley: Institute of Governmental Studies, University of California, 1970).

7. This discussion of Riggs' model is based on Fred W. Riggs, "Agraria and Industria — Toward a Typology of Comparative Administration," in Siffin, *Toward Comparative Study,* pp. 23–116.

8. Brian Chapman, *The Profession of Government* (London: George Allen & Unwin, 1959).

9. Harold F. Alderfer, *Local Government in Developing Countries* (New York: McGraw-Hill, 1964) and *Public Administration in Newer Nations* (New York: Praeger, 1967).

10. Barbara N. Rodgers with John Greve and John S. Morgan, *Comparative Social Administration* (New York: Atherton Press, 1968).

11. *Policy Studies Journal,* Symposium on Policy Studies Around the World, 1 (Spring 1973): 116–86.

12. One of the authors of this book served as a United States delegate to the conference. A fault of the conference, from the point of view of open and candid dialogue, was that too many of the delegates, especially from the less-developed nations, were government officials of the countries from which they came and had been designated as official delegates. Americans went to the conference, on the other hand, as unofficial representatives. This tended to constrain the academic dialogue.

13. Literature on the history and experience of the international development programs has become mountainous. The following are a sample of the more pertinent publications: Robert E. Asher, *Development Administration in the Seventies: Alternatives for the United States* (Washington, D.C.: The Brookings Institution, 1970); John C. Honey, *Toward Strategies for Public Administration Development in Latin America* (Syracuse, N.Y.: Syracuse University Press, 1968); Garth N. Jones, "Failure of Technical Assistance in Public Administration Abroad," *Journal of Comparative Administration* 2 (May 1970): 3–51; I.M.D. Little and J.M. Clifford, *International Aid* (Chicago: Aldine, 1966); *Partners*

in *Development: Report of the Commission on International Development*, Lester B. Pearson, chairman (New York: Praeger, 1969); Rutherford M. Poats, *Technology for Developing Nations: New Directions for U.S. Technical Assistance* (Washington, D.C.: The Brookings Institution, 1972); Arthur M. Schlesinger, Jr., *A Thousand Days: John F. Kennedy in the White House* (Boston, Mass.: Houghton Mifflin, 1965); Task Force on International Development, *U.S. Foreign Assistance in the 1970's: A New Approach*, Report to the President (Washington, D.C.: Government Printing Office, 1970).

14. Department of Economic and Social Affairs, Technical Assistance Programme, *A Handbook of Public Administration: Current Concepts and Practice with Special Reference to Developing Countries* (New York: United Nations Publication 61. II.H.2, 1961), p. 1.

15. Senate Committee on Foreign Relations, *The Operational Aspects of United States Foreign Policy*, A Study by the Maxwell Graduate School of Citizenship and Public Affairs, Syracuse University, 86th Cong., 1st sess., 1958 (Washington, D.C.: Government Printing Office, 1959).

16. Ibid., pp. 58–59.

17. Asher, *Development Administration*, pp. 72–81.

18. Milton J. Esman and John D. Montgomery, "Systems Approaches to Technical Cooperation: The Role of Development Administration," *Public Administration Review* 29, no. 5 (September-October 1969): 507–39.

19. Gilbert B. Siegel, "The Strategy of Public Administration Reform: The Case of Brazil," *Public Administration Review* 26, no. 1 (March 1966): 45–55.

20. House Committee on Appropriations, *Foreign Assistance and Related Agencies Appropriations for 1974*, Hearings, 93rd Cong., 1st sess., 1973 (Washington, D.C.: Government Printing Office, 1973), II, 1094.

21. Public Administration Division, *Public Administration in The Second United Nations Development Decade*, Report of the Second Meeting of Experts, 1971 (New York: United Nations Publication E.71.II.H. 3, 1971).

22. Ibid., p. 22.

23. Edward W. Weidner, *Public Administration Overseas: The Case of Development Administration* (Chicago: Public Administration Service, 1964), pp. 159–71. Used by permission.

24. From *Latin America*, 3rd Ed., by Preston E. James (p. 3, 1959 ed.), copyright © 1942, 1950, 1959 by Western Publishing Company, Inc., reprinted by permission of The Bobbs-Merrill Company, Inc.

25. United Nations, *Handbook*, p. vii.

26. Joseph L. Sutton, "Culture and Technical Assistance," paper prepared for delivery at the 1959 Annual Meeting of the American Political Science Association, Washington, D.C., September 10–12, 1959, pp. 6–7.

27. Daniel Lerner, *The Passing of Traditional Society: Modernizing the Middle East* (New York: Free Press, 1958), pp. 162–63.

28. Joseph A. Kahl, *The Measurement of Modernism: A Study of Values in Brazil and Mexico* (Austin: University of Texas Press, 1968), pp. 18–21.

29. This excerpt from "Failure of Technical Assistance in Public Administration Abroad: A Personal Note," by Garth N. Jones is reprinted from *Journal of Comparative Administration* Vol. 2, No. 1 (May 1970) p. 26 by permission of the Publisher, Sage Publications, Inc.

30. Hiram S. Phillips, *Guide for Development: Institution-Building and Reform* (New York: Praeger, 1969).

31. Herbert Emmerich, "The Public Administration Expert in the Second Development Decade," *International Review of Administrative Sciences* 37, no. 3 (1971): 240–44.

32. Stephen K. Bailey, "Opportunity and Responsibility of ASPA Members and Chapters to Advance Public Administration," *Public Administration News* (Washington, D.C.: American Society for Public Administration, 1967).

Public Administration in the Web of Government

5

Administering the Modern City

The rise of the modern city is one of the most profound developments of the past century. This chapter will discuss the special character of public administration in the urban community and consider the role played by public administrators in helping to govern the American city in this time of challenge and change.

Since the time of Jefferson, there has been a grass roots ideology in the United States which maintains that there is something special, something particularly healthy and benign about local government. James Bryce saw local self-government as the fountainhead of democracy, the source of honesty and efficiency, a bulwark against overbearing bureaucracy. Arthur Morgan, former chairman of the board of the Tennessee Valley Authority in the 1930s, perceived the local community "as a source of civilizing values," as the key factor in civilization and human progress. And in the 1940s, Elmer Schattschneider remarked that, "The most important thing about local government is that it is local." For the public administrator, proximity between governor and governed makes a difference.[1]

The public administrator operates "on the firing line." It is at the level of the delivery of municipal services where disputes over conflicting theories, ideologies, and broad policy objectives come face-to-face with the citizenry. It is at the level of the urban public administrator — mayor, city manager, police or fire chief, or department head — where controversial issues, such as equality of economic opportunity, land-use regulation, affirmative action, and collective bargaining in the public service, become personal, intense, and resistant to resolution.

Although it is on another level than these broad policy issues, the everyday practical work of urban administration — such as drafting laws and ordinances, processing all kinds of applications, coordinating a collection of different specialists, managing people and resources — is not unrelated to the larger issues of freedom, civility, and justice. Two decades ago, in a book co-authored by one of the authors of this book, it was pointed out that, while local officials of government do not play their roles on the world stage, these men and women exert a profound influence on the communities in which we live our daily lives.[2] That observation is still pertinent. If anyone in the American system of government has responsibility for furthering the quality of life in this country, it is the bureaucrat in city hall.

Finally, it should be noted here that the urban administrator carries a particularly heavy and complex burden. He or she plays many roles, some of which are contradictory: buyer and seller of goods, gatherer and user of information, maker of rules and adjudicator of cases involving those rules, defender of established institutions and agent of change, manager and arbitrator of conflict, collector and manager of money and other resources, coordinator of diverse and sometimes conflicting governmental machinery, leader and consensus builder, and person of action.

Rise of the Modern City

A historical theme in discussion of urban life in the twentieth century has been the so-called crisis of the cities. From Lincoln Steffens' *The Shame of the Cities* in 1904, to Jacob Riis' *How the Other Half Lives* in 1914, to Lewis Mumford's 1938 warning, in his book *The Culture of Cities,* that cities were in danger of becoming humanly intolerable, to a great rash of books and reports in the 1960s, prophecies of impending urban doom have been heard in the land.[3] In 1962, Luther H. Gulick, whom we have already met as one of the founders of modern public administration, ominously warned that there was accumulating evidence of failure everywhere. The failures of urban governments, he suggested, were partly due to some of the attempted solutions themselves.[4]

With the upheavals of the 1960s, which were related to the civil rights movement, the peace movement, the campus rebellions, and the "discovery" of urban poverty, there grew serious doubts about the viability of local institutions of government. As the implementers of public policies, compelled to operate on the "firing line," urban public administrators were the targets of much of the dissatisfaction.

Those critics who were more optimistic about the future and who were perhaps more knowledgeable about historical trends associated with urbanization talked not about imminent catastrophe, but rather about problems in need of resolution. Pessimists, on the other hand, who were understandably affected by past disappointments and failures and by the human costs of urban difficulties, perceived the cities as standing on the brink of disaster.

Whether the conditions in the cities that call for remedial action are called "problems" or "crises" is really not important here. What does matter is that urbanization has created new conditions that depart from generally desired norms and has complicated old unsatisfactory conditions. These conditions, which we choose to call "problems," involve both the ends of government as well as governmental means.

Problems Involving the Ends of City Government

Historically, municipal governments have exercised predominant responsibility in urban areas for enforcement of what constitutions call the "police power": law enforcement, nuisance abatement, fire protection, street maintenance, parking and traffic control, sewage treatment and refuse collection, and similar traditional public functions.[5] As long as there was social stability in the cities, municipal governments managed to serve these traditional ends reasonably well. But, where cities were inundated by the tide of urbanization, including especially rapid technological development, increase in population and its greater heterogeneity, and profound changes in values and attitudes, municipal governments were compelled to stretch themselves beyond their capacities in attempting to cope with new and more complex municipal maladies.

With over 18,000 recognized municipalities in the United States, it is dangerous, of course, to generalize too freely. Although the incidence and intensity of the problems of the cities vary from city to city, there is, nevertheless, a bundle of substantive problems that seem to defy satisfactory resolution:

1. Civil rights violations
2. Consumer rights violations
3. Crime and corruption
4. Energy shortages
5. Neglect of health needs
6. Housing shortage and decay
7. Pollution of air, land, and water
8. Failure to meet public school needs
9. Poverty and neglect of the aged
10. Failure to meet recreational needs
11. Racial and ethnic conflict
12. Inadequate slum clearance
13. Inadequate public transportation
14. Traffic congestion

There have been many attempts in recent years to explain such substantive failures. For instance, it is suggested that too many state constitutions and state legislatures tie the hands of municipal governments. Conflicts of interest are said to prevent the formulation of adequate public policies and to blunt the social purpose of otherwise adequate public programs. Citizens, we are told, too frequently demand much in service from city hall but are unwilling to pay the necessary taxes and other revenues. Conservatives argue that city hall is trying to do too much, and that many of the above problems should be left to individual initiative. Liberals, on the other hand, maintain that municipal governments are not granted sufficient power to achieve greater results. On one side there is the complaint that municipal governments do too little, too late and on the other that these governments over-promise and attempt too much, too fast. Finally, there is the suggestion that the problems listed above are too complex and deep-seated for substantial amelioration in our time, and that the necessary technical information and professional competence in such areas as urban planning, economic analysis, architecture and design, group dynamics, mass communication, public works, and law enforcement are inadequate to meet successfully the challenges of the times.

It is not productive to seek scapegoats for the malaise that the United States is suffering. Surely, there is sufficient blame to go around. Myopic lawmakers, petty politicians, elitist civic leaders, and parochial and over-confident professionals all bear some responsibility. Public administrators themselves are not blameless.

Problems Involving the Means of City Government

In a letter to a friend in 1816, Thomas Jefferson wrote a message that has meaning today:

> Forms and institutions must go hand in hand with the progress of the human mind. As that becomes more developed, more enlightened, as new discoveries are made, new truths discovered and manners and opinions change with the change of circumstances, institutions advance also to keep pace with the times. We might as well require a man to wear still the coat which fitted him when a boy as civilized society to remain ever under the regimen of their barbarous ancestors.[6]

In 1966, a century and a half later, Jefferson's memorable words were punctuated in a report by the Committee for Economic Development, drafted by some of the most knowledgeable and influential people in public service, academic life, industry, and governmental research and consulting. Granting that there are hazards in generalizing too readily about the myriad of munici-pal and other local units of government in the United States, the authors expressed concern about the continued viability of local governments, and cited several serious weaknesses:

1. Local units of government tend to be too small in population, terri-tory, and revenue base for modern methods of problem-solving and administration
2. Overlapping levels of government, involving municipalities, townships, counties, independent school districts, and special districts, inhibit ef-fective administration
3. Local government in the United States is weakened by ineffective and sporadic citizen control and by a low level of public interest in local politics and government
4. Weak policy-making institutions and methods

5. Outdated administrative organizations in most local governments
6. Unqualified personnel who hold public positions that require knowledge of modern technology[7]

Drafted in the immediate aftermath of the Watts riots of 1965, and prior to the stunning urban disorders that occurred during the second half of the decade of the 1960s, the CED report merely touched the surface. It is now clear that infusion of federal money, through revenue sharing and other devices, does not significantly affect the institutional, administrative, and other means-related problems facing city halls of America. Irrespective of the size and location of cities, and of the particular policy area, the following list suggests the difficult problems that public administrators are implicated in and, hopefully, can help to solve:

1. Politicization of public administration which injects public administrators and their agencies into conflict with interest groups in the community and into conflicts over different and competing conceptions of the general interest
2. Difficulties in specifying and measuring the "product" or "output" of municipal governments, especially in such policy areas as public health, welfare, education, law enforcement, and human relations: also, difficulties in developing appropriate "production strategies"
3. Lack of sufficient concern about the need for evaluating administrative performance and productivity
4. Shortages of trained and experienced personnel to perform new and more complex tasks
5. Increasing size and complexity of local governmental organization, resulting in growing distance between city hall and citizenry and in official remoteness
6. Increasing bureaucratization and professionalization of the municipal public services which, in some cities, tends to restrict access to public service for certain minority groups, and which tends to stifle governmental creativity
7. Confusion about what we mean and what we do when we "decentralize" the government of cities
8. Inadequate management information systems
9. Unimaginative and ineffective public information and public relations efforts by municipal governments

Involved in the substantive and administrative problems faced by the urban public administrator is a gap between *policy promise* and *administrative delivery*. The public policy-making process is influenced by a spirit of optimism regarding the capacity of governments to *solve* public problems. Public administration, on the other hand, is anchored to economic, political, legal, and technical constraints. Public administrators are especially concerned with feasibility, and they tend to limit themselves to *coping* with problems, *managing* problems, and with what has come to be called *satisficing* — the selection and adoption of satisfactory alternatives, rather than optimal alternatives, which leads not to the solution but to the amelioration of problems. "Democracy," Reinhold Niebuhr has declared, "is a method of finding proximate solutions for insoluble problems."

This gap between promise and performance has been receiving increasing attention during the 1970s. For instance, in 1972, Robert Aleshire, who was executive director of the National Association for Community Development, ascribed the gap — at least in the area of anti-poverty programs — to fickle national policies and priorities that build up the hopes of local people in the ghettos, barrios, and hollows, but then leave local governments alone to satisfy these expectations. In 1973, Norton Long saw hope in closing or bridging that gap by exploiting the slack resources of city governments and by cities freeing themselves from the dogma of their powerlessness. Further, in a provocative book in 1974, John Stewart, formerly communications director of the Democratic National Committee, argued that the major political issue of the 1970s is what he calls the "governing issue." That is, the people are demanding that the gap between governmental promise and performance be closed. In Stewart's view, this can be done only by politicians and political parties assuring that public administrators actually deliver on the goals that are set. Finally, the growing attention to performance evaluation and productivity in municipal government, reflected in the work of such organizations as the Council on Municipal Performance in New York, and the Urban Institute in Washington, are illustrative of the concern with closing the gap between the dream and its fulfillment.[8]

Disturbing though the contemporary governmental malaise in our cities may be, this discussion of the problems faced by city halls need not end on a note of despair. A great many cities in the United States are both well governed and well administered. The expanding citizen demands and expectations, the diminishing available resources, and the greater politicization of a hitherto more value-neutral public administration place enormous burdens on municipal governments. The larger and more troubled cities of the United States may receive the lion's share of public attention, but thousands of cities across this country, large and small, carry on remarkably well.

Relevant Structures

As mentioned in chapter 3, the environment of public administration includes a large number of social, economic, and political groups that interact with public administrators. In the discussion that follows, various governmental and nongovernmental structures that are part of the web of government in the city are examined.

Forms of Municipal Government

Organizational structure is an important variable in public administration. The form of municipal government — its organizational structure — makes a difference by influencing such important administrative details as the division of responsibility and work, the communication network, the decision-making process, the distribution of discretionary powers, the allocation of resources within the government, and the route of administrative review, evaluation, and control. But forms of government should not be mistaken for the substance of government. Democracy lies not in the organizational chart of a city government any more than the happiness of the family lies in the architectural drawings of the house in which the family resides. Mayor Richard J. Daley of Chicago is a strong mayor not because the form of government made him so, but rather because of the combination of his personal skill, the political history of the city, and the manner in which he and others use the governmental structure.

There are basically three forms of municipal government in the United States. These forms are ideal constructs, and no city has exactly the same structure as another. Much has been written during this century about the advantages and disadvantages of one form over another, sides have been drawn, and reform movements have been promoted. The distinguishing feature in these forms, from the overall systems point of view, is basically the separation of powers between the making of public policy and its administration.

First, there is the *mayor-council form*, depicted in figure 2. In general, this

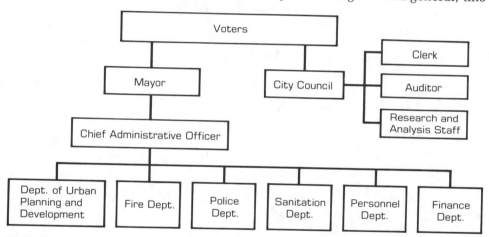

The structure depicted here is a simplified version of the "strong-mayor" arrangement, with a chief administrative officer appointed by and responsible to the mayor who is the chief executive. All of the departments are not included in the diagram. A more detailed diagram would include departments of water and power, human services, law, and others.

Figure 2   The Mayor-Council Form

form is characterized by the following features: separation of powers between the legislative and executive branches similar to the federal system; a popularly elected city council; an independent and popularly elected chief executive; partisan elections; and political rivalry between the council and mayor. The form is usually justified in terms of such claimed advantages as more effective political leadership in the city and executive leadership over city hall. Especially in cities with serious political cleavages, it is argued, a single executive can be more effective in mobilizing forces and resolving issues than can a many-headed deliberative body.

The power of the mayor and her or his relationships with the city council and other governmental bodies will depend upon which of the two variations of the form is being used. In the weak mayor-council form, the mayor is a weak administrator because she or he has little or no control over some top administrators who are popularly elected rather than appointed and limited appointive and removal power over the remainder of the administrative subordinates, restricted power over the preparation and management of the city's budget, and limited veto power over actions of the council. In short, the mayor is not the dominant administrative figure but shares power with other elected administrators and a council that is actively involved in administrative details. In the other variation, the strong mayor-council, only the mayor and council members are elected, and the mayor does have wide appointive and removal powers and control over budget preparation and execution. The occupant of the position has the tools needed to be a strong chief executive officer.

The critics of the mayor-council form argue that in this arrangement, political bossism, inefficiency, and partisan spoils are introduced into city government. On the other hand, defenders argue that city government is political by nature and therefore it takes a politician to provide the necessary leadership, that the *mayor-council form* more effectively counteracts the forces of dispersion and fragmentation in the community, and that the multiplicity of governmental units and jurisdictions in the American city require centralized executive direction.

The *mayor-council form* is employed in 47 percent of all American cities having populations of over 5,000 people. Of the twenty-six cities with over 500,000 people, twenty-one had the *mayor-council form* in 1974, while of the six cities with over one million people, all had the *mayor-council form*.[9]

A second form of city government is the *council-manager form*, depicted in figure 3. This arrangement, which originated in the early years of the present century as a part of the municipal reform movement, has been hailed by its champions as a major social invention. Some of its critics have described it as a triumph of technology over democracy. The *council-manager form* is generally characterized by no separation of powers between the legislative and executive branches; a popularly elected city council of laypersons who run for office in nonpartisan municipal elections; and a full-time professional administrator, appointed by and responsible to the city council — called either the city manager or the city administrator — and possessing all operational responsibility for the entire range of administrative tasks: appointment of subordinates, personnel management, budget preparation and execution, public information and relations, and the like. The key characteristic of this form of municipal government is professionalism.

City managers tend to be male, young, well-educated, nonpartisan with respect to political parties but not nonpolitical in the policy sense, and highly professional. They are organized nationally as the International City Management Association (ICMA), with headquarters in Washington, D.C. There are also junior professional associations of assistants to city managers, such as the Municipal Management Assistants of Southern California.

Permeating the city manager movement is a tendency to conceive of the manager's role in municipal government as something akin to "messiah." Here, as illustration, are the responsibilities which the city manager is ex-

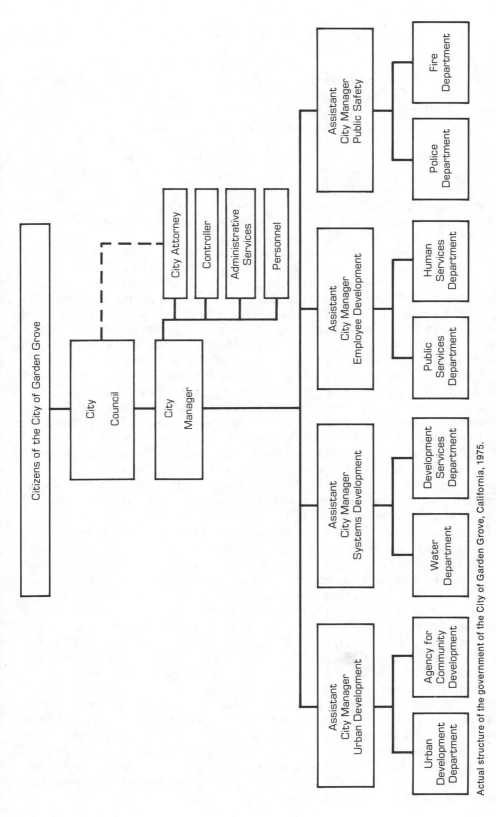

Actual structure of the government of the City of Garden Grove, California, 1975.

Figure 3 The Council-Manager Form

pected to fulfill: overseeing the enforcement of all laws and ordinances, making the major administrative appointments to the municipal service, controlling the work of all departments, making recommendations to the city council concerning alternative policies and programs, keeping the city council informed on all financial needs and problems, preparing and submitting to the council the annual municipal budget, preparing and submitting to the council all reports and other communications, and keeping the council — and through the council the public — informed about all appropriate municipal matters. In an effort to help assure professional performance in these tasks, the ICMA has for many years prescribed a Code of Ethics which stipulates in considerable detail the manner in which the city manager or administrator will behave.

As of 1974, 43 percent of the municipalities with over 5,000 people in the United States were governed by the council-manager form. Of the twenty-six cities with more than 500,000 people, only five had a council-manager system. None of the six cities having over one million people employed the council-manager form. The incidence of this form of municipal government is especially great in small suburban communities. There has been no experience with city managers seeking to cope with the titanic forces in cities such as New York, Los Angeles, Chicago, Philadelphia, and Detroit.[10]

Empirical research being conducted on the council-manager form of municipal government in the United States suggests, first, that some of the long-accepted notions about this form are invalid, and second, that the connections between this form and other aspects of municipal governance are not yet adequately understood. For instance, in 1962, Jeptha J. Carrell found six different kinds of conflict that exist in the supposedly amicable relationship between manager and council and urged that further research be conducted in a systematic manner. In 1971, Ronald O. Loveridge, on the basis of empirical study, found evidence of radical changes in the original theoretical justification and raison d'être of the city manager, such as the surprisingly high (policy) political role of the manager. In 1973, Cortus T. Koehler's evidence suggested that the notion that city councils make policy and city managers administer it may not be valid. And in 1974, Alan L. Saltzstein concluded from his evidence that scholars do not know enough about the differences that organizational structure makes in the roles and interrelationships of city councils, mayors, and city managers. In the communities that he studied, Saltzstein found that perceptions about these roles and relationships varied from official to official and among members of the communities. Despite these tentative findings and expressions of doubt, the council-manager system continues to spread among smaller suburban communities.[11]

A third and more rare form of municipal government is the commission. When, in 1900, a hurricane devastated Galveston, Texas, and the local government broke down, the governor of Texas appointed a commission of five businesspeople to govern and administer the city. All policy making and administrative functions were unified in the hands of the five commissioners who were the only elected officials of the city. As a collective body, they made policy; as individuals, they supervised the administration of particular municipal departments. Commissioners were elected in nonpartisan elections and they represented the city at large rather than separate wards or districts within the city. The arrangement was justified as a more "businesslike" form of government, a superior form because it removed local affairs from the hands of politicians and encouraged professional leaders and businesspeople to participate in local government.

The commission form grew in popularity until it was employed by almost 500 cities by 1918, most of which were from 5,000 to 25,000 in population. Since that time, the popularity of the form has waned, until by 1974 only 220 municipalities — most of which were under 25,000 in population — retained commissions.[12] Criticism of the form centered around the following weaknesses of the arrangement: inadequate coordination, weak political and administrative leadership, amateurism among commissioners, and the realization that business criteria are not entirely applicable to public administration.

Political Structures

A truism of political analysis is the realization that political systems are bounded not only by geography, but also by the interactions of individuals, institutions, and groups that seek to influence or control government. The modern urban administrator, as an actor in that system, must interrelate with a very complex web of economic, social, and political structures. This is basically true whether a particular city has an elitist or pluralist political system.

As will be seen more fully in the following chapter, the urban administrator has relationships with many other governmental and quasi-governmental structures: federal agencies, state agencies, county agencies, special and multipurpose districts, regional planning bodies, neighboring municipal governments, and councils of government. With the growth of urbanization and development of problems that ignore governmental boundaries and jurisdictions, the likelihood that any city hall might act in isolation is reduced.

With the enlargement of municipal responsibility for problem-solving in the city, accompanied by greater politicization of urban public administration which results from that deeper governmental involvement, the urban administrator is faced with a vast array of economic, social, and other structures that pay much attention to what happens in city hall and exert great efforts to influence or control what happens there:

Banks
Business associations
Communications media, including radio, television, and newspapers
Contractors and builders
Good government groups
Industrial firms
Liquor dealers
Minority groups
Municipal employee associations and labor unions
Neighborhood improvement associations
Professionals: lawyers, doctors, architects, engineers, etc.

Real estate developers
Religious institutions
Service organizations: Rotary, Kiwanis, Lions, etc.
Taxpayers' associations

The depth and complexity of the urban administrator's relationships with these structures varies from city to city. Francine F. Rabinovitz, for instance, found in Montclair, New Jersey, that the city's decision to participate in urban redevelopment was controversial, but was made in an elitist fashion — simply, quietly, efficiently. However, in neighboring New Brunswick, the decision making was more protracted. There, city officials attempted to make their decisions quietly, in accordance with professional planning criteria, but a storm of protest was provoked. Contenders in the struggle were the city commissioners (this is a commission-form city), the Zoning Advisory Commission, the Housing and Redevelopment Board, the former Democratic mayor of New Brunswick and, at the time of the dispute, a vice-president of the largest industrial taxpayer in the city, and others. Rabinovitz concluded on a provocative note: professional performance in urban administration may depend either on the conduct of elitist politics or on the ability of the professional urban planner and administrator to play politics.[13]

The urban administrator is compelled also to deal with specialized structures within the municipal government. Bureaucracies are not monolithic. There is a large body of empirical literature to support the view of a municipal bureaucracy as an aggregate of substructures — professionals, such as civil engineers, educators, lawyers, accountants, personnel managers, statisticians, and the like; work groups, such as building custodians and sanitarians, food handlers, secretaries and clerks, and the like; and groupings based on common race, religion, ethnic background, and national origin. Many of these groups are organized and make special demands on city hall that may conflict with certain established policies.

For instance, in 1967, Arthur Niederhoffer showed that the police department of New York City was intersected by a web of ethnic police societies or associations, as indicated in table 1.[14] While no New York City mayor or

Table 1   Ethnic Police Societies in New York City (1967)

Name of Society	Ethnic Group	Number of Members	% of Force
Emerald Society	Irish	8,500	42.0
Columbia Society	Italian	5,000	25.0
Shomrim Society	Jewish	2,270	11.2
Steuben Society	German	1,500	7.4
Guardians Association	Negro	1,320	6.5
Pulaski Asssociation	Polish	1,100	5.4
St. Paul Society	Greek and Russian	300	1.5
Hispanic Society	Puerto Rican and Spanish	250	1.0
		20,240	100.0

Source: Arthur Niederhoffer, *Behind the Shield: The Police in Urban Society* (Garden Grove, N.Y.: Doubleday, 1967), p. 135. Copyright © 1967 by Arthur Niederhoffer. Used by permission.

police commissioner has been dominated by these societies, their existence cannot be safely ignored. The fact that 42 percent of the force are organized Irishmen and the fact that more than two-thirds of the force are organized Catholics are significant data.

Similarly, Clement E. Vose has analyzed the important political and administrative impacts of municipal law officers, organized nationally as the National Institute of Municipal Law Officers (NIMLO). The NIMLO, acting as "a kind of semi-governmental institution," has exercised important influence in such policy areas as urban renewal, zoning, public utilities, tort liability, and others.[15]

Relevant Knowledge and Skills

A renaissance is occurring in the movement concerned with the generation of knowledge and skills that are needed for effective and responsible public administration in American cities. For instance, consider the change in the approach of the ICMA. In 1958, the ICMA published an influential textbook intended for use in the training of city managers. The volume was completely devoted to the more practical and specialized management-process tasks and procedures historically associated with Gulick's acronym POSDCORB. In sharp contrast, two recent textbooks have been published by the ICMA which deal extensively with topics that would have been regarded as esoteric in the 1950s: socioeconomic urban trends, management in a new milieu, political adjustments to change, community values, leadership styles and strategies, methods of influencing employee behavior, labor-management relations, and institutionalizing citizen participation.[16] The ICMA, like other professional associations in public administration, now fully understands that the modern urban administrator is operating in a new era calling for new and more complex knowledge and skills.

Areas of Knowledge

It is not an exaggeration to describe the contemporary state of relevant knowledge in most areas as an explosion. Old conventional notions are being challenged or overthrown; new bodies of knowledge are being generated. More specifically, the public administrator in city hall can draw on such emergent knowledge areas as:

1. The aged and their special needs
2. Untapped capacities of hitherto neglected racial and other minority groups
3. The causes and cures of poverty, ignorance, and disease
4. Technology — its diffusion and the assessment of its impact
5. Systems analysis — its use and abuse in the city
6. Governmental productivity
7. Alternative organizational arrangements
8. Planned communities
9. Alternative modes of communication between city hall and citizenry

In a significant forward step toward responsible professionalization, the National Association of Schools of Public Affairs and Administration (NASPAA) published a set of recommended guidelines and standards for graduate study in public administration. The document cites specifically the need for education in such knowledge areas as:

1. Political-social-economic context
2. Analytical tools: quantitative and nonquantitative
3. Individual, group, and organizational dynamics
4. Policy analysis
5. Administrative management processes.[17]

Meanwhile, an endless stream of new information, data, and insights is pouring from academic, governmental, and consultative research groups and individuals.

However, the existence of knowledge does not always lead to its application. Some knowledge, especially in the areas of nuclear power, biological manipulation, and behavior modification, is extremely powerful and should be employed — if at all — only with caution. As an implementer of public policy, the public administrator plays a key role in deciding when and how to use such knowledge. In the words of a sharecropper in the South many years ago, "We knows better than we does." Embedded in municipal and other governments are obstacles to the application of relevant and desirable bodies of knowledge, such as personal, political, and bureaucratic constraints. Before there can be a productive harnessing of the new knowledge and an overcoming of these impediments, it is necessary for urban administrators to seek self-consciously some consensus on what it is that they profess when they regard themselves as professionals. The contemporary efforts of the ICMA, the American Society for Public Administration, the American Society of Planning Officials, and other professional bodies are moving in that direction.

Relevant Skills

A persistent theme in critiques of contemporary municipal government is that city halls are being pushed beyond their capacities to cope with new and more difficult problems. Of course, this is partly a problem of inadequate or outdated legal, political, organizational, and procedural arrangements. But this is also a problem of human competency. The knowledge explosion mentioned above has profound implications for the training of urban public administrators.

In the NASPAA guidelines and standards previously cited, there is a carefully detailed listing of necessary skills that are related to the five important areas of knowledge. In that listing, the following verbs predominate: analyze, assess, communicate, comprehend, cope, decide, develop, evaluate, interpret, negotiate, persuade, plan, review, recommend, and study. A content analysis of public administration job announcements, especially for entry-level positions, reveals a high frequency in the use of these terms. The announcement of an opening for the position of "Administrative Analyst II" in the city hall of Anchorage, Alaska, in 1974, illustrates this:

> Analyzes need for, plans, develops and recommends management policies, practices, methods and procedures to insure administrative support of complex and technical governmental operations; serves on boards, committees and commissions as a representative of the City Administrator.

Or consider the following announcement of a similar position in the city of Garden Grove, California, in 1974:

> May assist in the preparation of annexation proposals; assists in the administration of a public relations program including such areas as preparing newsletters and annual reports for publication; makes special studies and investigations and prepares written reports; conducts research, surveys and analysis of municipal operations as required; performs budget analysis; may assist in some personnel functions. May assist in the planning, organizing and developing of budget recommendations for the annual and long range budget cycles; conducts organization and methods analyses of municipal operations and makes recommendations regarding administrative procedures, organizational structure, utilization of equipment and related work; assists in the application of approved programs and does other related work.

In addition to such universal skills, the urban public administrator must develop competence in performing tasks and coping with problems that reflect special circumstances in certain cities. For instance, as city halls have been subjected to greater demands for decentralization and citizen participation in public affairs, the requisite skills of the urban administrator have shifted from an emphasis on giving orders and processing papers, to greater concern with interpersonal and intergroup relations, bargaining, brokering, communicating, persuading, and the like. This point has been treated with considerable care by Adam W. Herbert. In his view, essential skills for the urban administrator in situations marked by decentralized governmental operation and citizen participation include the ability to handle conflict, familiarity with group relations, empathy with citizens, ability to work under bosses who disagree with each other, tolerance for ambiguity and uncertainty, readiness to accept a high degree of mobility in his or her professional development, political sensitivity and facility, ability to communicate in all directions within the system, and ability to relate in a nonelitist manner to citizens. Finally, Herbert ends on a moral note:

> Although proficiency in these areas will not guarantee success while operating within a participative administrative setting, it is a critical addition both to work experience and to fundamental understanding of basic management concepts. It must be emphasized, however, that skills, like technologies, can be used for good or evil purposes. The pertinence of these skills ultimately depends upon the administrator's philosophy and related sense of ethics. The critical question which we in the profession must address is whether our public administration programs are attempting to assist both students and practitioners in developing these management skills along with a philosophical frame of reference built around fundamental democratic principles.[18]

The need to temper technical competence with some commitment to public-interest values is the final point of concern in this chapter.

The Eternal Issue of Values

From its very beginning, the city management movement has been concerned with the issue of values. In 1924, the first city management code of
ethics was adopted, and several times since then the code has been revised,
most recently in 1972. Pervading the discussion of ethical principles governing the professional city manager is a concern with democracy, efficiency,
social responsibility, personal integrity, political nonpartisanship, continual
human growth and development, an informed citizenry, social equity and
justice, the administration of government on the basis of merit, and frugality
in the use of public resources.[19]

Most major decisions and actions of municipal governments are deeply
value-laden. Allocation of budgetary resources; hiring, firing, promoting, and
rewarding of public personnel; zoning, planning, and developing of land;
maintenance and policing of streets; purchasing of books for the public
library and electronic equipment and riot gear for the police department; prescribing of eligibility standards for public benefits — all are deeply entwined
in interpretations of right and wrong, justice and injustice, freedom and
tyranny. The technology of public administration — cost-benefit analysis,
systems design, operations research, organizational development, modeling, accountability control, productivity enhancement — cannot determine
whether a public park is "better" than a music hall, or whether a historic
building should make way for a parking lot. Urban government by nature
involves value trade-offs as well as technology.

It was appropriate, therefore, that the NASPAA included in its recommended guidelines and standards for the study of public administration a
suggestion that the ethical public administrator should have knowledge of
and commitment to the following:

1. Democratic traditions and practices, constitutionalism and the rule of law
2. The purposes and limitations of government as an instrument for foster-
   ing social and economic progress
3. Access for individuals and groups to centers of power and decision
   making
4. The political direction and responsibility of administration and administrators
5. Standards of official/personal conduct and ethics[20]

The NASPAA guidelines and standards further provided that in the work of
administrative management, public-interest values would be strengthened by
knowledge of and commitment to:

1. The role and use of organizations and administrative processes to achieve
   public objectives
2. Standards of efficiency and effectiveness in the conduct of the public's
   business
3. Standards of individual and organizational integrity and performance
4. Public surveillance and review by citizens and their elected representatives

5. A working environment conducive to individual fulfillment and the attainment of public confidence.[21]

The traumatic events of recent years associated with the Watergate Affair and with the Federal Bureau of Investigation, the Central Intelligence Agency, and the Internal Revenue Service were not the responsibility of local government. Yet, the climate produced by those offenses and by the *revelations* of those offenses has poisoned public trust in American institutions of government generally. Perhaps the transformations now taking place in the city halls of America, reinforced by such guidelines and standards as those suggested by NASPAA, will bring to pass the classical conception of local government as the fountainhead of honesty, efficiency, democracy, and justice in this country.

Conclusions

The complex web of government within which modern public administration takes place includes at its very center the force of urbanization. It is in the cities of America that the great issues of public administration take on especially intimate meaning. The problems accumulating in the cities and awaiting remedial action represent not imminent catastrophe, but rather increasingly difficult challenges. The story is told of the renowned architect, Frank Lloyd Wright, standing upon a promontory overlooking the city of Pittsburgh some years ago. In amazement he was transfixed by the panorama before him — river valleys filled with steel mills, railroad yards, industrial tracts, scabby houses, skyscrapers whose tops were lost in the murky fog. Asked what he, as an architect, would do with Pittsburgh, he replied: "I would abandon it."

But cities are not like old automobiles and refrigerators. They cannot be "junked." Nor can they be traded in for new models. As Barry Commoner has suggested, we are doomed to survive and struggle with our mess. The urban public administrator can be part of the solution.

NOTES

1. James Bryce, *Modern Democracies* (New York: Macmillan, 1921), I, 129–33; II, 435–37; Arthur E. Morgan, *The Small Community* (New York: Harper & Brothers, 1942), pp. 3–19.

2. Stephen K. Bailey, Howard D. Samuel, and Sidney Baldwin, *Government in America* (New York: Henry Holt, 1957), p. 455.

3. Mitchell Gordon, *Sick Cities* (New York: Macmillan, 1963); Jane Jacobs, *The Death and Life of Great American Cities* (New York: Random House, 1961); John Keats, *The Crack in the Picture Frame Window* (Boston, Mass.: Houghton Mifflin, 1956); Lewis Mumford, *The Culture of Cities* (New York: Harcourt Brace Jovanovich, 1938); Jeanne R. Lowe, *Cities in a Race with Time* (New York: Random House, 1967) Jacob A. Riis, *How the Other Half Lives: Studies Among the Tenements of New York* (New York: Scribner's, 1914); Lincoln Steffens, *The Shame of the Cities* (New York: McClure Phillips, 1904); York Willbern, *The Withering Away of the City* (Bloomington: Indiana University Press, 1964).

4. Luther H. Gulick, *The Metropolitan Problem and American Ideas* (New York: Alfred A. Knopf, 1962).

5. In this chapter, the term "municipal" is used as a synonym for the adjective "city." For the more technically correct use of the term "municipal," see chapter 7.

6. Thomas Jefferson, *The Writings of Thomas Jefferson,* definitive ed. (Washington, D.C.: Thomas Jefferson Memorial Association, 1905), XV, 40–41.

7. Committee for Economic Development, *Modernizing Local Government To Secure a Balanced Federalism* (New York: Committee for Economic Development, 1966), pp. 11–13. This study was conducted by the CED's Committee for Improvement of Management in Government, chaired by Marion B. Folsom of the Eastman Kodak Company, and John A. Perkins, president of the University of Delaware. The membership of the CIMG and its body of advisers and research consultants was an influential group of academic, consultative, and other leaders.

8. Robert A. Aleshire, "Power to the People: An Assessment of the Community Action and Model Cities Experience," *Public Administration Review* 32 (September 1972): 428–43; Norton E. Long, "Have Cities a Future?" *Public Administration Review,* Special Issue, 33 (November-December 1973): 543–52; and John G. Stewart, *One Last Chance* (New York: Praeger, 1974), pp. 156–67.

9. International City Management Association, *The Municipal Yearbook: 1974* (Washington, D.C.: ICMA, 1974).

10. Ibid.

11. Jeptha J. Carrell, "The City Manager and His Council: Sources of Conflict," *Public Administration Review* 22, no. 6 (December 1962): 203–12; Ronald O. Loveridge, *City Managers in Legislative Politics* (Indianapolis, Ind.: Bobbs-Merrill, 1971); Cortus T. Koehler, "Policy Development and Legislative Oversight in Council Manager Cities: An Information and Communication Analysis," *Public Administration Review* 33, no. 5 (September-October 1973): 433–41; and Alan L. Saltzstein, "City Managers and City Councils: Perceptions of the Division of Authority," *Western Political Quarterly* 27, no. 2 (June 1974): 275–88.

12. ICMA, *1974 Municipal Yearbook.*

13. Francine F. Rabinovitz, *City Politics and Planning* (New York: Atherton Press, 1969), pp. 31–58.

14. Arthur Niederhoffer, *Behind the Shield: The Police in Urban Society* (Garden City, N.Y.: Doubleday, 1967), pp. 134–36.

15. Clement E. Vose, "Interest Groups, Judicial Review, and Local Government," *Western Political Quarterly* 19, no. 1 (March 1966): 85–100.

16. International City Management Association, *The Technique of Municipal Administration,* 4th ed. (Chicago: ICMA, 1958); *Managing the Modern City* (Washington, D.C.: ICMA, 1971); and *Developing the Municipal Organization* (Washington, D.C.: ICMA, 1974).

17. National Association of Schools of Public Affairs and Administration, *Guidelines and Standards for Professional Masters Degree Programs in Public Affairs and Public Administration* (Washington, D.C.: NASPAA, 1974).

18. Adam W. Herbert, "Management Under Conditions of Decentralization and Citizen Participation," *Public Administration Review,* Special Issue, 32 (October 1972): 632.

19. International City Management Association, *City Management Code of Ethics* (Washington, D.C.: ICMA, 1972), pp. 8–9.

20. NASPAA, *Guidelines and Standards,* pp. 8–12.

21. Ibid., p. 12.

6

Intergovernmental Relations

Part II of this book is called "Public Administration in the Web of Government." The web, which is a set of closely intertwined relationships between the branches and levels of government, is the framework within which public administration must operate. In the preceding chapter, the focus was upon management in the metropolitan setting. In this chapter, the concentration will be on intergovernmental relationships within the federal form of government and their implications for public administration.

History

Since every independent nation has a choice of how it wants to organize in order to administer programs and deliver services, there are varied procedures and problems related to intergovernmental relations around the world. There are some similarities, however. With rare exceptions, countries do not function with only one level of government, but rather create various layers of subnational units. Within this context, two organizational aspects have a direct bearing on intergovernmental relations. First is the defining of relative power between the levels of government — the centralization-decentralization issue. Second is the choice of how to organize the administrative systems geographically — by area or by function.

Centralization versus Decentralization

What is the proper division of functions among the levels of government? Should it be a totally centralized (unitary) form with all powers lodged in the central government, with no subnational units of government, or should it be federal in form, providing for local governments? Should most of the authority be concentrated in the central government or should it be decentralized, with subnational units playing a more important role? In practice only a few small undeveloped nations function without some form of subnational government. But a country may choose to have varying degrees of centralization or decentralization for the various functions — legislative, judicial, and administrative.

In the administrative area, with which we are primarily concerned, the relative merits of centralization and decentralization were debated in the eighteenth-century constitutional convention and are still controversial issues today. Proponents of centralization argue that their system is more efficient, that the central government is the only one with a comprehensive overview of the problems and the only way to standardize and equalize programs and services, that the financial resources of the subnational governments are inadequate to cope with such problems, and that local governments lack the concentrated expertise available to the federal government for solving complex problems.

The advocates of decentralization, although conceding that centralization might permit a more efficient allocation of resources, insist that pluralism is essential. A decentralization of functions to many local power centers permits local citizen participation and control, makes government as a whole more responsive, permits tailoring solutions to meet particular local needs, and avoids a massive, impersonal bureaucracy at the center.

The United States Solution

The United States Constitution represents a compromise between centralization and decentralization. The constitution created a federal form of government and distributed powers between the federal and state governments. All powers not specifically delegated to the federal government, or which could be implied from those powers, were reserved to the states, with each level being supreme and free to operate independently in its own area of authority. However, the sixth amendment specified that the U.S. Constitution and laws were the supreme law of the land. It should be pointed out, however, that local government below the state level was not required, provided for, or mentioned in the Constitution. Authority to create this structure was reserved to the states. Substate governments — regional entities, counties, cities, and special districts — are either provided for in the state constitutions, created directly by state law, or established under the authority of state enabling statutes. But, in any case, their powers, organization, and authority are prescribed by the states.

Area versus Function

Governments have some choices as to how they organize their administrative systems geographically. But since none but the smallest units can deliver services from the center, most governments, and especially national governments, have to create some method of reaching their client groups in the field. As James Fesler says, "National field administration systems come in two principal models: one we may call the prefectoral where a single official is in charge of all national government activities in his field area; the other we shall call the functional. . . . In the functional system, each national functional department or bureau establishes its own field administration system — with regions it chooses, with staff it chooses, and with direct supervision from departmental or bureau headquarters in the capital."[1]

France is a good example of a prefectoral system. The nation is divided geographically into areas called departments. The administrative structure in each department, which is staffed by employees of the central government in Paris, is headed by a prefect. The prefect, appointed by and responsible to the central government, is a powerful individual. As the representative of the central government, he or she serves as the administrative supervisor, as the political liaison between the area and Paris and as the channel of communication between the central and field administrations. The net effect is that the country is administered from the center with little or no local autonomy.

The United States adopted the functional model as the technique for delivering services to the field. This model produced a series of distinguishing characteristics. Until the creation of the Regional Councils, discussed later in this chapter, there was no commonality in the boundaries of the administrative regions, but rather a hodgepodge of overlapping ones created by each of the departments in Washington. Some departments were highly regionalized while others had little organization outside Washington. Each agency selected the city that would serve as its regional headquarters. Each field employee of a department was a functional specialist responsible to the central department, with little interest in the programs of other departments, and there was no mechanism for forcing coordination among functional units. The result was that each agency pursued its own ends independently with little or no thought of cooperation or coordination to avoid duplication, permit unified rather than segmental attack on common problems, and improve the delivery of services in general.

The subnational levels also adopted a functional organization. When states and other units create field structures, the organization is quite similar, and the field representatives report to their specialist bosses in the central office.

The Changing Scene

As it was pointed out in chapter 3, the environment in which all governments operate changes continually. In some nations change comes slowly, but in the United States it has been rapid. The historic system functioned at an acceptable level during the early years in the life of the nation. However, the changes brought by the Industrial Revolution, World War I, the economic depression of the 1930s, World War II, and the rapid postwar expansion in governmental programs and bureaucracy created an environmental climate quite different from that when the Constitution was written.

These changes, which placed the system under stress, forced modifications in various areas of our federal system. The areas most directly affected have been federal field administration, federal-subnational relations, relations between subnational governments, and regionalism. We will discuss the changes in that order.

Federal Field Administration

The functional model for delivering services and the system it created, discussed earlier in the chapter, have been criticized for years for concentration of authority in Washington, lack of coordination among federal agencies in the field, and unresponsiveness to clientele groups. Modifications in the field operations have occurred over the years and these operations are currently being reorganized again.

In view of the variety and independence of agencies, numerous techniques designed to encourage joint action on common problems have been attempted. These techniques, however, normally represented an attempt to secure cooperation, but not coordination, which is a different concept. As Fesler points out, "Cooperation is horizontal, i.e., cooperation among equals; coordination involves a Coordinator."[2] While cooperation is essentially voluntary, coordination implies that someone has the authority and power to compel compliance to a plan of joint action.

Cooperative activities have taken a variety of forms. At the national level, both in Washington and the field, they include interagency agreements, special task forces, commissions, councils, lead agencies, and boards. Prior to the creation of the Federal Regional Councils, the best-known device was the Federal Executive Board.

The Federal Executive Boards, created in 1961, consisted of the federal executives who headed major programs in cities with large concentrations of federal programs and employees.[3] These were designed to encourage better Washington field communication, interagency cooperation, and exchange of information, while attempting some coordination of federal programs in the area to improve the delivery of federal services to the citizens. The boards, which operated in most metropolitan areas, were an improvement over the old system. They did provide a forum for the exchange of information and plans among federal program managers in the area, a contact point for local officials, and a clearinghouse for federal employees. But they functioned under two handicaps. First, they operated only within a metropolitan area and not on an interstate or regional basis. Second, they were not organized to produce coordinated programs. The boards simply provided a meeting among equals, each administrator having a personal programmatic interest to protect. Any cooperation was strictly voluntary, either because it did not pose a threat or was mutually advantageous. No individual had any authority to demand coordinated effort. To expect detailed program coordination on such a basis was unrealistic.

Federal-Subnational Relations

The changing environment made the historic division of powers between these levels of governments obsolete. Some subjects reserved to the states became interstate and national problems beyond the capacity of individual states to fund or control. That the need for modification to meet the demands of the changing environment has been recognized is evidenced by the numerous commissions which have been appointed over the years to study the problem. The most recent one, created by Congress in 1959, is the permanent Advisory Commission on Intergovernmental Relations.[4] The law which created the commission recognized the problem of changes by stating, "because the complexity of modern life intensifies, in a federal form of government for the fullest cooperation and coordination of activities between the levels of government, and because population growth and scientific developments portend an increasingly complex society in future years, it is essential that an appropriate agency be established to give continuing attention to intergovernmental problems."[5]

The permanent bipartisan commission is composed of twenty-six members with nine representing the federal government, fourteen representing state and local governments, and three the general public.[6] Its role is to give continuing attention to intergovernmental problems in the federal-state, federal-local, and state-local, as well as interstate and interlocal areas. The commission not only researches problem areas but also works directly with the Office of Management and Budget, congressional committees, Executive Office of the President, and state officials in drafting legislation, executive orders, and model state laws to implement their recommendations.

Although modifications have occurred throughout the nation's history, major emphasis on the topic seems to occur in cycles, which often coincide with an incoming president's attempt to implement a personal philosophy. As Robert Wood noted, we have passed through phases labeled as dual federalism, cooperative federalism, creative federalism, and new federalism.[7] It should be pointed out, however, that these terms have been used as "catchy" labels and do not identify any particular period. At no time has there been such an abrupt change as to permit talking about an old and a new system of federalism. Institutions, especially within a democratic framework, evolve at an extremely slow rate with no sharp breaks with the past. Such a slow, cumbersome evolutionary process, unlike revolutionary change, provides continuity and stability, but it also creates a problem. The problem is that institutional modifications are occurring too slowly to respond to the challenges produced by the rapidly changing environment. And this is a real danger, because the arrangements and techniques that produced adequate results in the past may be obstacles under present conditions.

Methods of Change

Within a democratic society, modifications in intergovernmental relationships must be accomplished through prescribed and acceptable methods. In the United States, they have occurred through three techniques. One is by following the prescribed method for formally amending the U.S. Constitution — a complex, deliberately slow process designed to discourage rapid change. The second has been by judicial review. The U.S. Supreme Court, in deciding cases, constantly reinterprets the meaning of the Constitution. Some of these decisions, which involve the implied powers doctrine, either add to or subtract from the powers of the national government. A final and important method of change has been federal manipulation of the system by which it provides essential financial resources to subnational governments, which is discussed in a later section called "Fiscal Federalism."

Although there have been many variations, much experimentation, and considerable confusion, the modifications may be discussed under two categories: centralization versus decentralization and fiscal federalism.[8]

Centralization-Decentralization

Before we proceed with the discussion, we should review the concepts of centralization and decentralization to avoid confusion.[9] The earlier use of the terms concentration (centralization) or dispersion (decentralization) of powers was in reference to the newly created nation. In the context of discussing changes which have occurred and are occurring that alter the original distribution of authority between the levels of government, centralization means the transfer of administrative authority and control which constitutionally belongs to a lower unit of government to a higher unit — state to federal and city or county to the state. Decentralization is the delegation of decision-making authority from the central agency responsible for the program to one of its units in the field — for example, the Office of Education in Washington to its directors in the regional office, or city hall to regional sub-city halls. Nevertheless, this is delegated authority, which means that the central office retains ultimate control and can modify the delegation at any time. Decentralization is thus different from *devolution*, where authority and control is actually relinquished by a higher level and returned to a lower unit of government.[10]

Centralization.   Although the centralization-decentralization issue has been periodically debated, the federal and state governments historically functioned in their respective areas of authority without much conflict. The economic depression of the 1930s, however, put the system to a severe test and reopened the centralization issue.

The collapse of the economic structure created catastrophic problems which affected every individual and government in the nation. Only the federal government had the financial resources needed to launch a unified attack on problems of such magnitude and scope. In response to the situation, President Franklin D. Roosevelt created the New Deal program. A vast array of new federal recovery agencies and programs were spawned under this new label. Although the Supreme Court declared some of them unconstitutional on the basis that the federal government had no constitutional authority over the subject, others survived. The centralization trend, which was reinforced by the necessities of World War II, continued under Presidents Truman, Eisenhower, and Kennedy. Then, President Johnson, under the rubric of the Great Society, greatly expanded programs — especially in the social area — and made them available to new segments of the society. The centralization of power in the federal government became even more pronounced. As Dwight Ink said, "one difference between the Great Society approach and that of past administrations was a greater recognition that administrative centralization or direct federal leverage was required in order to reach federal goals — civil rights in particular."[11]

This centralization was accomplished primarily through the use of federal conditional grants-in-aid and not through amendment of the U.S. Constitution. The federal government offers financial assistance for specified purposes to state and local governments. If the subnational unit accepts the money, it also accepts the conditions imposed by the federal level. This technique, used in areas where the federal government has no authority to act directly, is used to induce subnational governments to do something the national government thinks should be done. Since the money and conditions do not have to be accepted, this "carrot" approach does not violate the constitutional division of powers. Although state and local governments may reject the money on the basis that the conditions inject the federal government too deeply into their affairs, few have been able or willing to refuse the proffered assistance.

Reasons for Centralization. Centralization is often blamed on federal bureaucrats who, it is assumed, have encouraged the transfer of power in order to acquire more administrative authority. While bureaucratic desires were probably a factor, there were other reasons. One reason was that many problems which historically were state and local became regional, interstate, and national. Second, many of the problems were and are beyond the financial capacity of the responsible government to solve them. Third, national policy makers thought that some needs and services, which should be considered as national goals, could only be achieved by a centralization of authority. Finally, there was an elitist attitude among federal legislators and bureaucrats and a feeling that state and local people were comparatively incompetent and could not be trusted to achieve the goals.[12]

Results of Centralization. The centralization trend resulted in the concentration of administrative power in Washington at the expense of subnational governments. Programs and topics historically reserved to the states now came under the purview of the federal government. Subnational governments either completely lost administrative control or shared it with an increasingly powerful central government. Such a centralization of administrative power made it possible to launch nationwide programs in many areas of national concern — crime, welfare, poverty, community programs, and so on — and to standardize programs and procedures. However, in the process, the fact that there are great regional and local differences was ignored; decisions were made without much if any input by those affected; locally elected officials were isolated from the decision process; red tape, delay, confusion, and frustration greeted state and local officials seeking grants; and individual citizens were disenchanted, alienated, and had a feeling of powerlessness in making any impact on their government.

As Ink says, "the defects of centralization began to outweigh the advantages. People felt that government was remote; that they could not communicate with the decision makers."[13] The director of the Center for the Study of Federalism at Temple University says there is a crisis in the federal system. The crisis was created because power, which has been increasingly concentrated in the presidency, is administered through an administrative pyramid which has "become too large to be controlled from the top yet too horizontal to be controlled at any other point."[14]

As the American Council on Intergovernmental Relations has consistently pointed out, there is a serious lack of balance in the federal system. "Balance is central to the concept of federalism — balance in decision-making power, balance in fiscal resources, balance in program responsibilities. Yet a decade of probing study by the Commission documents the fact that the federal system now lacks that essential element."[15] In 1974, the Commission stated that there is general concurrence that "the power of the Federal establishment should be reduced, while the autonomous authority of state and local government should be augmented."[16]

Decentralization.   In answer to some of the criticisms of centralization, the federal government has periodically gone through phases of attempting to decentralize its operations. However, until the advent of regional councils (discussed in the section on fiscal federalism), decentralization at the national level was haphazard. Some central administrative departments delegated extensive decision-making authority to their field representatives; others delegated much less or none; lines of authority were subject to frequent modification; and no one had any authority to direct or coordinate the activities of the field officers of the various departments. There was no uniform national policy or commitment to decentralization of federal decision making to the field offices.

Decentralization, however, refers only to the delegation of federal decision making from Washington to the field offices. It did not transfer decision making to subnational governments. Since such delegation does move the decision centers closer to the users, it does make the federal government more accessible, reduces the red tape, and permits closer liaison; it represents a considerable improvement.

Fiscal Federalism

While other aspects of intergovernmental relations are important, the crucial ingredient is money. Since money is power, who controls the supply becomes the decision center for establishing the philosophy, goals, and programs of government. In the United States, there has been a great disparity in the financial capacity of the various levels of government. The federal government, due to the revenue from the flexible and efficiently managed income tax, has been in the superior position.

Because of this fiscal imbalance, subnational governments have to rely upon financial assistance from the federal government. Such aid, which has been a historic practice, became a more significant factor in public expenditures after World War II. The progression has been rather steady—$2 billion in 1950, $7 billion in 1960, $46.1 billion in 1974, and $56.0 billion (projected) in 1976. This 1976 amount represents about 22 percent of state and local expenditures for the year.[17]

The principal techniques for distributing federal money to subnational governments have been categorical grants, block grants, and revenue sharing.

Categorical Grants. Historically, federal financial assistance to state and local governments was provided through a system of "categorical" grants. The program had a number of characteristics: (1) there were numerous programs (more than 1,000, at one time); (2) each one addressed a specific narrow problem; (3) each program, usually created by separate federal legislation, had its own individualized guidelines, application procedure, time frame, processing methods, and specialized requirements; (4) most programs required the recipient government to put up a specified percentage of its own funds as "matching" money; (5) the federal money came with "conditions" or strings, which state and local governments had to accept if they wanted the money (the conditions, which varied with each program, specified the purposes for which money could be spent and usually established performance standards, operating procedures, accounting methods, reporting requirements, and any other conditions which Congress saw fit to include in the legislation); (6) administrative authority over grants was not centralized, but dispersed among many federal agencies, each responsible for specific programs; (7) final decision making on all aspects of each grant program, in most cases, was located in Washington; (8) the "lead time," which varied with the type of grant, was very long (each unit of government had to apply formally for each category of grant months in advance).

The general status was that "each of these programs was enacted with a national purpose in mind and is endowed with its own matching and allocation formulas and with a plethora of detailed strings relating to administrative organization, program content, application processing, planning, auditing, and reporting."[18]

This financial input, which was crucial to many governments, produced both positive and negative results. The positive results were a unified nationwide attack on selected problems, as well as a strengthening of the management capacity of subnational governments as reflected by modernization in budgeting and accounting procedures, better organized and more professional planning departments, and the creation of special departments to deal with intergovernmental affairs. However, the numerous negative aspects — negative in the eyes of the state and local recipients — have been criticized for years. A major criticism is that the grant system does not allow for local options. It is designed to attack problems thought to be important nationally — social welfare, highways, police, education — but if a choice were possible, subnational governments might select other problems they thought more crucial. The second criticism pertains to the federal government's attempt to standardize the funding and methodology for approaching these problems, which vary in character and intensity among the regions of the country. A third complaint is a possible improper allocation of nonfederal funds. Subnational governments, knowing that federal matching money is available for a particular topic, may be tempted to commit scarce money to these areas and underfinance other programs. A fourth criticism is that such grants induce governments to overextend themselves both financially and in scope or complexity. While it may be possible to discover sufficient matching money to qualify to receive the federal grant, it would be impossible to sustain the organization or fund the program if the federal money was withdrawn. A fifth and standard complaint is the red tape involved in securing federal money — different agencies handling different programs; the difficulty and time invested in preparing applications, conflicting regulations, time delays, expense and confusion in reporting, and a host of other irritations. Finally, the hundreds of assistance programs created in the 1960s were responses to individual problems and in no sense represented a planned, comprehensive, and coordinated program.

Because of these criticisms, but especially because of the number of grants, the dispersion of decision-making authority, and the horrendous red tape, two important modifications have been made in the grant program — block grants and the Federal Assistance Review procedures.

Block Grants.   Block grants attempted to remove the detailed conditions and red tape associated with categorical grants. Under this system, a recipient of the funds may allocate and spend the funds to accomplish any legitimate purpose within a broad problem area defined by the federal government — such as safe streets, transportation, employment, community development. Removal of the detailed constraints permitted governments to decide on the specific techniques for attacking a problem, to allocate funds to fit local conditions, to encourage comprehensive planning in a whole related area, rather than focusing on artificially isolated components of the problem, and to reduce the red tape in securing and administering grants.

While this was some improvement, it was not totally satisfactory for numerous reasons. In the first place, Congress has been reluctant to authorize the extensive use of such grants. They have been limited to a comparatively few areas on a trial basis. However, the Community Development grant program, which begins its first full year of operation in fiscal 1976, will replace ten categorical grant and loan programs. Second, although they were exempt from many procedural details, these are still controlled by the federal government. Third, since the general topic was selected by the federal government, subnational governments often reallocated scarce resources to take advantage of the federal money. Finally, this program escalated the city-state conflict. The states, who received the money, decided on what basis it would be allocated to the cities. However, most cities are convinced that state legislatures, dominated by the rural areas in many states, do not understand urban problems.

The categorical grant program remained the major format for providing financial aid to subnational governments. After the block grant system offered only a minimal improvement, the thrust became to improve the process. The major effort in this area was the Federal Assistance Review (FAR) program.

Federal Assistance Review Program.   Decentralization of the delivery of grants to subnational governments, which became an integral component of President Nixon's New Federalism, took shape under the Federal Assistance Review (FAR) program, initiated on March 27, 1969.[19] As this program evolved, some basic changes were made. In addition to a variety of FAR planning teams and committees, which produced numerous documents, the federal agencies involved in providing financial assistance were required to establish ten regions with common geographic boundaries for their field operation, to locate their regional offices in the same city, to decentralize decision making to the regions, to standardize and simplify forms and procedures, to cooperate more closely with state and local governments, and to make other changes.[20] One of the major changes was the creation of the Federal Regional Councils.

Regional Councils. In January 1971, the president ordered the regional directors of the major social agencies in each region to form themselves into a Federal Regional Council. These new councils, unlike the Federal Executive Boards, which served as voluntary coordinating agencies, were specifically charged with coordinating federal functions in the region and developing and maintaining close working relationships with state and local governments, coordinating their grant programs, and, when necessary, convening their counterparts from other federal departments and agencies to develop means to react better to specific regional, state, and local problems.

However, the councils have been modified in a variety of ways since their initial creation.[21] First, the membership on the councils has been expanded until each is now composed of the regional directors of the major federal domestic agencies, which provide over 90 percent of the federal grants. Second, the regional directors are usually general administrators rather than specialists in a particular functional field. Third, the regional directors are no longer career employees of a functional department, but are political appointees selected by the secretary of the parent unit in Washington. This status change has important implications. If a person is a career employee protected by civil service rules, the political leadership in Washington has limited control. But if the person is a political appointee, he or she serves at the pleasure of the appointing authority and is more susceptible to direction and control. Because of this, the top administrators in Washington are much more willing to decentralize decision-making authority, involving a variety of programs and billions of dollars, to their regional people.

Finally, in addition to the political nature of the regional directors, the leadership of the councils has been politicized. On each council, one of the directors is designated as chairperson by the president. This action bestows considerable power, which the "President's Man" may then use to achieve the desired action. As Kolberg said, "the philosophy behind it was simple — no longer would there be laissez-faire secretarial domination of the regions. Somehow or another the President as the head of the Executive Branch of the federal government has a responsibility to see that goals are accomplished and work is done in the regions."[22]

To increase the presidential presence, the Office of Management and Budget (OMB) now has a representative assigned to each region. The representative attends council meetings and works with the chairperson and staff. Since OMB is a part of the Executive Office of the president, the chief executive actually has two representatives through whom to communicate in influencing actions. In addition, the Deputy Director of OMB was given responsibility for coordinating the policy committee of the regional councils.

Functions of the Councils.   Although the councils play no role in general revenue sharing, their responsibilities are numerous.[23] The principal one, however, is in the area of conditional grants-in-aid. In an attempt to reduce the massive red tape, delay, and centralized authority, Washington has decentralized the authority to process and make final decisions on applications for categorical grants from state and local governments. Rather than having to relate to approximately 1,200 different funding programs, applicants relate to the council in their region which serves as a clearinghouse. The respective directors can process, approve, disapprove, negotiate, and make final decisions on applications. However, in practice, there are variations in the amount of decision authority which the respective departments have delegated to their regional directors.

The councils also serve as a mechanism for permitting coordination among federal grant programs which impact on the same topic or program. They also develop common administrative policies and procedures for agencies in the region. Through developing personal contact with governors and other elected officials, the councils serve as a catalyst to receive and process program inputs from politicians in an effort to explore possibilities for and encourage intergovernmental relations. Another, comparatively new activity, which has been attempted on a demonstration basis, is the Chief Executive Review and Comment (CERC) program. In this, the councils work with mayors to inform them of the amounts and sources of federal money coming into their municipalities and to assist them in developing organizations, techniques, and procedures for monitoring or controlling such money.

An additional function of the councils is administration of the Integrated Grant Administration (IGA) Program.[24] Under this, public agencies may apply for a number of Federal Assistance grants by a single application. The procedure is intended to permit the applicant to select programs from different agencies that relate to various aspects of a common problem, rather than being required to file a separate application for each grant. Each application is processed by a task force composed of representatives from participating agencies, but under the auspices and supervision of the regional council.

Success of Federal Assistance Review.   The program has made some very significant changes — standardization of regional boundaries, one city designated as a regional center, simplification of grant processing — but it did not achieve all of its objectives. The regional councils, the most visible product, have not realized their full potential for a variety of reasons — variations in the amount of authority delegated to the regions, unstandardized operating procedures, and the changing composition of the councils.[25]

This lack of complete success should not surprise anyone. The program, initiated by the president, attempted to make a variety of basic organizational and procedural changes which — like the block grant concept — immediately threatened vested interests, especially those of the bureaucrats. Any change disrupts "the functional status quo and directly challenges the security of the various bureaucratic fiefdoms that have built up over the years around the narrow-purpose program . . . . "[26] Faced with a threat to "their" program, bureaucrats mobilized support from their client groups, supportive legislators, and other concerned administrative organizations to resist modifications in the laws. Such administrative resistance creates a significant barrier to reorganization, because the narrowly defined programs, each of which affects only a small segment of the population, does not generate any massive public support for the changes.

Revenue Sharing

Revenue sharing is not a new idea. States have shared their income from a variety of taxes — gasoline, roads, liquor, gambling, sales — with local governments for years. And, the idea had been discussed frequently at the federal level.[27] However, President Nixon, in his message to Congress on January 4, 1971, proposed it as a major component of his "New Federalism."

As we have discussed, much of the centralization of power at the federal level has been accomplished through the conditions imposed on grants made to state and local governments. This is made possible because the escalating revenue generated by the federal income tax represents vast sums of money when compared with that produced by the revenue sources available to state and local government. Due to the federal revenue superiority, subnational governments have to rely on the federal level for resources. Revenue sharing is designed to lessen the dependence by requiring the federal government to return a specified portion of the federal income tax revenue without the restrictions found in categorical grants. "Revenue sharing establishes the principle that state and local governments should have a guaranteed, albeit limited, access to the Nation's prime power source — the Federal personal income tax."[28]

The program takes two forms — general and special revenue sharing.

General Revenue Sharing. The general revenue sharing legislation, signed by the president in October 1972, will return 30.2 billion dollars of federal revenue to state and local government over a five-year period. Money is distributed to the states on the basis of two formulae. One, the three-factor formula, bases the distribution on comparative population, tax effort, and per capita income. The five-factor formula adds urbanized population and state income tax collections. The share distributed to each state is based on the formula that produces the greatest amount of money. But, if the calculations total more than the money available, all shares are reduced proportionally. After the calculations, each state receives one-third of the calculated amount and two-thirds is assigned to its units of local government on the basis of the three-factor formula.

How have the subnational governments, free from detailed federal controls for the first time, used the money? Experience has been mixed.[29] Money has been spent on things ranging from exotic computers to uniforms for the municipal band. In general, some jurisdictions have used the money to fund programs in a cross section of the nine broad program categories authorized by the law, but most of the emphasis has been in two categories — public safety and capital improvements. Social services, health, environment, and the other categories have been assigned a much less significant priority.

This emphasis on material things rather than on people has been criticized by many.

There were a variety of reasons for this emphasis, such as the desire of police and fire departments to have the latest equipment, the need for new buildings, sewer and water lines, some degree of insensitivity to the human element, and a variety of other reasons. However, a basic reason was uncertainty. The most sensitive and conscientious decision maker, knowing that the experiment has a five-year life span but unsure of whether it will be extended and if so for how long, has to be cautious. Projects which can be completed during the five-year period are fiscally and politically safe. However, committing the money to create, staff, and fund programs with long-range and usually escalating costs (such as social services and health delivery systems), is a high-risk decision. If revenue sharing is discontinued, such programs might have to be drastically cut back or eliminated because local revenue could not support them.

Special Revenue Sharing.   Special revenue sharing was mentioned in President Nixon's 1972 State of the Union Message and included in his 1974 budget. This proposal would have consolidated approximately seventy categorical grants into four areas — education, law enforcement and criminal justice, manpower training, and urban community development.[30] A specified amount of federal money would have been made available, on a formula basis, to state and local governments to fund projects. Unlike categorical grants, the money could be spent in the generally prescribed areas with no requirements for matching and freedom from federal conditions and control.

Congress has not been very receptive to this form of sharing, since the program would have control and political implications. "Congress, with an interest in supervising the administration of individual grants for which it must appropriate the money, has steadfastly opposed special revenue sharing."[31]

The Subnational Scene

State-City

The state-city relationship is quite different than the federal-state relationship. Cities, not mentioned in the distribution of power in the federal constitution, are creatures of state government. After incorporation, under procedures specified by state constitutions or laws, their organization, powers, taxing authority, financial procedures, and almost all other conditions are dictated in varying degrees of detail by the state government. It is a unitary rather than a federal relationship.

But, the same environmental changes that influenced federal-state relationships are also affecting the relationship between each state and its cities. The historic division of power, responsibility, and money is obsolete. Problems that were historically local are now statewide problems. Structure and procedures created for a rural milieu are not adequate to meet the demands created by an urbanized area. In most states, there are conflicts and competition for resources between urban and rural areas and between large and small cities. Big cities usually feel that the state government really does not understand the nature, complexity, and intensity of their problem.[32]

The result of these changes, especially the inadequacy of local revenue, has led to administrative centralization. States, largely through subsidy and conditional grant programs, have invaded what used to be the local domain.

State-Other Local Units

The relations between the state and other local units — such as school districts, other special districts and counties — are also changing. Problems no longer fit the boundaries of the responsible units and program costs have escalated beyond the local units' capacities to fund them from their revenue sources. Again, the state has been forced to create regional entities and to channel money into the local areas. Since administrative control accompanies both practices, the traditional independence of these units has been reduced.

Metropolitan Area

Relationships in metropolitan areas are especially difficult. In a typical metropolitan area there will be eighty-five general and special-purpose governments — two counties, thirteen townships, twenty-one municipalities, eighteen school districts, and thirty-one special districts, three or four federally supported areawide planning districts, and one clearinghouse to review and comment on the area impact of certain federal grant applications.[33] If one were to draw the boundary of each unit on a piece of acetate and overlay these pieces on a map of the area, the overlapping duplication and utter chaos would become evident. Each of these units has its own authority, objectives, operating procedures, revenue base, personnel, and independence. Although coordination would probably reduce costs, or at least improve services, securing even cooperation is extremely difficult. For example, consider the frequent difficulties in cooperation between adjoining cities in the location of fire and police stations, cooperation between school districts and cities in locating new schools to reduce the traffic and safety problem, and a variety of other decisions and programs of mutual concern.

To solve some of the relationship problems, special metropolitan areawide committees and councils have been voluntarily created. In other cases, such organizations have been mandated by state law or induced by federal requirements as a condition for receiving federal grants. Another coordinating technique is the use of joint powers agreements where units agree to support each other in police and fire, to use facilities jointly, and to undertake other activities that are mutually beneficial.

But negotiating voluntary coordinating ventures is difficult. Each agency has its own geographic turf, elected governing body, history, tradition, identity, budget, and all of the other emotional and political characteristics that militate against enthusiastic cooperation.

Regionalism as a Solution

Since many problems no longer conform to the boundaries of the responsible government — state, county, or city — regional governments have been created to fill the authority gap. The regions are of two general types. The first is the multistate region created to handle problems which cross state boundaries and require the cooperation of two or more states for their solution.[34] The second and largest category is substate regions, dealing with areas that are smaller than states but larger than cities or counties.[35]

These substate regions, each with its own governing board, have proliferated rapidly due either to local initiative or as a condition for participating in certain federal grant programs. At the end of 1973, there were more than 600 regional councils of government (COG's) which are confederations of governments, usually cities and counties, created to coordinate efforts on areawide problems; approximately 25,000 special districts and authorities (for cemetery, school, irrigation, fire protection, transportation, and other services) created under state enabling legislation with their own elected governing boards and taxing and borrowing authority; approximately 1,800 special-purpose regional districts, either required or encouraged to qualify local government for federal funds in specified programs (law enforcement, health planning, transportation, waste treatment, air quality, manpower programs, community action, and a variety of others); and 524 substate regional councils (required by Office of Management and Budget Circular A–95) which have the responsibility for receiving applications for specified federal grants from individual governments, commenting on their areawide impact and recommending action.[36]

Problems Created by Regionalism

This level of government, not provided for by the Constitution, has proliferated rapidly to meet changing conditions. The development has added to the complexity of the governmental structure and created many problems.[37] The root of one of the basic problems is that each level of government — federal, state, and local — has created such entities to meet its own needs, with no provision made for an effective regional decision-making body. The product has been a complete lack of coordination, overlapping, and duplication. A second cluster of concerns revolves around the nature of these organizations. Some of these agencies were created years ago, some provide no or comparatively little service, many people do not understand their roles, most have their own governing boards which operate with little public control, and some have taxing authority which influences the general tax burden.

To provide for coordination and decision making at the substate level, the Advisory Commission on Intergovernmental Relations has proposed the creation of a regional mechanism called an "umbrella multi-jurisdictional organization (UMJO)."[38] Although examples of such agencies already exist, this concept would standardize procedures. The legal status of the new units, which would actually be a new level of local government, would be established by state legislation. The governing body would consist of representatives from state and local governments, with the latter having at least 60 percent of the representation. All local government units would be required to join as a condition for receiving certain types of federal assistance. The ACIR has drafted proposed state legislation which would assign varied duties to the agencies, including assuming "responsibility for implementing all federally encouraged areawide planning, programming, coordinating, or even servicing programs as well as for similar state undertakings."[39]

Conclusions

In this chapter we have discussed the system and problems of intergovernmental relations, with emphasis on the changes which have occurred and are occurring. The main theme was the centralization trend which transferred administrative authority from lower units to higher governmental units. In the process, and primarily through the financial assistance program, state governments have lost administrative control over programs and subjects historically within their domain. The dysfunctional results of extreme centralization have created dissatisfaction and demand for change. Recent modifications—such as revenue sharing, block grants, and regional councils—have made some improvements, but the preponderance of administrative power is still concentrated in Washington. The Advisory Commission on Intergovernmental Relations believes that to correct the authority imbalance which exists in our federal system it "will require major changes in our governmental institutions, programs, and procedures . . . . Those changes are needed to revitalize the federal system and to achieve a strong partnership of strong partners."[40] The changes not only involve relationships, but also modernization of all levels of government. In 1974, the Commission summarized the problem of balancing the components of the federal system when it said that " . . . true equilibrium can never be reached, for federalism is as dynamic as the forces that shape the society it serves."[41]

Although many of the problems in intergovernmental relations have been created by the changing world, the fundamental cause is the historic federal form of government which distributed powers between the levels of government. Since this distribution is specified in the U.S. Constitution, it is difficult to make any fundamental changes. Moreover, constitutional law is only one of the legal constraints under which public administration functions. In the next chapter, the general legal environment of public administration will be reviewed.

NOTES

1. James W. Fesler, "The Basic Theoretical Question: How to Relate Area to Function," *Public Administration Review,* Special Publication (September 1973), p. 6. For a more comprehensive discussion by the same author, see *Area and Administration* (University: University of Alabama Press, 1964).

2. James W. Fesler, "The Basic Theoretical Question: How to Relate Area to Function," in *The Administration of the New Federalism,* American Society for Public Administration, Special Publication (September 1973), p. 9.

3. For a description of the boards by one who was instrumental in their creation, see John W. Macy, Jr., "To Decentralize and to Delegate," *Public Administration Review* 30, no. 4 (July-August 1970): 438–44.

4. Public Law 380, first session of the 86th Congress and approved by the president on September 24, 1959; for the report of a previous commission see *The Final Report of the*

Commission on Intergovernmental Relations (Kestnbaum Report), U.S. House of Representatives, Committee on Government Operations, House Document No. 198, 84th Cong., 1st sess., June 1955.

5. Section 2 of Public Law 380.

6. For how the members are appointed, the membership and programs, see Advisory Commission on Intergovernmental Relations (ACIR), *15th Annual Report,* Report M-80 (Washington, D.C.: Government Printing Office, January 1974).

7. Robert Wood, "Needs and Perspectives," in "Symposium on Needs and Prospects for Research in Governmental Relations," *Public Administration Review* 30, no. 3 (May-June 1970): 265. Also, for a discussion of the meaning and components of New Federalism see American Society for Public Administration, *The Administration of the New Federalism: Objectives and Issues,* Special Publication (September 1973).

8. A review of ten years of developments in the federal system is contained in ACIR, *Eleventh Annual Report,* Report M-40 (Washington, D.C.: Government Printing Office, January 1970); the 174-page special issue of the *Public Administration Review* (October 1972) contains articles on the topic, as well as 1,278 citations to other materials and thirteen films; and the Annual Reports of the ACIR survey each year's events.

9. For a discussion of this area, see James W. Fesler, "Approaches to the Understanding of Decentralization," *Journal of Politics* 27 (August 1965): 536–66; Herbert Kaufman, "Administrative Decentralization and Political Power," *Public Administration Review* 29, no. 1, (January-February 1969): 3–14; the *Annual Reports* of the ACIR surveys of each year's events; *Public Administration Review,* Special Issue, 32 (October 1972); the American Society for Public Administration, Special Publication, *The Administration of the New Federalism: Objectives and Issues* (September 1973) — devoted entirely to the question; and Irving Kristol, "Decentralization For What," *The Public Interest,* no. 11 (Spring 1968): 17–25.

10. For a discussion of devolution, see Frank P. Sherwood, "Devolution as a Problem of Organization Strategy," in Robert T. Daland, ed., *Comparative Urban Research: The Administration and Politics of Cities* (Beverly Hills, Calif.: Sage Publications, 1969), pp. 60–87.

11. Dwight Ink, "The Origin and Thrust of the New Federalism: Objectives and Issues," in *The Administration of the New Federalism: Objectives and Issues,* American Society for Public Administration, Special Publication (September 1973), p. 29.

12. For a discussion of some of the myths about the inadequacies of the states, see Daniel J. Elazar, "The New Federalism: Can the States Be Trusted," *The Public Interest,* no. 35 (Spring 1974): 89–102.

13. Ink, "Origin and Thrust of New Federalism," p. 30.

14. Daniel J. Elazar, "Authentic Federalism for America," *National Civic Review* 62, no. 9 (October 1973): 475.

15. ACIR, *Federalism in 1970,* Twelfth Annual Report (Washington, D.C.: Government Printing Office, January 3, 1971), p. 1.

16. ACIR, *Federalism in 1973: The System Under Stress,* Report M–81 (Washington, D.C.: Government Printing Office, January 1974), p. 1.

17. For a description of grants, see Executive Office of the President, *Special Analyses, Budget of the United States Government, Fiscal Year 1976* (Washington, D.C.: Government Printing Office, 1975), pp. 235–51. For some history, see ACIR, *Trends in Fiscal Federalism, 1954–1974* (Washington, D.C.: Government Printing Office, February 1975).

18. ACIR, *Special Revenue Sharing: An Analysis of the Administration's Grant Consolidation Proposals,* Report M–70 (Washington, D.C.: Government Printing Office, December 1971), p. 2.

19. For a discussion of the conceptual framework of the move toward decentralization by top administrators in the Nixon administration, see Dwight Ink and Alan Dean, "A Concept of Decentralization," *Public Administration Review* 30, no. 1 (January-February 1970): 60–63.

20. For a detailed report of activities, see *Simplifying Federal Aid to States and Communities*, First Annual Report to the President, Executive Office of the President, Washington, D.C. (March 1970); *Restoring the Balance of Federalism*, Second Annual Report to the President, Executive Office of the President, Washington, D.C. (July 1971); and *Federal Assistance Review*, Agency Field Organization, FAR, 1016 16th Street, NW, Washington, D.C. (June 30, 1971).

21. For a description of the councils and possible new activities, see William H. Kolberg, "The New Federalism: Regional Council and Program Coordination Efforts," *Public Administration Review*, Special Publication (September 1973), pp. 51–64; Melvin B. Mogulof, "Federal Interagency Action and Inaction: The Federal Regional Council Experience," *Public Administration Review* 32, no. 3 (May-June 1972): 232–40.

22. Kolberg, "The New Federalism," p. 54.

23. These councils deal essentially with agencies in the urban areas. To coordinate an attack on problems in the rural areas, Congress passed the Rural Development Act in 1972. For a discussion of the problems and coordination efforts, see William A. Carlson, "New Federalism and a New Program — The Rural Development Act of 1972," *American Society for Public Administration*, Special Publication (September 1973), pp. 65–76.

24. For a complete description of the objectives, organization and procedures, see Executive Office of the President, Office of Management and Budget, *The Integrated Grant Administration (IGA) Program* (Washington, D.C.: Government Printing Office, January 14, 1972). Also, for a discussion of the Joint Funding Simplification Act of December 5, 1974, which extended the IGA experiment, see ACIR, *Federalism in 1974: The Tensions of Interdependence* (Washington, D.C.: Government Printing Office, February 1975), pp. 18–19.

25. For a description of some of the operating problems and suggested modifications, see Mogulof, "Federal Interagency Action and Inaction," pp. 232–40.

26. ACIR, *Special Revenue Sharing*, p. 4.

27. For an early appraisal of revenue sharing, see C. Lowell Harriss, *Federal Revenue Sharing: A New Appraisal* (New York: Tax Foundation, Inc., 1969).

28. ACIR, *Revenue Sharing — An Idea Whose Time Has Come*, Report M-54 (Washington, D.C.: Government Printing Office, December 1970), p. 2.

29. For a detailed listing of the expenditures and a discussion of the area, see the Comptroller General of the United States, *Report to the Congress, Revenue Sharing: Its Use by and Impact on Local Government* (Washington, D.C.: U.S. General Accounting Office, April 25, 1974); John C. Murphy, "General Revenue Sharing's Impact on County Government," *Public Administration Review* 35, no. 2 (March-April 1975): 131–35; David A. Caputo and Richard L. Cole, "General Revenue Sharing Expenditure Decisions in Cities over 50,000," *Public Administration Review* 35, no. 2 (March-April 1975): 136–42; and Michael A. Carroll, "The Impact of General Revenue Sharing on the Urban Planning Process," *Public Administration Review* 35, no. 2 (March-April 1975): 143–49.

30. For a discussion, see ACIR, *Special Revenue Sharing*.

31. ACIR, *Federalism in 1973*, p. 11.

32. For a discussion of what states are doing on local problems, see ACIR, *State Action on Local Problems* (Washington, D.C.: Government Printing Office, Annual).

33. ACIR, *15th Annual Report*, p. 6.

34. For a description of these, see ACIR, *Multistate Regionalism*, Report A–39 (April 1972), p. 271.

35. The ACIR has published a six-volume study in *Substate Regionalism and the Federal System*, Vol. I, *Regional Decision Making: New Strategies for Substate Districts*, Report A–43 (October 1973); Vol. II, *Regional Governance: Promise and Performance*, Report A–41 (May 1973); Vol. III, *The Challenge of Local Governmental Reorganization*, Report A–44 (February 1974); *Governmental Functions and Processes: Local and Area-wide*, Report A–45 (February 1974); Vol. V, *A Look to the North: Canadian Regional Experience*, Report A–46 (February 1974); Vol. VI, *Hearings on Substate Regionalism*,

Report A–43a (October 1973). Also, see David B. Walker, "The Quandary of Substate Regionalism," *Public Administration Review*, Special Publication (September 1973), pp. 79–84.

36. For a description, see ACIR, *15th Annual Report*, p. 6.

37. The whole issue of *Public Management* 56, no. 1 (January 1974), is devoted to "How Will Regionalism Work?" See also David B. Walker and Carl W. Stenberg, "A Substate Districting Strategy," *National Civic Review* 63, no. 1 (January 1974): 5–9.

38. For a description, see ACIR, *15th Annual Report*.

39. Robert E. Merriam, "State-Designated Districts and Local Modernization," *National Civic Review* 63, no. 2 (February 1974): 68.

40. ACIR, *Twelfth Annual Report*, Report M–59 (Washington, D.C.: Government Printing Office, January 1971), p. 1.

41. ACIR, *American Federalism: Into the Third Century*, Report M–85 (Washington, D. C.: Government Printing Office, May 1974), p. 3. See also *16th Annual Report, ACIR: The Year in Review*, January 1975.

7

Public Administration Under Law

In chapter 2 it was noted that for many years the legal perspective in public administration has been in eclipse. It was also suggested that contemporary challenges to established governmental institutions and practices are encouraging a rediscovery of some matters long associated with the study of administrative law. The turbulent challenges, in which public administration is deeply implicated, include the following: official corruption, disputes over eligibility for welfare benefits, affirmative action in the hiring and development of public employees, the growth of unionization in the public service, relations between police forces and the community, charges of administrative coercion in fields such as welfare and education, extraordinary methods of investigation by public agencies, and the rise of new public interest-oriented groups seeking to influence public policy and administration in environmental protection, economic planning and regulation, community development, and civil liberties.

These challenges, in turn, are causing renewed interest among public administrationists in such hitherto neglected matters as the legal powers and obligations of public officers, justice, social equity, remedies against arbitrary official action, and the requirements of "due process" in administration. Long neglected in the textbooks of public administration, these matters are beginning to attract greater interest in the professional journals and the classrooms of this field.

Law in the Web of Government

The Rule of Law

Few words defy clear-cut and universally accepted definition more than does the word "law." But, one attribute of the law which is particularly important in the context of public administration is its primacy. This primacy is sometimes obscured by such factors as the growth in the size and power of governments, the rise of the administrative state, aggrandizement of the executive power relative to legislative bodies and courts, disturbing cases of official corruption and lawlessness, and affairs such as "Watergate" and the fall of the Nixon administration. However it may be construed, though, public administration in the American system of government is not a law unto itself.

The role of law in society is diverse and complex, but the idea of law as supreme is central in the American system. For example, law is viewed in this country as a body of rules which defines certain actions as right or wrong, which incorporates the principle of certainty, and which is regarded to be binding on all members of society. Law is also conceived as an instrument of social order and social justice and as a paramount means for societies and individuals to achieve the "good life." As a regulator of the conduct of individuals living in organized society, law is regarded as an instrument of constraint over both the governed and the governors. Moreover, law provides the "raw materials" from which the rules of governance are formulated and supplies the basic criteria by which the behavior of both citizen and official are measured and judged. In the words of our second president, John Adams, "we have a government of laws, not of men." Violations of this principle in actual practice do not alter the fact that law enjoys a special place in Western society and is clothed with almost sacred robes.[1]

The "rule of law" implies limited government, government in accordance with predetermined rules and criteria, and government on the basis of certainty rather than whim. Further, "rule of law" implies a monopolization of the use of force, of the power of judgment, and of the application of sanctions and penalties. These concepts are symbolized in the scales and the sword in the hands of the figure of "Justice" displayed around courts of law, and they are symbolized on a policeman's badge. The public administrator who forgets the "rule of law" may do so at his or her peril as well as at a peril to society.

Categories of Law

The body of law with which the public administrator is concerned is called *public law,* which is composed of two closely related subdivisions: (1) *constitutional law,* concerned with the fundamental structure of the state, including especially the powers, duties, and obligations of officers of the state, which in the American system are incorporated in the Constitution of the United States, in the constitutions of the separate states, and in court cases where these constitutional prescriptions are interpreted; and (2) *administrative law,* concerned primarily with such matters as the powers and procedures of public administrators, legal limitations on administrative discretion, and provisions for judicial review of administrative actions — all of which are incorporated in constitutions, statutes, compacts, charters, ordinances, resolutions, and interpretive court cases.

Another way of categorizing the law for the public administrator is as sources of direction and guidance. From *public law* (including both constitutional law and administrative law) come rules and prescriptions concerning powers and duties of office. From *common law* come precedents and leading cases settled by courts (sometimes called "judge-made law"). And from *statutory law,* made by legislative bodies, the public administrator receives the mandate to act or to desist from acting.

Constitutional Law

Central Principles

In a sense, we may say that *constitutional law* is the basic architecture of a political system. As an important part of that system, public administration is affected by that law. Embodied in American constitutional law and expressed in the Constitution of the United States and in the constitutions of many of the individual states are such central principles as:

1. The principle of *federalism,* with governmental power in the United States divided between a central government (the government of the United States of America) and several individual states that enjoy certain powers, either specified or latent in the constitutional document
2. The principle of *checks and balances,* through which the powers of the central government are divided and shared among three branches of government — legislative, executive, and judicial
3. The principles of *popular sovereignty* and *limited government,* which are institutionalized through various representative bodies, and through judicial review of legislative and executive action
4. The principle of *change,* expressed in the provisions for interpretation and amendment of the written constitutional document, and thus providing for a *living* constitution
5. The principle of *national supremacy,* in which it is specifically provided in the Constitution that in various ways the central government is superior to the governments of the individual states.[2]

Practical Implications for Public Administration

For the contemporary public administrator, these constitutional principles have more than antiquarian interest. For instance, the principle of *federalism* governs the complex web of interrelationships among Washington, D.C., state capitals, county seats, and city halls. Involved are such important administrative issues as revenue sharing and other fiscal devices and the division of responsibility and allocation of power in coping with such policy areas as law enforcement, social welfare, and population planning.

The principle of *checks and balances,* as embodied in the Constitution of the United States and many of the individual state constitutions, is an important factor in determining presidential and gubernatorial powers over budgeting, appointment, and firing of subordinates, and the power to veto legislation; the exercise of the power of judicial review by the courts over the actions of administrators; and the power of executives to go over the heads of the legislatures and courts and appeal directly to the people.

The principles of *popular sovereignty* and *limited government* are behind a wide range of limitations and restrictions on the freedom of public executives and public administrators to act. These include the indirect election of the president; the necessity of legislative advice and consent for various executive appointments by presidents, governors, and mayors; constitutional provisions for popular referenda on various policy issues and for the popular recall of elected executives and administrators; and constitutional limitations on such important administrative matters as the organizational structure of the bureaucracy, the collection of public revenues, the expenditure of public funds, the determination of which officers will be popularly elected and which appointed, terms and conditions of office, and the power to reorganize executive establishments.

The constitutional principle of *change* has inspired a mood of tentativeness and adaptability in American public administration. This is reflected in such developments as the assumption of new and diverse responsibilities by the bureaucracy; changes in the administrative relationships within the central government and between the central government and the states and municipalities; various administrative reforms, such as the reorganization of the executive branches of government and changes in administrative procedure; and the movement to decentralize the administration of government from offices in Washington, D.C., to regional, state, and local governments.

Finally, the principle of *national supremacy* has implications for public administration at all levels of government. Much has been said and written about this exceedingly complex, and often ambiguous, principle, but in general it is fairly clear that in the motto of the American republic, *E pluribus Unum*, there is especially heavy reliance on the supremacy of unity over diversity. This commitment to national unity is reflected in the way Americans have coped with such problem areas as war and peace, fiscal affairs, business regulation, and the like.

Constitutional Provisions Governing Public Administration

The responsible public administrator has an obligation to be as familiar with certain features of constitutional documents as with the other technical literature of the profession. Familiarity with the following specific provisions of the United States Constitution is imperative:

1. The *"commerce power,"* which is provided for in Article I, section 8, paragraph 3, assigns to the Congress and its agencies and instrumentalities — in other words, the administrative bureaucracy — the power to regulate a host of economic activities that involve the movement of goods and services across state boundaries.

2. *The taxing and spending power*, prescribed in Article I, section 8, paragraph 1, delegates to the Congress the power "to lay and collect taxes,

duties, imposts, and excises," specifies the purposes for which revenues may be raised, and thus imposes a connection between the raising of funds and their expenditures. Through the processes of legislation, these powers are delegated to public administrators for their execution.

3. *Fiscal-monetary powers,* provided for in Article I, section 8, paragraphs 2, 5, and 6, empower Congress to borrow money "on the credit of the United States," to "coin money, regulate the value thereof," and "provide for the punishment of counterfeiting the securities and current coin of the United States." All of these, which include the regulation of banking, protecting national banks from state taxation, the issuing of paper money and making it legal tender, and the establishment and maintenance of the Federal Reserve System and other banking institutions, are essentially the tasks of the public administrator.

4. *The war or emergency power,* embodied in Article 1, section 8, paragraphs 11-16, empower Congress, and through Congress the bureaucracy, to raise and support armies, provide and maintain navies, call out the militia, formulate and enforce rules for the government and regulation of land and naval forces, and the like. Much of the expansion that has occurred in the power and impact of the bureaucracy since the founding of the republic 200 years ago is rooted in this constitutional power.

5. *The power of weights and measures,* provided for in Article I, section 8, paragraph 5, empowers Congress, and derivatively public administrators, to regulate the standards of weights and measures, which becomes especially important in a society experiencing vast and rapid technological change.

6. *Limitations on state taxation,* provided for in Article I, section 10, paragraph 2, include a provision that, except where absolutely necessary for inspectional purposes, the states may not tax imports or exports.

7. *Limitations on state monetary powers,* provided for in Article I, section 10, paragraph 1, forbid the states to coin money, issue bills of credit, or make anything but gold and silver coin tender for payments of debts.

8. *Interstate privileges and immunities of citizens,* contained in Article IV, section 2, paragraph 1, provide that the citizens of each state shall enjoy "all privileges and immunities of citizens in the several states." This provision, which makes national unity superior to state diversity, has profound impact on the administration of such policy areas as education, law enforcement, and social welfare.

9. *Due process of law and equal protection of the laws,* guaranteed in the Fourteenth Amendment to the United States Constitution, which was ratified in 1868 as a result of the Civil War, provides that no state shall "deprive any person of life, liberty or property without due process of law," and that no state shall "deny to any person within its jurisdiction the equal protection of the laws." The term "person" includes corporations. This set of guarantees has been violated in practice, especially where minority people, poor people, and other relatively helpless citizens are involved. But it remains an important limitation on the public administrator.

10. *The "elastic clause,"* provided for in Article I, section 8, paragraph 18, empowers Congress "To make all laws which shall be necessary and proper for carrying into execution the foregoing powers, and all other powers vested by this Constitution in the Government of the United States, or in any department or officer thereof." As interpreted over the years, this provision has helped to enlarge greatly the power and the responsibilities of public administrators in the unfolding national system.

11. *The provision for certain powers to be reserved to the states,* expressed as the Tenth Amendment to the United States Constitution, ratified in 1791 as the last of the Bill of Rights, reads: "The powers not delegated to the United States by the Constitution, nor prohibited by it to the States, are reserved to the States respectively, or to the people." This provision has allowed enhancement of the scope of decision and action for public administrators at the state and local levels of government.

State Constitutional Constraints on Public Administration

It is beyond our scope here to devote comparable close scrutiny to relevant provisions of the fifty individual state constitutions. Let it suffice to summarize briefly some of the main provisions that constrain public administration at the state and local levels of government:

1. Provisions designating the principal executive officers and agencies of state government, including especially the so-called constitutional officers that are specified in some detail, such as governor, lieutenant governor, secretary of state, state treasurer, auditor or controller, attorney general, and superintendent of public instruction.

2. Provisions governing the powers of state bureaucracies to reorganize and to conduct other important administrative reforms.

3. Limitations on the powers of state and local governments to collect revenues, borrow money, expend funds for certain purposes, and practice administrative flexibility in the allocation and reallocation of appropriated funds.

4. Limitations on the powers of state and local public administrators to modernize outdated civil service systems.

5. Provisions for direct legislation, such as the *initiative* and *referendum*, and for the *recall* of officials.

6. Restrictions on the powers of local self-government generally, which we shall discuss more fully below under *municipal law.*

7. A tendency for state constitutions to be excessively detailed with respect to administrative and other matters. State constitutions average in length about twice that of the United States Constitution.

The Living Constitution

In the United States, constitutional documents may be encased in airtight compartments and preserved in museums and archives, but the constitutional system, of which these documents and their written interpretations are a part, is a living and dynamic thing. The traditional theory of American constitutional law, embodied in the principles and provisions discussed above, has been substantially challenged, modified, and changed by political and administrative practices. For instance, political parties and special-interest groups, which were not provided for in the United States Constitution and state constitutions, play a role in government generally and they influence public administration beyond anything anticipated by the founders of the republic. Similarly, the separation between the central government, seated in Washington, D.C., and the individual state governments has been bridged in a thousand ways, as administrators from both sides have learned to work together on common problems. Furthermore, the theory of the separation of powers and checks and balances between the three major branches of government — legislative, executive, and judicial — has been twisted and warped over the years by the shifts in relative power among them, such as the twentieth-century aggrandizement of the national executive branch. Of special interest to us in this regard is the substantial delegation of legislative and judicial powers by Congress to the administrative bureaucracy.

For 200 years there has been continuing dialogue and debate about the "true" intents and purposes of the founders of the republic and of the state governments about the meanings of words, phrases, and punctuation in the written documents. But while the dialogue and debate have raged, the work of government — much of which is administrative work — has continued. The authors of the constitutions purposely built conflict and controversy into the system, but — for good or ill — it has been with the help of public administrators that we have escaped some of the difficulties, contradictions, ambiguities, and mysteries of the constitutional system. Therein lies much of the meaning of the term "the living constitution."

Administrative Law

The Legal Problems of the Administrative State

Administrative law is the other face of *public law*. It has developed contemporaneously with the great social changes of the past century and a half and with the rise of the "administrative state." When the American republic was in its infancy, governments were expected to do less, the problems of society were simpler, and it was more feasible for legislatures and courts to bear the major burdens of governance. But all of that changed.[3]

First of all, the Industrial Revolution and associated changes in society began to be felt early in the nineteenth century. Governments were faced with more complex problems, and legislatures were compelled to depend more heavily on administrators for technical expertise. The need for technical specialization in public administration increased. There arose many different kinds of regulatory agencies to enforce and oversee new governmental regulations on commerce, industry, transportation, the professions, and the like. With these developments came the realization that traditional legislative and judicial processes could not cope effectively with this revolutionary increase in the scope and complexity of governance. Also, there came the discovery of the need for more technical competence in the administration of public policy.

One consequence of these trends was the greater delegation of responsibility for administrative work by superior officers of government to their subordinates. Another was the great enlargement of administrative discretion exercised by administrators who were less visible to the public and less easily controllable by legislatures, courts, and other political bodies.[4]

One important concern in administrative law, which was greatly emphasized in earlier years but is receiving less attention now, is the need for proper criteria and control in the processes of administrative delegation. Another important concern, which is of special interest to modern students of administrative law, is the need for proper criteria and control over the exercise of administrative discretion, especially in carrying out inspection, investigation, licensing, and similar powers. A third problem area which has emerged from the rise of the administrative state in a democratic society is the conflict between the requirements of efficient administrative performance on the one hand and respect for the legal and human rights of individual citizens on the other. According to Kenneth Culp Davis in 1973, an emergent area of concern is not the procedural safeguards necessary where public administrators are making courtlike judgments, but the exercise of administrative discretion in the general administrative process, as in the processing of taxpayers' returns, a police officer's decision to arrest someone, the granting of visas to foreigners, and the making of environmental-protection decisions.[5] In conclusion, the contemporary public administrator should pay attention to program effectiveness, productivity and efficiency, and justice.

Two Branches of Administrative Law: Internal and External

It is dangerous to posit too sharp a distinction between the internal and external aspects of public administration, but for analytical purposes the distinction is useful here. It may be said that one branch of administrative law concentrates on *internal* matters, such as:

1. The legal basis of public office — what distinguishes the mayor, the police chief, the tax collector, or the superintendent of public schools from ordinary citizens
2. Legal limitations and legal empowering that are at the basis of administrative agencies of government
3. Legal aspects of various administrative processes, such as fiscal administration, budgeting, personnel administration, data collection and processing, and organizational planning and development
4. Legal qualifications and disqualifications for serving in public administrative posts
5. Legal aspects of such matters as appointment, tenure, removal, compensation, and pensioning of public officers and employees
6. Legal aspects of such matters as supervision, delegation, discretion, authority, negligence, and the structure of authority within a public administrative agency

Another major branch of administrative law is concerned with the law of *external* public administration, that is, with those duties and powers that are exercised by public administrators having direct relationship to and impact upon the interests and rights of citizens. Included here is the analysis of the nature, scope, and limits of:

1. *The power of inspection*
2. *The licensing power*
3. *The dispensing power*, the power to permit deviations from established standards and norms
4. *The directing power*, the power to issue orders and enforce compliance, such as the removal of nuisances, the rehiring and restoration of job rights to a public servant who had been erroneously fired (this includes the power to issue and enforce cease-and-desist orders)
5. *The rule-making power*, the power to formulate rules of conduct by members of the public having future effect and having general or particular applicability, such as rules applying to the relocation of persons displaced by urban renewal
6. *The power of administrative adjudication*, the resolution of controversies in situations involving the legal rights and duties of particular individuals such as the resolution of a rate dispute by a state public utilities commission

Principles and Procedures

Administrative law has been greatly influenced by legal theory generally and by a sense of defensiveness against those who were hostile to the rise of the administrative state altogether. Therefore, the development of administrative law has been subjected over the years to efforts to "judicialize" it — that is, to make it more "judgelike" and to make administrative agencies more "courtlike."[6] The distinctive principles and procedures of administrative law include:

1. Public administrators should always be especially sensitive to who is being helped and who is being hurt by the working of the administrative process.
2. Every citizen who is affected by a particular administrative decision or action is entitled to procedural guarantees, or what might be called "administrative due process."
3. The principle of separation of powers (between legislative, executive, and judicial functions) is not entirely applicable to decision making and action in an administrative agency. Attempts to separate sharply, organizationally, and personally, the making of administrative rules, the enforcement of those rules, and the adjudication of cases involving those rules would make public administration impossible.
4. Public administrators should take care to assure that administrative judgments affecting the rights and interests of citizens should be based on impartiality.
5. Since more justice (and perhaps some injustice also) is dispensed in administrative hearings than in judicial courts, the procedures by which administrative hearings are conducted should conform to the principle of "administrative due process," which includes fairness, giving the

affected citizen prior notice, statement of the charges or issue, care in determining the admissability of evidence, the right of a citizen to appear in his or her own behalf, the right of representation by an attorney, the right of administrative review of the order resulting from the hearing by higher administrative authority, the right of appeal to the regular courts under certain circumstances, and under certain circumstances, the availability of the extraordinary remedies, including *habeas corpus*, *injunction* and *quo warranto* (a challenge to a public official's right to exercise the powers of office, an action against usurpation of office).

6. Judicial review of administration by the courts is an important procedure by which public administrators can be held accountable, but not all challenges to administrative decisions can or should be thrown to the courts for review and settlement.

The Danger of Administrative Injustice

The growth of the administrative state, the bureaucratization of the public service, the "politicization" of government and its more intimate involvement in the lives of citizens, and the increasing anxieties of those who feared powerful and arbitrary government converged earlier in this century and produced a movement to "judicialize" public administration. Passage of the Administrative Procedure Act in 1946 by Congress, the studies and recommendations of the Task Force on Regulatory Commissions of the first Hoover Commission in 1949, the work of the Task Force of the second Hoover Commission which reported in 1955, the efforts of the American Bar Association's Special Committee on Legal Services and Procedure during the 1960s, and the promulgation of a "Model State Administrative Procedure Act" by the National Conference of Commissioners on Uniform State Laws illustrate the movement to "judicialize" public administration. Resistance of those who are more management-minded, however, has helped to maintain the principle that there are important intrinsic differences between the work of the courts and the work of administrative bureaucracies.

While the issue, like the legal perspective in public administration generally, has been neglected in the literature of public administration, there is evidence of growing awareness among students and practitioners of the dangers of administrative injustice. In virtually every policy area of public administration, unprecedented challenges are being made by individual citizens and by citizens organized in various kinds of groups. A common denominator in these challenges is the demand not so much for administrative efficiency as for administrative equity and justice.

The review of contemporary legal literature reveals a growing number of court cases involving the decisions and actions of public administrators that are being challenged on the grounds of equity and justice. Some of these include: employment discrimination in state and local governments, administration of municipal rent control, the administration of revenue sharing, pension administration, entrance examinations in the recruitment of firefighters, enforcement of height and weight requirements for appointment to positions in law enforcement, retroactive denial of Medicare and Medicaid benefits, and the denial of unemployment benefits because of the use of vulgarity and profanity.[7]

Also, scholars have begun to produce disturbing studies about the tendencies toward administrative coercion in dealing with aggrieved and damaged citizens.[8] This is especially true in such fields as law enforcement, public school administration, prison administration, social welfare administration, and the administration of urban renewal and poverty programs. It is a temptation for critics to jump to the conclusion that there are authoritarian and punitive tendencies among people who become public administrators, but truth probably lies partly in the administrative situation itself. Urgent problems call for urgent action. Too frequently, busy and goal-oriented public administrators, subjected to complex tensions and pressures, neglect to observe the rights of individual citizens. In the opinion of Kenneth Culp Davis, one of the relatively few scholars who has maintained an abiding concern about these issues, arbitrary and unjust exercise of administrative discretion by public administrators in the United States represents one of the most serious threats to our system of government and one of the least researched.

There is reason to believe that the serious decline of citizen trust in government in the United States during the 1970s may be due in part to administrative injustices. The injustices committed by public administrators in certain kinds of governmental agencies and institutions, such as tax collecting offices, poverty agencies, public hospitals and clinics, public schools, colleges and universities, police and fire departments, and jails and prisons, have a particularly important and personal impact on individual citizens. The rise of the ombudsman, citizen review boards, and various Nader-like organizations are symptomatic of the problem.

Municipal Law

Especially of importance to public administrators and others who are involved in the governance of cities and other local entities is a category of law which is called *municipal law* — the law of the municipal corporation. Since local units of government do not enjoy the clear constitutional recognition accorded to the republic and to the states, municipal law for many people appears to be mysterious, shadowy, excessively abstract, and irrelevant to practical problems. Also, since the city is a creature of the state and thus can be made and unmade by the state, municipal law is dominated by the state constitution, the state statutes, and the case law of that state in which the city is located. Where constitutional law and administrative law have a constraining effect on public administration — that is, both empowerment and restraint on power — municipal law tends to be more concerned with what shall *not* be done in government.

The Municipal Corporation

There is no precise and generally recognized definition of the term "municipal corporation." In the eyes of the law, the municipal corporation is an artificial person, like any corporation, which may own property, enter into contracts, enjoy legal rights and observe legal obligations, sue and be sued, and the like. But the municipal corporation in the United States is not legally recognized as a sovereign body possessing power of its own over a particular territory and the inhabitants thereof. This is very different, for instance, from the legal status of the Corporation of the City of London, England, which may be traced to constitutional recognition beginning with a charter granted by William the Conqueror in 1070.

The municipal corporation — the "municipality" in short — is the legal abstraction for a variety of local governmental units. These include incorporated cities, towns, villages, and boroughs as well as various quasi-corporations representing such governmental units as counties, unincorporated towns, special districts, and the like.

The basic legal instrument on which the municipality is built is the municipal charter, granted by the state and usually consisting of all the state statutes and judicial opinions that affect the structure, powers, and mode of operation of the corporation. Charters may be of various types: *special charters*, based on separate action of the state legislature; *general charters*, based on the attempt to standardize municipal government by having all municipalities organized under the same state statutes; *classified charters*, whereby municipalities are classed together on the basis of population and are then treated alike by the state within each class; and *home-rule charters*, which permit a relatively larger measure of power to the municipal corporation to design, adopt, and amend its charter. Over the years, much has been said and written about the pros and cons of these various types of charters, but for the public administrator it does not necessarily make a great deal of difference how the charter is characterized.

In California, for instance, where cities generally enjoy a larger measure of freedom of operation than in many other states, much care has been given to distinguishing between "General-Law Cities" based on general statutes of the legislature and "Charter Cities" based on charters that may, under certain conditions, be framed and adopted by the cities themselves. But the distinction is relatively insignificant for the administration of these cities.

The Problem of Excessive Abstractness in Municipal Law

For the practical-minded urban administrator, trained and inclined to cope with tangible things like parks, recreation, streets and roads, public utilities, traffic, fires, and riots, the excessive abstractness of municipal law is a source of frustration. For example, some of the "legalisms" that must be faced are:

1. *Ultra vires*, which applies to actions that are legally beyond the power of the municipal corporation or its officers
2. *Tort liability*, which is the liability of an official for committing an act against an individual
3. *Governmental functions*, which are the functions that a city performs when it acts as an agent of the state
4. *Proprietary functions*, which are those that a city performs when it acts as an agent of the local citizenry and for their convenience and comfort

5. *Discretionary acts*, which are those that a city performs in the making of public policy rather than in actions that apply to individual citizens
6. *Respondeat superior*, which is the common law principle that the master is responsible for the actions of his servant where those actions can be considered to have resulted from orders by the master

Surely, these are important concepts in the courtroom, where litigation over actions of municipal officers may be involved, but the body of municipal law, which has been relatively unchanged over the years, exercises significant *restraint* over the urban public administrator. The young and aspiring public administrator tends to be confused and fearful about legal abstractions that are rooted in a time and set of circumstances long past. State legislatures, especially those still dominated by rural interests, do not have much interest in clearing out the legalistic underbrush that ties the hands of urban bureaucrats. If the real problems of the cities are to be ameliorated, there will surely have to be some modernization. Otherwise, Americans shall be doomed to endure the curse of Faust, as phrased by Goethe: "Laws and statutes are inherited / Like some eternal disease."

Conclusions

In this chapter it has been argued that there is a continuing tension between the logic and values of law and the logic and values of administrative work. But such tension need not be destructive. A strong system of public administration is neither intrinsically good nor bad, liberal nor conservative, malignant nor benign. Executive energy, as it was called by Alexander Hamilton 200 years ago, and managerial efficiency, which remains important to the modern public administrator, can serve democratic statesmen and autocratic despots equally well. There is probably no happy medium or golden mean between efficiency, equity, and justice.

Many dilemmas are involved in public administration under the law. The proper task is not to try to escape the law. Responsibility means strengthening the capacity of government to perform its tasks effectively without violating the rights and interests of individual citizens. There is still great value in our legal heritage. Is it too much to hope that the same technological genius that has been demonstrated in commerce and war might be harnessed to the balancing of this crucial equation between efficiency, equity, and justice?

With the discussion of public administration in the web of government now complete, we turn our attention to a discussion of the great tasks for which public administration is intended. These include formulating public policy, decision making, leadership, and communication.

NOTES

1. Huntington Cairns, "The Community as the Legal Order," in *Community*, Nomos II, ed. Carl J. Friedrich (New York: Liberal Arts Press, 1959), pp. 25–37; Benjamin N. Cardozo, *The Growth of the Law* (New Haven, Conn.: Yale University Press, 1924);

Morris Rafael Cohen, *Law and Social Order: Essays in Legal Philosophy* (New York: Archon Books, 1933); A.V. Dicey, *Introduction to the Study of the Law of the Constitution,* 9th ed. (London: Macmillan, 1939); Carl J. Friedrich, *Constitutional Government and Democracy* (Boston, Mass.: Little, Brown, 1941); Herbert Jacob, *Justice in America: Courts, Lawyers, and the Judicial Process,* 3rd ed. (Boston, Mass.: Little, Brown, 1972); Hans Kelsen, *General Theory of Law and State* (New York: Russell & Russell, 1961).

2. United States Constitution, Article VI.

3. Kenneth Culp Davis, *Administrative Law: Cases, Text, Problems,* 5th ed. (St. Paul, Minn.: West Publishing Co., 1973); Walter Gellhorn and Clark Byse, *Administrative Law: Cases and Comments,* 6th ed. (Mineola, N.Y.: Foundation Press, 1974); Philippe Nonet, *Administrative Justice: Advocacy and Change in a Government Agency* (New York: Russell Sage Foundation, 1969).

4. Kenneth Culp Davis, *Discretionary Justice* (Baton Rouge: Louisiana State University Press, 1969).

5. Davis, *Administrative Law,* p. 2.

6. Robert S. Lorch, "Toward Administrative Judges," *Public Administration Review* 30 (January-February 1970): 50–55; Peter Woll, "Administrative Law in the Seventies," *Public Administration Review* 32 (September-October 1972): 557–64.

7. Joel F. Handler and Ellen J. Hollingsworth, *The "Deserving Poor": A Study of Welfare Administration* (Chicago: Markham, 1971); Handler, *The Coercive Social Worker;* and issues of *Clearinghouse Review* (Chicago: National Clearinghouse for Legal Services, School of Law, Northwestern University, 1973–74).

8. Theodore L. Becker and Vernon G. Murray, eds., *Government Lawlessness in America* (New York: Oxford University Press, 1971); Walter Gellhorn, *When Americans Complain: Governmental Grievance Procedures* (Cambridge, Mass.: Harvard University Press, 1966): *Public Administration Review,* "Symposium on Regulatory Administration: Are We Getting Anywhere?" ed. Michael D. Reagan 32 (July-August 1972): 283–310; Jerome H. Skolnick, *Justice Without Trial: Law Enforcement in a Democratic Society* (New York: John Wiley, 1966).

PART THREE

The
Tasks
of
Public
Administration

Policy
Making
and
Analysis

Governments are not great slot machines in which you insert your money, pull the handles, and await the outcomes. Rather, as suggested in the first chapter, there is a generally universal and highly complex process through which ideas are translated into action, and dreams are converted into tangible governmental programs. The great tasks that must be performed in this work of translating thought into action — policy making and analysis, decision making, leadership, and communication — constitute an important part of public administration. This chapter discusses the first of these great tasks — the making and analysis of public policy.

Public Policy

Toward Definition

The term *public policy*, like so many other terms in public affairs, defies attempts to formulate a universally applicable and acceptable definition. But all knowledge is limited, tentative, and approximate, and therefore one need not be deterred from employing this fertile term.

The way a person defines a particular term reflects his or her perceptions of the phenomenon that the term is intended to describe. For instance, those who, like David Easton in political science, have perceived public policy making as "the authoritative allocation of values for the whole society" emphasize the body of authoritative rules governing future decision making and behaivor. Those who concentrate on the end products or outputs of government see public policy in terms of goals, values, practices, and programs. Running through the continuing efforts toward definition are the following attributes often ascribed to the term *public policy*:

1. Deliberate rational application of thought and knowledge to the solving of or coping with public problems
2. Formulation of rules, norms, and prescriptions intended to govern the subsequent decisions and actions of governments
3. Futurist and course-setting orientation, and a concern with the factors of uncertainty and prediction
4. Focus upon projected goals, objectives, purposes, conditions, and outcomes
5. Striving toward fulfillment of the public interest[1]

However defined, public policy involves a type of decision making. It is not the kind of decision making discussed in the next chapter, which is concerned primarily with decisions made by individuals and groups within particular organizations and aimed at coping with immediate and specific problems and situations, but rather with more general and future-oriented issues. For example, the term *public policy* is normally not applied to the decision of a city hall to spend funds on a recreational park instead of a municipal parking lot. Nor does the term *public policy* apply to the decision of the federal Office of Management and Budget to recommend the funding of a new multilane superhighway from Chicago to St. Louis. But the term *does* apply to a municipal government's commitment to promote recreation in the city over the next ten years. When a father resolves that his son or daughter may not use the family automobile tonight, that is what we call a *decision*; but, when the father determines that the son or daughter may use the automobile only on weekends, that is what we regard as a *policy*.

Public Policy Studies

An important distinction between conventional and more innovative approaches to public administration is the relationship perceived between public administration and public policy. Where the conventional view is to see them separate and distinct, we see these two fields very closely intertwined. The contemporary trend toward establishment of Schools of Policy Studies and Public Administration, unified and under one roof, testifies to the intimate relationship between these two fields.

The field of public policy studies is rooted in the history of western civilization. In a sense, Joseph served as a policy maker and policy analyst in the Egyptian court of Pharaoh. We might also characterize Machiavelli's *The Prince* as a work of policy studies. But the modern movement toward development of a scholarly and professional field is an outgrowth of the Great Depression of the 1930s and of World War II. An important beginning occurred in 1938 when Robert S. Lynd, professor of sociology at Columbia University, delivered his lecture entitled "Knowledge for What?" Viewing a world that was in deep social, economic, and political upheaval, Lynd criticized academic colleagues for their failure to harness their knowledge and analytical skills to the task of coping with urgent public problems.[2] This movement toward a field of policy studies was reinforced by lessons learned in World War II, in the space program of the 1960s, and in the various social programs launched by Presidents Kennedy and Johnson in the 1960s.

Public policy studies is an interdisciplinary approach designed to draw upon a variety of academic disciplines and professional fields in identifying variables that are implicated in effective policy making and analysis. A purpose of policy studies is not to add to the general body of knowledge, but to improve the performance of government. An important feature of contemporary policy studies is the belief that sophisticated problem-solving technology, such as information retrieval, systems analysis, and gaming and simulation, can raise the effectiveness of government.

It was the development of such technology during the 1960s that led Yehezkel Dror in 1968 to call for a distinct but interdisciplinary field, dedicated to the development and application of policy knowledge and skills to governmental problems. He would call such a field "policy science" after the phrase introduced in 1951 by Daniel Lerner and Harold D. Lasswell.[3]

The professionalization of public policy studies is reflected in the establishment during the past few years of academic schools and institutes of public policy studies at some of the leading universities in the United States. For instance, the Institute of Public Administration, founded in 1914 at the University of Michigan, was reconstituted in 1968 as the Institute of Public Policy Studies, with the mission of creating graduate programs designed "to develop professional decision-makers and administrators who will eventually advance to high-level policy making, general management, or consulting positions in the public sector."[4] One of the graduate degrees offered at the Michigan Institute is the Master of Public Policy.

The rising interest among scholars in public policy studies was reflected at the 1971 annual convention of the American Political Science Association when Robert Lane and Thomas Dye issued a call for an organization to spearhead the development of a more serious study of public policy. With a steering committee of eighteen academic leaders who have devoted attention to policy studies in recent years, a "Policy Studies Organization" was created, and in the autumn of 1972, the first issue of a new periodical, *Policy Studies Journal*, appeared. A pervasive theme in that and other policy journals has been an emphasis on the need for an interdisciplinary approach in the making and analysis of public policy, and also the need for at least as much care and insight in the *making* of public policy as in its *implementation*.

The Political Nature of Public Policy

While public policy studies are and should be interdisciplinary, the political nature of this work deserves special attention. Public policy making is not simply the "discovering" of the economic and social laws of nature and the enacting of these "laws" into official statutes, ordinances, and regulations. The making of public policy is permeated with conflict, controversy, coalition-building, conciliation, and compromise. Public policy making has to do with what Lasswell saw as the essence of politics — "Who Gets What, When, How." Public policy involves the allocating of values and resources for society, which is Easton's idea of politics. The political character of public policy making and analysis is eloquently expressed in the following statement by the federal judge, Learned Hand, in an important case in 1943 involving federal policy governing regulation of the milk industry:

> ... the 'milk problem' is exquisitely complicated. The citydweller or poet who regards the cow as a symbol of bucolic serenity is indeed naive. From the udders of that placid animal flows a bland fluid indispensable to human health but often provoking as much human strife and nastiness as strong alcoholic beverages. The milking of animals in order to make use of their lactic secretions for human food was one of the greatest human inventions, but the domestication of milk has not been accompanied by a successful domestication of some of the meaner human impulses in all those engaged in the milk industry .... The pressure of milk is indeed powerful .... The milk problem is so vast that fully to comprehend it would require an almost universal knowledge ranging from geology, biology, chemistry, and medicine to the niceties of the legislative, judicial, and administrative processes of government.[5]

Categories of Analysis

What are the analytical categories that might be employed in the study of public policy? First, there are categories that have to do with the *making* of public policy, such as identification of a policy problem, determination and evaluation of alternative routes of action, the formulation of the policy and its enactment and announcement, implementation, and review. Second, there are *institutional* and *jurisdictional* categories, such as congressional policy, presidential policy, gubernatorial policy, county policy, municipal policy and the like. Third, there are temporal (time-related) categories, such as nineteenth-century policy, wartime policy, depression-years policy, and the policy of the Kennedy-Johnson years. Fourth, we employ *valuational* categories in the study of public policy, such as "good" policy, "bad" policy, "desirable" policy, and "hurtful" policy. Fifth, there are *ideological* categories, such as radical, liberal, conservative, and reactionary policies. Finally, policy analysts might focus on *clientele* categories which have to do with the groups and sectors of society being served or regulated, such as apple growers, butchers, consumers, doctors, and engineers.

With the development of a more self-consciously systematic approach to policy studies in recent years, there has been greater attention devoted to more complex and sophisticated categories of analysis. These concentrate not on the outcomes of public policy, such as agriculture, economic regulation, and taxation and finance, but rather on the processes of *making* public policy. We discuss these in the section that follows.

The Making of Public Policy

The making of public policy is a complex process involving the totality of the political system. The elementary model of the process suggested earlier in this chapter — identification of a problem, choice among alternative routes of governmental action, and implementation — is oversimplified. In reality, whether we are dealing with the making of public policy in city halls, county buildings, state capitols, or Washington, D.C., we are faced with a very complex process that involves rational calculation as well as the vagaries of chance. In recent years, scholars in the field of public policy studies have attempted to learn whether there is a regular pattern in the way public policies are made, whether there are certain functional needs that must be satisfied in order for public policies to be properly formulated and implemented. If there is such a pattern of functional needs, then one of the practical implications would be that there are certain policy-making skills that may be learned.

The Policy Process

There is no one dominant model of the public policy process. In 1969, Edward V. Schneider edited a collection of readings on public policy in which he posited six functional stages through which public policies pass: *formulation* of policy issues and selection of the mode of governmental response; *articulation* or relating things through manipulation of the factors of timing, location, and phrasing of policy statements; *mobilization* of support among elements of the constituency; *codification*, that is, translation of general policy into specific detailed operational rules and guidelines that "hang together" and fit into the overall system; *application*, essentially the enforcement of policy with respect to particular cases, problems, and situations — the traditional idea of public administration; and *redefinition*, which emphasizes the ongoing or cyclical nature of the public policy process and includes the tasks of evaluation and assessment of impacts and the making of necessary changes in policy.[6]

A similar, but slightly more detailed set of functional stages is suggested by Charles Jones. In his view, public policies proceed through a complex process that begins with *perception* and *definition* of a public problem requiring governmental action or response; the *aggregation* and *organization* of individuals and groups who have interests in the policy being formulated; *representation*, which serves as a bridge upon which proposed policies are brought to the government; and *formulation*, which is essentially the preparation of a plan of action. Once a plan has been formulated, a policy proposal passes through *legitimation*, which includes the conferring of official status on the policy as *public* policy, usually through legislative enactment; *application* and *administration* of the plan of action, followed by careful consideration of the reactions to the policy as administered; *evaluation* and *appraisal* of policy impacts; and *resolution* and *termination*, by which is meant either the solving of the problem and the ending of the policy, revision of the policy, or beginning of a new policy cycle.[7]

Such a process is not a tight sequential and compartmentalized mold through which all public policies must pass in their formulation, adoption, and administration. In reality, public policies vary greatly in terms of (1) complexity of the problem to which the particular policy is addressed; (2) the state of the art on which remedial public action may be based; (3) the degree of political conflict and controversy surrounding the particular policy area; (4) the degree of governmental commitment and determination regarding the solving or amelioration of the public problem addressed; (5) the nature and strength of the political and other forces furnishing the thrust for adoption and implementation of the policy; and (6) the quality of governmental and extragovernmental leadership exercised on behalf of the policy. These differences help to explain variations in the policy-making process as suggested above.

For instance, the genesis of certain public policies that enjoy much public consensus and are supported and advanced by powerful interests may be very different from the genesis of a policy that is highly controversial and not championed by powerful friends. The difference between defense policies and anti-poverty policies in the United States during the second half of the 1960s is illustrative. One of the authors of this book has shown the difference in the policy-making process involved in two related policies — one supported by influential bankers, landowners, and the established power centers in the federal government, and one supported primarily by impoverished and landless sharecroppers, farm tenants, and their friends.[8] In some policy areas, the perception and definition of a problem, the aggregation and organization of supporters, and the representation to the government may be telescoped. In other policy areas, the legitimation stage may be escaped, postponed, or may prove to be the burial ground for that proposed policy. In a particularly complex and difficult policy area, such as money and banking, revenue and taxation, or poverty, perception and definition may represent insurmountable challenges, while policy aimed at the eradication of a specific and understood affliction — such as polio or malaria — is easier to perceive and define. Thus, it should be recognized that typologies offered to explain the making of public policy should be likened more to road maps than to blueprints.

Who Makes Public Policy?

In a satirical novelette published in 1968, John Kenneth Galbraith of Harvard University portrays an automatic policy-making machine capable of generating computerized foreign policy.[9] In reality, we have not yet arrived at such a questionable nirvana. It is still people who make governments work, who think, plan, act, and react. This fact becomes especially important in trying to understand how public policies are made. Policy making is a deliberative process among people, not among machines and legal abstractions called governments, corporations, agencies, institutions, and the like. The parameters of viable public policy are set, in part, by physical, technical, and other tangible constraints, but also by the imaginations, perceptions, and preconceptions of individual human beings acting in various roles. For instance, accumulating empirical literature on the experience of the anti-poverty programs in the United States during the 1960s suggests that an important cause of failure was the misperceptions and misjudgments of people who participated in or influenced the making of anti-poverty policies during those years.[10]

The question has been asked, "Who makes public policy?" A simple, but not incorrect, answer might be a comprehensive listing of those who do participate in varying ways and degrees:

1. Bureaucrats from all levels of government
2. Citizens and community leaders

3. Clientele — the target populations and their leaders
4. Elected and appointed executives in government
5. International leaders
6. Legislators at all levels of government
7. Mass communicators in press, radio, and television
8. Policy analysts in government, academic institutions, and consulting firms, such as the Rand Corporation
9. Political party leaders
10. Professional specialists, such as business managers, educators, engineers, lawyers, scientists, and scholars
11. Religious leaders
12. Special-interest lobbyists

Simply offering such a listing does not adequately answer this question, because making public policy, like making automobiles and dishwashers, is complex, as we have seen. The question, "Who made your automobile?" would be equally difficult to answer.

In his search for an answer to the question of who makes public policy, Charles Lindblom has distinguished between what he calls "proximate" makers of policy, such as public officials who are closest to the arena of the policy process and who share immediate legal responsibility, and those who are more remote policy makers and policy influencers, such as ordinary citizens, voters and political party workers, interest group leaders, and the like. Viewing politics pluralistically, Lindblom emphasizes such variables as the following: disparities in the measure of power and influence enjoyed by policy makers, proximity to the center of official action, skill in persuasion and negotiation, personal biases, and the politics of association — who interacts with whom and how often.[11]

With such variables in mind, it is necessary to distinguish between the roles of the actors. The mere fact that a person's name may appear on a petition or memorandum urging a particular policy course should not be exaggerated. Conversely, the *apparent* absence of a person from the stage on which public policy evolves should not be automatically construed to mean that the person was not involved in the process. In the making of public policy, much happens not in the spotlight, but in the shadows. However, anyone who launches a campaign for enactment of a particular public policy should at least be familiar with the possible *dramatis personae*. The art of ascertaining who helped to make a particular public policy should appeal to the person who is a detective by nature.

Analyzing Public Policy

The art or science of analyzing public policy, including especially the assessment of outcomes and impacts, is still too young and experimental to have developed a truly dependable methodology. One of the problems is that much of the work of policy analysis in the past has been done by academic people who have not distinguished carefully between disciplinary research and policy research. This problem is easing, now that policy studies is emerging as an interdisciplinary field, but there is still a tendency for academics to examine life in piecemeal fashion — that is, they tend to make sharp distinctions between the history, the economics, the political science, the psychology, the sociology, and the technology of a public problem. On the other hand, practitioners in government tend to be thin-skinned and defensive in their attempts to analyze policies and assess outcomes in which they have had a hand.

Evaluative Criteria

A central purpose of policy analysis is the assessment of policy outcomes and impacts, evaluation of successes and failures in coping with the problem toward which the policy is addressed, and the application of the findings to policy reform and improvement. The growing professional interest in governmental productivity is helping to focus attention on the importance of adequate evaluative criteria. A list of appropriate criteria might include the following:

1. The clarity and specificity of the objectives and goals toward which the policy is aimed
2. The completeness and quality of the data on which the policy is based
3. The independence of the analysts from any self-serving and protectionist influences exercised by those who are responsible for the policy and its administration
4. Provision for evaluative findings to be received by policy makers and administrators and to be translated into appropriate policy changes
5. The existence of adequate policy output indicators on the basis of which judgments can be made about the level of performance and productivity
6. Consideration of policy impacts on such public values as democratic participation, equality of opportunity, political responsibility, managerial accountability, justice and equity, and humaneness in internal and external relationships

Each policy area has special criteria that are particularly appropriate to that area. For instance, Seeman and Evans in 1961 emphasized that policy evaluation in the area of hospital care should employ criteria that address such factors as distinguishing among people with different medical needs, distributing personnel and other resources, providing direct services to patients, generating and distributing information, advancing medical knowledge, and providing opportunities for relevant training and instruction.[12] Similarly, evaluation of agricultural policy should be based not only on the question of productivity of certain crops, but also on intelligent land use, equity in providing federal subsidies and other supports to farmers and in pricing arrangements, consideration of the interests and needs of processers and consumers of agricultural products, and balance and coherence between agricultural policy, land-use policy, water resources policy, and policy governing the forests.[13]

Analytical Knowledge and Skills

As the size and complexity of government and its problems grow, the tasks of policy analysis become more difficult. If, as shown in this chapter, the

problem of milk in 1943 was complex, how much greater are today's problems of poverty, crime, pollution, population explosion, energy shortage,
urban blight, and economic upheaval. To be truly an expert in policy analysis
is to possess almost universal knowledge and skill. For example, Yehezkel
Dror, who is widely recognized as a leader in the movement toward "policy
science," suggested to the United Nations that an intensive workshop on
policy analysis be offered for senior public administrators. Coverage of the
workshop would include the following:

1. The role of values, science, and intuition in the analysis of public policy
2. Alternative models of decision making based on various degrees of
   rationality
3. Quantitative methods, including operations research, gaming and simulation, and related techniques
4. Systems analysis
5. Value analysis, including logical skills, value costing, sensitivity testing,
   consistency testing, and the like
6. The uses of uncertainty and prediction, including futures studies and
   forecasting
7. The uses of innovation and creativity in policy making
8. The political, social, and psychological constraints on public policy making and implementation[14]

A more authoritative statement of analytical knowledge and skills needed
by policy analysts was published in the NASPAA document in 1974 and
adopted unanimously by the delegates to the annual conference that year.
According to that important statement, policy analysis requires knowledge
about the various analytical and administrative tools employed in efforts to
solve public problems; the processes by which policy is made, administered,
and evaluated; optimizing strategies; and specialized knowledge of substantive policy areas, such as health and transportation. Further, the NASPAA
document calls for policy analysts to develop skill in socioeconomic analysis,
political diagnosis, problem identification and problem-solving, quantitative
analysis of policy output, and program impact measurement.[15]

A Balance Sheet on Successes and Failures

As Peter Drucker and others have pointed out, ours is becoming a knowledge-
based society in which the great frontiers lie where scientific knowledge and
social action converge. Policy analysis represents an important sector of that
frontier land. Policy studies — such as those in education, crime and delinquency, and agriculture — have exerted over the years a substantial influence on public actions.[16] But in the United States, the physical sciences enjoy
much greater prestige than do the social sciences.

During the 1960s, many of the important public policies designed to combat racial discrimination, poverty, urban blight, and other social pathologies
had found their inspiration in the researches and writings of social science
scholars. Where the physical sciences were acclaimed for landing men on the
moon and encircling the planets, the social sciences were condemned for

contributing to social and political upheaval. In 1969, for instance, the columnist Joseph Alsop laid much of the blame for the disorders of the 1960s at the doors of social scientists who allegedly misled public policy makers. Alsop would turn his back on the social scientists, in making such public policies, and turn instead to the NASA scientists who helped to make the Apollo space program a success.[17] But a more fair-minded judgment was rendered by Harold Orlans of the Brookings Institution as a consultant to the House Committee on Government Operations:

> The social sciences face difficulties unknown to the physical sciences. The laws of nature do not change, but each nation and each Congress writes, and can change, its own laws. It is not easy for students of modern society adequately and accurately to comprehend the complex social trends of our time. But, insofar as they succeed, they give the nation that self-knowledge which is necessary to rational action . . . . Just as objective qualifications have gradually replaced political influence as a test of employment in the civil service, so objective knowledge is gradually replacing subjective judgments in the evaluation and direction of government programs.[18]

Finally, any attempt to judge the accomplishments of policy analysis should take into consideration that some public policies are subjected to more intense and continuous evaluative scrutiny than others, not because of the intrinsic seriousness of the problem addressed by the particular policy, but rather for political purposes. Policy analysis can be employed as a weapon against a particular governmental program, agency, policy, or regime. For example, Thomas Morehouse has concluded that the evaluation of certain federal policies during the late 1960s was motivated by political rather than analytical purposes:

> The demand for program evaluation research grew out of a federal policy of program consolidation and retrenchment in the late 1960's. Evaluation requirements were initially applied to the most controversial of the innovative social-action programs associated with the "war on poverty," and they spread elsewhere. Significantly, none of the older, well-established, and "safe" domestic programs — e.g., urban renewal, federal highways, farm subsidies, etc. — are subject to similar requirements to prove their "effectiveness." It thus appears that, in addition to and beyond reflecting a genuine interest in learning what works and how well, program evaluation requirements were an important by-product of a general policy of bringing controversial programs under control. . . .[19]

Conclusions

In this chapter it has been suggested that the making and analysis of public policy is an important and difficult task which serves as one of the pillars on which the strength and effectiveness of government rest. Second, it has been argued that the making and analysis of public policy is a major task of public administration. Third, it has been emphasized that the making and analysis of public policy is an interdisciplinary enterprise which calls for a range of knowledge and skills, but that this enterprise is thoroughly political.

There is much talk about public administration as change agentry, and about the need for clear statement of purpose, operational data, analytical insight, creativity, and innovative skill in governance. It is in the making and analysis of public policies that these attributes can be realized.

Finally, it should be remembered that this task is particularly hazardous and calls for people who know how to deal with the unknown. The administrative specialist, such as the budget or personnel analyst working within the bureaucracy, is buffered from the great political and social storms that rage over governmental goals and methods. The public policy maker and analyst, on the other hand, must work on a more public stage, open to the hot demands and expectations of the constituency. As Paul Appleby, who was one of the first public administrationists to understand this matter, saw it in the 1950s, the public policy maker must operate in a goldfish bowl. When an important public policy fails or boomerangs, it is usually the heads of the policy makers that roll. Nowhere does President Harry Truman's admonition about bearing the heat of the kitchen apply more forcefully than it does for those who make and evaluate public policy.

Attention is now turned to an examination of decision making in public administration, which occurs within the parameters of the public policy process.

NOTES

1. The literature on public policy and problems of definition is voluminous and growing luxuriantly. The following are useful and representative: Yehezkel Dror, *Public Policymaking Reexamined* (San Francisco: Chandler, 1968), pp. 12–17; Thomas R. Dye, *Understanding Public Policy*, 2d ed. (Englewood Cliffs, N.J.: Prentice-Hall, 1975), pp. 1–3; David Easton, *The Political System* (New York: Alfred A. Knopf, 1953), p. 129; Heinz Eulau and Robert Eyestone, "Policy Maps of City Councils and Policy Outcomes: A Development Analysis," *American Political Science Review* 72, no. 1 (March 1968): 126; Carl J. Friedrich, *Man and His Government* (New York: McGraw-Hill, 1963), p. 70; Herbert J. Gans, "Social Science for Social Policy," in *The Use and Abuse of Social Science*, ed. Irving L. Horowitz (New Brunswick, N.J.: E.P. Dutton, 1971), p. 14; Charles O. Jones, *An Introduction to the Study of Public Policy* (Belmont, Calif.: Wadsworth, 1970), pp. 1–16; Morton Kroll, "Policy and Administration," in *Policies, Decisions, and Organizations*, ed. Fremont J. Lyden et al. (New York: Appleton-Century-Crofts, 1969), p. 9; Harold D. Lasswell and Abraham Kaplan, *Power and Society* (New Haven, Conn.: Yale University Press, 1970), p. 71; Theodore Lowi, "Decision Making vs. Policy Making: Toward an Antidote for Technocracy," *Public Administration Review* 30, no. 3 (May-June 1970): 314–25; Austin Ranney, ed., *Political Science and Public Policy* (Chicago: Markham, 1968), pp. 6–9; and Ira Sharkansky, "Environment, Policy, Output and Impact: Problems of Theory and Method in the Analysis of Public Policy," in *Policy Analysis in Political Science*, ed. Ira Sharkansky (Chicago: Markham, 1970), p. 63.

2. Robert S. Lynd, *Knowledge for What?* (Princeton, N.J.: Princeton University Press, 1939), pp. 3, 140, 177, 207.

3. Dror, *Public Policymaking Reexamined*, pp. 240–45. Dror acknowledged his debt to an earlier book, *The Policy Sciences*, ed. Daniel Lerner and Harold D. Lasswell (Stanford University Press, 1951), in which the term "policy science" was coined to designate the work being done by scholars in the social sciences emphasizing the following: (1) the methodology of public policy making, (2) the results or fruits of such study, and

(3) the knowledge of insights of the various disciplines that might contribute to a better understanding of and skill in public problem solving.

4. *University of Michigan Bulletin,* Institute of Public Policy Studies, 1972–73 (Ann Arbor: University of Michigan, 1972), p. 7.

5. *Queensboro Farms Products v. Wickard,* 137 F.2d 969 (1943).

6. Edward V. Schneider, ed., *Policy-Making in American Government* (New York: Basic Books, 1969).

7. Charles Jones, *An Introduction to the Study of Public Policy.*

8. Sidney Baldwin, *Poverty and Politics* (Chapel Hill: University of North Carolina Press, 1968).

9. John Kenneth Galbraith, *The McLandress Dimension* (New York: New American Library, 1968).

10. See, for instance, the following: Warner Bloomberg, Jr., and Henry J. Schmandt, eds., *Power, Poverty, and Urban Policy* (Beverly Hills, Calif.: Sage Publications, 1968); John C. Donovan, *The Politics of Poverty* (New York: Western Publishing Co., 1967); Daniel P. Moynihan, *Maximum Feasible Misunderstanding* (New York: Free Press, 1969); Daniel P. Moynihan, ed., *On Understanding Poverty* (New York: Basic Books, 1969); Frances Fox Piven and Richard A. Cloward, *Regulating the Poor: The Functions of Public Welfare* (New York: Random House, 1971); and James L. Sundquist, ed., *On Fighting Poverty, Perspectives From Experience* (New York: Basic Books, 1969).

11. Charles E. Lindblom, *The Policy-Making Process* (Englewood Cliffs, N.J.: Prentice-Hall, 1968).

12. Melvin Seeman and John W. Evans, "Stratification and Hospital Care: The Objective Criteria for Performance," *American Sociological Review* 26, no. 2 (April 1961): 193–204.

13. Ross B. Talbot and Don F. Hadwiger, *The Policy Process in American Agriculture* (San Francisco: Chandler, 1968).

14. Yehezkel Dror, "Outline of Ten-Session Workshop in Policy Analysis," *Public Administration Newsletter* (New York: United Nations Department of Economic and Social Affairs, 1972), pp. 33–34.

15. NASPAA, *Guidelines and Standards,* pp. 10–11.

16. The following are illustrative: James S. Coleman et al., *Equality of Educational Opportunity* (Washington, D.C.: Government Printing Office, 1966); Charles S. Johnson et al., *The Collapse of Cotton Tenancy* (Chapel Hill: University of North Carolina Press, 1935); and President's Task Force on Manpower Conservation, *One-Third of a Nation* (Washington, D.C.: Government Printing Office, 1964).

17. Joseph Alsop, "Bankruptcy of Social Science," *Los Angeles Times,* 29 May 1969.

18. Harold Orlans, "Federally Financed Social Research — Expenditures, Status, and Objectives," in House Committee on Government Operations, *The Use of Social Research in Federal Domestic Programs,* A Staff Study for the Research and Technical Programs Subcommittee, 90th Cong., 1st sess., 1967 (Washington, D.C.: Government Printing Office, 1967), pp. 1–2.

19. Thomas A. Morehouse, "Program Evaluation: Social Research Versus Public Policy," *Public Administration Review* 32, no. 6 (November-December 1972): 872–73.

Decision Making

Decision making, simply stated, is the process of choosing one course of action from among the choices available. Individuals make many decisions every day that affect their lives in a variety of ways. Administrative organizations also have to make decisions to establish goals, priorities, procedures, and programs, and to mount responses to problem situations.

Individual decision making, however, is different from decisions made within the setting of a complex organization. Most basic organizational decisions are collective decisions, "collective" in the sense that there are many actors, from both inside and outside the organization, involved in the process. Who are the actors in the process? The actors include any individual or groups that would be affected by the decision — individual employees, supervisors, administrative decision makers, elected legislators and chief executives, political parties, pressure groups, unions, and competing administrative units, to name a few. Because all of these actors make inputs into decision making, it is a terribly complex process which normally involves numerous meetings, consultations, trade-offs, and compromises. To be effective, decisions have to be acceptable to the actors, or at least within limits of what they will tolerate. It is a slow, time-consuming, tedious process which involves a lot of "selling" of ideas, bargaining, and brokerage among competing alternatives and groups.

Decision making is central to administration. It is what administration is all about. Administrative and organizational theories, communications, supervision, and all other aspects are meaningless without decisions, which are the mechanism for triggering a product from organizations. As Herbert Simon said, "the task of 'deciding' pervades the entire administrative organization quite as much as does the task of 'doing'—indeed, it is integrally tied up with the latter."[1] The same author, in discussing the present society where most organizations now produce services rather than tangible products, believes that the major organizational problem "is not how to organize to produce efficiently (although this will always remain an important consideration), but how to organize to make decisions—that is, to process information."[2]

The Decision Makers

The formal organization chart theoretically indicates the hierarchy of decision making and decision makers. But, since it presents only the formal side of an organization, it does not present a true picture. In practice, decisions are also made by those who do not occupy any formally prescribed supervisory position. Actually, decisions are made throughout an organization from the lowest paid nonprofessional to the top administrator.

Formal Decision Makers

The formal decision makers are those who occupy supervisory positions in the hierarchy. With the position comes the authority or legitimate right to make decisions which can be expected to influence the behavior of subordinates. The subordinates, on the other hand, expect such behavior from the superior and are conditioned to respond to directives. It is actually a system of expected behavior—supervisors expect to have the right to make decisions and have them executed and subordinates expect to receive directives and to obey them.

Few decision makers, even though they may have the right to do so, make decisions unilaterally and simply issue orders. They understand that ordering something to happen is no guarantee that it will occur. If there has been no prior consultation or advance preparation, the directive may be in conflict with the expectations of the informal organization, in which case the order may be followed for fear of sanctions, but it may be executed with less than enthusiasm and to the minimal degree possible.

Informal Decision Makers

A considerable number of organizational decisions are made by those who are not in the formal decision hierarchy and with no decision authority. Specialists in functional fields, administrative assistants, secretaries, and a variety of other employees either make or influence decisions.

Types of Decisions

Decisions, both individual and organizational, are not of the same complexity. Simon has classified decisions into two general categories—programmed and unprogrammed. Programmed decisions are those triggered by stimuli which are recurring, known and familiar. There are standardized operating procedures and programs which have been developed for meeting similar situations in the past. These programs may be recalled, modified if necessary, and applied to the problem. This does not imply that alternatives are not considered, but it requires no extensive gathering of new data or much conscious deliberation. Many decisions fall in this category.

Unprogrammed decisions are of a different order. The situation is either totally new, involves conditions that recur infrequently, or consists of conditions that have changed drastically. In such situations, there is no routine, automatic response or existing program which may be used and the decision process becomes much more complex. There is uncertainty about the scope of the problem, possible alternative solutions, the consequences of alternatives and the methodology in general. Such issues may be value-laden, involve controversial areas, and have a variety of political implications.

Decision Models

How do administrators make nonprogrammed decisions? Administrative theorists have developed a variety of decision-making models which have generated considerable debate. The models come in essentially two variations — "normative" and "descriptive." The "normative" model attempts to show the decision maker how he or she should make the decision. The "descriptive model," on the other hand, describes or simulates the behavior followed by decision makers. Of course, no one model is acceptable to all. We will look at some of the models and comment on their utility for the practitioner.

Rational Comprehensive Model

Rationality has been a historic theme, not only in decision making, but in the whole area of administrative theory.[3] In fact, most democratic political theory as well as economic theory is based on the concept of the rationality of man.

When faced with a nonprogrammed decision, the rational comprehensive model assumes that a decision maker would:

1. Identify the problem
2. Clarify his goals, and then rank them in their order of importance
3. List all possible means — or policies — for achieving each of these goals
4. Assess all the costs of the policies and the benefits that would seem to follow from each of the alternatives
5. Select the package of goals and associated policies that would bring the greatest relative benefits or the least relative disadvantages[4]

If such a model is followed, a completely rational choice which produces an "optimal" or best possible choice from all possible alternatives should result. However, for the day-to-day decision maker the model is of little use due to inherent problems.

Problems with Rationality

All administrators take pride in the fact that their decisions are rational. But administrators, functioning under the daily pressures of the real world, operate in an environment quite different from that of the purely rational model. In addition to their own preferences, administrators receive a mass of conflicting inputs from inside — which Sharkansky calls "withinputs" — and from outside the organization.[5] These conditions create problems in utilizing the rational model. The major obstacles include individual differences, organizational barriers, the outside environment, time constraints, the civil service and the securing and processing of information.

Individual Differences

The setting of goals and decision making in general is complicated by the goals, preferences, and vested interests of the individuals that make up the organization. These complications arise from three sources. First, all employees have their own values, need system, and set of goals for their own personal improvement and well-being. "Therefore, the goals of every bureau member are different to at least some degree from those of every other member."[6]

Second, the operating style of each administrator is shaped by his or her own value system, experience, personality, and preferences. "Bureaucratic officials in general have a complex set of goals including power, income, prestige, security, convenience, loyalty (to an idea, an institution, or the nation), pride in excellent work, and desire to serve the public interest. But, each is significantly motivated by his own self-interest even when acting in a purely official capacity."[7] The third factor, which is essentially a product of the first two, is the matter of bias. There is not only disagreement on goals among members, but also a divergence between the stated goals of the organization and those of its members. These conflicts introduce a variety of biases that enter into decision making.[8]

Organizational Barriers

The structure and processes of most bureaucratic organizations inhibit the use of a rational decision-making model. The inhibiting characteristics include size, geography, structure, specialization, and established procedures.

The size of an organization plays an important part in determining the decision process. The process in a small organization is quite different from that of a large complex one. A small organization permits more face-to-face contact, and closer interpersonal relations, as well as decreasing the problems of communication and consultation.

Geography is also important. If an organization is geographically dispersed, with field units in various locations, the decision process is complicated by obstacles to the flow of data, information, and directives. In addition, the loyalties and goals of the field personnel may be different from those in the central office.

The structure of an organization has an impact. The traditional, layered, hierarchical organization imposes a variety of obstacles, such as competition among the subunits, differing priorities, different client and support groups, filtering of communications, distance between top decision makers and the level of policy execution, and alienation of personnel. On the other hand, if the organization is set up on the newer concept of transient task forces or as a more horizontal, flatter structure, the decision process could be more direct and participative.

The fragmentation of organizations into specialized units can also create an important obstacle. These units, staffed by personnel with a particular expertise or profession, have their own language, codes of conduct, expectations, and behavioral patterns, which may or may not coincide with those of the organization. Such units, which naturally think their function is vital, will struggle to establish organizational goals which emphasize their role. The potential for conflict between the administrators of specialized functions and the administrator with the overall responsibility is always present and is usually a given in practice.

Administrative procedures and the accompanying "red tape" are impediments to decision making. Any large organization develops procedures — usually contained in operating manuals — covering almost all phases of the administrative process. This has the advantage of standardizing and making procedures predictable, but it also creates red tape and a resistance to change. The manuals and directives become the "bible," cited as the basis for legitimizing all actions. This documentation often becomes a type of "security blanket" and, hence, a major obstacle to innovative decision making and change. Since established procedures define lines of authority, document routing, roles, and other characteristics, employees become comfortable with them and resist decisions that would alter the status quo.

Inputs from Outside the Organization

Each administrative unit has transactions with others outside its own immediate environment — political parties, legislature, chief executive, pressure groups, citizens, and other administrative units. These outside forces expect to have some influence in making the decisions that will affect them. In a pluralistic society, their attitudes, demands, and expectations must be considered. However, they are not interested in following all of the steps prescribed by the rational decision model. Their inputs are designed to influence decisions in such a manner as to protect or enhance their positions, which to them is a rational process.

Time Frame

The time element is an important obstacle. In the first place, problems requiring decisions always come with a time frame attached. Some decisions have to be made quickly while others may be more leisurely, but none exist without some time concept. Secondly, time is always in short supply. Time must be allocated among decision making and the myriad of other administrative functions. Because of these two pressures, the time needed to follow all of the steps prescribed by the rational decision-making model is not available to the practicing administrator.

The Civil Service

The merit system can be an obstacle to decision making. The system makes it difficult to remove or impose other sanctions against employees and thus complicates the decision process. Since subordinates see no great risk, they

feel comparatively free to oppose the apparent desires of the top administrator and to be less than enthusiastic in executing a policy with which they do
not agree. Unless these actions are so visible or violent that they constitute
gross insubordination or some other sanctionable action, the administrator
has little control. But even if administrators believe there are sufficient
grounds for disciplinary action, they may decide that the potential gain is
not worth the time and trauma of going through all of the procedures prescribed by the civil service rules.

Securing and Processing Information

The rational model assumes that all information is available to the decision
maker. This is usually not possible. Anthony Downs indicates the major
obstacles as follows:

1. Information is costly because it takes time, effort and sometimes money
   to obtain data and comprehend their meaning.
2. Decision makers have only limited capabilities regarding the amount
   of time they can spend making decisions, the number of issues they
   can consider simultaneously, and the amount of data they can absorb
   regarding any one problem.
3. Although some uncertainty can be eliminated by acquiring information,
   an important degree of ineradicable uncertainty is usually involved in
   making decisions.[9]

Even if every piece of information could be accumulated and processed,
decisions would still be affected by two additional constraints. First, it is
impossible to think of all the possible alternative solutions to a problem. As
Herbert Simon says, "imagination falls down also in conceiving all the possible patterns of behavior that the individual might take."[10] Second, decisions
would still be influenced by the forces inside and outside the organization.

Because of the problems involved here, most organizations do not attempt
a total search. The extent depends upon the inclination of the decision maker,
time, availability of resources, intensity of the internal and external interest
in the issue, and the level of organizational tolerance for uncertainty and
ambiguity.

Impact of the Rational Model

From the above problems, it is evident that the rational model is impractical.
Most decisions are not "optimal" but represent compromise solutions to
problems. As Simon says, "the alternative that is finally selected never permits a complete or perfect achievement of objectives, but is merely the best
solution that is available under the circumstances. The environmental situation invariably limits the alternatives that are available."[11]

This does not mean that decisions are not based on data, analysis, consultation, and consideration of alternatives — in short, totally irrational.
But, administrators look for a satisfactory solution, which is the next model.

Satisficing Model

In the rational model, the decision maker follows the prescribed procedures
and reaches an optimal decision — the alternative that provides the greatest

benefit at the least cost. In contrast, the "satisficing" model allows the decision maker to select a satisfactory decision based on the information and alternatives available. As Herbert Simon says, " . . . administrative man satisfices — looks for a course of action that is satisfactory or good enough."[12] Such decisions not only meet the needs of the organization but also are acceptable to the competing forces active in the decision process. March and Simon believe that "most human decision making, whether individual or organizational, is concerned with the discovery and selection of satisfactory alternatives: only in exceptional cases is it concerned with the discovery and selection of optimal alternatives."[13]

Heuristic Model

William J. Gore also argues that the rational choice model is not appropriate for all occasions. When that which rationality dictates is too far removed from what can practically be done, employees seek solutions that are within their concepts and understanding of the situation. Substituting these choices for the purely rational is called the "heuristic" process. He feels that the "concept of an organization as a rational system of action will coexist with a conception of organization as a social system or as a collective, heuristic strategy."[14] In such a social system, human emotions, desires, personalities, and irrationality enter into decision making.

Incremental Decision Making

As a substitute model, Charles Lindblom proposed a "muddling through" model of incremental decision making.[15] In this model there is no attempt to be comprehensive and analyze all possible alternatives. Relying on past organizational decisions and policies, the decision maker: (1) attacks only the issues that differ from existing policies or norms, (2) reevaluates problems on a case-by-case basis, (3) approaches each problem in a piecemeal, incremental fashion, and (4) proceeds through a succession of limited comparisons among only a few selected alternatives. Such a procedure is a process of compromise and accommodation because it is less threatening and therefore can secure the support needed to implement the decision.

This model was praised by some and criticized by others. Dror attacked it on a variety of bases including its emphasis on past experience as a guide and its conservatism, both of which provide "reinforcement of the pro-inertia and anti-innovative forces prevalent in all human organizations."[16] He said that acceptance of the model "reflects the widespread disposition of administrators and students of public administration to accept the present as a guide to the future, and to regard contemporary practice as a norm for the future."[17] As a suggestion, Dror proposed what he called a "normative optimum" model which was a compromise between the rational model and the incremental model.

Mixed Scanning

Amitai Etzioni, after discussing the defects of the rational-comprehensive and disjointed incremental models, proposed a "mixed scanning" model as a substitute. In this model, decisions are divided into two categories — fundamental and incremental — and each requires a different technique for scanning or searching for information and alternatives. The fundamental decisions, which establish policy, require a detailed (rationalistic) search for information, while a truncated search is adequate for incremental decisions. He says that "fundamental decisions are made by exploring the main alternatives the actor seeks in view of his conception of his goals, but — unlike what rationalism would indicate — details and specifications are omitted so that an overview is feasible. Incremental decisions are made but within the contexts set by fundamental decisions (and fundamental reviews). Thus, each of the two elements in mixed scanning helps to reduce the effects of the particular shortcomings of the other; incrementalism reduces the unrealistic aspects of rationalism by limiting the details required for decisions, and contextuating rationalism helps to overcome the conservative slant of incrementalism by exploring longer-run alternatives."[18]

Impact of Models on Practical Decision Making

Models serve some very valuable functions in administration. By focusing on the complexities and defects of decision making, they serve as "think" pieces to induce administrators to look at and evaluate their techniques. But most administrators do not adopt a prescribed model and follow it in their daily routine. This is not to say that decision makers do not follow logical procedures. But since the environment of decision making will vary with the type, size, and location of administrative units, most administrators develop a more or less personalized decision model which will incorporate elements from the various models as well as what has worked in their past experience. Administrators must also rely on a particular brand of acquired sensitivity similar to radar: they have to be able to receive and translate the signals received from within the organization, from politicians, from pressure groups and other power groups, into decisions that generate the support necessary to insure implementation of the policy, or possibly survival of the organization. This support can come in the form of budgets, clientele support, and/or acceptability to the employees.

The model and techniques developed will vary with the administrator and the conditions under which he or she operates. The ability to read and evaluate what these environmental factors are is crucial to the success of an administrator. As an illustration, a highly successful city manager moves to another city, uses the models that had been productive, and soon becomes unacceptable to the new city council. As one administrator said, there is little evidence "that decision making by following a difficult model is an inescapable requirement for success in the life of a public administrator."[19] He concluded by saying that administrators "will continue to be skeptical of prescribed methodology as a road to administrative salvation."[20]

The Role of Citizens in Decision Making

Citizen participation and control of government has been a consistent theme since the American republic was founded.[21] In an attempt to guarantee this objective, a variety of control and participative mechanisms have been created. Among them are the principle of limited government — all powers not given to government belong to the people — popularly elected legislators, executives, and, in some cases, judges, a federal form of government to insure the creation of local government where participation could be more immediate, lowering the requirements and age for voting, recall and referendum elections, and increased ease of getting on the election ballot.

In addition to these provisions, which principally guarantee political participation, citizen inputs into public policy making is not a new idea. Citizens have historically served on planning commissions, architectural review committees, zoning boards, human rights commissions, parks and recreation boards, and a wide variety of advisory committees. Some of these groups may be required by law or ordinance, but many are created voluntarily and have no statutory authority.

The Creation of Committees

Since, in the political and administrative world, voluntarily sharing power is not a normal procedure, why public agencies would voluntarily create citizens advisory committees is an interesting question. There are a variety of reasons. In the first place, some public agencies do not know the scope of a particular problem, what the alternate solutions might be, or the appropriate approaches to the problem and are sincerely seeking advice and guidance from such citizen groups. In other cases, committees may be created for less legitimate purposes. James A. Riedel classifies these other uses into three categories — supportive, put-off, and put-on — each subdivided into three variations.[22]

In the supportive category, committees are used to generate a solution already chosen by the agency, to propose alternate solutions to an unacceptable answer facing the agency, and legitimating agency decisions.

The put-off and put-on tactics include a variety of ploys, such as structuring committees in such a way to impede their functioning, careful selection of the "right" committee members, overloading the group with problems, burying committees with an excessive amount of complex data, and balancing opposing forces to name a few. The intent of the agency is either to delay decision making or to avoid any action at all.

The traditional advisory capacity did not provide citizens with direct participation in the policy making and decision process. The citizens wanted a more direct voice in the policies that affected them.

Changes at the Federal Level

In federal programs, more direct participation has been granted in varying degrees in a number of programs, especially since World War II. The initial programs, such as Urban Renewal and Juvenile Delinquency Demonstration Projects, involved citizens directly through serving on the Community Action Councils (CAC's) for Urban Renewal and on the boards of Delinquency Demonstration projects. The membership of such committees, however, usually had no direct representation from the neighborhood or affected groups. The representatives, appointed by government, were recognized community leaders selected from business and other organized groups.

The idea was that the broad-based community groups, which would understand the local situation and problems, would be able to provide an assessment of needs, recommend solutions, and pressure for action. In practice, the groups often did not fulfill their role, because some understood the general community goals but not those of the affected groups, adequate organizational structure and staffing did not exist, the conflict level in meetings was high, meetings often became marathon affairs, nonrepresented groups were resentful, and the competition for the leadership role was intense. As a result, public officials, instead of being advised, often had to advise and provide leadership in identifying problems and suggesting solutions.

Because of these defects, groups — especially minorities and the poor — continued to pressure for more direct participation. As a result, the federal government started in 1964 to redefine participants and participation. The changes, which started with the Community Action and Model Cities programs, was due to the language of the laws. The legal language in the Community Action Program, which was a major component of the Economic Opportunity Act, specified that the program would be administered "with the maximum feasible participation of the poor." The Model Cities legislation required "widespread participation" by the affected groups.

This broad language, subject to many possible interpretations, was used by groups interested in more direct participation with two principal results. First, while participants in earlier programs were predominantly affluent, white, middle-class, and community-oriented, the representatives in these programs were primarily from ethnic minorities, poor, with an immediate neighborhood rather than city-wide orientation. Second, some citizens directly affected by the programs became members of the policy-making bodies and many were hired as either administrators or workers in the programs.

As a result, in each program the extent of citizen participation and the type of participation varied greatly from region to region and with the times. "In some cities participation has not amounted to critical shared decision making or resulted in citizens having coequal status with public officials and bureaucrats. Collaboration and placation, rather than control and power, characterized the citizen role here."[23] In other cases citizens did share decision-making power, which in some cases happened only after some basic confrontations with the representatives from the other segments.

The Subnational Scene

The demand for participation has not been confined to federal programs but has spread throughout the federal system. At the local level, there is involvement in a variety of advisory boards, neighborhood councils have been created, regional city halls more accessible to citizens have been established, community liaison officers have been appointed to serve as a link between city hall and the people, and the position of ombudsman has been created to hear citizen complaints.

Future Decision Making

Decisions will always have to be made by someone, but what will the future decision-making process look like? The possible changes which have been suggested span a wide range of options. It seems clear that there will be some changes. The more important ones will probably include the following:

1. The process will become more complex. The rapidity of change in all areas of society will undoubtedly continue. Changes will occur not only in the technical areas, but in the areas of values and expectations as well. Such change intensifies existing problems, creates new concerns, creates a closer interdependence among the segments of society, and affects more people which will increase the interest and expectations of more people and groups and make solutions even more critical.

2. There will be an increasing demand for more participation by the affected groups. This pressure will come from inside and outside the organizations. The inside demands which already exist will be intensified as the educational level and professionalization of the public servant increases. The professionals, accustomed to being consulted on professional matters as a team member, expect the same role in administrative decisions which affect them. This, combined with increasing unionization of the white-collar labor force, will force more participation by employees.

   The outside pressures for participation will increase. The demands of an ever-growing number of groups and interests — women, minorities, the aging, conservationists and a host of other groups — will be heard. As Kaufman says, organizations "will routinely be obliged to take explicit account of groups of people and types of demands hitherto neglected by or excluded from the processes of decision in many social institutions."[24]

3. Structural changes will alter the decision process. If the organizational form shifts from the hierarchical pyramid toward the temporary, task force format, work groups will be smaller with more direct participation by the team members.

4. The computer will probably have an increasingly important impact. Humans will not be replaced, but decisions may be shared with machines. Simon points out that with computers there is a tremendous capacity for information storage, data collection, modeling, simulation and other techniques for decision making. The problem is not a lack of information but how administrators organize to select alternatives and find the time they need to process the information, assess alternatives and make decisions.[25]

Decision makers, then, will have to accommodate to these modifications. Some will welcome the changes and others will resist; but all will have to adjust to their new role in the decision process.

Conclusions

In this chapter the complexity of the decision-making process was discussed. Decision makers, with their own value systems and preferences, receive and process a wide variety of conflicting inputs from both inside and outside the organization. The decision makers serve as brokers in the process, brokers in the sense that they attempt to achieve a solution — usually a compromise — that the major competing groups can accept or at least live with. We also looked at decision-making models pointing out the environmental constraints which make the rational model impractical for daily use. Nevertheless, although decision making may not meet the test of total rationality, it is not an unplanned or irrational process. The choices, made by conscientious people in our pluralistic system, may not be optimal but represent the best alternative available under the conditions that existed at the time. It should be remembered that environmental conditions change and new decisions are made in response to new stimuli. In our rapidly changing society, the future decision maker must be responsive to demands for more participation and willing to accept a modified role in the decision process.

Although decision making occurs at all levels of any organization, there is a hierarchy to legitimate those organizational decisions and to hold people accountable. Decision making is a major function of leadership which is discussed in the following chapter.

NOTES

1. Herbert A. Simon, *Administrative Behavior: A Study of Decision-Making Processes in Administrative Organization,* 2d ed. (New York: Free Press, 1957), p. 1. Copyright 1945, 1947, 1957 by Herbert A. Simon. Used by permission.

2. Herbert A. Simon, "Applying Information Technology to Organization Design," *Public Administration Review* 33, no. 3 (May-June 1973): 269–70.

3. The rationality theme is discussed in the writings of Chester Barnard, Herbert Simon, James March, March and Simon, Cyert and March, Charles Lindblom and Chris Argyris, to name a few. Some current controversy is reflected in Chris Argyris, "Some Limits of Rational Man Organizational Theory," *Public Administration Review* 33, no. 3 (May-June 1973): 253–67. In this article, he critiqued some of the work done by others, including Simon. For the response, see Herbert Simon, "Organizational Man: Rational or Self-Actualizing," *Public Administration Review* 33, no. 4 (July-August 1973): 346–353. Argyris responds in pages 354–57 of no. 4.

4. Charles E. Lindblom, *The Policy Making Process* (Englewood Cliffs, N.J.: Prentice-Hall, 1968), p. 13. Adapted with permission.

5. Ira Sharkansky, *Public Administration: Policy Making in Government Agencies* (Chicago: Markham, 1970), p. 35.

6. Anthony Downs, *Inside Bureaucracy* (Boston: Little, Brown, 1967), p. 76. Used by permission.

7. Downs, *Inside Bureaucracy*, p. 2. Used by permission.

8. For a discussion of these ideas as well as five types of bureaucratic officials and their behavior patterns, see Downs, chapter VII.

9. Downs, *Inside Bureaucracy*, p. 3. Used by permission.

10. Simon, *Administrative Behavior*, p. 84. Used by permission.

11. Ibid., p. 6. Used by permission.

12. Ibid., p. xxv. Used by permission. For other discussion of the concept see James March and Herbert Simon, *Organizations* (New York: John Wiley, 1958); Sharkansky, *Public Administration*, chapter 3.

13. March and Simon, *Organizations*, pp. 141–42. Used by permission.

14. William J. Gore, *Administrative Decision Making: A Heuristic Model* (New York: John Wiley, 1964), p. 17. Used by permission.

15. Charles Lindblom, "The Science of Muddling Through," *Public Administration Review* 19 (Spring 1959): 79–88. He later changed the title from "incremental decision

making" to "disjointed incrementalism" in David Braybrooke and Charles E. Lindblom, *A Strategy of Decision* (New York: The Free Press of Glencoe, 1963). See also Charles E. Lindblom, *The Intelligence of Democracy* (New York: Free Press, 1965), and John J. Bailey and Robert J. O'Connor, "Operationalizing Incrementalism: Measuring the Muddles," *Public Administration Review* 35, no. 1 (January-February 1975): 60–66.

16. Yehezkel Dror, "Muddling Through — 'Science' or Intertia?" *Public Administration Review* 24, no. 3 (September 1964): 155. Lindblom's reply to the Dror article is contained in the same issue.

17. Ibid., p. 156.

18. Amitai Etzioni, "Mixed Scanning: A Third Approach to Decision Making," *Public Administration Review* 27, no. 5 (December 1967): 389–90.

19. Roger W. Jones, "The Model as a Decision Maker's Dilemma," *Public Administration Review* 24, no. 3 (September 1964): 159.

20. Ibid., p. 160.

21. For a thorough discussion of citizen participation, see the *Public Administration Review* 32, no. 3 (May-June 1972) and 32, Special Issue (September 1972) which are devoted to the topic.

22. James A. Riedel, "Citizen Participation: Myths and Realities," *Public Administration Review* 32, no. 3 (May-June 1972): 211–20.

23. Carl W. Stenberg, "Citizens and the Administrative State: From Participation to Power," *Public Administration Review* 32, no. 3 (May-June 1972): 192.

24. Herbert Kaufman, "The Direction of Organizational Evolution," *Public Administration Review* 33, no. 4 (July-August 1973): 302.

25. See Simon, "Applying Information Technology," pp. 268–88.

Leadership

"Leadership" is a word commonly used to describe a process considered to be vital to any group effort, an especially vital process in complex modern organizations. Ralph Stogdill said that "the survival of a group is dependent upon a type of leadership able to keep members and subgroups working together toward a common purpose, maintain productivity at a level sufficient to sustain the group or to justify its existence, and satisfy member expectations regarding leader and group."[1]

Although everyone agrees that this extensively (and intensively) studied topic is important, there is no common agreement on what it is. As Philip Selznick pointed out, it is an elusive, slippery phenomenon whose functions are not self-evident or precise.[2] Fred Luthans says "it is known to exist and to have a tremendous influence on human performance, but its inner workings and specific dimensions cannot be precisely spelled out."[3]

However, the most commonly accepted definition of leadership is that it is a process through which one individual influences the attitudes, beliefs, and especially behavior of one or more persons. Ideally, in organizational terms, a leader is one who attempts to induce others to behave in a manner that will assist the organization in achieving its goals.

What characteristics distinguish leaders from followers, what precise functions leaders perform, the effectiveness of different leadership styles, and how leadership styles are chosen are subject to continuing research and debate.

Theories of Leadership

The theory on leadership, like that on other administrative concepts, has progressed through phases, and continues to be under review at the present time. As one theory proves inadequate to explain the leadership phenomenon, the search for a replacement intensifies.

Trait Theory

Historically, the study of leadership focused on individuals. The research attempted to identify and analyze the specific characteristics or traits evidenced by successful leaders. The earliest trait theory was the "great man" concept of leadership, which stated that leaders were born with these traits, they were "natural" leaders. Some believed that such leaders came only from the aristocratic classes, while others thought that they could come from any social stratum. Regardless of the source, the traits were believed to be inherited and could not be acquired.

Later the "great man" theory was abandoned in favor of a modified theory, which accepted the idea that the essential traits did not have to be inherited, but could be acquired through the learning process. This expanded theory led to intensive research to isolate the traits.

Prior to World War II, research in leadership had attempted to identify leaders in terms of isolated, individual traits or personal characteristics of leadership. Success was evaluated in terms of a particular trait or personality of the individual. A long series of traits were considered, including intelligence, judgment, adaptability, dominance, responsibility, ambition, integrity, emotional control, social skills, social and economic status, and even physical characteristics such as height, weight, and general appearance. These traits, taken individually, were considered to be predictive of leadership selection and success.

After the war, the search for a valid trait theory continued. Stogdill, after comparing surveys done in 1948 and 1970, summarized the findings: "the leader is characterized by a strong drive for responsibility and task completion, vigor and persistence in the pursuit of goals, venturesomeness and originality in problem solving, drive to exercise initiative in social situations, self-confidence and sense of personal identity, willingness to accept consequences of decision and action, readiness to absorb interpersonal stress, willingness to tolerate frustration and delay, ability to influence other persons' behavior, and capacity to structure social interaction systems to the purpose at hand."[4] These characteristics were more general than those listed from the older trait approach which viewed each characteristic as a separate entity. While the older trait approach had proved unsatisfactory, Stogdill believes that even the more general characteristics, if considered singly, hold little significance in predicting leadership capacity or success. But, "in combination, it would appear that they interact to generate personality dynamics advantageous to the person seeking the responsibilities of leadership."[5]

These characteristics, of course, do not guarantee that such individuals will be selected as leaders. If such a person is fortunate enough to be in the right place at the right time to be selected as a leader, these characteristics might enhance the chances for selection. Also, these characteristics may improve the chances for success, although they will not guarantee it.

However, as Stogdill notes, analysis of this research "indicated (1) that little success had been attained in attempts to select leaders in terms of traits, (2) that numerous traits differentiated leaders from followers, (3) that traits demanded in a leader varied from one situation to another, and (4) that the trait approach ignored the interaction between the leader and his group."[6]

Situational Theory

The failure of trait theory to predict leadership success satisfactorily forced theorists to shift their attention from the individual to the environment of the leader. The situational approach represents the opposite end of the theory spectrum from traits. Theorists in this group believe that the characteristics of the situation and not traits dictate leadership selection and success. The situation represents the total environment in which the organization operates. Situational factors would include (1) the type, structure, size and purpose of an organization, (2) the external environment in which it operates, (3) the orientation, values, goals and expectations of the leader, the leader's superiors and those of the subordinates, and (4) the expert or professional knowledge required of the position.[7] The list could continue, but the preceding illustrates the types of forces in the situation, rather than traits, which dictate the characteristics of acceptable leadership behavior.

Formal and Informal Leaders

The situational factors explain the phenomenon of two types of leaders in organizations — formal and informal. The formal leaders, selected by superiors and not the work group, are leaders because of the positions they occupy in the hierarchy. Occupants of supervisory positions at each level, in addition to having a certain status, acquire the formal authority assigned to the position (for a discussion of authority and power, see chapter 12). This authority includes the legitimate right to use organizational control techniques, including sanctions, to enforce their leadership role. Persons in such positions are leaders regardless of their personalities, operating styles, competency, or reputations among subordinates.

Informal leaders are in a different category. They do not occupy supervisory positions; they are not designated leaders by the formal organization and, although they have no formal authority, they have power. Such informal or natural leaders acquire power — the capacity to influence the actions of others without having the formally assigned authority to do so — influence, and status due to a variety of situational factors. Functional expertise or specialized knowledge is an example. If an individual is an expert in computerization, systems, or any other specialty needed by the organization, formal leaders have to come to that person for information, advice, and leadership. Another basis for informal leadership is personality. An informal leader may be a person who relates well with people, inspires their confidence, and to whom they look for on-the-job leadership. Seniority can also be a foundation for power. Senior employees, simply on the basis of length of service, acquire a knowledge of the procedures, rules, regulations, and precedents that are of sufficient value that others seek their advice and guidance. The above are a few examples of the situational conditions that generate informal leaders.

Other Theories

Between the extremes of the trait and situational concepts, other theories have been developed. One attempts to combine some elements from both the trait and situational concepts. This approach recognizes that both work in combination, with a great deal of interaction between the leader and the situation. The situational factors important in this theory include the inter-relationship between the leader and the group with the differing personalities, goals, values, and norms.

Another category consists of exchange theories. These are based on the concept of mutual benefit to the leader and followers. The leader receives status, esteem, authority, and support, which are important to him or her, in exchange for the things the leader can provide the group — protection, goal achievement, and association with the leader.[8] It is a system of social inter-action in which mutual benefits are exchanged.

Luthans and others proposed yet another kind of theory, which is some-what a combination of the above two. It holds that leadership should be viewed as an influence-system model, which combines the leader, the situa-tion, and the group (followers). "Each of the three major subsystems influ-ences, and is influenced by the other."[9]

Leadership Functions

There is no complete agreement on the role of a leader in an organization. The definitions of leadership and the functions of leaders have evolved as components of the various periods of administrative theory — Weber, sci-entific management, humanist, and behavioralist.

Initially, the functions were rather narrowly confined to planning, orga-nizing, and coordinating — the POCO out of the Planning, Organizing, Staff-ing, Directing, Coordinating (POSDCORB) model discussed in chapter 12. These were expanded and added to by the human relations and behavioral movements. The functions now include establishing goals and objectives, integrating individuals into the organization, insuring group cohesiveness, creating mechanisms for motivating and satisfying the personal needs of workers, facilitating interpersonal and group interaction through communi-cation and group processes, maintenance of the organization, and concern with the achievement of organizational goals.

The shift in the emphasis was pointed out by Stogdill when he said that the functions proposed by the behavioralists "focus attention on the perfor-mances, interactions, and satisfactions of members engaged in the group task. Those proposed by the classical theorists, on the other hand, are con-cerned with the rationalized processes of formal organizations."[10]

Some theorists group the functions under two major headings — control and system maintenance. The control functions, sometimes called TASK functions, include decision making ranging from goal setting to deciding detailed matters, planning, organizing, and insuring personnel compliance through a variety of methods, including sanctions. The system maintenance functions, which focus on people and their interactions in the group process, are designed to develop and maintain the viability of the organization to insure achievement of objectives. These functions include communicating the desires of superiors downward and the problems and expectations of subordinates upward, serving as a broker between higher authority and the worker, protecting subordinates against unreasonable demands, creating a desirable work environment, maintaining the unity of the group, attempting to balance organizational goal achievement with individual goals to insure worker satisfaction, and facilitating interaction among members of the group.

The importance assigned to each of these groups of functions has varied. Historically, the control function was emphasized. Even today, position descriptions tend to emphasize the control aspects, due not only to the desire for that emphasis, but also to the difficulty in describing and assessing the qualities needed for system maintenance. As Cyril Sofer says, "in the long run the two pairs of functions coincide in the sense that performance cannot be maintained or long range objectives reached if the way managers go about this disintegrates the group effort."[11]

Leadership Styles

The manner in which a leader interacts with subordinates has been the subject of considerable research in business organizations, schools, and public organizations. The research attempts to identify various styles of leadership and to evaluate the impact on group behavior, satisfaction with the leader, personnel turnover, production, efficiency and other organizational factors.[12] Three general patterns of behavior have been identified — democratic, autocratic, and laissez-faire.[13]

Autocratic Leadership

In the pure autocratic style, which is also referred to as task-oriented leadership, the leader is an authoritarian figure who remains aloof from close, personal contact with the group. Policies, goals, task assignments, procedures, and expectations are dictated by the leader. It is a one-person process with no participation by, or consultation with, the members of the work group. The leader supervises performance closely and constantly.

Democratic Leadership

In the democratic pattern, which is also referred to as people-oriented leadership, the decision-making process is a group effort. The leader retains responsibility for decisions, but the group members are consulted and make inputs before decisions which affect the groups are finalized. The leader presents the problems and possible legitimate options to the group, receives their comments, and then decides. It is a participative process coupled with much less supervision than is characteristic of the authoritarian model.

Laissez-faire Leadership

This style is the complete opposite of the autocratic behavior and is more loosely structured than the democratic pattern. In this style, the leader serves more as a facilitator and is not a dominant figure. The leader may identify and bring problems to the group, but the group makes the decisions with minimal or no direction by the group leader. If the leader participates, it is more in the nature of a peer rather than in the role of a "boss." It is a completely permissive atmosphere with almost total worker freedom.

Few leaders, of course, fit any one of the pure categories. There are many gradations or degrees on the continuum between the extremes. A leader may move across the scale as the situation dictates.

The Continuum of Behavior

Robert Tannenbaum and Warren Schmidt developed the concept of a continuum of leadership behavior. Figure 4 graphically depicts the schema. From the autocratic style on the left of the figure to the laissez-faire on the right, each step reduces the authority role of the leader in decision making and increases the participation and freedom of subordinates.

Results of Leadership Styles

Considerable research findings suggest that the democratic, participative or people-oriented style has produced desirable results in many cases. Due to the intensified charges that bureaucratic organizations are dehumanizing and the increasing demands by workers, unions, and community groups for participation, the pressure to adopt this pattern will intensify. But, there is no one *best* pattern. What produces desired results with one group at a particular time and place may be totally inappropriate for another group in a different setting. For example, a strong directive style might be appropriate for a production unit, but unacceptable to a professional staff of planners or research scientists.

Choice of Leadership Style

From among the variety of choices, it might be assumed that a leader would automatically select the style expected to be the most productive. However, an individual does not have an unlimited choice. Tannenbaum and Schmidt identified three forces that influence the choice — "forces in the manager," "forces in the subordinates," and "forces in the situation."[14]

Forces in the Manager

Every person comes to a managerial position with his or her own personality, beliefs, and values. Some people are authoritarian by nature, while others may be democratic. Individuals, then, prefer a style in keeping with their inclination and with which they are comfortable. Any person who attempts to adopt a leadership style which conflicts drastically with his or her inclination or concept of how groups should be led, will not only be uncomfortable, but the incompatibility will be readily apparent to subordinates. To reverse roles completely is difficult. For an authoritarian type, the participation game is dangerous. If the leader accepts the group decisions, he or she will suffer personal conflict and doubts about the wisdom of the decision. But, if the leader invites and then constantly rejects group decisions, group morale, effectiveness, personal interrelationships, and organizational cohesiveness

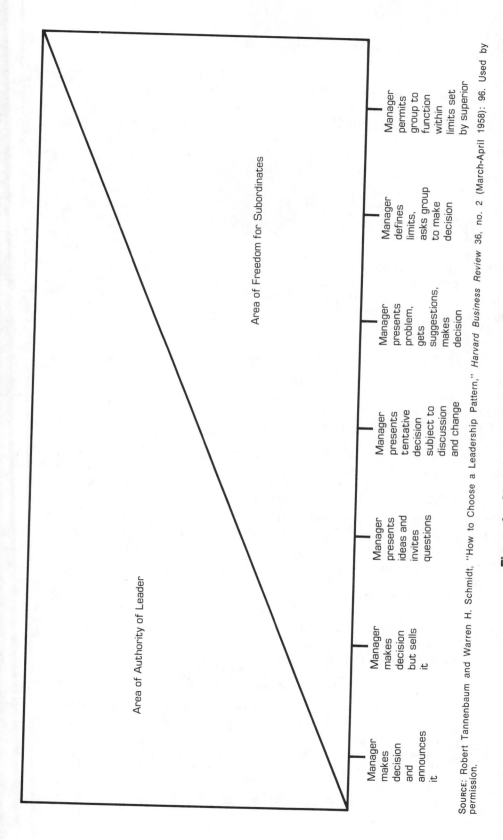

Area of Authority of Leader

Area of Freedom for Subordinates

| Manager makes decision and announces it | Manager makes decision but sells it | Manager presents ideas and invites questions | Manager presents tentative decision subject to discussion and change | Manager presents problem, gets suggestions, makes decision | Manager defines limits, asks group to make decision | Manager permits group to function within limits set by superior |

SOURCE: Robert Tannenbaum and Warren H. Schmidt, "How to Choose a Leadership Pattern," *Harvard Business Review* 36, no. 2 (March-April 1958): 96. Used by permission.

Figure 4   Continuum of Leadership Behavior

will be adversely affected. On the other hand, if a democratic type attempts to be an autocrat, he or she will probably be tested and challenged to determine his or her commitment to the chosen style. If the leader consistently gives in, then there is no real leadership being provided.

Forces in the Subordinates

This category of constraints is based on how subordinates expect the supervisor to relate to them. Such things as the degree to which they expect to participate in decision making and their willingness to accept responsibility are important factors. If they want to participate and have the necessary knowledge and willingness to accept responsibility, an autocratic leader who attempts to make all decisions will have problems. But conversely, a democratic leader who attempts to force a participative style on subordinates who do not want to or are not qualified to participate will also have trouble. In either case, the subordinates will be frustrated, morale will be low, personnel turnover will be high, and production will suffer.

Forces in the Situation

Situational factors are forces in the environment that surround the manager. There are numerous forces over which the manager has little if any control. First are the behavioral patterns the organization expects. Over the years, the leaders who have passed through an organization have left their imprint on how leaders behave. This accumulated legacy becomes the organizational style which is passed along through the organizational socialization process. An employee who hopes to advance to a supervisory position or a supervisor interested in upward mobility tends to behave in the expected manner. Second are the objectives of the organization: is it geared to production, service, or research and development? A third situational determinant is the size, geographic dispersion, complexity, and degree of specialization of the unit. Fourth is the time factor. If a decision must be made quickly, a supervisor may not have the time to consult, even if he or she desired to do so. The fifth classification includes the skill and experience of the work group: is the group competent to handle the particular problem? Sixth, the social, political, and economic system within which an organization functions is important. The culture and general social system determine how a worker expects to be treated on the job. As consultants have found, a style which might be successful in the United States might be inappropriate in Japan, Brazil, Chile, or other countries with different outside environments.

Loyalty and Identification

With whom does a formal leader relate? Does the leader identify closely with subordinates or with superiors? The issue of role definition is faced by anyone in a leadership capacity.

How an individual relates will depend on a variety of factors. One is the individual's level of desire for promotion and the status, authority, and money that comes with promotion, a decision made by superiors. The overly ambitious person may be tempted to "look upward" and neglect his or her role as protector and buffer for subordinates. In such a case, the leader loses the confidence of his or her subordinates, morale falls, and in the end the formal leader may be rejected. This rejection will normally not take the form of open insubordination, but the workers may turn to a natural leader and sabotage the formal leader in subtle ways without jeopardizing their positions. On the other hand, complete identification with subordinates may preclude promotion.

The successful leader is faced with a balancing act. He or she must attempt to balance loyalty to superiors with loyalty and support to subordinates. This is really a dual role. One role demands that the leader use his or her unit to support achievement of the goals of the total organization. The other role, expected by the subordinates, is that the leader will protect their interests, values, and goals in case of conflict with organizational objectives. The work group expects the leader "to be on their side and to use his [or her] prestige and ability — and that of his [or her] superiors, if possible — to protect the group."[15]

This role identification and associated problems are common to all organizations. But the role expectation may change, depending upon the level of the position in the hierarchy and the nature of the position. Quite often, those in the lower levels of leadership identify more closely with the work group than do the higher levels. This may be due to the closer personal daily contact, which engenders closer friendships, or even to a limited understanding of the goals of the total organization. The type of work group is also important. This often is evident in professional groups, such as scientists and research and development units. In such groups, the leader, chosen from that profession, has a professional loyalty, and the relationship is often that of a peer or colleague rather than boss.

Conclusions

Although all of these theories have made important contributions, it is quite evident that there is no single leadership theory. Leadership is not based strictly on the individual or group but is considered to be a product of the interaction between individual personalities and the demands of the situation. As Stogdill says, "most recent theorists maintain that leader characteristics and situational demands interact to determine the extent to which a given leader will prove successful in a group."[16]

Leadership is not necessarily transferrable. A successful leader in one type of organization may not be successful in another agency which differs from the previous assignment. Also, problems may be encountered in transferring from one agency to a similar position in another organization, given the different environment. As an example, a city manager who has been highly successful transfers to a new city of the same size and may fail completely. Similarly, a successful leader at a lower organizational level may fail after moving up in the hierarchy. Each level carries a different role which includes different acceptable norms or patterns of behavior expected by superiors, peers, and subordinates. Some people cannot make the role change and modify their behavior to comply with the new expectations.

The formal leader plays an assigned role within a bureaucratic organization. The leader has authority and power which goes with the hierarchical position and may be enforced partly through the use of sanctions. But as Sofer points out, it depends on much more than the formal delegation of authority. It also depends "largely on the existence of a value system shared with those whom they are formally entitled to command" as well as the acceptance of the legitimacy of that power by subordinates.[17] "This automatically makes the study of leadership or any other form of organizational control, a study of social structure, of social relationships and of social interaction."[18]

The tasks which have been discussed — policy making, decision making, and leadership — are fundamental to public administration. But unless the policies, decisions and influence of the leaders can be effectively introduced into an organization, they will not influence the behavior of individuals. This information must be communicated, which is the topic of the following chapter.

NOTES

1. Ralph M. Stogdill, *Handbook of Leadership: A Survey of Theory and Research* (New York: Free Press, 1974), pp. 419–20 and chapter III. Used by permission.

2. For a complete discussion of leadership, see Philip Selznick's *Leadership in Administration* (New York: Harper & Row, 1957).

3. Fred Luthans, *Organizational Behavior: A Modern Behavioral Approach to Management* (New York: McGraw-Hill, 1973), p. 498. Used by permission.

4. Stogdill, *Handbook of Leadership*, p. 81, used by permission. For other lists see Keith Davis, *Human Behavior at Work* (New York: McGraw-Hill, 1972), pp. 103–4.

5. Stogdill, *Handbook of Leadership*, p. 82. Used by permission.

6. Ibid., p. 128. Used by permission.

7. For another list, see Alan C. Filley and Robert J. House, *Managerial Process and Organizational Behavior* (Glenview, Ill.: Scott, Foresman, 1969), p. 409.

8. For a discussion of the needs of both leaders and followers and their influence see Max D. Richards and Paul S. Greenlaw, *Management, Decisions and Behavior*, rev. ed. (Homewood, Ill.: Richard D. Irwin, 1972), pp. 167–75.

9. Luthans, *Organizational Behavior*, p. 504. Used by permission.

10. Stogdill, *Handbook of Leadership*, p. 31, used by permission. For some earlier studies, see Ralph M. Stogdill and Alvin E. Coons, eds., *Leader Behavior: Its Descriptions and Measurement* (Columbus: Ohio State University, Bureau of Business Research, 1957).

11. Cyril Sofer, *Organizations in Theory and Practice* (New York: Basic Books, 1972), p. 273. Used by permission.

12. There has been considerable research on this topic. Some examples of the pioneering work would include Henry C. Metcalf and L. Urwick, eds., *Dynamic Administration: The Collected Papers of Mary Parker Follett* (New York: Harper and Brothers, 1942); Fritz J. Roethlisberger and William J. Dickson, *Management and the Worker* (Cambridge, Mass.: Harvard University Press, 1939); Henry A. Landsberger, *Hawthorne Revisited* (Ithaca, N. Y.: Cornell University Press, 1958); Daniel Katz, Nathan Maccoby and Nancy C. Morse, *Productivity, Supervision and Morale in an Office Situation* (Ann Arbor: Uni-

versity of Michigan, Survey Research Center, 1950); Rensis Likert, *New Patterns of Management* (New York: McGraw-Hill, 1961); Douglas McGregor, *The Human Side of Enterprise* (New York: McGraw-Hill, 1960).

13. For another more structured model for determining leadership effectiveness, Fiedler developed a contingency model. See Fred E. Fiedler, *A Theory of Leadership Effectiveness* (New York: McGraw-Hill, 1967).

14. Robert Tannenbaum and Warren H. Schmidt, "How to Choose a Leadership Pattern," *Harvard Business Review* 36, no. 2 (March-April 1958): 95–101.

15. Herbert A. Simon, Donald W. Smithburg, and Victor A. Thompson, *Public Administration* (New York: Alfred A. Knopf, 1964), p. 108.

16. Stogdill, *Handbook of Leadership,* p. 411. Used by permission.

17. Sofer, *Organization in Theory and Practice,* p. 271. Used by permission.

18. Ibid., p. 271. Used by permission.

Communication – Internal and External

11

Communication, the last of the tasks, is crucial to public administration. Information, the raw material of communication, "has become a critical resource in modern democratic politics."[1] As it was recognized long ago, information in its various forms — data, expertise, knowledge of policy decisions — is the basis of power.[2] Who controls or has access to information has a competitive advantage in the distribution of power in the administrative, political, and economic arenas. In the political arena, at all levels of government, this is recognized by the drive of legislative bodies to improve their information-gathering capacity to reduce the current reliance on the executive branch for information and by the efforts of public groups to force administrative agencies to open their files and meetings.

Communication is the process through which all forms of information are transmitted. These transmissions flow internally, within administrative organizations, and externally, between organizations and their environment.

Internal Communication

Internal communication is the process through which information, data, and decisions are transmitted to members at all levels of the organization. This flow of information is a crucial element in the functions of leadership, coordination, goal achievement, power, group behavior, morale, motivation, control, decision making, and almost all aspects of organizational life. The validity of the decision process, a core element in organizations, depends upon accurate, timely information flowing from all parts of the organization to the decision centers and decisions flowing to those responsible for carrying them out.

As Chester Barnard put it, "in an exhaustive theory of organization, communications would occupy a central place, because the structure, extensiveness and scope of the organization are almost entirely determined by communication technique."[3] Simon emphasized the behavioral implications when he said, "it is obvious that without communication there can be no organization, for there is no possibility then of the group influencing the behavior of the individual."[4] This influence on behavior is designed to induce predictability, without which an organization not only may be unable to function but may also be destroyed by internal conflict.

Because of its importance, communication has been the subject of intensive study by psychologists, sociologists, management theorists, managers, and others. Nevertheless, satisfactory communications is still a major problem between individuals in private, within organizations, and among groups in society. When problems arise, we constantly hear that they were caused by a "communications gap."

However, since communication involves individuals, it is necessary to look at the problems of interpersonal communication before proceeding to the system of information exchange within organizations.

Barriers to Interpersonal Communication

In communication between individuals there are many barriers, which of course carry into organizational communications. Communication is a two-way process which requires a sender and a receiver. Conversation is just noise unless someone receives the sound waves and responds. Some of the more common barriers in the process are described below.

1. In the first place, the English language may be a barrier. Words are not especially precise and are subject to many interpretations, even among those with common cultural and educational backgrounds. This problem is intensified when individuals with different backgrounds are communicating. The individual to whom English is a second language or one who is in the process of learning the difficult language may interpret the meaning of words differently from what was intended by the speaker.

2. The differing backgrounds of individuals is another obstacle. Due to variations in education, experience, traditions, values, and other factors, people have different perceptions and differing degrees of sensitivity. Because of these differences, there is a tendency to evaluate, judge, approve, or disapprove statements of others from one's own frame of reference. Messages are received and evaluated in light of the receiver's total personality and background, which may be different from that of the sender. Distortion or misinterpretation may result.

3. Listening is an additional barrier. The word "listening" is a common word with an apparently straightforward meaning, but listening is a very complex procedure. It is quite different from hearing. Hearing is a mechanical process by which sound waves vibrate on the eardrum. Listening involves not only the ear, but the brain as well: the sound waves have to activate

the brain and thought processes. Most people can hear, but few have developed the art of listening. Listening is hard work and must be consciously cultivated. An old saying that "nature has given to man one tongue, but two ears, that he may hear from others twice as much as we speak" makes good sense; but it is usually not practiced.

In listening, one should concentrate on several characteristics of the communication process:

1. The real meaning of the words spoken may be quite different from the dictionary definition of the words themselves. A secretary, returning from a coffee break, finds her boss digging madly through the files in search of something. She really does not mean it when she says "looking for something?" She is probably saying "could I help you" or "you couldn't find your desk without me; move over and I'll find it" or a variety of other possibilities.
2. It is wise to listen for feelings. Many statements are backed by some feeling or emotion, such as boredom, annoyance, self-pity, indifference, resentment, enthusiasm, excitement, or a host of other possibilities. These emotions are evidenced by words that reflect feeling, such as "prejudiced," "arbitrary," "unreasonable," "impossible," "great," and other traditional words as well as expressive slang words. The tone and inflection placed on such words are also indicators of feeling.
3. The nonverbal or silent language is a form of communication that is also important as an indicator. Mannerisms, facial expressions, gestures, and use of hands are important indicators of internal feelings. This is especially important in the United States. Through the socialization process, we have been educated against a visible and straightforward display of emotions, such as anger, hatred, fear, distrust, or indignation, in our interpersonal relationships. These feelings are usually veiled or hidden from view.
4. Feedback is important in listening. Unless a listener reflects, summarizes or in some other way indicates that the speaker is coming through, the speaker has no way of knowing whether the listener is really hearing. If a listener simply sits and looks and offers no inputs, an exchange can be an experiment in frustration rather than in communication.

Elements of the Internal System

As we have stated, communication within organizations is crucial to the survival of the unit. March and Simon state that "the capacity of an organization to maintain a complex, highly interdependent pattern of activity is limited in part by its capacity to handle the communications required for coordination."[5] The communication system normally develops into two networks — the formal and informal systems.

Formal Communication System

The formal or officially recognized communication system is indicated by the hierarchy which is shown in an organization chart. Theoretically, it is a three-directional model. The first direction consists of orders and directives flowing from the top decision makers down through the organization to those who will execute the order. In organization theory, the assumption is that those in the superior hierarchical positions have the legitimate right to issue orders and directives with every expectation that the directives will be followed by those responsible for carrying them out. Decisions theoretically come from the top down.

The second direction assumes that communications in the form of reports, data, and information will flow from the bottom to the top. This is the process of "administrative feedback" by which leaders and decision makers monitor performance to determine whether subordinates are complying with directives. Such feedback is a "vital element in organizations because subordinate compliance does not automatically follow upon the issuance of orders and instructions."[6] If subordinates do not comply, organizational leadership is weakened to the extent of their noncompliance. Administrative feedback is essential to permit the leaders to "correct and redirect subordinate behavior when it starts to drift away from the patterns they desire."[7] Corrective action may take the form of some type of sanction, but it may also include clarifying instructions, improving training, restructuring the authority pattern, or a reanalysis of the incentive system used to induce compliance.

What are the techniques which may be used to reinforce the vertical (upward-downward) communications system? A variety of techniques, found in all organizations, will include use of manuals which specify in detail the procedures and routes to be used in processing personnel documents, financial reports, and other data; routing of standardized reporting forms completed by individuals in the lower echelons upward through prescribed channels; authority directives indicating who has the authority to issue the various types of orders as well as who must review and approve them before they may be executed; and distribution charts indicating who should be informed about what information. Of course, most of the information flowing from the bottom to the top is contained in standardized reports; but few organizations rely solely on the reports filed by employees, who may be biased about their own work and organization units. As an additional check, most organizations have people from the higher echelons make periodic, routine on-site inspection visits to the lower units. In addition, departmental meetings of field and headquarters personnel may be used to open face-to-face communication.

If the system fails, the usual remedy is to conduct an investigation to determine why the organization is not functioning properly. The result will usually be a report which may determine the cause, recommend some personnel changes, and possibly propose some reorganization plan.

The third direction of communication is horizontal. Besides upward and downward, communication flows horizontally across organizations. These horizontal contacts normally are between individuals on the same status and authority levels heading units within the same department or across departmental lines. They may also be between persons at different authority levels in different units, but not where a superior-subordinate relationship exists.

Such communication is an essential, but difficult process. An individual who occupies a certain authority position in the hierarchy must work with and relate to his or her counterparts on the same level in the organization as well as with those from agencies other than his or her own. This essential coordination process is difficult, because units are basically competing for functions, role, status, and budgets; individuals come into the process with different personalities, needs, goals, and personal objectives; each administrator is concerned with his or her own career advancement and some administrators may be generalists while others are specialists, which introduces language problems.

Because of these difficulties, there may be frequent contacts, but little true communication. In the competitive situation, there is often a tendency not to share information that would reduce the advantage of the owner of the data. In fact, this tactic can degenerate into a game where administrators manipulate information in order to place other units or individuals, perceived as competitors, at a competitive disadvantage.

The prescribed formal plan, by defining and restricting the officially sanctioned channels of communication, is designed to enhance or reinforce the authority structure indicated by the formal organization chart. The individuals in the legitimate decision centers are informed, which is the basis for decision making, control, and coordination. The formal structure is important, but there are obstacles to its full implementation.

Problems of Implementation

Communicating through the formally prescribed channels has some serious limitations. The major obstacles are:

1. The sheer size and geographic dispersion of organizations makes it difficult to move communications quickly. The distribution of a memo or directive is a time-consuming process. This is especially true if a number of people have to review and "sign off" on the documents before they are distributed. Such a clearance process can consume days.
2. Specialization is another obstacle. Modern organizations are fragmented into specialized units, each with its own expertise, knowledge, loyalties, and often technical language. This creates some problems. One is that the units may become isolated, not understand the mission of the whole organization or their role in it, and honestly not appreciate the necessity of communicating information. Second, however, is the possibility of an intentional failure to communicate. Units often own and jealously guard their pieces of knowledge, and share it when it is advantageous.
3. Individual personalities can also be a barrier. People join organizations as adults with their personality and behavior patterns developed. Some are dominant personalities, others are passive; some are secure individuals, others are insecure; some are social creatures, others are shy; and all have prejudices and needs. These differences may block communication when people try to enhance their position or penalize that of others.
4. The hierarchical concept, with its superior-subordinate relationships, creates barriers to the free flow of information. The major evidence of this is the "filtering" process. "Filtering" works in both directions. Orders or

directives from the top have to be interpreted as they flow down through the various levels in the chain of command. At each level there is the possibility that the order may be added to, subtracted from or modified. By the time the order reaches the operating level, it may communicate something quite different than the originator intended.

The same filtering process operates on information and reports flowing from the bottom to the top. The information put in the report by the originator may have been complete and accurate or it may have been incomplete and biased. As it progresses through the channels, each level reviews and makes inputs into the original. At each level, new information from other sources may be added, data and conclusions may be reinterpreted, and the report rewritten and synthesized for submission up the hierarchy. As the reports progress upward through many levels, there is a good chance that their content, character, and emphasis may be altered.

This filtration on the way up is encouraged by two factors common to all organizations. The first is a normal human reaction to "look good" as an individual or to have one's organization look good. So, in reporting there is often either a conscious or unconscious tendency to be selective in what one reports. The information is usually not dishonest, but it is probably presented in such a way as to accentuate the positive achievements and downplay the less successful aspects. Second is the desire to report what the "boss wants to hear." Most decision makers are interested in achieving the stated objectives of the organization. They like to think that the combination of their leadership and their personnel will yield positive, desirable results. So, sometimes there is a tendency to report work progress in those terms rather than pointing out the difficulties and obstacles which have developed in achieving the stated goals.

If we assume everyone in the process is attempting to be totally honest, filtration will still occur due to the problems discussed under interpersonal communications — especially since an individual's pattern of behavior is influenced by personal perceptions of the orders and reports. In perceiving and making judgments, an individual's value system, background, and experience play an important role.

Because of these problems, the formal communication system not only generates a mass of paper work but also is slow, inflexible, unresponsive, sometimes inaccurate, and lacking in the subtle nuances which are important. In addition, it does not meet the human need to communicate within the organization. If administrators at all levels relied solely on the formal system and followed only prescribed procedures, group behavior, morale, and efficiency would be adversely affected and decision making would be all but impossible. To meet these problems, every organization develops an informal communication structure.

Informal Communications

An informal communication network, like an informal organization, develops to meet the needs of employees and to correct deficiencies in the formal system. As the formal communication system becomes more obstructed and less satisfactory, the "grapevine" becomes more important.

Where the formal system prescribes that the information flow will be vertically up and down the hierarchy, the informal net crosses the organization in every possible direction — vertically, horizontally, and tangentially within each agency, across departmental lines, and even outside the organization. If the conversation flow is charted, it might look like a line puzzle or a piece of abstract art. The informal system may be based upon a variety of factors. Some of the more important ones follow:

1. Friendships are a frequent basis. Friendships may have developed outside the organization through common membership in bowling leagues, bridge clubs, or other social clubs. Or, they may have developed within the organization. People meet and are attracted to each other through serving on committees, task forces, union groups, departmental associations, orientation and training sessions, as well as through more unstructured contacts such as coffee breaks, retirement parties, and other chance encounters. There is also another side. These encounters also produce negative results ranging from tolerance of other's differences to utter dislike and repulsion. All are a part of the social nature of organizations.
2. Status can be a basis. There is a tendency for those of equivalent status to communicate freely across departmental lines. One bureau chief may contact another bureau chief to exchange information, impressions, and inside information.
3. Liaison among professionals is quite common. The professional groups — medical personnel, personnel directors, finance people, engineers, computer center directors, and so on — can be a close knit fraternity. The members of each group have essentially the same educational background, professional standards, and expectations. In addition, each has its own professional language, and sometimes abbreviations and jargon, which is unintelligible to the uninitiated outsider. Their input, which often cannot be challenged by an outsider, will become more vital as the administrative process becomes more technically oriented.

Within the informal communications "net," the tendency is to contact directly the individual or source which can provide the needed information, without going through the prescribed channels. Thus, the informal network is a casual, unstructured system which functions in different directions in different situations. It is apparent, then, that there are many networks operating at the same time, but covering different segments of the organization. The telephone, coffee breaks, and lunch are important channels for communicating information, sensitivity, and feeling for what is going on in the organization. The "grapevine" is an efficient mechanism for transmitting information quickly and widely.

Such an informal communication system has both a positive and a negative side. On the positive side, it permits the exchange of information needed for decision making and other processes that permit the organization to function.

Also, through the friendship linkages, it may be used selectively to "feed" information, feelings, and concerns to subordinates and superiors. On the negative side, it can be and usually is a "rumor factory." Gossip, guesses, half-truths and false information, which start with one person and soon spread throughout the organization, are further distorted as they are orally received and transmitted by each additional person in the chain. This, of course, can be damaging to an organization. Nevertheless, such an informal network will always exist. The best chance of mitigating the negative impact is for management to transmit information officially that is of importance to employees as quickly as possible and thereby reduce the anxiety and uncertainty level which feeds the "grapevine."

External Communication

As we have pointed out, public management does not function in a vacuum, but within the expectations, constraints, and pressures of its environment, which vary with the level of government and the geographic areas of the nation. Every public organization, as an open system, also has transactions with its environment. Communication with the environment is a two-way process — inputs to the governmental process are received from innumerable sources and outputs are transmitted to the public at large as well as to specific groups. This transmission is accomplished through a process which can be broadly defined as public relations.

Public Relations

Public organizations, like those in the private sector, must be conscious of the public image they project. While there are great variations in the size of the budgets and professional staffs allotted for this effort, every administrative agency at every level of government carries on a public relations program. Although some people view public relations activities by governmental agencies as somewhat illegitimate and as an expensive form of ego enhancement, they are much more than that. Public relations, in addition to informing the public, has a direct bearing not only on the health of the organization as measured in terms of programs, financial support, staffing, prestige, and other indicators, but on its survival as well. If an agency can sell the idea that its programs provide a vital service and that it is an efficient operation, it will muster the support to guarantee that it receives the necessary resources in the competitive resource allocation process. Conversely, if it fails to do this, it will decline in importance and possibly be abolished.

Public relations is complicated by the many publics to which a governmental agency must relate — the general population, the legislative body, the chief executive, other administrative agencies within the same level of government, agency client groups, political parties, and often counterpart agencies at other levels of government. Relations with each of the various publics may require different techniques.

Directing the Information

Although the targets for public relations attention will shift depending on the circumstances and timing, the major emphasis will be directed to cultivating the support of the organized client or pressure groups — farmers, labor, business, veterans, environmentalists, minorities—which the agency serves.[8] Under our governmental system, this is a logical choice, because such established, organized and recognizable groups, competing with each other in the political arena, play a major role in determining governmental policies.[9] If an agency can muster the support of its group or groups, it may not only represent a sizable voting block but also may be used to mount a pressure campaign on Congress and the executive branch. Since the allocation of resources is a political process, such organized support provides an agency with some leverage and an advantage in the competition with other administrative agencies for money.

This process involves a two-way, mutually beneficial communication flow in which the agency supplies information to the groups and receives information in return. Government, in our complex society, not only cannot rely upon its own capacity to collect information but also needs the cooperation of organized groups in administering programs. Government has to receive not only hard data, but also feedback on attitudes, expectations, and problems in order to do program planning. On the other hand, since government has a direct impact on and is so closely entwined with the economy, private groups need advance information so they can organize to protect or improve the subsidies, preferred treatment, prestige, or role they have gained over the years.

The general or unorganized public is a different matter. While all governments find it important to keep the general public informed and hopefully favorably impressed, the importance of public opinion in administrative decisions — not political futures — varies with the level of government. It is most important in the smaller jurisdictions where the "public" has face-to-face access to the administration, but decreases in importance as administration is further removed. In actuality, there is rarely such a thing as a public opinion, but rather many public opinions. Among these opinions, the portions of the population which are organized either temporarily or permanently are the ones with access to the decision-making centers. Unorganized segments of the population are essentially a neutral force neither fighting for nor against administrative programs.

Special Uses of the News Media

While the news media are normally used to disseminate information to the public, they may also be a means by which bureaucrats disseminate information to officials in the executive and congressional branches in order to influence policy decisions.[10] As Leon Sigal says, "news management encompasses more than just keeping secrets secret, officials want to disclose the information they want, when they want, and in the way they want."[11] Releasing information to the press, on which officials rely for much of their information, is a useful method of signaling a policy, alerting and involving other administrative agencies, eliciting support from client groups and accomplishing numerous other purposes.

How is the information passed to the media? The information may be provided through press releases, press conferences, and background briefings, which are available to senior officials. However, a fourth method, the "leak," is also used by senior people, most often by those who do not have the status or authority to use the other methods. The "leak" is information passed by an official to a selected reporter. The process represents a mutually beneficial exchange. The reporter gets an exclusive story but protects the identity of the source, and the bureaucrat circulates the information in an attempt to achieve the desired objective.

The Problem of Secrecy

A historic issue has been the question of the right of the administration to withhold information from Congress, the courts, and the public.[12] The practice of bureaucratic secrecy, in addition to serving as a cover for improper and illegal actions, has serious implications for the democratic process. How can Congress establish policy and the voters participate intelligently if information is withheld from them?

In this section, the problem will be explored from the perspectives of history and current practice.

Historic Techniques of Withholding Information

A variety of methods for withholding information have historically been used.[13] We will look at the three most common ones — classification, executive privilege, and refusal to respond.

The Classification System

The practice of withholding information on the basis that it was classified data involving national security has been used since the country was founded. Under Executive Order 10501, issued by President Eisenhower in 1953, federal agencies had the authority to classify information on the basis of national security and refuse to release it to anyone, including the courts and Congress. While much of the material was legitimately classified, vast numbers of documents were stamped "classified" simply as a convenience to the responsible agency. A companion problem was the question of declassification. Records once classified tended to retain that designation and be unavailable to the public for years after there was any valid reason for the secrecy, if there was a valid reason in the first place.

Executive Privilege

Executive privilege, which is somewhat related to classification, is the right of the president to refuse to release documents or information which in his (or her) opinion would adversely affect the national interest. In addition, the president may refuse to permit close advisors to testify on such matters before congressional committees. The right of the executive to withhold information has a long tradition as an administrative practice in the United States. Few would argue that the president should not have the right to consult with advisors without disclosing the contents of the conversations or to withhold information that has implications for national security. Conversely, the practice should not be used to conceal illegal activities, as was done in the Watergate case.

Historically, questions of executive privilege have been negotiated between Congress and the president through the political process. In case of a refusal to release information sought by Congress, that body through consultation, political pressure, threats of retaliation on programs desired by the president, delaying the confirmation of presidential appointees, and other tactics has attempted to force the release of the information. But in the process, each side has usually modified its position: Congress reduces its demands and the president agrees to release some information in order to avoid a complete impasse which would have serious constitutional and political implications. The courts have been reluctant to enter into such congressional-executive conflicts.

In the Watergate case, the historic procedures did not work and an impasse resulted. The courts accepted jurisdiction on the basis that the administration was withholding information on possible illegal activities, which is not privileged information. The results were that many top-level political appointees in the administration were convicted and a president was forced to resign.

Refusal to Respond

Some agencies function under the theory that what they do is no one's business. Without ever invoking the protection of executive privilege or classification, administrative agencies have neglected to respond to requests for information from the public.

The Current Situation

Bureaucratic secrecy, criticized for years, has become more suspect and unacceptable in recent years. Cambodia, Viet Nam, and Watergate, the products of secrecy, provided more ammunition for individuals and groups insisting on a more open government.[14] As Francis E. Rourke says, "No aspect of administration in modern times has aroused more heated political controversy than the practice of withholding information from the public — or what is loosely called 'bureaucratic secrecy.' "[15]

But does the public have a right to know everything? Would it be beneficial and appropriate for the general public to know the details, current status, and progress of sensitive diplomatic relations in progress; the number, type, and distribution of our military hardware; the daily proceedings of a grand jury investigation; the past court records on individuals anyone cares to ask about; the tax returns of a neighbor one happened to be curious about, and so on? Obviously, secrecy can be a way of covering mistakes and establishing policy without interference from the public, but "even the most ardent supporters of open government acknowledge that there are situations in which official information can legitimately be withheld from the public in order to protect individual privacy or community welfare."[16] In short, there must be a balance.

What the balance will be in a democratic society will not be determined by some theoretical model, but in the political arena. While most administrative agencies resist full disclosure, those connected with defense, national security, diplomacy, and law enforcement are the most secrecy-conscious. Counterbalancing these agencies are a variety of groups, such as public unions, congressional committees, citizens lobbies (Common Cause and Ralph Nader's Public Citizens Inc., for example), good government groups, investigative reporters, the news media, and others who insist on full disclosure.[17] As Rourke says, "The task of striking a balance between the legitimate claims for withholding information and the essential right of the public to know what is going on in their own government is largely accomplished in the American system of democracy by the interplay of competing organizations."[18]

The forces for full disclosure have made some important gains in reducing governmental secrecy at all levels of government. We will look at some of the changes at the federal and subnational levels.

Federal Level

At the national level, where most of the effort has been concentrated, some legislation has been passed and more is pending in the area of secrecy. Some of the more important recent developments include those discussed below.[19]

Freedom of Information Act

The federal Freedom of Information Act, passed in 1966, guarantees all persons the right to see the records of all administrative agencies, except those exempt by the statute. There are nine classes of exempt material, "which can be summarized as covering: (1) classified national defense and foreign relations secrets, (2) purely internal management matters, (3) such records as income tax returns, that are withheld by some other law, (4) trade secrets and certain other confidential or privileged information, usually of a business nature, (5) government employee's advice and similar expressions in aid of deciding upon various agency actions, (6) medical and personnel files and other individual privacy information, (7) investigatory files compiled for law enforcement purposes, (8) bank examination records, and (9) certain mineral geology information."[20] Responding to requests for information, assuming a cooperative bureaucracy, is a complex, time-consuming process for three reasons.[21] First, organizationally, the records are dispersed among thousands of agencies, there is no centralized processing section for the whole government, and individual agencies are not staffed or budgeted to handle the load. Second, in the process area, someone has to decide what is being requested, which agency or unit has custody of the records, find the information, decide if it can be released, copy, and send the information. Third, the nature of the requests can create problems. The requester, who does not have to state a reason for wanting the information, may not only be imprecise in language but may also demand an unlimited amount of records from a variety of sources.

Federal agencies, who opposed the legislation, have been criticized for less than complete cooperation with the law. Some of the criticism included long delays in responding to requests, excessive charges for copying and processing material, insistence on precise description of the document or material requested, inability to locate documents, and ruling that nonexempt documents fall into the exempt class.

If an agency refuses to honor a request on the basis that it is exempt information, the requester may take the case to court. In such cases, the normal procedure is reversed and the defendant — the government — has to prove that the denial was logical and proper, which tends to encourage governmental caution.

Classification Changes

President Nixon, based on the Freedom of Information Act, issued Executive Order 11652 entitled "Classification and De-Classification of the National Security Information and Material," which applied to thirty-four agencies. The Interagency Classification Review Committee, established by the order, has drastically reduced the number of people authorized to classify documents, speeded up the declassification process, and issued guidelines for future classification actions.

Advisory Committee Meetings

The federal government uses approximately 2,000 committees to advise administrative agencies. Such committees make important inputs into the decision process and as such are important channels of communication.[22] Should the meetings of such influential groups be public? Congress thought so when it passed the Federal Advisory Committee Act (P.L. 92–463) in 1973. "Patterned after the Freedom of Information law, the statute presumes all advisory panel meetings will be open to public scrutiny unless the President or the head of the agency to which the advisory committee reports determines the subject matter of a particular session is concerned with matters listed in . . . the exemption provisions of the Freedom of Information Act."[23]

The act has not really opened such meetings to public scrutiny. Too often the public is excluded when the responsible official closes the meeting by simply declaring that the subject under discussion falls into the exempt category of the Freedom of Information Act or fails to adequately publicize the time and place of the meetings.

Other Federal Proposals

A variety of bills to make the federal government more open, introduced in Congress in 1974, will be heard from again in 1975.[24] Based on the 1971 report of the National Commission on Reform of Federal Criminal Law and encouraged by the Pentagon Papers incident, various bills have been introduced into both Houses to rewrite the criminal law section of the U.S. Code to redefine the penalties for releasing national defense information. Another bill would open most meetings of congressional committees and administrative agencies, unless the subject matter fell within the exempt category. Yet another bill would grant individuals not only access to any files maintained on them, but also the right to purge any false information and impose restrictions on the access to and dissemination of information in the file.

Subnational Level

While secrecy in most subnational governments has been less an issue than at the federal level, the demand for access to information has accelerated.

More citizens groups, insisting on the "right to know," have been formed and are becoming more active. However, at this level, and especially in local government, the "right to know" has now been expanded to include the "right to participate," which is discussed in chapter 9.

Conclusions

This chapter recognizes the importance of information and the communication process, both internally and externally, as well as the problem of withholding information. Effective communication, broadly defined, is an absolutely essential process in the life of an organization. Internally, it is crucial to leadership, decision making, control, morale, efficiency, cohesiveness, and the other basic organizational concerns. Externally, it is an essential technique for generating the support needed to guarantee the well-being and survival of the organization.

The problem of secrecy will not be completely eliminated by legislation. At the federal level, the president, by invoking executive privilege, can still refuse to release information. And at all levels, withholding information is a complex problem, involving bureaucratic attitudes, values, careers, and long-standing behavioral patterns, which are not altered simply by passing a law. But, a start has been made toward making administration more open. The pressure for full disclosure will undoubtedly continue.

The sheer volume of communications in any organization is astounding, communications expressed in written documents as well as in verbal and non-verbal forms. An amazing amount of an administrator's time is invested in the communication process: communicating in staff, committee, and other group formats; in one-to-one situations with superiors, equals, and subordinates; on the telephone with people inside and outside the organization; writing memos upward in response to memos from higher authority, as well as downward; answering correspondence from legislators, pressure groups, disgruntled citizens and a variety of other sources; and especially at the local level, belonging to community groups, attending community functions, speaking to civic groups, and using other techniques of relating with and communicating to client groups. In fact, some days — actually most days — middle managers and above are buried in people and paper.

Administrators often resent these communication demands, but a good administrator recognizes the importance of being a part of the communication net. This is how goals are defined, decisions are made, leadership is exerted, and the organization integrated.

NOTES

1. Francis E. Rourke, "A Symposium, Administrative Secrecy: A Comparative Perspective," *Public Administration Review* 35, no. 1 (January-February 1975): 2.

2. Early writers on bureaucracy, including Max Weber, discussed this concept.

3. Chester I. Barnard, *The Functions of the Executive* (Cambridge, Mass.: Harvard University Press, 1938), p. 91. Used by permission.

4. Herbert A. Simon, *Administrative Behavior: A study of Decision-Making Processes in Administrative Organization,* 2d. ed. (New York: Free Press, 1957), p. 154. Copyright 1945, 1947, 1957 by Herbert A. Simon. Used by permission.

5. James G. March and Herbert A. Simon, *Organizations* (New York: John Wiley, 1958), p. 162. Used by permission.

6. Herbert Kaufman, *Administrative Feedback: Monitoring Subordinates' Behavior* (©1973 by the Brookings Institution, Washington, D.C.), p. 2. Used by permission.

7. Ibid., p. 5. Used by permission.

8. For a discussion of the relationship, see Itzhak Galnoor, "Government Secrecy: Exchanges, Intermediaries and Middlemen," *Public Administration Review* 35, no. 1 (January-February 1975): 32–42.

9. There is a vast literature on the subject of pressure groups.

10. For a discussion of this, see Leon V. Sigal, "Bureaucratic Objectives and Tactical Uses of the Press," *Public Administration Review* 33, no. 14 (July-August 1973): 336–45.

11. Ibid., p. 343.

12. There is extensive literature on governmental secrecy. Some examples are Itzhak Galnoor, ed., *Government Secrecy: An International Perspective* (New York: Harper & Row, 1975); Francis E. Rourke, "Bureaucratic Secrecy and Its Constituents," *The Bureaucrat* 1, no. 2 (Summer 1972); Edward A. Skils, *The Torment of Secrecy* (Glencoe, Ill.: Free Press, 1956); Francis E. Rourke, *Secrecy and Publicity: Dilemmas of Democracy* (Baltimore: Johns Hopkins, 1966); and Norman Dorsen and Stephen Gillers, eds., *None of Your Business: Government Secrecy in America* (New York: Viking, 1974).

13. For the results of approximately eleven years of hearings on the availability of information, see U.S. Congress, Committee on Government Operations, *Availability of Information from Federal Departments and Agencies* (17 parts), Hearings, 84th–86th Congresses (Washington, D.C.: Government Printing Office, 1956–59).

14. For a discussion of the changes and a good bibliography of government publications on the topic, see Harold C. Relyea, "Opening Government to Public Scrutiny: A Decade of Federal Efforts," *Public Administration Review* 35, no. 1 (January-February 1975): 3–10.

15. Rourke, "A Symposium, Administrative Secrecy," p. 1.

16. Ibid., p. 1.

17. For some of the attitudes and activities of one group, see Ralph Nader et al., eds., *Whistle Blowing* (New York: Bantam Books, 1972).

18. Rourke, "A Symposium, Administrative Secrecy," p. 2.

19. However, for a general bibliography documenting most of the efforts, see U.S. Congress, House Committee on Government Operations, *U.S. Government Information Policies and Practices — Administration and Operation of the Freedom of Information Act* (Part 5), Hearings, 92nd Cong., 2nd sess. (Washington, D.C.: Government Printing Office, 1972), pp. 1463–71.

20. Robert L. Saloschin, "The Freedom of Information Act: A Governmental Perspective," *Public Administration Review* 35, no. 1 (January-February 1975): 11.

21. For some of the problems in administering the Act, see U.S. Congress, House Committee on Government Operations, *Administration of the Freedom of Information Act,* House Report 92–1419 (Washington, D.C.: Government Printing Office, 1972), pp. 12–19.

22. For a good collection of readings on the role of these committees, see Thomas E. Cronin and Sanford D. Greenberg, eds., *The Presidential Advisory System* (New York: Harper & Row, 1969).

23. Relyea, "Opening Government to Public Scrutiny," p. 5.

24. Ibid., pp. 3–10.

PART FOUR

Administration as Management

Organization
Theory

In the preceding sections of this book, the orienting themes have been the study of public administration, public administration in the web of government, and the tasks of public administration. The management function is also a major component of public administration. In the following eight chapters, the management perspective will be explored in some detail. This first chapter, on Organization Theory, will establish the theoretical framework within which the management process occurs.

Organizations

Organizations, excluding natural units such as the family, are artificial, human-created social institutions brought into being whenever the achievement of any goal or objective requires the utilization of the talents and services of a number of people. "They are 'social units (or human groupings)' deliberately constructed and reconstructed to seek specific goals."[1] Organizations are nothing new, but the scope, pervasiveness, and intensity of "organized society" as we know it is a product of the demands created by the complexity of a modern, industrialized society subject to rapid change.[2] In the present period which Peter Drucker has labeled as a "post-industrial society," we are a society of organizations.[3] As Amitai Etzioni says, "earlier societies had some organizations, but modern society is a society of organizations."[4] Drucker expresses the development by saying that our society "has become a pluralist society in which every major social task has been entrusted to large organizations. . . . "[5] Whether we like it or not — and many people do not appreciate it — formal bureaucratic organizations are a fact of life in developed nations. In some countries, bureaucratization is even more intense than in the United States. As was indicated in chapter 1, organizations influence most people from the cradle to the grave; and "most of us spend all of our working day and a great deal of our non-working day in a unique and extremely durable social arrangement called bureaucracy."[6]

Since public organizations are a given fact in modern life, the basic concerns become how they should be structured, whom they should serve, what their goals should be, how they should be managed, what their impact is on workers and client groups, and so on — all in the realm of theory.

The Evolution of Organization Theory

The field of organization theory has been an area of conflict over the years and is still in turmoil. There is no single acceptable theory of organization. As Dwight Waldo says, the opinions "represent much diversity among those who might be said to have an informed opinion. Some may find this a discouraging fact, but others will probably find it a reason for optimism. At least we are offered alternative as well as complementary views; the future is not captive to a unanimous present opinion."[7] The appropriateness of each organizational model, developed for a particular time in history, has been challenged as environmental conditions and social values have changed.

As was pointed out briefly in chapter 2, organization theory has evolved through a variety of schools of thought or models. However, it is impossible to cover the vast body of literature in an introductory book. We have deliberately chosen to comment briefly on the models which have had the most impact on modern organizations. Although scientific management and behavioralism were discussed as perspectives of public administration in chapter 2, they will be briefly reviewed here to show the chronology. For convenience, we will discuss the topic under two headings — classical theory and challenges to classical theory.

Classical Theory

The term "classical theory" is applied to the earlier theories of organizations which emphasized organizational structures and administrative procedures designed to insure rational and predictable employee behavior. The major classical theories may be grouped under scientific management, principles of organization, and the bureaucratic models.

Scientific Management

The scientific management period started in the United States with Frederick Winslow Taylor, in the late nineteenth and early twentieth century. Taylor, an American engineer, developed his theories about the same time Henri Fayol was working on the same topic in France.

Taylor was writing during a transition period. "During the Industrial Revolution, emphasis was chiefly on the entrepreneur rather than the executive—

on starting business concerns and innovating change rather than on maintaining continuity of operations or establishing and keeping to routines."[8] In such an atmosphere, technological change and machines, not workers, were the focus of interest. By the late nineteenth and early twentieth century, however, when Taylor was managing and writing, the role and importance of the worker in increasing productivity was recognized. The orientation of management shifted from "machine problems" to "labor problems." Taylor's theoretical construct of management, based on his experience, was expressed in *Introduction to the Principles of Scientific Management.*[9]

Taylor was searching for the one best way to achieve results by concentrating on the workers. In his view, labor was not very bright, economic rewards were the only motivating force for labor, workers produced as little as they could get away with, jobs had to be broken into minute parts, bonus systems should be used to encourage production over the norms, and workers should adapt to the technological requirements of the job. His other organizational concepts included the use of time and motion studies to determine the most efficient way to perform each operation, clearly defined roles for labor and management, and work flow rationally organized by proper plant layout and work scheduling. His philosophy was summed up when he said "the fundamental principles of scientific management are applicable to all kinds of human activities from our simplest individual acts to the work of our great corporations, which call for the most elaborate cooperation."[10] If it could be analyzed, there was *one best way* to organize to solve all human problems.

As is evident, scientific management was concerned with "the use of men as adjuncts to machines in the performance of routine productive tasks. The emphasis was on repetitive tasks which required no decision making or problem solving. The theories on organizational problems approached the subject from an engineering viewpoint."[11]

Principles of Organization

A variety of other writers expanded on the Taylor model, but with a different thrust. Whereas Taylor concentrated primarily on time and motion and activities of the individual engaged in performing a specific task, the new thrust was searching for the best way to organize to perform the assigned tasks — the principles of organization. Among the leaders of this group were Gulick, Urwick, Mooney and Reiley.[12]

This period generated many concepts which were to become the orthodoxy of public administration in the United States for some time to come. One of Gulick's contributions was POSDCORB which he coined to describe the work of the public administrator — planning, organizing, staffing, directing, coordinating, reporting, and budgeting.[13]

This model, which incorporated much of Taylor's thought, had certain distinguishing "principles" which may be summarized as follows:

1. *Division of Labor* — The functions of the organization should be divided into small, defined duties which are assigned to a position to permit acquiring expertise and defining responsibility.

2. *Functional Organization* — These individually defined positions should be grouped into specialized units — sections, bureaus, departments — according to their particular functions or specialty.
3. *Unifunctional Organization* — Any major department should deal with only one general topic. Units within the larger unit should be specialized — section on recruiting, section on position classification, section on pay standardization, etc., within a personnel department.
4. *Unity of Command* — Although authority may be delegated, it ultimately ends in the hands of the top executive. Such a principle is needed to provide unified direction, coordination, and decision making to guarantee the attainment of organizational goals.
5. *Authority Structure* — The principles specified that authority, the power to issue orders, filtered from the top of the organization down through the levels to the lower units. The lower units had the responsibility of reporting which flowed from the bottom to the top.
6. *Span of Control* — The principle was that the top decision maker could supervise, control, and meet with only a limited number of people. Therefore, the organization should be structured so that only a few reported to the top executive. Although the magic number was never specified, the span of control concept was embedded in the thinking of academics, practitioners, and those responsible for reorganization efforts.

Bureaucratic Theory

The bureaucratic model, proposed around 1900 by Max Weber, a German sociologist, was introduced into the United States in the 1930s but did not receive wide attention until translations became readily available after World War II. Since then, the theory has had a tremendous influence in the United States.

The theory was developed during the early stages of the industrial revolution and the factory system. During this period, labor was just another commodity to be exploited as an ingredient of production, inhumane treatment was a common practice, workers had absolutely no rights or protections and managerial decisions were based on emotion, whim, and dictatorial powers. It was a brutal, exploitative, unpredictable system.

Although Weber's model came somewhat later and varied from classical theory in its recognition of the role of human personalities, it is usually included under this category because it attempted to establish a framework in which roles and relationships were formally prescribed and "rationality and predictability were sought in order to eliminate chaos and unanticipated consequences."[14]

What are the basic distinguishing components of the bureaucratic model?[15] The major characteristics can be summarized as follows:

1. A division of labor based on functional specialization. Work is divided into small manageable parts and each assigned to a position so that an employee becomes a technical expert in that function.
2. Positions are organized into a hierarchical authority structure which takes the form of a pyramid. In the pyramid, each level has authority over the

level or person below with ultimate authority in the hands of one individual at the apex. As George Berkley says, "the well wrought pyramid stands as the symbol, the coat of arms, of modern bureaucracy."[16]

3. A system of rules covering the rights and duties of employees to formalize and routinize the process.

4. A system of procedures for dealing with work situations to insure uniformity of actions, continuity, and predictability in achieving organizational goals.

5. Impersonality of interpersonal relations with workers and clients to remove factors such as personal emotion, love, likes, dislikes, and values. This was designed to remove extraneous factors that might adversely affect impartiality and rational decision making.

6. Selection, retention, and promotion of employees should be based strictly on an objective evaluation of their technical competence. Politics, friendship, connections, and other considerations should play no role.[17]

Weber thought that the adoption of these concepts of organization would introduce rational decision making, efficiency, and predictability into administration. As Peter Blau and Richard Scott say, Weber believed that "bureaucracy is the most efficient form of administrative organization, because experts with much experience are best qualified to make technically correct decisions, and because disciplined performance governed by abstract rules and coordinated by the authority hierarchy fosters a rational and consistent pursuit of organizational goals."[18]

Weber's Concept of Authority

Another important part of Weber's philosophy was his concept of power and authority. Power is a situation where one person can impose his or her will on another and force the other person to comply unwillingly through a threat of violence, manipulation, control over the other's livelihood, and other means. Authority is a different concept. It has two distinguishing characteristics. First, people willingly comply with legitimate commands or orders because they consider that a person occupying a leadership position has a right to direct them. The power is legitimate because it resides in a position and not in an individual. Second, the recipient of the order suspends personal judgment as to the correctness of the order or decision. He or she does not inject personal feelings into the situation and resist or evaluate the decision.

Weber identified three sources or methods of legitimizing authority. One type of authority is supported by tradition. In traditional authority, religious beliefs, divine right, heredity, subjectivity, and other factors cause people to believe that a person has a right to rule. Absolute monarchies and tribal structures would be examples. The second type is charismatic authority. This is the cult of one person who gathers followers because she or he claims to have supernatural powers, was designated from a supreme authority, has a cause, proposes a revolutionary idea or some other factor that induces people to believe in her or him and follow directions. Such organizations run the great risk of collapsing when the leader dies, unless provisions have been made for succession. The third type is legal authority which is made legitimate by law. "In such a system obedience is owed not to a person — whether a traditional chief or charismatic leader — but to a set of impersonal principles. Those principles include the requirement to follow directives originating from an office superior to one's own."[19] The societal norms, value system, and socialization process lead people to accept such control as proper, expected, and legitimate.

Impact of Classical Theory

Classical theory, especially the principles of organization and Weber's concept of bureaucracy, became the gospel of organizations in the United States. The combination became the model for organization and reorganization. The basic principles became the guiding framework for work by the Brownlow Commission, for President Franklin Roosevelt's Committee on Administrative Management and the two Hoover Commissions established by Presidents Truman and Eisenhower, and for other groups charged with administrative reform at the federal level. Many reorganization efforts at the state and local levels were also guided by these doctrines.

These fundamentals of organizations became tremendously important when the demands of the economic depression expanded the role of government. As existing organizations expanded and new ones were created, they were organized to mirror the model. The bureaucrats, those persons who staffed the bureaucracy, "assumed roles of near heroes as they proceeded to battle big business and to ride roughshod over local elites and political bigwigs in order to extend the benefits of the welfare state to one and all."[20]

Challenges to Classical Theory

The classical theory — scientific management, principles and bureaucracy — did not go unchallenged.[21] In fact, Weber himself later expressed deep concern over his bureaucratic model. Although he thought the model was inevitable, he expressed some of the fears and criticism of bureaucratic organization that are currently controversial topics: that bureaucratic organizations would become oppressive, dictatorial, and generally dehumanizing for the individual employee. Since then, the challenges have intensified.

Although various classifications have been used to delineate the schools of thought, we will group the challenges under three headings — the behavioralists, systems theory, and the new public administration.

The Behavioralists

This school was essentially a revolt against the classical theorist's view of human beings, their motivation and needs, and the impact of bureaucracy on individuals. In classical theory "man was viewed as a passive, inert instrument, performing the tasks assigned to him."[22] Motivations other than money, individual differences, and human feelings were unimportant and did not have to be considered in achieving the production goals of the organization. With this view of people "the only road to efficiency and productivity was to surrender man's needs to the service of the bloodless machine."[23]

The serious challenge to classical theory originated in the late 1920s and early 1930s when Elton Mayo and some of his colleagues in the Harvard Business School conducted a series of studies of workers at the Hawthorne plant of the Western Electric Company.[24] These studies of the behavior of workers in an organizational setting developed findings which were in direct opposition to the principles developed by Taylor and others in the classical school. The major findings were that organizations are social systems, that a variety of incentives other than money motivate workers to produce, that the behavior of individuals in small groups was important, that an informal organization developed, that informal leaders recognized by the workers competed with the formally designated leaders, and that the informal groups rather than the work supervisor established and enforced work norms through group sanctions.

In general, the importance of interpersonal relations and communication between formal leaders and the workers, as well as the importance of worker participation in setting production goals, were recognized as having more impact on production than the older concepts of hierarchy, chain of command, and formal structure.

Influenced by the work done in the early 1940s by a group of psychologists such as Maslow, Rogers, and Fromm, the challenge to classical theory intensified after World War II. An important influence was Maslow's hierarchy of needs model in which self-esteem and self-actualization were the highest needs of man. Challenges and suggested modifications were made by such people as Dwight Waldo,[25] Kenneth Boulding,[26] William H. Whyte,[27] Chris Argyris,[28] Douglas MacGregor,[29] Herbert Simon,[30] James March and Herbert Simon,[31] Rensis Likert,[32] Warren Bennis,[33] Robert T. Golembiewski,[34] and John Pfiffner and Frank Sherwood.[35]

The behavioral emphasis of these theorists, as opposed to classical theory, focused its attention on the human being and his or her relations to the organization, rather than on organizational structure. The key was the linkages between the individual members of the organization and the patterns of organizational activity. As Herbert Simon says, "the principle normative concern here was to create organizational environments in which employees would be motivated to join the organization, to remain in it, and to contribute vigorously and effectively to its goals."[36]

The movement focused on the complexities of people and their motivations, on factors such as how to integrate the individual into the organization, noneconomic forms of motivation, redesigning positions to expand and enrich them to reduce their repetitive, boring nature, making workers feel more a part of the organization by developing participative techniques in decision making, "self direction" to replace authoritarian direction by the organization, small-group behavior, and the role and importance of the informal organization that develops within the formal organizations.[37] This movement not only challenged the structure but also the actual historic concepts of efficiency and production. Theorists asked, should everything be geared to efficiency or should organizations be willing to sacrifice some efficiency in order to make working a more enjoyable, satisfying experience?

Systems Theory

Systems theory is yet another way of looking at organizations. System theorists charge that the scientific management, Weberian bureaucratic, and human relations models erroneously viewed an organization as a closed system in which values, objectives, procedures and other variables were known. They argue that organizations are not closed but rather open entities.[38]

If one looks at the whole nation, there are many systems operating — social, economic, educational, religious, family, governmental, and so on. None of these systems operates independently or in a vacuum, but all are interrelated, interdependent, and interwoven. What happens in one has an impact, either good or bad but rarely neutral, on the others. If only the governmental system is analyzed, it will be composed of a political system (elections, political parties, legislatures, pressure groups, policy making), a judicial system, and an administrative system. The total administrative system is composed of a variety of systems — federal, state, and local — and any given organization, such as a city, can be viewed as being composed of a series of subsystems.

If only a particular organizational unit such as a bureau, department, board, or other unit is considered, it is also an open system. It is not an isolated independent entity, but a part of the total environment in which it is located. It is affected by the environment and influences it in return. This openness can be viewed as an input-conversion-output model. The organization receives inputs (demands, support, opposition) from individuals and groups of citizens as well as from other administrative agencies and the legislative body. These are fed into the organizational conversion mechanism, which is often referred to as the black box. The conversion machinery is the internal decision-making process where the inputs are interpreted, conflicting solutions are aired, and compromises are made. The outputs are goods, services, regulations, support, controls, and other actions that affect the citizens and possibly other public agencies. These outputs trigger a reaction from those who were adversely affected. This activates the feedback mechanism through which the reactions are communicated back to the organization as new inputs.

As can be seen in figure 5, the input-conversion-output-feedback system is a continuous, never-ending cycle representing an organization's transactions with its environment.

The New Public Administration

One of the impacts on public administration in general, and organization theory in particular, was the movement which was labeled the "New Public Administration." The movement, initiated primarily by the younger members of the profession and especially by those in the academic world, developed over a period of time but came to fruition during a vary turbulent period in our history. In the latter part of the 1960s, the youth movement was in full swing, riots were occurring on university campuses, political turmoil was prevalent, professional societies were factionalized over issues involving

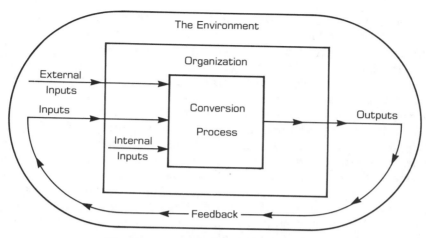

Figure 5   An Administrative System

goals and control, and many forms of traditional organizations and authority were being challenged in a variety of ways.

The movement was formally launched in 1968 when a number of younger academics and practitioners were invited to attend a conference which came to be known as the Minnowbrook Conference.[39] This was followed by a series of panels with the orienting theme "Public Administration in a Time of Turbulence," at the 1969 meeting of the American Political Science Association.[40] A conference, principally for private executives, with a similar theme was held in 1970.[41] Since these conferences, the literature has included material in support of, in opposition to, and expanding on the concerns reflected in books published as a result of these conferences.[42]

Themes of the New Public Administration.   What are the major themes of the new public administration? A summary is difficult because the challenges are extremely broad, and indeed there is no common agreement among the new revisionists.[43] A major theme is the bitter attack on complex, bureaucratic organizations with their current concepts. None of the basic aspects of bureaucratic organization escape attention. The charges include the misuse of authority and the dysfunctional impact of the authority structure itself, the undue emphasis on efficiency and effectiveness, the emphasis on rationality to the exclusion of other human characteristics, organizational and bureaucratic tendencies to retain the status quo, the trust placed in theoretically value-free professionalism, improper goal setting to accommodate the politically powerful at the expense of those who lack political and economic resources, the lack of accountability to client groups, the absence of participation by employees and client groups in decision making and goal setting, the elitism of the merit system in personnel administration, the morality of organizations and the dehumanizing impact bureaucratic organizations have on workers and client groups, to name some. Dehumanization of employees was an important theme. Modern organizations are viewed as not only oppressive places to work, but also as forces which inhibit individual growth and development, alienate the workers, and are destructive to the individual employee in general. Waldo summarized his general impression of the movement's view of dehumanization by saying that bureaucratic organizations "squeeze the joy, the warmth, the very humanness from life."[44]

The main objective and plea of this movement is to create a new organizational and administrative theory. In addition to organizational changes, discussed under the section in this chapter titled "Organizations for the Future," the major thrust may be illustrated by a few quotes. LaPorte says that "our primary normative premise should be that the purpose of public organization is the reduction of economic, social and psychic suffering and the enhancement of life opportunities for those inside and outside the organization."[45] Frederickson stated that, "simply put, new public administration seeks to change those policies and structures that systematically inhibit social equity."[46] Equity, morality, humanism, participation, and the human condition were to be major considerations.[47]

Other Voices.   In addition to the results of the conferences discussed above, other people have written on the same theme — some for the first time and others as a continuation of earlier comments. George Berkley, citing experiences from other countries, agrees that an administrative revolution is in progress and the bureaucratic organization has outlived its usefulness and is crumbling.[48]

Warren Bennis has been a leader in condemning the bureaucratic business organization. He argues that "this form of organization is becoming less and less effective, that it is hopelessly out of joint with contemporary realities . . . so within the next twenty-five to fifty years, we should all be witness to and participate in, the end of bureaucracy. . . ."[49]

Organizations for the Future

Given the rapidly changing society and the criticisms leveled against today's organizations, what will the organizations of the future look like? The possibilities and suggestions run the gamut from no or little change in the structure of our present organizations to totally new organizational forms, goals, and directions.

Little Change

Some argue that organizations will become more pervasive. Alberto Guerreiro Ramos states that "it is not enough today to manage organizations. . . . It is necessary to manage the whole society."[50] Bertram Gross has also discussed the possibilities and options for a totally managed society.[51] Some, like Herbert Kaufman, believe that change will occur but that "the main outlines and features of organizations as we know them will obtain in the near future — in 2001, say, not to mention 1984."[52] Those that support this view argue that organizations, although human creations, are products of an evolutionary process and are not susceptible to rapid change. Every organization has built-in barriers which resist modifications — barriers such as human inertia and human resistance to change. Change is threatening because it affects behavioral patterns, avenues of communication, power structures, personal relationships, operating procedures, possible loss of status, author- ity, and prestige, and thus creates uncertainty.[53] In fact, Kaufman worries about the apparent "view of mankind as currently possessing the capacity to exercise full control over the evolution of all our institutions. It perpetu- ates a myth of managerial omnipotence."[54] Such a belief may generate expec- tations which probably cannot be fulfilled, leading to dangerous levels of frustration.

Basic Changes

The opposite view holds that organizations as we know them will completely disappear due to their inefficiency, problems of control, dehumanization of employees and other factors. What will replace it? The range again is tre- mendous. Many see the future organizations as being more democratic, flexible, adaptable, susceptible to quick change. Warren Bennis says that "adaptive, temporary systems of diverse specialists, solving problems, linked together by task evaluative specialists in organic flux, will gradually replace bureaucracy as we know it," which he labels an "organic-adaptive" struc- ture.[55] These temporary systems or task forces will be put together to solve specific problems and will consist "of relative strangers who represent a set of diverse professional skills. People will be differentiated not vertically according to rank and role but flexibly according to skill and professional training."[56]

Bennis also argues that organizations will inevitably become democratic. Although he is discussing private business organizations, the same pressures will probably force government in this direction. His democracy consists of a set of values which include:

1. Full and free communications, regardless of rank and power
2. A reliance on consensus, rather than on the more customary forms of coer- cion or compromise, to manage conflict
3. The idea that influence is based on technical competence and knowledge rather than on the vagaries of personal whims or prerogatives of power
4. An atmosphere that permits and even encourages emotional expression as well as task-oriented acts
5. A basically human bias, one which accepts the inevitability of conflict between the organization and the individual but which is willing to cope with and mediate this conflict on rational grounds.[57]

He does not advance the democratic argument on political or moral grounds, but as a matter of efficiency and response to change. He sums up by saying "democracy becomes a functional necessity whenever a social system is competing for survival under conditions of chronic change."[58] Richard Chapman and Frederic Cleaveland, based on a Delphi exercise which included academics and practitioners, agree that organizations will become flatter "with shorter chains of authority but a broader network for providing information and advice" and that greater use will be made of temporary, special groups assembled to solve a problem or complete a project.[59]

James D. Thompson believes that organizations will not only exist in the future but also will be more prevalent and believes that the emphasis may be placed on the administration of temporarily organized activities built around administrative teams or cadres. Perhaps complex organizations of the future will be known not for their components but by their cadres, with each cadre devoted to mobilizing and deploying resources in shifting configurations, in order to employ changing technologies to meet changing demands.[60]

Orin White, Jr., criticizes the bureaucratic organization on the basis of its treatment of people, inability to plan effectively, effectiveness of operations, and the problems of "making job roles compatible with the healthy human personality."[61] White is concerned with the organization's relationship to the client. Using Victor Thompson's models of maturity of clients, White argues that current administration is based on the "client-as-a-child model."[62] This leads to administrative structures which are "too powerful, inhumanely impersonal, pry too far and too often into individuals' lives and exact too heavy a price from individuals through the use of rules."[63] His solution he calls the "dialectical organization." Such an organization, somewhat like the Bennis organic-adaptive model, would have a nonhierarchical structure where "roles would not be strictly defined, but would be fluid according to functional necessity. Also, policy would be set in a 'balance of power' fashion by laterally related groups instead of at the top."[64]

Another possibility is behavioral modification which would allow people to influence their own evolution.[65] The techniques could include drugs, electrical manipulation of the brain, and techniques of positive and negative stimuli to create the desired results. The possible uses for such behavioral modification are extremely broad with a range of both positive and negative objectives. However, William G. Scott thinks the mind techniques should be used on or used by the administrative elite — the decision makers in key positions — to increase their sensitivity, awareness, and effectiveness which will benefit the mass of society.[66]

A Synthesis

While the controversy over the hierarchical versus nonhierarchical organization continues, many authors have insisted that a solution lies not in an either-or situation but in a combination. Every organization needs a hierarchical structure for stability and the performing of certain tasks, but it should also be cognizant of the needs of the employees and sufficiently flexible to restructure itself to respond to changing environmental conditions.

Peter Drucker discusses the controversy over hierarchical versus free-form organizations under a section he calls "What We Need to Unlearn."[67] He criticizes traditional theorists for insisting that the hierarchical or scalar model is the one best form for all types of organizations and the non-hierarchical free form on the basis that the overemphasis on interpersonal relations dictates that "the purpose of the structure is to make it possible for each person to 'do his thing.'"[68] He argues that the hierarchical form actually protects workers by defining roles and responsibilities, whereas in a team effort individuals have less freedom because of group demands. He concludes that a sound organizational structure needs "both a hierarchical structure of authority, decision-making and pyramid and the capacity to organize task forces, teams and individuals for work both on a permanent and temporary basis."[69] But in lieu of a final answer, "the right answer is whatever structure enables people to perform and contribute."[70]

Conclusions

In this chapter we have reviewed the major thrusts in the theory of organization. It is quite evident that no theory has gone unchallenged. While most of the movements and schools of thought have enjoyed a period of popularity and have made contributions, there is no single universally accepted theory on how organizations should be constructed. The field is in great turmoil and much of the controversy revolves around the potential adverse impact that organizations — especially those characterized by the bureaucratic hierarchical model — has on employees. Since we are a society of organizations and will probably become more so in the future, the search for an organizational form which will permit the accomplishment of objectives and at the same time be more able to accommodate the desires and needs of workers will continue.

In the next chapter we will look at organizations in practice, focusing on their structure, operation, and complexity.

NOTES

1. Talcott Parsons, *Structure and Process in Modern Societies* (Glencoe, Ill.: Free Press, 1960), p. 17. Copyright ©1960 by The Free Press. Used by permission.

2. For a discussion of organized society, see Robert Presthus, *The Organizational Society* (New York: Alfred A. Knopf, 1962).

3. "Post-industrial" because organizations now provide services more than they manufacture tangible products.

4. Amitai Etzioni, *Modern Organizations* (Englewood Cliffs, N.J.: Prentice-Hall, 1964), p. 106. Used by permission.

5. Peter Drucker, *Management: Tasks, Responsibilities, Practices* (New York: Harper & Row, 1974), Preface, ix. Used by permission.

6. Warren Bennis, *Changing Organizations, Essays on the Development and Evolution of Human Organizations* (New York: McGraw-Hill, 1966), p. 3. Used by permission.

7. Introductory note in "Symposium on Organizations for the Future," *Public Administration Review* 33, no. 4 (July-August 1973): 299.

8. Cyril Sofer, *Organizations in Theory and Practice* (New York: Basic Books, 1972), p. 22. Used by permission.

9. Frederick W. Taylor, *Introduction to the Principles of Scientific Management* (New York: Harper, 1911, reprinted 1942).

10. Frederick W. Taylor, *The Principles of Scientific Management* (New York: Norton, 1967), first published in 1911. Used by permission.

11. James G. March and Herbert H. Simon, *Organizations* (New York: John Wiley, 1958), p. 13. Used by permission.

12. Luther Gulick and L. Urwick, eds., *Papers on the Science of Administration* (New York: Institute of Public Administration, 1937); J.D. Mooney and A.C. Reiley, *The Principles of Organization* (New York: Harper, 1939).

13. Luther Gulick, "Notes on the Theory of Organizations" in Gulick and Urwick, *Papers on the Science of Administration.*

14. Bennis, *Changing Organizations*, p. 5. Used by permission.

15. For additional information on Weber's philosophy, see: Max Weber, *The Theory of Social and Economic Organizations*, A.M. Henderson and Talcott Parsons, trans., and Talcott Parsons, ed. (Glencoe, Ill.: Free Press and Falcon's Wing Press, 1947); Reinhard Bendix, *Max Weber: An Intellectual Portrait* (Garden City, N.Y.: Doubleday, 1960).

16. George Berkley, *The Administrative Revolution, Notes on the Passing of Organization Man* (Englewood Cliffs, N.J.: Prentice-Hall, 1971), p. 19. Used by permission.

17. Although there are various summaries, this list was taken from Bennis, *Changing Organizations*, p. 5.

18. Peter M. Blau and W. Richard Scott, *Formal Organizations: A Comparative Approach* (San Francisco: Chandler, 1962), p. 33. Used by permission.

19. Ibid., p. 32. Used by permission.

20. Berkley, *The Administrative Revolution*, p. 11. Used by permission.

21. For a critique of the scientific management school and its deficiencies, see March and Simon, *Organizations.*

22. Bennis, *Changing Organizations*, p. 67. Used by permission.

23. Ibid. Used by permission.

24. For a description and the results of the research, see F.J. Roethlisberger and W.J. Dickson, *Management and the Worker* (Cambridge: Harvard University Press, 1939).

25. Dwight Waldo, *The Administrative State* (New York: Ronald Press, 1948).

26. Kenneth Boulding, *Organization Revolution: A Study in the Ethics of Economic Organization* (New York: Harper & Row, 1953).

27. William H. Whyte, Jr., *The Organization Man* (Garden Grove, N.Y.: Doubleday, 1957).

28. Chris Argyris, *Personality and Organization* (New York: Harper & Row, 1957), and *Integrating the Individual and the Organization* (New York: John Wiley, 1964).

29. Douglas MacGregor, *The Human Side of Enterprise* (New York: McGraw-Hill, 1960).

30. Herbert Simon, *Administrative Behavior: A Study of Decision-Making Process in Administrative Organization*, 2d ed. (New York: Free Press, 1957), first edition published in 1945.

31. March and Simon, *Organizations.*

32. Rensis Likert, *New Patterns of Management* (New York: McGraw-Hill, 1961).

33. Bennis, *Changing Organizations.*

34. Robert T. Golembiewski, *Men, Management and Morality: Toward a New Organizational Ethic* (New York: McGraw-Hill, 1965).

35. John M. Pfiffner and Frank P. Sherwood, *Administrative Organization* (Englewood Cliffs, N.J.: Prentice-Hall, 1960).

36. Herbert A. Simon, "Applying Information Technology to Organization Design," *Public Administration Review* 33, no. 3 (May-June 1973): 268.

37. MacGregor called his new, expanded role of the worker Theory Y, as opposed to the older concept which he labelled Theory X.

38. For additional sources, see Daniel Katz and Robert L. Kahn, *The Social Psychology of Organizations* (New York: John Wiley, 1966); C. West Churchman, *The System Approach* (New York: Dell, 1968); and for comments, including the use and abuse of systems theory, with special emphasis on the comparative aspects, see Fred W. Riggs, "Structure and Function: A Dialectic Approach," paper delivered at the 1967 Annual Meeting of the American Political Science Association, Chicago.

39. The papers presented at this conference were included in Frank Marini, ed., *Toward a New Public Administration: The Minnowbrook Perspective* (Scranton: Chandler, 1971).

40. Some of these papers as well as some additional ones may be found in Dwight Waldo, ed., *Public Administration in a Time of Turbulence* (Scranton: Chandler, 1971).

41. Warren H. Schmidt, *Organizational Frontiers and Human Values* (Belmont, Calif.: Wadsworth, 1970).

42. Alan K. Campbell, "Old and New Public Administration in the 1970s," *Public Administration Review* 33, no. 4 (July-August 1972): 343.

43. A summary may be found in the concluding chapters of Waldo, *Public Administration in Time of Turbulence,* and Waldo's introduction to Marini, *Toward a New Public Administration.* Additional analyses may be found in York Wilburn, "Is the New Public Administration Still With Us?" *Public Administration Review* 33, no. 4 (July-August 1973): 373–78; Campbell, "Old and New Public Administration," pp. 343–46.

44. Dwight Waldo, "Some Thoughts on Alternatives, Dilemmas, and Paradoxes in a Time of Turbulence" in Waldo, *Public Administration in Time of Turbulence,* p. 272.

45. Marini, *Toward a New Public Administration,* p. 32. Used by permission.

46. Ibid., p. 312. Used by permission.

47. For a critique of bureaucracy and a plea for a new direction, see Eugene P. Dvorin and Robert H. Simmons, *From Amoral to Humane Bureaucracy* (San Francisco: Canfield Press, 1972).

48. Berkley, *The Administrative Revolution.*

49. Bennis, *Changing Organizations,* p. 51. Used by permission.

50. Alberto Guerreiro Ramos, "Models of Man and Administrative Theory," *Public Administration Review* 32, no. 3 (May-June 1972): 245.

51. Bertram Gross, "An Organized Society," *Public Administration Review* 33, no. 4 (July-August 1973): 323–27.

52. Herbert Kaufman, "The Direction of Organizational Evolution," *Public Administration Review* 33, no. 4 (July-August 1973): 300.

53. For a discussion of the barriers to and consequences of change, see Herbert Kaufman, *The Limits of Organizational Change* (University: University of Alabama Press, 1971).

54. Kaufman, "Direction of Organizational Evolution," p. 307.

55. Bennis, *Changing Organizations,* p. 12. Used by permission.

56. Ibid. Used by permission.

57. Ibid., p. 19. Used by permission.

58. Ibid. Used by permission.

59. Richard L. Chapman and Frederic N. Cleaveland, "The Changing Character of the Public Service and the Administrator of the 1980s," *Public Administration Review* 33, no. 4 (July-August 1973): 361.

60. James D. Thompson, "Society's Frontiers for Organizing Activities," *Public Administration Review* 33, no. 4 (July-August 1973): 335.

61. Orin White, Jr., "The Dialectical Organization: An Alternative to Bureaucracy," *Public Administration Review* 29, no. 1 (January-February 1969): 32.

62. Victor Thompson, *Modern Organization* (New York: Alfred A. Knopf, 1965).

63. White, "The Dialectical Organization," p. 34.

64. Ibid, p. 38.

65. For some of the research and possibilities, see B.F. Skinner, *Beyond Freedom and Dignity* (New York: Alfred A. Knopf, 1971); Jose M.F. Delgado, *Physical Control of the Mind* (New York: Harper & Row, 1969); and John G. Taylor, *The Shape of Minds to Come* (New York: Weybright and Talley, 1970).

66. See William G. Scott, "The Theory of Significant People," *Public Administration Review* 33, no. 4 (July-August 1973): 308–13.

67. Drucker, *Management: Tasks, Responsibilities, Practices,* pp. 524–28.

68. Ibid., p. 525. Used by permission.

69. Ibid., p. 526. Used by permission.

70. Ibid., p. 528. Used by permission.

13

Organizations in Practice

The turmoil in organization theory, combined with the unionization of public employees, affirmative action programs, citizen demands for participation, decentralization, and other events, have had their impact. However, much of the impact has been reflected in procedural rather than structural changes in most public agencies. Although project teams, which are not totally new, are being used, there is more participation in the decision-making process and administrators are more cognizant of the new pressures, public organizations have not become free-form, flat, temporary, or any of the other terms used to describe organizations of the future. In practice many of the basic concepts of traditional theory are still the orienting themes for present public organizations.

In this chapter we will discuss the creation of public agencies, review the characteristics of formal organizations, look at factors modifying the formal organizational structure, analyze the informal organization which always develops, and comment on some of the problems faced by the practicing administrator.

The Creation of Organizations

Public organizations in a democratic society are created by basic documents (constitutions and charters) or by laws and executive orders. All are created to administer a program or deliver a service to meet a perceived demand. Although the demands and pressure for a new activity usually come from potential client groups, the idea may originate with the bureaucrats. In either case, the bureaucracy is usually more than willing to expand an existing function or add a new one.

Conflict, with varying degrees of intensity, always accompanies the creation of a new agency or program. Conflict revolves around three issues. First, it must be determined whether the activity is necessary. Rarely is there unanimous agreement on this basic question. Some individuals and groups will oppose any new agency on the philosophical basis that government is already playing too large a role in society. Others — bureaucrats, administrative units, and client groups — will resist because the new program may compete with their programs for resources, power, and prestige. Second, after the program idea has been accepted, the next issue becomes the organizational location of the activity. Should the program be added to an existing administrative department, administered by a newly created department, or established as an independent agency? Since the locational question has power, status, and budgetary implications, it becomes an issue of intense interest to those involved. Third, a decision must be made about the level of the initial funding for the program.

These conflicts will be resolved in the political decision-making process. The outcomes, which are normally compromise solutions, will depend upon the relative interest and power positions of the legislators, bureaucrats, pressure groups, and other interested and competing parties.

Regardless of the outcome, the legal document will specify goals and provide some "start-up" money and staff. From a small start, organizations usually expand and grow into large complex units with formal organizational structures.

The Formal Organization

The organization chart, with its solid and dotted lines and boxes, graphically depicts the structure of the organization. A glance at the organization chart in figure 6 indicates:

1. The general configuration of the organization and its component parts
2. The functions or subject matter of each unit by the labels assigned to each, normally on a traditional unifunctional basis
3. The many individual positions to allow specialization at the base
4. The grouping of positions into departments, bureaus, divisions, and sections staffed by bureaucrats
5. A pyramidal structure with each level having its assigned responsibilities, duties, role, authority, and expected behavioral pattern
6. Few positions at the second level from the top of the pyramid, indicating the concept of limited "span of control"
7. The peak of the hierarchy is the chief executive — mayor, governor, director, president, chairman — who thus has unity of command
8. The official lines of communication, authority and decision centers, and superior-subordinate relationships
9. A division between line agencies — those in the hierarchy — and staff agencies — those outside the pyramid

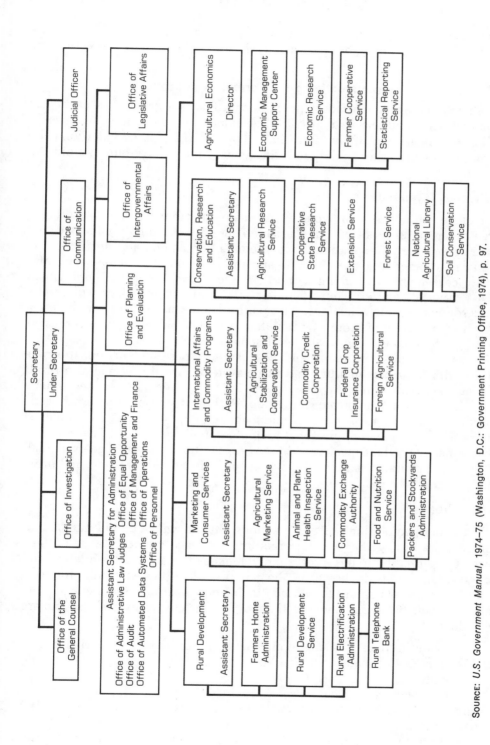

Figure 6 Department of Agriculture

SOURCE: *U.S. Government Manual, 1974–75* (Washington, D.C.: Government Printing Office, 1974), p. 97.

The chart indicates how the organization should function, but how it functions in practice might be and usually is quite different for a variety of reasons.

Factors Modifying the Formal Organization

Organizations are composed of people operating as a group at a particular time and place and within a specific environment. As such, they are susceptible to change. Two of the more important internal forces modifying the formal organization are individual differences and small groups within the organization.

Individual Differences

The range and variety of women and men — the bureaucrats — staffing a large organization is often quite broad. There are the highly educated and those with minimal educational backgrounds, the skilled and unskilled, the young newcomer and the older organization person, and some who enter with a career objective along with others who consider public employment as a temporary matter. These people come in all shapes, sizes, colors and backgrounds — social, economic, and political. This mixture, due to the pressure from a variety of groups, will undoubtedly become even more representative of the composition of the total society in the future.

These differences are important, because all types enter organizations as adults with their personalities and value systems already formed as a result of their background and life experiences. It is unreasonable to expect such a labor force to be a homogeneous group. Rather, it will be a heterogeneous mixture of needs, expectations, and behavioral patterns. Each employee brings to the organization personal prejudices, political beliefs, likes and dislikes, a need system, capacity, ambition, expectations, personal goals, and all of the other characteristics that make people different, interesting, and often difficult to deal with.

Small Groups

When many people think of organizations, they visualize untold numbers of people working together and interrelating with each other. This would be a correct picture if an observer simply looked at personnel statistics and budgets. On the inside, however, the actual work is done in small groups.

Such groups, which are the foundation of organizations, are important because of their behavior. Some of the more important behavioral aspects are as follows:

1. They can become a social group with all of the characteristics that this implies — friendships, dislikes, hatred, factions, cooperation, and competition.
2. Informal leaders emerge.
3. The work group establishes and enforces expected roles, behavior, and work norms.
4. Loyalty to the subunit or group may become more important than loyalty to the total organization.

These group behavioral patterns may either serve to support or oppose the achievement of organizational objectives.

The formal structure and prescribed relationships cannot meet the needs of individuals and small groups. The result is that a complex informal organization develops within the formal structure.

Informal Organization

The informal organization develops in large measure as a response to the artificial system created by the formal organization. The informal structure is a spontaneous thing which Victor Thompson calls the "natural system." Thompson indicates that this structure develops because employees are interested in protection, conservation and survival—in warding off the dangers and threats deriving from the artificial system, such as threats of subordination, injustice, failure, ridicule, dull work and so on."[1]

Since the informal organization is based on human relationships, it might be called "people-oriented" as opposed to structure-oriented. This organization cannot be diagrammed on a chart. It is not static, but changes with the circumstances and personnel, and its presence is known and felt but not readily visible. One might say that it is based on a sensitivity or knowledge of the organization. It is something that cannot be described to a new employee but is acquired through observation, experimentation, conversation, and trial and error. Although not included as a part of a formal training program, it might be considered a part of "on-the-job training," because it is a part of the learning process for new employees.

A good way of looking at the informal organization is the overlay system suggested by John M. Pfiffner and Frank P. Sherwood.[2] They visualize the informal structure as a series of overlays which are superimposed on the formal organization. These overlays may be peeled off for analysis and discussion, but in practice all of these relationships are operating simultaneously. According to Pfiffner and Sherwood, there are five overlays — sociometric, functional, decision, power, and communication.

Sociometric Overlay

This overlay consists of modifications in the formal structure due to social and personal relationships among people. Friendships, which often have been developed outside the organization, serve to create a network of confidences, contacts, communications, and decision making not indicated in the organization chart. However, there are other results from this overlay. In addition to personal friendships, personality clashes, dislikes, and even hatreds also develop. Thus, this overlay — in most organizations — will indicate that the relationships among people run the continuum from friendship and positive attraction to hatred and total repulsion.

Functional Overlay

Functional relationships develop because a person possesses expertise, knowledge, and information others need but do not have. Such persons, even though they may be in a staff position without authortiy over line personnel, will develop a significant amount of influence. For example, the people in the department of data services who understand and can use the electronic equipment normally become centers of influence due to the lack of skill and understanding of most people in the organization.

Decision Overlay

Where are the decision-making centers in the organization? The final decision-making authority and responsibility are located in the spots indicated by the organization chart. However, in practice decisions are made or at least influenced by other individuals or groups at every level of the organization.

Power Overlay

Before discussing the power overlay, we should once again distinguish it from authority. Authority is the right of an employee to enforce his or her decisions by the use of sanctions. Various degrees of authority are assigned to positions rather than to individuals. The individual occupying a position at any given time inherits the authority, but loses it if demoted or transferred. Power, on the other hand, is the ability or capacity to influence others to behave in certain ways or to influence decisions or actually to make decisions in certain cases. Power can accrue to people at any level in the organization for a variety of reasons. Seniority and a resulting knowledge of the organization, expertise, personality and leadership characteristics which generate confidence and attract others, connections and relationships with higher echelons are a few foundations of power in a career (nonpolitical) organizational structure.

A few examples will illustrate the distinction. A city manager has authority because of his or her position. But, this person also has power to influence others. This form of power is referred to as legitimate power because it is visible, expected, and accepted in the formal organization. On the other hand, the secretary to the city manager is not in an authority position in the hierarchy. Nevertheless, he or she screens phone calls, sets up appointments, answers innumerable questions, handles sensitive correspondence, makes decisions within guidelines established by the manager, prepares agendas, and protects the manager's time. That is power.

Communication Overlay

The organization chart indicates the theoretical chain through which communications, orders, direction, information, and other matters will flow from the top to the bottom and the bottom to the top of the organization. An informal network develops in communications because of the social nature of the organization. Inside the organization, communications flow in every conceivable direction — direct telephone calls flow among friends, members of the same profession or specialty, and employees of similar rank. Outside the organization, information is exchanged in social groups — bridge clubs, bowling leagues, luncheon groups, and a variety of other social contacts.

Importance of Informal Organization

Despite its elusive nature, the informal organization is an important public administration topic, because of its potential for both negative and positive effects. On the negative side, the informal organization may have actually developed to protect quietly the workers against arbitrary decisions, to oppose or subvert the official leadership pattern to modify the procedures and objectives of the organization, or for any of a variety of other purposes. The net result is that the tension, conflict, and general climate which develops imposes obstacles which make it difficult or impossible for an organization to meet its objectives. On the positive side, the informal organization by speeding communications, supporting the felt needs of personnel, and in general smoothing out the inflexibility of the formal structure may be a positive force which makes the organization function more efficiently.

With these two possibilities, then, what administrators do with the informal organization may have a significant impact on their success. In the final analysis, the informal structure cannot be prevented. Thus, an administrator can use it to advantage. There is, of course, no "one" way to do it. The successful technique will depend upon a host of factors, including the personality and style of the leader, the type of organization, the type of personnel involved, and the environment in which the organization operates, to name a few. No successful administrator will insist that everything happen exactly as the formal organization chart indicates.

Management Problems

Because of the characteristics of living organizations, practicing administrators have no shortage of problems with which to cope. In addition to problems in decision making, leadership, communication, and personnel which are discussed in separate chapters, there are such problems as conflict resolution, integrating the individual into the organization, and reorganization. Although these problems are inherent in organizations, they do not require daily decisions. Administrators should, however, be cognizant of them and be prepared to decide when issues arise.

Conflict in Organizations

In our personal and social lives, most people strive to keep tension-producing conflict to a minimum. In organizations, conflict is a fact of life which cannot be avoided but hopefully can be reduced and controlled. Conflicts, which may originate from any source in complex organizations, may take a variety of forms. We will discuss the topic under two headings — staff-line conflicts and other conflicts. Some methods will be suggested for handling each type of conflict.

Staff-Line Conflicts. Defining the proper role of staff and line organizations and mediating the conflicts that develop is a problem common to all organizations. Theoretically, line agencies — indicated by the vertical chain of command on the organization chart — are responsible for delivering the services (police, fire, social welfare, and so on) to the public. Directors of the line departments are accountable for and judged on the level of services provided by their units. At a higher level, top managers (such as city managers) are evaluated on the overall performance of all of their line departments. Such judgment has political overtones in the manager's case: if the citizens are unhappy with the way services are provided or the service levels, it may have an impact on future elections.

Also according to theory, staff agencies — indicated on a separate horizontal line and not in the chain of command on organization charts — are support units. Such functions as personnel, purchasing, business services, and planning are created to provide advice and services needed by all line departments. The specialists who staff these bodies have no authority to direct, order, or command line units.

In practice, the picture of the distinction is much less clear-cut. Although most organizations still retain the staff-line organization format, there is not the separation between the two that traditional theory would indicate. The line is still responsible for the delivery system and the staff provides the supportive services, but staff plays a much more significant role than just facilitating. A personnel director refuses a departmental request to hire someone because the applicant does not meet the minimum qualifications. The affirmative action coordinator directs a department to extend its recruiting effort to attract more minorities. The finance department orders a line department to change its procedures to meet legal and audit requirements. To a line department head, such events are not viewed as advice, but rather as directives; and they are. An organization could not function without this interaction. If these staff agencies, which were created to provide specialized talent to the chief administrative officer, had to pass every ruling or decision to the executive officer who would then relay it to the line through the prescribed chain of command, the result would be a time-wasting muddle of paper work. The executive could not fulfill the expected role, the communications chain would be extended, the red tape and delay would be horrendous, and the organization, which would be an excellent example of the ultimate in bureaucratic form, would be severely crippled and possibly cease to function.

Nevertheless, because of the interaction between line and staff, there will be conflicts. A responsible line administrator normally does resent a staff decision which denies what she or he considers to be a perfectly legitimate and legal request, especially when the staff decision may adversely affect her or his operation. On the other hand, a specialist in a staff agency feels pressure to enforce policy, professional and legal standards.

Reducing Staff-Line Conflicts.   Although staff-line conflicts can never be completely eliminated, the leadership does have some options for reducing conflict. These would include, first, a precise definition of the role and expectations the executive has of staff agencies. Each administrator may have a different concept, but the different concepts should be clearly communicated to all those involved. Second, the leaders of each group should be exposed to each other through staff meetings, workshops, seminars, and other group activities. In such group encounters, information is exchanged, staff and line people gain a better mutual understanding, and facilitating personal relationships are established. Third, the top leadership should attempt to establish an organizational atmosphere within which staff and line people feel free to communicate and discuss concerns before they develop into serious confrontations. Finally, some theorists have suggested a rotation of personnel between staff and line assignments. But, this is difficult to establish in practice due to the difficulty of acquiring the technical knowledge required in some staff and line positions and resistance from those involved.

Other Types of Conflict.   Conflicts may involve people and components of the organization as well as outside agencies. We will look at personal-organizational, interpersonal, organizational, interorganizational, and revolutionary conflict.[3]

Personal-Organizational Conflict.   Personal-organizational conflict is always present. It is generated by employee dissatisfaction with the organization due to conflict between personal and organizational goals, dull and nonchallenging jobs, the impersonal nature of large organizations, resistance to the red tape, and organizational constraints, to name a few. But the result is an unhappy nonmotivated employee who will not be a committed organization person.

Interpersonal.   Interpersonal conflict is generated because the organization is an open social system staffed by people. In the outside world, we select those with whom we want to associate. In organizations a person's position dictates those with whom he or she must relate and interact for eight hours a day. Differing individual personalities, needs, and values make conflict inevitable.

Organizational.   Organizational conflicts are usually due to system-wide actions, such as an emphasis on hiring and promoting ethnic minorities and women to meet the goals of an affirmative action plan, procedures adopted for reducing the labor force, mandatory training programs, and proposed plans for reorganization. Such policies create tensions which have to be dealt with from the top.

Interorganizational.   Interorganizational conflict, a type of subdued civil war, is always present. An organization is rarely a unified whole, but rather a loose confederation of competing units. Every component, concerned with its own self-interest, competes with every other unit for the limited available resources, prestige, power, status, and for survival. In this type of conflict, agencies enlist the support of their external clientele and political groups.

Revolutionary.   Revolutionary conflict, as conceived by C. Brooklyn Derr and others, challenges the legitimacy of the organization. The tactics, which include bombing, arson, threats, marches, sit-ins, and physical violence, are designed to destroy an organization, policy, or program.

Conflict Resolution.   There is a tendency to view all conflict as undesirable, to be avoided if possible. Many disagree with this concept, however. Some conflict, if it is handled correctly, can lead to changes and modifications which will make the organization more efficient and effective as well as making it a better place in which to work.[4] The problem remains of distinguishing between those conflicts which are functional and those which are dysfunctional, as well as determining the relative seriousness of the conflicts. Since all do not carry the same potential organizational impact, there has to be a priority system for solution. Conflict resolution is an extremely complex process, but unlike other administrative functions, there has been no comparable outpouring of theory and models. This may be due to the situational nature of most conflict. Each conflict has its own peculiar causes, actors, and characteristics. Derr does suggest three ways to approach this problem. First, administrators should be exposed to training, including simulation exercises and games, to equip them to cope with various types of conflict. Second, organizational development techniques are needed to alter the agency's structure and internal processes to accommodate and respond to change and conflict. Third, the fundamental causes of conflict must be analyzed and corrected, rather than reacting to the symptoms in the hope that the causes will go away.

Integrating the Individual into the Organization

Since the labor force represents such a heterogeneous mass of individuals, management has the problem of integrating them into the organization. Integration, designed to encourage desired behavioral patterns, has two components: first, inducing employees to accept the goals and values of the organization which may conflict with their own; and second, encouraging them to accept legitimate influence, leadership, and decisions. This integrative process is accomplished in three basic ways — pre-employment socialization, the employment process, organizational socialization, and the use of rewards and sanctions.

Pre-employment Socialization

Organizations depend upon the pre-employment socialization process — family, school, church, and so on — to prepare people for organizational life. Conformity, respect for authority, appreciation of the expected conduct in different roles, acceptance of authority, responsibility, and other personal characteristics important to organizations are acquired early in life. Due to different backgrounds and different reactions among those with the same background, the socialization process does not create a uniform product, however. The heterogeneous product coming into organizations as employees creates the necessity of reconciling the needs of the organization — efficiency, standardization, predictability, and effectiveness in achieving organizational goals — with the varying value systems, needs and expectations of employees — job satisfaction, happiness, individual growth, individuality, responsibility, promotion, and so on. These need systems are rarely identical. As Etzioni points out, "most organizations most of the time cannot rely on most of their participants to internalize their obligations, to carry out their assignments voluntarily, without additional incentives."[5]

Faced with such a conflict situation, an organization may resort to using the employment process and manipulating rewards and sanctions as ways of avoiding conflict.

The Employment Process

An organization may attempt to use the employment process to reduce conflict. In the recruiting and hiring process, organizations may attempt to avoid selecting those whose personalities and goals deviate significantly from those of the organization. This can be followed by using the probationary period to rid the organization of those who do not fit. However, this approach is often not possible due to legal problems, the problem of hiring large numbers, challenges by ethnic groups and women, and the difficulty of accurately predicting how the attitudes of an individual will develop over the years.

Organizational Socialization

After an employee is hired, organizations attempt to induce individuals to accept organizational goals, and to develop loyalty, commitment, and a sense of belonging. A variety of techniques — such as orientation meetings, workshops, training sessions, lectures, movie and slide presentations, systems for making suggestions, and organization-sponsored activites — are used.

Rewards and Sanctions

All organizations have to resort to some system of "formally structured distribution of rewards and sanctions to support compliance with their norms, regulations and orders."[6] Rewards, given to those whose performance meets organizational expectations, include promotions, salary increases, titles, prestige indicators, recognition — such as letters of commendation and names in published material — and other intangible rewards. The sanctions for those who perform below expectations might include pressure from higher authority or peer groups, reprimand, transfer to an undesirable "outpost," lack of promotion, demotion, and dismissal. However, the excessive use of these negative sanctions is limited by civil services rules and the impact that their indiscriminate use could have on the morale and efficiency of the organization. A major aspect of sanctions is the knowledge that they are available. Employees consider the anticipated organizational response in making their decisions on how to behave. If negative sanctions have to be actually used extensively, an organization is in trouble.

Results of Integrative Efforts

Regardless of the efforts, few organizations succeed in completely integrating all individuals. Few persons will completely sublimate their own goals to those of the organization. The best that can be hoped for is a mutual accommodation in which employees participate sincerely in helping the organization reach its goals.

The Problem of Reorganization

Organizations, created to respond to a particular problem at a specific time, must change as internal and external conditions shift. Reorganization, as one response to change, may have a wide variety of objectives, some of which may be stated publicly and others which must remain unstated. Reasons may include the desire of the chief executive to inject her or his philosophy and programs, the necessity of breaking up an undesirable situation, revitalization by injecting new leadership into key organizations, an efficiency move to avoid overlapping and duplication, or reform to avoid entrenched procedures and traditions. One reason always given is the increase in efficiency and effectiveness in responding to new demands and delivering services to the public such a reorganization will provide.

At the federal level, the reorganization of structure and responsibilities is nothing new.[7] Although the executive branch is constantly evolving, major dramatic overhauls occur in cycles. As an example we will examine a recent reorganization which occurred under President Nixon.

In April, 1969, President Nixon created the President's Advisory Council on Executive Organization and gave it responsibility for reorganizing the Executive Office of the President to make it a more effective management arm of the president. On July 1, 1970, based on the recommendations of this committee, the president issued Reorganization Plan Number Two and Executive Order 11541 to put the plan into operation. The plan, recognizing that the Executive Office performs two separate, but closely related functions, created special agencies and procedures to perform each task.

The first task is policy determination, deciding what government should and should not do in the domestic area, which was assigned to the newly created Domestic Council. The cabinet-level group, chaired by the president, replaced the Council for Urban Affairs, Cabinet Committee on the Environment, and the Council of Rural Affairs, all of which had been created by earlier executive orders. The Domestic Council had a broad range of responsibilities, including assessing national needs, proposing alternate methods of meeting these needs, advising the president on domestic affairs, coordinating the establishment of national priorities for the allocation of resources among the possible programs, conducting a continuous review of existing programs and proposing reforms in priorities, procedures, and administration. The Council plays a role in the domestic area similar to that of the Security Council in the area of foreign affairs.

The other function of the Executive Office of the President is to develop procedures and techniques to be used in implementing policy decisions and evaluating program effectiveness in meeting objectives — executive management. The new agency responsible for implementing the policies developed by the Domestic Council is the Office of Management and Budget, which became operational on July 1, 1970. The procedural method of creating the new office was simply to rename the existing Bureau of the Budget and expand its role, responsibilities, and functions. Although the agency is still responsible for budget preparation and execution, these functions are no longer its all-consuming concern. The role was expanded to make it more of a management tool, as was originally envisioned when it was created by the Budget and Accounting Act of 1921. Management aspects include evaluating program performance, expanding federal interagency cooperation in the field, working to improve intergovernmental relations, improving the information and management systems, recommending organizational change, and promoting executive manpower development. Since executive manpower development had been the responsibility of the Civil Service Commission, this change created some apprehension and indicates further internal reorganization.

While the reorganization of the Executive Office of the President was a fundamental change, that office is considered to be more or less presidential territory and within the prerogative of the president. Nixon moved the reorganization into the traditional executive departments in 1970 by reorganizing the Post Office department. This department, somewhat unique in that it charged for its services, had been criticized for losing money, although it also had tremendous support from publishers and advertisers whose materials were processed well below cost. Effective in 1971, the department became a federally chartered corporation and functions as a business enterprise rather than as a service organization.

This initial foray into the ranks of the cabinet-level departments was mild compared with what was to follow. On March 26, 1971, President Nixon submitted to Congress a plan to restructure the remaining eleven cabinet-level executive departments.[8] The plan would have abolished the departments of Interior, Agriculture, Labor, Commerce, Transportation, Housing and Urban Development, and Health, Education and Welfare. The functions of these seven would have been redistributed among four newly created "super-departments" of Human Resources, Community Development, Economic Affairs, and Natural Resources. Only the departments of Defense, State, Justice, and Treasury and the numerous regulatory agencies (Federal Communications Commission, Federal Trade, Interstate Commerce, and so on) would not have been reorganized. However, due to pressure from the farm groups, the president announced in November, 1971, that Agriculture would remain as a separate cabinet-level department. These new departments would not have followed the traditional unifunctional structure dealing with a single topic but would have been organized around broad program areas. Different aspects of a program or problem, to be handled by numerous departments, would have been collected into one organizational unit. The plan was not, however, accepted by Congress.

Resistance to Reorganization

The word reorganization has a nice modern sound to most people when discussed in the abstract, but the reactions are different when a reorganization is actually proposed or ordered — especially if it is one's unit that is being reorganized. Both structural and functional reorganizational and realignments create a variety of problems, apprehensions, and opposition from a variety of sources.

One problem is that reorganization cannot be done quickly, since it requires a considerable period of time for definition and readjustment. Procedures, responsibilities, lines of authority, interagency relationships, individual roles, leadership patterns, funding, and innumerable other administrative aspects are affected.

A crucial problem is the human factor — personnel. From the first rumor of a possible reorganization, employees view any plan as a threat. They worry about how it will affect their unit, but — more importantly — what impact it will have on them personally in terms of status and role, relocation, promotional opportunities, and so on. These and a host of other career questions run through the minds of bureaucrats. The basic concern is whether there will still be a job for oneself. Since reorganizations are theoretically designed to increase efficiency, reduce overlapping, duplication, and costs, a "reduction in force" — commonly referred to as a RIF — is always a possibility. Even when no RIF is promised, it does not mean that positions and employees will not be reassigned and transferred. These tensions remain.

Reorganization also has an impact outside the organization. The client groups served by the organizations are vitally concerned.[9] The knowledge of how an old agency will probably react in a given situation and its procedures is replaced by the uncertainty of how a new organization will respond. Personal contacts, friendships, alliances, and entrees developed over the years, along with the accepted methods of doing business with the old agency are drastically changed. The clients, and their paid Washington representative, must "read" the new organization and work to construct new avenues into its personnel and procedures.

Another problem is that administrative reorganization plans proposed by the president (and effective within sixty days unless Congress takes positive action to disapprove them) are not purely administrative questions but have many political implications for legislators. One impact is on the legislators' political futures. Voters in the home area — especially organized groups — measure a legislator's success by what he or she has delivered and the services provided. Any reorganization disturbs the working relationships legislators and their staff people have developed with the executive departments and personnel over the years.

Another impact is on the internal structure and power distribution in Congress. For example, the congressional practice of having specialized standing committees to deal with the subject matter of individual executive departments — labor, agriculture, commerce, and so on — would have been affected by Nixon's proposed executive reorganization along program rather than single-topic lines. The congressional committee structure would also have been required to reorganize. This would have had two important results. First, the move would have reduced the number of the extremely powerful committee chairmanships available to legislators. Second, it would have considerably reduced the power, role, and influence the triumvirate of congressional committee, executive department, and organized groups have played in setting policy in the subject-matter areas.

A final problem with basic reorganization such as that proposed by President Nixon is that it violates tradition. Historically, we have followed the practice of creating unifunctional departments — one department for each subject. The new proposal would have completely altered that approach by organizing around program areas.

Conclusions

In this chapter, what a formal organization chart indicates about an organization and the factors which modify the formal structure have been reviewed. The informal organization, which always exists and which may be functional or dysfunctional, is a system which must be understood by administrators. We also discussed some of the general problems which confront administrators in managing actual organizations. Managers must be conscious of these problems, but they should also remember that there are no perfect solutions. Organizations and conditions are simply too dynamic to permit a permanent solution. At best, satisfactory solutions can be found which will regularize the process for as long a time span as possible. The alternative is managing by crisis — bouncing from crisis to crisis and attempting to solve them individually — a rather nonproductive and nerve-wracking procedure.

NOTES

1. Victor A. Thompson, *Organizations as Systems* (Morristown, N.J.: General Learning Press, 1973), p. 10. Used by permission.

2. John M. Pfiffner and Frank P. Sherwood, *Administrative Organization* (Englewood Cliffs, N.J.: Prentice-Hall, 1960). The material on overlays in the following discussion is adapted by permission.

3. The section on conflict relies heavily on C. Brooklyn Derr, "Conflict Resolution in Organizations: Views from the Field of Educational Administration," *Public Administration Review* 32, no. 5 (September-October 1972): 495–501.

4. See Richard Beckhard, *Organizational Development: Strategies and Models* (Reading, Mass.: Addison-Wesley, 1969); Robert R. Black and Jane S. Mouton, *Corporate Excellence Through Grid Organizational Development* (Houston: Gulf Publications, 1968).

5. Amitai Etzioni, *Modern Organizations* (Englewood Cliffs, N.J.: Prentice-Hall, 1964), p. 59. Used by permission.

6. Ibid., p. 59. Used by permission.

7. For discussion of some previous efforts, see Frederick C. Mosher, ed., *Governmental Reorganization* (Indianapolis: Bobbs-Merrill, 1967); Dominic del Giudice and Charles Warren, *Reorganization by Presidential Plan* (Washington, D.C.: National Academy of Public Administration, April 1971); Harvey C. Mansfield, "Federal Executive Reorganization: Thirty Years of Experience," *Public Administration Review* 29, no. 4 (July-August 1969): 332–45.

8. For a discussion of President Nixon's proposals, see Douglas M. Fox, "The President's Proposals for Executive Reorganization: A Critique," *Public Administration Review* 33, no. 5 (September-October 1973): 401–6. For more background, see *Papers Relating to the President's Departmental Reorganization Proposal: A Reference Compilation* (Washington, D.C.: Government Printing Office, 1971); *Executive Reorganization: A Summary Analysis,* Eleventh Report by the Committee on Government Operations, House of Representatives (Washington, D.C.: Government Printing Office, 1972); and Fox, ed., "A Mini-Symposium, President Nixon's Proposals for Executive Reorganization," *Public Administration Review* 34, no. 5 (September-October 1974): 487–95.

9. For a description of the importance of clientele politics, see Peri E. Arnold, "Reorganization and Politics: A Reflection on the Adequacy of Administrative Theory," *Public Administration Review* 34, no. 3 (May-June 1974): 205–11.

History
of
Personnel
Management

A formal organization chart can be drawn so it is a precise and impressive diagram hanging on the wall. It does not truly represent the organization, however, until people — the flesh, blood, heart, and problems — are inserted into the neat squares. In a very real sense, organizational behavior, leadership, decision making, goal setting and policy formulation, ethics, responsibility — in fact, all administrative functions — are concerned with people and their behavior in organizations. This focus, combined with the fact that salaries and wages consume well over half of the financial resources of most public organizations, illustrates the importance of personnel management. The success of any public or private organization depends not only upon the quality of the employees, but also upon their motivation and commitment to the organization and its objectives.

Before discussing in succeeding chapters the specific personnel functions and the challenges posed by unionization and minorities, we will review briefly the historical foundation on which present personnel administration in the United States is based.

Phases of Personnel Management

Personnel management, like the whole field of public administration, has evolved over the years.[1] The theory and practice have been influenced by and modified in response to the changing perspectives of administration discussed in chapter 2 as well as the environmental changes discussed in chapter 3. It has evolved through four general historical periods — competency, spoils, reform, and post-reform — and is in the process of being reevaluated again in the 1970s.[2]

Although the periods are usually assigned dates, which vary with the author, these are offered simply to indicate a general time frame. As Frederick C. Mosher says, "clearly each began before the beginning date assigned, and the influence of none of these has yet ended."[3]

Period of Competency

During this phase, which lasted essentially through the administration of the first six presidents at the federal level, employees were selected primarily on the basis of ability or proven merit. Merit, however, had a particular meaning. It was not measured by competitive examinations but was defined in terms of (1) breeding — if the candidate came from an old aristocratic family, his or her traditions, upbringing, and values probably qualified the candidate to serve; (2) educational background — admission to a university indicated that the candidate was among the select few and graduation was evidence of capacity; and (3) status and prestige — success in a nonpublic career or profession demonstrated ability which could be transferred to the public sector. Merit, then, was based on an elitist concept, with no participation by the masses.

Although merit was the fundamental criteria, selection had some political overtones in terms of loyalty to the leadership and programs of the group in control of the executive branch of government. Even during this period, an elected leader would rarely select an outspoken opponent of his philosophy and program. The net effect was that from among the meritorious, the leadership selected those who were loyal and supportive.

When a new president was elected, the system was susceptible to complete political manipulation, since it was based on custom and not law. However, no president chose to break the merit principle. In order to influence governmental policy and direction, a new chief executive would replace a large percentage of those holding high-level decision-making and leadership positions with his own supporters. But, there was no mass removal of the appointees of the preceding presidents. Those below the top echelon were retained, which provided a cadre of experienced employees to provide continuity. Although political leadership was provided for, the idea of merit and a career service were retained.

A variety of explanations have been given for the evolution and perpetuation of such a system, and most are due to the environment of the time. Some of the specific reasons that made it possible would include the fact that political parties as we know them did not exist; government, which provided few public services and played a comparatively insignificant role in the daily lives of the people, was not very complex and had a simple administrative structure staffed by a limited number of people; a new nation was attempting to demonstrate that its system would work; and government service was prestigious and sought after.

Spoils System

The second period saw the introduction of the "spoils system" and a complete reversal of the earlier concept of merit and life-time careers for the mass of employees.[4] The motto became "To the victor belongs the spoils," which were government jobs as well as contracts and other favors government could bestow. In its most flagrant form, it meant that the winning political party had a monopoly on all government jobs. A newly elected chief executive — president, governor, mayor, board of supervisors — would fire most or all of the employees appointed by the preceding chief executive and replace them with members of his own political party. Party affiliation and not ability was the criteria for employment.

Although the spoils system had been practiced in some state and local jurisdictions for years, President Jackson is usually blamed for creating the climate for its introduction at the federal level in 1829. Jackson, whose election campaign had been built on the "cult of the common man," believed that administration was simple, required no special skills, could be performed by any intelligent person with good common sense, and that no person had property rights to a job. Under this philosophy, to have public positions filled by only members of the upper class was not only unnecessary, but it also violated the spirit of frontier democracy so important to President Jackson and his followers. Under his egalitarian philosophy, many lower-level employees were removed, but there were no mass dismissals, which were expected. Although there seems to be rather general agreement that the removals were accomplished on philosophical rather than purely political grounds, the precedent had been established. Succeeding presidents, using this philosophy and precedent, not only began to increase the numbers removed, but dismissals were also made for strictly political rather than philosophical reasons. Government jobs, the "spoils," became the payoff for the party faithful and the glue that held political machines together. By 1860, the spoils system, with rare exceptions, was entrenched at all levels of government in the United States.

The spoils system not only reduced the competency level of government employees, but resulted in some fantastic, innovative, and brazen ways of defrauding the government. Payoffs, kickbacks, bribery, misuse of public funds, and assorted other examples of graft and corruption were widespread and were often practiced by top officials. Government positions, contracts, and decisions often carried a price tag. The political machine, which was sustained by graft and the ability to deliver jobs to the party faithful, became an integral part of the political scene, especially at the state and local levels.

Reform Period

Although changes had been sought by a comparatively small group of civil service reformers for some time, the twin products of the spoils system — inefficiency and corruption — made reform much easier. However, as some have pointed out, inefficiency alone probably would have been insufficient to produce reform. The corruption and recurring scandals became a moral issue and "the moral argument for civil service reform soon caught hold in an

America that, at that time, thought largely in moral terms."[5] Reformers were able to muster the support of a morally offended and aroused public, which can be frightening to incumbent politicians.

In 1871, as a result of the pressure from the reinforced civil service reform movement, Congress authorized the beginning of a merit system which President Grant used to create a Civil Service Commission. In the following congressional elections (1872), the leadership of both the Democratic and Republican parties, translating this moral mood of the public into votes and election odds, included personnel reform as an item in their platforms. After the election, however, no fundamental changes were made in the system, and in 1873, Congress effectively killed the embryonic Civil Service Commission by failing to appropriate any money for its operation.

Subsequently, the reform issue which had been sustained by the dedicated reform groups was given added impetus in 1881, when President Garfield was assassinated by one who failed to receive a spoils position to which he thought he was entitled. The shock of this act aroused much of the previously uncommitted general public who now joined the reformers in their demand for a new personnel system. The product of the increased pressure was the passage of the Pendleton Act in 1882, which was signed into law by the president in 1883. This law became the basis for the present civil service system, creating the Civil Service Commission and instituting the concepts of selecting personnel on the basis of merit through competitive examinations. It provided for a politically neutral career service protected from removal for political reasons. However, because of the politics of the situation, the supporters of the legislation had to compromise in order to secure its passage. One of the compromises was that the law was not all-inclusive but applied to only approximately 10.5 percent of the federal employees. Nevertheless, the foot was in the door and the law did authorize presidents to extend the coverage of the merit system by executive decree. This grant of authority was to become the technique for future expansions of the merit system.

Reform was not confined to the federal level. Civil service reform groups had been active in fighting the spoils system in many states and in some local jurisdictions. The state organizations, which had formed into a national organization called the National Civil Service Reform League, supported the reform movement at the federal level. Actually, the bill that Senator Pendleton sponsored through Congress originated with the New York Civil Service Reform Association. Success at the federal level provided added impetus for the reform effort in the states.

Politics of Reform. The politics of change are always interesting. Why would federal legislators vote to adopt a merit system which would eliminate the spoils system which had provided the basic support for party organizations? In general, the fact that it was good practical politics, rather than some altruistic, ethical or moral consideration was the major motivating factor.

According to Van Riper, the Pendleton Act probably would have been passed even without the assassination of the president. At that time, the

Republican party, which had lost many seats in the congressional elections of 1882, thought that a Democratic president would be elected in 1884. Since the Republican president elected in 1880 had replaced the Democratic appointees of his predecessor with "good" Republicans, it made practical political sense to cover these Republicans with the merit, nonpartisan label so they could not be removed if a Democrat were elected. Consequently, the Republicans supported the passage of the Pendleton Act in 1882 to hedge against this possibility. Moral commitment or politics?

Extension of the merit system to cover more positions was also frequently made for political reasons. An outgoing president, realizing the great value of the merit system late in his term and especially after the November elections had produced a president from the opposition party, would issue an executive order "blanketing in" many previously exempt positions under the protection of the civil service. The party faithful then became a permanent part of the nonpartisan civil service, unless the incoming president removed the positions from coverage as permitted by the Pendleton Act, which most were reluctant to do. So, political expediency, even though some presidents did not like it, played an important part in the creation and expansion of the merit system.

This does not mean to imply that politics was the sole motivating factor for reform. Changing times and relationships were important influences. The increasing complexity of government required specialized talents; industrialization, efficiency, and the machine model made their impact; the number of employees had increased tremendously; and dispensing a large volume of jobs, which was always less than the number of claimants, created more conflict and enemies than benefits.

Post-reform Period

Since the merit principle was accepted, its orienting theme has varied with conditions.[6] As Mosher points out, initially it was morally oriented, with an emphasis on political neutrality of the bureaucrats and tight mechanisms to insure honesty. In the second period, which coincided with the scientific management phase in public administration, the basic theme was efficiency, which spawned position descriptions, position classification, work measurement, testing, and techniques for personnel evaluation. In the third period, largely due to the changed character of the role of government necessitated by the economic depression of the thirties, personnel administration shifted to a management theme. The emphasis shifted again, after World War II, to the professionalization of the public service.[7]

Professionalization of the Public Service. Education, expertise, and technical competence were not highly prized attributes for public employees during the spoils system period. In fact, throughout much of our history there was a reluctance to impose education and training requirements as a qualification for public employment. This attitude has changed.

Actually, the adoption of the merit system itself, by removing politics as a criteria for employment, might be considered to be the start of professionalizing the public service. Since that essentially negative action, positive steps have been taken to increase the technical and professional competence of employees. This new direction has been largely due to the changing environment and role of government in society rather than the influence of a widely accepted new philosophy. Government over the years has assumed administrative responsibility for a vast array of programs which require not only personnel with administrative expertise but also highly trained specialists in a variety of professional fields. This professionalization is evidenced in three major ways — the entrance qualifications for administrative generalists which now require a specified educational background; the increased emphasis on personnel training and development after employment; and the escalating number of individuals employed from the traditionally recognized professions such as law, engineering, medicine, social welfare, public health, accounting and others.

This increasing professionalization, and especially the last category of employees, has caused some concern:

1. There is a feeling that the professional may not be sensitive to the needs of some client groups, and especially the minorities and the socially and economically disadvantaged.
2. It appears that a professional elite, based on expertise and knowledge, is being created.
3. Since a professional enjoys the same orientation as others of the same profession, there is a danger that loyalty might be to the goals of that group rather than to those of the organization.
4. The desire of the members of a professional group to establish work standards, dictate personnel requirements for hiring, and administer their own programs can create conflicts with those responsible for overall operations as well as personnel administration.
5. Professionals may be given favored treatment. Since most professionals are selected on the basis of a review of their education and background, and not through the competitive examination process, the professional societies through their licensing procedures determine who is qualified.

There is every reason to believe that the professionalization trend will not decrease significantly, and it will be a continuing concern in the future.

The Present Personnel System

To talk about personnel management in the United States as though there were a single system is misleading. There are many systems tailored to fit the particular needs of each governmental jurisdiction as well as to accommodate the environment and political culture in which it operates. In most governments, personnel management is actually a hybrid system combining merit and politics in varying mixtures.

Merit Principles

As previously indicated, the definition of "merit" has evolved over the years. The merit principles, as defined by the Intergovernmental Personnel Act of 1970, are as follows:

1. Recruiting, selecting and advancing employees on the basis of their relative ability, knowledge, and skills, including open consideration of qualified applicants for initial appointment.
2. Providing equitable and adequate compensation.
3. Training employees, as needed, to assure high-quality performance.
4. Retaining employees on the basis of the adequacy of their performance, correcting inadequate performance, and separating employees whose inadequate performance cannot be corrected.
5. Assuring fair treatment of applicants and employees in all aspects of personnel administration without regard to political affiliation, race, color, national origin, sex, or religious creed and with proper regard for their private and constitutional rights as citizens.
6. Assuring that employees are protected against coercion for partisan political purposes and are prohibited from using their official authority for the purpose of interfering with or affecting the results of an election or a nomination for office.[8]

The above principles, then, should be included if a personnel system is based on merit.

Patronage Appointments

Patronage appointments are in keeping with democratic theory which assumes that a few political types in top leadership, policy making, and decision-making positions can influence the behavior of permanent career employees and make them responsive to changes in the political leadership. This is not only the justification for political appointments, but is also the logic behind the "short ballot" where only a few members of the executive branch are elected by popular vote. Because of this theory, every level of government exempts some positions from the career protection of the merit system. The positions are available for appointment by the incoming leadership.

There are, however, great variations in the number of positions filled by political appointees. The number ranges from a very few to a large percentage of the labor force, bordering on the old spoils system. Political machines, based on the ability to deliver government positions to the "faithful," still exist. The extent of political appointments, of course, is in inverse proportion to the status of the merit system in the jurisdiction. The mere existence of a comprehensive merit system does not guarantee that it will be enforced. If there is a dedicated will to violate the concept, it can be done in a variety of ways.

Merit Systems

Although the basic concepts are similar, there are many merit systems each with its own special peculiarities. Each level and, in some cases, units at the same level define merit in their own terms and create procedures for determining it, within the guidelines established by the constitution, charter, laws, and court decisions.

Federal Level.   At this level, there is not a single system, but a variety. In 1974, the number of employees covered by merit approached 100 percent, with only approximately 6,000 positions reserved for political appointees. Most of the positions were covered under the Civil Service Act administered by the U.S. Civil Service Commission and its regional and district offices. The remaining covered positions, exempt from these civil service requirements by law or the Civil Service Commission, are under the merit system of the Foreign Service, FBI, Atomic Energy Commission, Postal Service, and other agencies that are authorized to establish their own systems.

State and Local Level.   Although approximately 30 percent of the states did not have comprehensive merit systems in 1974, every state had some employees covered, because federal law requires that certain programs partially funded by federal money be administered by "merit employees."

At the local level, there is more variation in the systems. All cities over 250,000, except Washington, D.C., have a comprehensive civil service system. In addition, most cities between 100,000 and 250,000 have a system covering most or all employees. Smaller cities show a great variation with some having no system, some covering all employees, and others covering only specified groups such as police and firemen.[9] Counties have lagged behind the other levels in adopting the merit concept.

Challenges to the Merit System.   The concepts and procedures of the civil service system of the United States, thought to be one of the great contributions to public administration and copied by many nations, is under serious attack for a variety of reasons and from a number of sources. However, much of the problem is due to the lack of precision in terms and definitions. The words merit, merit principles, merit system, classified service, and civil service are often used interchangeably. The basic concept of merit — employing people on the basis of ability — is quite generally accepted, but the process and procedures — the system discussed in chapter 15 for determining merit for initial employment, retention, promotion, and other personnel decisions — is being challenged.

There is a growing general dissatisfaction among present employees, from those attempting to enter the service, from unions, minority groups, and the public at large. The general charges against the system include that (1) it affords too much protection to employees thus limiting opportunities to remove marginal employees;[10] (2) the system selects the best from among the worst;[11] (3) entrance tests have little, if any, correlation with success on the job; (4) that the proper techniques and procedures, rather than the end product — top-quality employees — has become the orienting theme of the personnel process. However, specific charges, which are having a major impact, are coming from principally two groups: minorities — including women — and unions.

Because of these challenges, the personnel systems, including merit, are being reevaluated at all levels of government. We discuss these pressures and changes in chapters 15, 16, and 17.

The Career Service

A merit system implies that people may make a career out of public service. In a career service, employees and employers have certain expectations.

Employee Expectations

Employees expect certain protections — all personnel actions based on ability, no discrimination on the basis of race, sex, national origin or religion, permanency of employment, and no removal for political reasons. In addition, they expect promotion opportunities, training opportunities, an adequate retirement system, decent pay, and more recently, a voice in setting policies that affect them, as discussed in chapter 16 on unionization. One of the historic concerns has been the pay system.

The Pay System. Again, as in the classification system, there may not be a single salary schedule. The federal government has a variety of scales keyed into the respective classification systems. Excluding the Executive Schedule, reserved for high-level political employees, there are three basic pay structures. First, the salaries assigned to positions under the General Schedule are set by law and apply worldwide. Second, agencies with their own classification system have separate pay scales set by law. Third, employees working as manual laborers or in the crafts area were traditionally paid under the Coordinated Federal Wage System, which had been introduced by Executive Order. In 1972, the Prevailing Rate System Act placed the wage system under statutory authority.[12] In addition, the coverage of the Federal Wage System was expanded to include approximately 70,000 employees paid from nonappropriated funds (NAF). These positions, whose salaries had been established by the employing agency, are primarily in military post exchanges and canteens operated by the Veterans Administration.

Under the "prevailing rate" system, the government matches the salaries paid for similar work by private employers in the specific geographic area, which means that the wages paid for similar work vary with the section of the country.

Pay Comparability. Should public employees, both salaried and hourly, be paid at the same level as their counterparts in private industry? While some say that public employees are overpaid, most people would agree that if governments are to compete successfully for quality talent, public salaries should be competitive with those paid comparable positions in private industry.[13] Nevertheless, the methods of setting salaries for federal white- and blue-collar workers have created problems.

Federal White-Collar Workers. As Raymond Jacobson says, "at the federal level the method of determining the salary of 'white collar' workers was a nonsystem of unstructured pay adjustment practices during the 1940s and 50s."[14] The president would periodically recommend a salary increase to Congress. Congress, if it thought the increase was justified and that it would not have any adverse political implications, would authorize it. The increase might be the same percentage for all employees, it might apply different rates to different groups, and it could exclude specified classes. In the process, pay scales were reevaluated infrequently, no prescribed procedures were followed, and public salaries lagged far behind those in the private sector. The pay lag, which was most noticeable at the middle and upper levels, made it difficult for the federal government to compete for managerial talent.

This problem as well as concern for the equity in the situation and pressure from employees led to a study of the pay structure in 1957. This committee report, which recommended pay comparability, encouraged further studies which reinforced the concept and began preliminary work on developing a general plan. After President Kennedy urged the adoption of the principle of pay comparability in his 1962 Budget Message, Congress passed the Federal Salary Reform Act of 1962 requiring pay comparability and establishing the machinery for its implementation.

The foundation of the plan is the basic data collected in the annual salary survey conducted by the U.S. Bureau of Labor Statistics. The survey compares the salaries paid to approximately eighty positions, representing the various levels of positions covered by the General Schedule, with that paid comparable white-collar positions in approximately 30,000 private organizations. The law also required that an agent, appointed by and responsible to the president, would analyze the data and make recommendations to the president. However, the president was not authorized to adjust salaries but had to present his recommendations to the Congress, where the proposed increases became political issues. The time-consuming political process meant that federal salaries usually lagged about eighteen months behind those paid in the private sector. This delay was attacked by the Federal Salary Reform Act of 1967 which specifically authorized the president to make salary adjustments, without congressional approval, in a series of stages designed to achieve full comparability by July, 1969.

As a result of pressure by the now more militant and unionized public employees, who were dissatisfied with the unilateral procedure and wanted a voice in salary setting, the Federal Pay Comparability Act was passed in 1970. The law retained the president's agent who is responsible for making recommendations, but it also created the Federal Employees Pay Council, consisting of five representatives of employee organizations, and an independent Advisory Committee on Federal Pay, consisting of three experts from outside government. The president's agent, working with the Pay Council representing employees and the Advisory Committee representing the public, makes the recommendation to the president who can implement the adjustments by executive action. Because of the simplified process, the law required that adjustments be made within six months after the survey, which reduced the previous eighteen-month time lag.

Federal Blue-Collar Workers. Although blue-collar workers are paid the rate which prevails in their labor area, pay comparability is still a problem. The procedure for maintaining comparability is separate from the system for white-collar workers. In 1972, soon after passage of the Prevailing Rate System Act, the Federal Advisory Committee Act which created the Federal Prevailing Rate Advisory Committee was passed.

Although the composition of the new committee is the same as that of the National Wage Policy Committee which preceded it, the organization and procedures were changed. The committee is composed of a representative from each of five federal agencies and five representing the major labor organizations. On the management side, the representatives include one from the Civil Service Commission and representatives from the agencies who are the largest users of this type of labor — one from the Veterans Administration, one from the Department of Defense and two rotated on a two-year basis among the Departments of Navy, Army, and Air Force.

This system for salary determination differs from that for white-collar workers in two major respects. First, the recommendations are implemented by the Civil Service Commission and not the president. Committee decisions, which are arrived at by consensus, are forwarded to the Bureau of Policies and Standards of the Civil Service Commission for implementation. In case of an impasse, the results of a formal vote, with supporting documents, are sent to the Civil Service Commission for a decision. The second difference is in procedures. Rather than the essentially consultative process used in the white-collar determinations, this is basically across-the-table labor-management relations conducted by representatives from these groups in the single committee. As Jean Stewart says, "what goes on in the Federal Prevailing Rate Advisory Committee may not be collective bargaining in a technical sense, but it is a close first cousin."[15]

State and Local Levels.   Most subnational governments have also theoretically adopted the concept of pay comparability. As at the federal level, the starting point is a salary survey. The survey usually collects data on the salary paid comparable positions in industry. Where there are no comparable private positions, the comparison will be made with similar institutions. For example, a city might compare positions with those in similar cities in its region, and likewise a school district with other school districts.

Limitations on Pay Comparability.   While pay comparability is an accepted principle, there are some limitations on its full implementation. Some of these are:

1. The emotional overtones. Some people view public employees as less productive than private employees and believe, therefore, that there should be a pay differential.
2. The large sums of money involved. A 1 percent salary increase does not sound like much, until it is converted into dollars. At the federal level, where the white-collar payroll is approximately 17.8 billion dollars, a 1 percent increase means around $178 million, plus the corresponding increase in fringe benefits. Moreover, since military pay is now tied in with the civilian pay scale, the impact of increases is intensified.
3. The political realities of the time. Since the cost of salary increases must be paid by the taxpayer, all legislative bodies are reluctant to grant increases — regardless of how justified they are — if such an action will necessitate a tax increase.
4. The absence of comparable jobs in the private sector can make meaningful comparisons difficult.
5. The ceilings imposed by the salaries paid to noncareer employees — elected officials, top political appointees. There is a great reluctance to authorize salaries for career employees that are higher than those paid the governor or the political appointees at the federal level.

Expectations of Government

Government not only expects dedicated loyal employees, but it also imposes restrictions on their activities. In addition to the prohibitions usually found against striking, employees are expected to be inactive in the political arena. At the federal level, we have attempted to insure their political neutrality by two major means. First, employees may not be coerced into making financial contributions to or working in a campaign for a political party. Second, employees and their immediate families are prohibited from engaging voluntarily in partisan political activities. Although there were previous regulations, the major prohibitions on federal employees were contained in the Hatch Political Activities Act of 1939.[16] Later amendments to the law extended its coverage to state and local employees working in all federally funded programs and to employees of private organizations working in specified programs funded by the federal Economic Opportunity Act. Workers may not become candidates for elective office but, in addition, they may not campaign for nor endorse a candidate, attend political meetings, speak on a political issue, nor in any other way be visibly active in political life at the federal, state, or local levels. About the only privilege they retain is the right to vote and to vote quietly. The federal prohibitions have disenfranchised millions of people and made employees second-class citizens in the political life of the nation.

In addition to the federal regulations, many state and local governments have legislated to prohibit partisan activity by career civil servants. The regulations vary in detail from extremely restrictive to fairly permissive.

The laws at all levels have been challenged in the courts as an infringement of the employees' civil rights — the right to assemble and to petition the government, but usually as a denial of freedom of speech.[17] The courts have declared some nonfederal laws unconstitutional, but the Hatch Act was upheld by the U.S. Supreme Court in 1973.

What will be the future of such laws? Although challenged in the past, the increased militancy, unionization, and desire for participation by employees will increase opposition to these laws. The opposition will probably take three forms — political participation, especially in local politics, through the creation of artificial nonpartisan parties composed solely of government employees in cities or areas where there is a large concentration of federal employees, continued challenges through the courts, and intensified pressure on legislative bodies to modify the laws. Since the first is a doubtful subterfuge and the second has had little success, the attempt to secure modifications in the laws would appear to be the most likely approach.

Conclusions

Personnel administration has evolved through a variety of phases in the United States. Actually it has come full circle from an initial merit system through political spoils back to the present merit system. Our system, the culmination of a long struggle to professionalize the career service, became a model which was adopted by many other nations. However, beginning in the 1960s and continuing into the 1970s, all aspects of American personnel administration, and especially the merit system on which it is based, have been under severe and sustained attack. Many groups, from both inside and outside government, insist that the historic merit system no longer meets the needs of society. The attack comes from inside government, as evidenced by the unionization of employees, and from outside, by groups who feel discriminated against. These challenges and their impact on personnel management will be discussed in chapters 15, 16, and 17.

NOTES

1. For a detailed discussion of the evolution of the system, see Paul P. Van Riper, *History of the United States Civil Service* (New York: Harper & Row, 1958).

2. Frederick C. Mosher divides the history into five periods: 1789–1829, Government by Gentlemen; 1829–83, Government by the Common Man; 1883–1906, Government by the Good; 1906–1937, Government by the Efficient; 1937–55, Government by the Administrators. See his *Democracy in the Public Service* (New York: Oxford University Press, 1968).

3. Ibid., p. 54. Used by permission.

4. This period is described in James D. Norris and Arthur H. Shaffer, eds., *Politics and Patronage in the Gilded Age* (Madison: State Historical Society of Wisconsin, 1970).

5. Felix A. Nigro and Lloyd G. Nigro, *Modern Public Administration*, 3rd ed. (New York: Harper & Row, 1973), p. 264. Used by permission.

6. For a discussion of these various phases, see Mosher, *Democracy in the Public Service*, pp. 53–98.

7. For a discussion of various aspects of professionalization, see Mosher, *Democracy in the Public Service*, chapter 4; for the characteristics of 28,000 federal executives, see "Characteristics of the Federal Executive," *Public Administration Review* 30, no. 2 (March-April 1970): 169–80; also Richard L. Chapman and Frederic N. Cleaveland, "The Changing Character of the Public Service and the Administrator of the 1980s," *Public Administration Review* 33, no. 4 (July-August 1973): 358–66; and David Garnham, "Foreign Service Elitism and U.S. Foreign Affairs," *Public Administration Review* 35, no. 1 (January-February 1975): 44–51.

8. For a list of these principles and specific examples of what some governments are doing to implement each one, see *On The Move: Personnel Systems Improvements in State and Local Government* (Washington, D.C.: U.S. Civil Service Commission, March 1974).

9. For a discussion of this level, see Albert H. Aronson, "Personnel Administration: The State and Local Picture," *Civil Service Journal* 13, no. 3 (January-March 1973): 37–42.

10. Enid F. Beaumont, "A Pivotal Point for the Merit System," *Public Administration Review* 34, no. 5 (September-October 1974): 426–30.

11. E.S. Saurs and Sigmund G. Ginsburg, "The Civil Service: A Meritless System?" *The Public Interest*, no. 32 (Summer 1973).

12. Public Law 92–392, 19 August 1972.

13. For a good discussion of comparability and its evolution at the federal level, see Raymond Jacobson, "Pay Comparability: How Comparable?" *Civil Service Journal* 14, no. 4 (April-June 1974): 9–12.

14. Ibid., p. 10.

15. Jean Stewart, "Advising the CSC on Blue-Collar Pay," *Civil Service Journal* 14, no. 4 (April-June 1974): 23.

16. Merit employees under systems other than the Classification Act are covered by separate legislation. For a discussion of the Hatch Act, see Philip L. Martin, "The Hatch Act in Court: Some Recent Developments," *Public Administration Review* 33, no. 5 (September-October 1973): 443–47.

17. For a discussion of some of the challenges, see Philip L. Martin, "The Hatch Act: The Current Movement for Reform," *Public Personnel Management* 3, no. 3 (May-June 1974): 180–84.

Personnel Management

15

From rather humble beginnings, the career civil service concept has evolved to its present status. Initially the effort at the federal, state, and local levels could be classified as a minimally funded, limited program aimed almost completely at preventing any political considerations from creeping back into the personnel process. Civil service commissions, relying on the extensive use of competitive examinations as the basic technique for keeping the "bad guys" out, served as watchdogs but provided few positive personnel services. The system has now evolved into a more positive process. Government is interested in actually doing something to enhance the quality of public employees, while still being conscious of the possibility of political interference. Positive "people management" under a merit system runs the full gamut of activities from recruiting employees to utilizing them to achieve the objectives of the organization until their employment is terminated by dismissal or retirement.

However, before discussing the specific functions of personnel management, we will look at the location of responsibility, constraints on the administrator, and the nature of those being managed.

Responsibility for Personnel Management

How the personnel function is structured will depend upon the size of the organization, geographic distribution, and the volume and complexity of the personnel transactions. In smaller units, such as cities, there may be a personnel officer with a limited staff or no staff at all to provide limited services, but most of the work in such a case is done by the operating units. In larger organizations, there will usually be a central personnel department with a professional staff, such as the U.S. Civil Service Commission. Some individual departments may be so large, complex, and geographically dispersed as to have their own professional personnel staff. In the larger organizations, the central department normally establishes guidelines and policies, develops tests, does position classification work, bargains with employee organizations, and may do centralized testing, recruitment, and training. Its primary function is to standardize and monitor procedures, which insures equality of treatment throughout the organization, permits transfers and promotions across departmental lines, and guards against political influence in the personnel process.

Most of the day-to-day personnel work is performed in the operating units. Here line supervisors — engineers, accountants, secretaries, administrative generalists, and so on — with little or no personnel training, are responsible for interviewing, hiring, motivating, evaluating, promoting, firing, and other aspects of personnel administration. This is the action level where formally prescribed regulations have to be interpreted and applied in a personal face-to-face situation. This is where the personnel process ceases to be a technical process. It is influenced by human judgment, feelings, personalities, impressions, value systems, and other subjective considerations.

Constraints on the System

The personnel function under a merit system, regardless of how it is organized, is a legalistic system surrounded by constitutional and charter provisions, laws and ordinances, executive orders, court decisions, and rules and regulations issued by central personnel departments, and also by compliance agencies responsible for enforcing the affirmative action programs for minorities and women. The legal framework, which injects some inflexibility into the system and may be narrowly interpreted to justify resistance to change, is intended to standardize the personnel process and achieve the objectives of the merit system, including the protection of employees and applicants. Moreover, if the prescribed procedures are not followed, such a failure may serve as the basis for a grievance or a court case.

Those Being Managed

The growing importance of government as an employer in the economy cannot be overemphasized.[1] In 1947, of the average of 43,881,000 people employed in the United States, 5,474,000 or approximately 12 percent worked for government. By 1974, the total number employed had risen to 78,334,000 of which 14,285,000 or approximately 18 percent worked for public agencies. These figures do not tell the complete story, however. Governments, for a variety of reasons, often use private individuals and organizations to provide consulting, research, management, and other services on a contractual, grant, or subsidy basis, for example, management of government research laboratories contract to universities, city trash collecting contracts with private companies, and highway construction. Technically, these people are not government employees, although the money for their salaries originates from a public agency. If these figures, which are not available, could be added, the total number paid from the public treasury would be much higher.

The distribution of the employees by level of government is important. While many people think of the federal government as the expanding giant, this is not the case. While the number employed by the federal government increased rather steadily from 1,892,000 in 1947 to 2,724,000 in 1974, the number of state and local employees jumped from 3,582,000 to 11,560,000 during the same period. In terms of employment, subnational government can be considered to be one of the fastest growth industries in the United States.

Unless the role of government changes and the level of services demanded by residents decreases drastically, the numbers will increase, making public employees an increasingly important factor in the economy and a more potent force on the labor scene.

The Public Labor Force

This public labor force represents the full range of talents from the unskilled to the highly skilled, from the minimally educated to the highly educated, and from the nonprofessional to the professional. The talents run the full gamut of the existing occupations. At the federal level in 1974, approximately one-half million were classified as "blue-collar" workers and the remainder as "white-collar."

Are these millions an elitist group selected from a narrow segment of society or are they representative of the total population? Since a person's background may influence his or her approach to problems and decision making, such questions are important in a democratic society where the bureaucracy has such an important impact on the general population. If the bureaucracy is to be responsive to and representative of the total population, it should closely mirror that population. This issue of a representative bureaucracy is discussed in chapter 17 on Equal Employment.

Personnel Functions

As Gerald E. Caiden says, "as every public employee has to be recruited, paid, trained, supplied with proper tools and working space, and generally serviced, personnel administration involves much more than routine salary administration. It spreads over into manpower planning, image building, motivation and morale, staff development, performance evaluation, conflict resolution, productivity, safety standards, work-place environment, health facilities and collective bargaining."[2] We will look at the major functions in four categories — position classification, employment process, post-employment activities, and unplanned events.

Position Classification

At some point in the history of every public organization, a position classification system — the basis for the personnel system — has been developed, While there are numerous approaches, the general starting point is examination of the thousands of individual positions. Each position and not the occupant of the position is analyzed to determine the duties, responsibilities, and level of difficulty as well as the experience, educational level, and special requirements an individual needs to fill the position.[3] The information is listed in the position description as assigned duties and in qualification standards, which indicate the qualifications an employee must have to fill the position.[4] All of the positions providing a similar service or using the same speciality are grouped into larger classes — Secretarial, Administrative Assistant, Engineer, Urban Planner. Based on the level of difficulty, responsibility, and personal requirements, the classes are subdivided — Administrative Assistant I, II, III or Accountant I, II, III, IV — and a pay grade with a minimum and maximum range is assigned to each level. Comparable positions in each class, regardless of organizational location, are assigned the same pay grade. Also, positions requiring the same education level and carrying similar responsibilities, regardless of the specializations — nursing, engineering, planning — should be assigned the same salary level. At the federal level, the techniques are the same, but the system is much more complex. Positions are grouped into larger and larger categories.

However, the federal government, like some state and local governments, does not have a single classification system for all employees. Although most employees are covered under the General Schedule (GS) administered by the Civic Service Commission, there is also an Executive Schedule for political appointees as well as special systems created by a variety of laws to meet the specialized needs of the Foreign Service, Central Intelligence Agency, Atomic Energy Commission, and other agencies. Regardless of the system, each follows the same general procedures in classifying employees and developing position descriptions.

Uses of Position Classification. Position classification is used for four purposes — recruitment, career ladders, pay standardization, and reclassification. The first use is to allow recruiting and testing for a large number of positions rather than by individual positions. For example, any large organization knows that due to resignations, promotions, and other reasons for turnover, it will have to hire a large number of people to fill the position of Clerk Typist I. Since the position description indicates the duties and the qualifications needed, large groups may be recruited, tested, put on the "eligible list" and made available for appointment throughout the organization over a designated period of time.

The second use is to indicate career ladders. Grouping of the classes in a series showing a hierarchy of positions provides an indication of the career ladder within each specialty — Secretary I, Secretary II, Administrative Secretary, Executive Secretary, or Urban Planner GS 5 through GS 15.

It is designed to guarantee "equal pay for equal work." To illustrate this point, the federal General Schedule (GS) is divided into eighteen grades, each with a minimum and maximum salary assigned to each. Positions requiring the same education, experience, and having the same degree of responsibility, regardless of the subject matter or organizational unit, will be assigned the same pay grade. A grade of GS 9, for example, will be assigned to comparable positions in nursing, engineering, administration, finance, and all other functional fields dispersed throughout the government.

Finally, position classification serves as a comparative benchmark for reclassification work, a continuous process. Since the characteristics and duties of positions change, they must be rather constantly monitored and audited to check the present duties against those included in the position description. What will be done if they differ will depend upon the legal provisions and the rigidity of the system. In many jurisdictions, there are several options. If the duties are less demanding than those specified, additional duties may always be added, nothing may be done, depending upon the circumstances, or the position might be reclassified downward, although this is actually done rather infrequently. If the duties of the position have expanded, some of them may be reassigned or the position may be reclassified to the next higher class — Administrative Assistant I to a II. If an employee is performing more complex and responsible duties than are required by the standards, the employee is working out of class, which may be the basis of a grievance.

The Employment Process

The employment process, which involves getting people on the payroll, includes recruitment, selection, and appointment. Since these activities supply the talent with which an organization must work, they are crucial. If the process works as it should, future personnel management problems will hopefully be reduced.

Recruitment. The recruitment process consists of making people aware of job opportunities and attempting to induce those who meet minimum qualifications to file an application. The recruiting techniques vary but may include the traditional announcements in professional journals for specialized positions, advertisements in newspapers, bulletin board announcements, direct contact with university placement offices, and direct mailing to organized groups.

However, it is not enough simply to announce openings, wait the required length of time, and test whoever happened to notice the announcements and wandered in — the method historically used by government. A positive program of "head hunting," which has been practiced in industry for years, is more important in the public sector for a couple of reasons. In the first place, public employment in general is less desirable to many people than private employment, which imposes a recruiting disadvantage. Although government employment is attractive during periods of economic depression or recession, in periods of full employment, the potential salary, working conditions, prestige, and status of private employment is higher than that of public employment in the minds of many people. Second, the recent emphasis on recruiting from minority and disadvantaged groups requires a special effort and technique. Such groups, often with little or no positive contact with public agencies and suspicious of government, are not recruitable through the traditional methods.

The federal government, as well as many state and local governments, are now using the activist, positive approach. Application forms and procedures are being simplified and made more intelligible; the time lag between application and employment is being reduced; testing methods are being reevaluated; examinations are being given at more frequent intervals or continuously; and women and minority groups are being given intensive attention.

Selection.   The selection process is a screening device to evaluate and rank those who meet the minimum qualifications contained in the job announcement. Depending upon the position being filled, the evaluative procedures may include performance tests, reference checks, evaluation of education and experience, and written and oral examinations — either singly or in various combinations. Most of these procedures are well accepted, but the written and oral interviews have some problems.

Written Examinations.   Written examinations, which are usually of the multiple-choice variety suitable for machine grading, may test achievement (can applicants perform the duties of the specific job for which they applied) or aptitude (what is an applicant's potential for learning, growth, and value to the organization in the future). The traditional written examination is under attack, however, as being discriminatory and totally unfair to ethnic minorities and other culturally and educationally disadvantaged groups (these challenges are discussed in chapter 17). The instructions and language of the tests emphasize the ability to read and discriminate between word meanings and are thus constructed to evaluate those with the traditional educational, cultural, and economic background. Minorities, often with less or inferior education, less experience with taking written examinations, less facility with the language and often raised in a subculture with a different set of values and a different sub-language, are at a competitive disadvantage. The examinations do not test their actual achievement, native mentality, or even aptitude. This charge of cultural bias has forced a reevaluation and analysis of the structure and language of written examinations.

Another challenge is based on the validity of the examinations. Considerable research indicates that there is little or no correlation between success on the examination and success on the job.

Oral Interview.   The oral examination may be used in conjunction with the written examination or as a supplement to the evaluation of an applicant's written record of training and experience. The purpose of an oral examination is to evaluate characteristics that are impossible to assess by a written test or records, but which are essential for the success of a person in dealing with colleagues on the job as well as with the public. These characteristics may include appearance, poise, verbal ability, thought processes, mental alertness, attitudes, concepts, sensitivity to others, or response to pressure. In the case of technical or professional positions, specific questions pertaining to education and experience may be asked to determine a person's competency as well as his or her personality traits.

While interviewing techniques will differ, questions may run the gamut from the straightforward, information-seeking type to veiled questions and loaded, hypothetical situations which attempt to elicit a response that will illustrate an applicant's grasp of the position, her or his sensitivity, sense of loyalty and fair play, value orientation, degree and quality of ambition, and other pertinent factors. The following example will illustrate the point.

> You are an applicant for the position of Assistant City Manager. The oral interview board consists of two city managers, one assistant city manager, a personnel director, and a university professor. One member of the panel poses this hypothetical situation to you: You are the assistant city manager. The mayor comes to you and says, "We want to get rid of the city manager. If you will help us by supplying us with some inside information on his activities, we will make you the city manager." What would you do?

The above is just a simple example of an almost endless variety of hypothetical questions that can make an applicant fairly uncomfortable. Just a simple, straightforward question like "Tell us why you want to enter the city management profession" can be difficult to answer without sounding like either the heavenly solution to all municipal problems or a money and power-hungry undesirable. Try answering it.

Like the written examination, the oral is being challenged principally on the basis that it is subjective. Each evaluator rates on the basis of his or her own experience, expectations, and value system. Some charge that the oral evaluation is not subject to proof and is susceptible to prejudice and bias, which is true. Evaluators, however, conscious of the possibility of bias, try to guard against it especially where a sex or minority bias could be charged.

Eligible Lists.   The names of those who survive whatever screening process is dictated by the particular government are placed on the appropriate eligible list or register in the order of their scores. A register, normally created for each class of positions, may remain active indefinitely or be cancelled after a stated period of time. These lists represent the available supply of qualified talent from which appointments may be made. In smaller agencies, the limited job opportunities and personnel turnover do not justify using eligible lists.

Appointment.   While the specialized central or departmental personnel office may do the screening and maintain the eligible lists, it does not make appointments. The operating departments, when a vacancy occurs, send requisitions on approved forms for a "person" to fill the position. How the personnel agency responds to this request will depend upon the laws or civil service regulations in force. At the federal level, following the "rule of three," the personnel agency sends over (certifies) the top three names on the proper list to the requesting department (other levels of government may certify other numbers). The department, usually after interviewing those certified, selects the person it will employ, with no legal compulsion to appoint the one with the top score. The names of those not hired are returned to the eligible list in their proper order.

Probation.   After appointment, the public employee enters the position in a probationary status, which should be considered as the final phase of the selection process. During the probationary period, which varies in length, the person's performance and behavior on the job are observed and evaluated at stated intervals. In most jurisdictions, a probationer has none of the job protections that apply to a permanent employee and can normally be terminated without any problems. In practice, the probationary period is usually not used as a final phase of the testing process as it was intended. Rarely is there a high mortality rate among probationary employees. Initial appointment in effect is permanent appointment. Some of the reasons for this include the normal human reluctance of a supervisor to deprive a person of a livelihood, the desire to give an employee the benefit of the doubt, inertia, unwillingness to make a decision, the feeling that the employee is a "nice person," friendships that develop, no terribly objective criteria for measuring performance in many positions or the fear of a discrimination charge where minorities and women are involved.

Permanent Appointment.   After an individual survives the probationary period, the provisional appointment becomes permanent. This is an important step because the status carries with it certain employee expectations, rights, and protections. The expectations include career concepts with training opportunities, promotion possibilities, transfers, and individual growth and retirement, to name a few. The protections will vary but usually include dismissal only for cause, accompanied by the right of a hearing and appeal.

Post-employment Functions

Although the employment procedures of recruitment, selection, and appointment are not totally routine, managing personnel within the organization is a more difficult task. It is complex because adult people, in all shapes, sizes, colors, and backgrounds, arrive in the organization with their own needs, value systems, expectations, personalities, and attitudes, which may or may not coincide with those of the organization. In short, "a new employee is not a blank sheet of paper on which the organization can write what it wills. There are definite limits on the ability of the organization to direct or influence his behavior."[5]

How does the personnel process of an organization attempt to influence behavior in order to mold the heterogeneous mass of humanity into a working team to accomplish the objectives of the organization with at least a tolerable level of conflict? Most of the activities can be discussed under some major headings — training, organization development, evaluation, promotion, and discipline.

Training.   In any organization, training is essential — whether it is "on the job" training or a program outside the organization. Both kinds of programs serve a variety of purposes, such as selling the organization and its objectives to employees; increasing the skills of employees in functional fields as well as in supervision, communication, human relations, leadership, and a variety of other areas, and opening channels for mobility and promotion which enhance the concept of a career service. Programs may range from orientation sessions for new employees up to high-level executive development and "retooling" operations.

Since middle and top managers create the working climate for an organization, executive development is an important element in a training program.[6] This development actually should focus on two groups — the middle manager and the top career executives. The first group is the middle managers who not only have current needs but who also will be the future top executives. As an individual moves up the promotion ladder into middle management, she or he becomes less and less an engineer, planner, or whatever the initial specialty was and becomes more and more an administrator. As the role changes so do the needs. The specialized technical knowledge is no longer adequate to meet the new responsibilities as leader, decision maker, coordinator, and "tone setter." Some method of identifying and training those approaching this role change in their career is essential. Such programs may be provided by specialized agencies, such as the federal training centers at Berkeley, California; Kings Point, New York; and Oak Ridge, Tennessee; through interagency training; by governmental training divisions; on university campuses; or in classes conducted by professional societies.

The other types of executive development is the "retooling" of high-level career administrators. These senior people, on the job for years and totally consumed by the duties of the position, have not had the time, opportunity, incentive and perhaps inclination to keep abreast of the changing concepts, theory, and practice of public administration. They are out-of-date, which creates problems for the organization in general and raises the frustration level of younger people who have recently graduated from universities or participated in intensive training experiences.

A variety of techniques ranging from long intensive weekend training sessions to governmentally funded educational leaves are being used to meet the needs of such senior employees. However, senior people, seeing less advantage to such training than a younger person on the rise, are reluctant to leave the job for any extended period of time. In an attempt to overcome this resistance, the federal government in 1968 created the Federal Executive Institute in Charlottesville, Virginia, where groups of senior executives (super grades GS 16 through 18) are sent for intensive eight-week training sessions conducted by a staff consisting of academic professionals on leave from their educational institutions and career government employees.[7]

Problems with Management Development. Although executive development programs are highly desirable, they do have a built-in frustration problem which is especially acute if only a limited number of people are singled out for such training. The employee, while attending a university or training center, acquires new ideas, concepts, techniques, and approaches. He or she gets excited and returns to the home agency ready to apply the hot new ideas which would improve the organization. The employee often finds that the organization is not really ready for these ideas. Fellow employees may not understand the ideas or changes proposed, may be less than interested in the ideas, and at best will be slow to restructure the organization or its procedures. There is no real communication of new ideas when the forces for the status quo are operative. The returnee is a stranger in his or her own organization, not understood, not listened to and frustrated because change is not easily effected.

Such a problem can be guarded against in smaller jurisdictions. One technique being used is the group technique. The county or city manager and all of the department heads will participate in a series of long weekend training sessions over the course of a year with outside resource people exploring topics of common interest. This technique at least exposes all top personnel to the concepts. If this exposure can be reinforced by succeeding sessions for middle managers, the chances of making an impact on an organization are improved — especially if the activity can be an annual affair.

Extent of Training.   While training of various types and comprehensiveness occurs at all levels of government, the federal government presently has the most highly developed organization and program directed by the various divisions of the U.S. Civil Service Commission.[8] However, many states, counties, and cities do have large, well-staffed training departments which conduct a wide variety of programs. To assist this subnational effort, the Intergovernmental Personnel Act of 1970 made federal money available to fund a variety of training and development programs; opened up avenues for temporary interchange of personnel; made federal training facilities available to state and local employees; created a mechanism for collecting, coordinating, and disseminating data on personnel administration; and developed procedures to assist state and local governments in improving their personnel systems and employees.[9]

Organization Development.   The concept of organization development (OD) is quite different from training. Traditional training focuses on improving employee skills to increase employees' efficiency and modify their attitudes so they can better fit into prescribed organizational roles. It ignored, however, the organizational framework within which the "changed" individuals had to return and function, which create the problems of receptivity discussed in the previous section. Organization development, on the other hand, approaches organizational and individual change as a package. It attempts to modify individual behavioral patterns, but at the same time to analyze and alter the organizational structure so it will be supportive of these new behavioral patterns. As Warren G. Bennis says, "Organization development (OD) is . . . a complex educational strategy intended to change the beliefs, attitudes, values and structure of organizations so that they can better adapt to new technologies, markets, and challenges, and the dizzying rate of change itself."[10] Organization development — especially the laboratory training aspects — does not reinforce prescribed roles, but attempts to alter behavior to force structural and procedural changes.

Organization development is often conducted by consultants from outside the organization and thus involves strategies for intervening in an organization to effect change. The targets may be building a more effective management team, improving communications, modifying individual behavior, increasing personal well-being, altering leadership patterns, securing attitudinal

changes, or any of a variety of other orientations. The strategies for intervention include a tremendous variety running from the comparatively simple to
the complex. The following examples will illustrate some of the techniques.[11]

Feedback. The simplest form of organization development is a system,
which may be structured in many ways, to feed information back into the
organization to influence the behavior of its members. Data may be collected
by structured questionnaires, open-ended questionnaires which encourage
written comments, personal and group interviews, observation, problem
census instruments, and a variety of other techniques. This information,
which might range from perception and feelings on organizational goals,
structure, and procedures to interpersonal relationships and personal feelings, is fed back to the group by the trainer. The value of this technique is
that by reflecting feelings, perception, and attitudes, it introduces formerly
suppressed data which force individuals to reassess their behavioral patterns in light of how they are perceived by others. At the same time, the
trainer tries to analyze the organizational environment.

Confrontation Sessions. Confrontation sessions, which go under other
names, are often used. The participant group may consist of only the top
management of an organization, the employees from all levels of a complete
department, department heads from all units, or a variety of other combinations. Although the strategies will vary, a common procedure is to divide the
group into small subgroups which spend a specified amount of time "brain-
storming" on the problems of the organization. Each problem is written on a
separate piece of paper. Back in a group session, all of these individual sheets
of paper are taped to the walls. The individual problems are then grouped
under major problem headings — such as leadership, decision making, group
relationships, and other categories which seem appropriate. The result is a
problem census which serves as the basis for "eyeball to eyeball" discussions
as to why perceived problems occurred, who or what was responsible for
creating the problems, and what can be done to alleviate the problems. As
the name implies, this is a confrontation, which can be uncomfortable for
all participants, since "leveling" (honestly putting your feelings out in the
open) is against our cultural pattern. Especially uncomfortable will be those
singled out as the principal creators of the problems.

Sensitivity Training. Sensitivity training, one of the early techniques, is
known by a variety of names — laboratory approach, encounter groups,
training groups (T-Groups), human dynamics groups, therapy for normals, and
"bod business," a name assigned to some of the groups that emphasize touch
and feel.[12] The technique, pioneered by Kurt Lewin and his staff at the
Research Center for Group Dynamics at MIT, served as the basis for the
formation of the National Training Laboratory (NTL), which offered its first
course in 1947.[13] Since then, the technique, with many variations and approaches, is now used by hundreds of groups across the country.

   Although there are many variations, T-Groups are usually constructed in
two ways. The first approach is the basic T-Group, composed of strangers, or
at least people who do not work together. The second type, variously referred

to as the variant T-Group, family group, core group, and action group, is composed of people who work together. The latter type of group, which might include personnel at all levels of a particular organization, department heads, or other combinations, is more threatening to the participants than the first type.

The theory behind sensitivity training is quite different from traditional training or education. While traditional approaches emphasize the rational aspects of man, the sensitivity style "takes man's emotional life as its central issue and seeks to determine how these emotions affect his relationships with others and his capacity for attaining high competence."[14] In the jargon of the profession, the objective is to "free up" the individual, which means getting participants to drop the traditional social mask we all carry and express their ideas, feelings, and impressions in an honest, open, and frank manner. The product should be individuals with changed behavioral patterns who will force structural and procedural changes upon their return to the organization.

To achieve these objectives, a variety of techniques may be used. T-Groups, which should function under the direction of a skilled leader, usually operate in an unstructured situation — unstructured in the sense that the group does not operate from an agenda or from defined tasks or goal statements. The group uses the "here and now" principle, taking what develops from the group as the information base.[15] The interchange or "feedback" process is an integral part of the program. The participants tell each other what they heard them say, how they felt about the statement, their reactions to the statements and behavior of other group members. In a sense, the feedback from others holds a mirror to a person and forces him to look at himself as others see him.

A variation of the type of sensitivity training discussed above is the encounter group. Whereas the sensitivity training conducted by most organizations probes emotions within limits, encounter groups operate with few restraints. The intent is to force individuals, by group pressure, to probe, expose and discuss their innermost true feelings — many of which may have been hidden for years — and to have those feelings discussed, challenged, criticized and attacked by the group. When the session — often structured as an around-the-clock exercise — is over, fundamental beliefs may have been challenged and most everyone has bluntly told a person how he or she "comes across" to them. Unless properly handled, this can be a destructive experience for a person with emotional problems and threatening to even very secure individuals.

Problems. Organization development is not a panacea for organizational problems. There are risks and problems involved.[16] Some of the problems include: (1) the absence of a commonly accepted theory of organizational development; (2) defining what change is needed; (3) determining how to measure the change impact the laboratory experience has had; (4) deciding how to sustain changed behavior once a trainee returns to the organization; and (5) assessing to what extent it is legitimate to engineer the social and behavioral change of individuals.

The Evaluation Process

The process of evaluation is an integral part of "people management." Employees at every level are constantly being evaluated, especially during the probationary period. As a supervisor — from first line to top management — a difficult responsibility is to evaluate and pass judgment on subordinates. Although supervisors observe, gather impressions, and make mental notes constantly, formal written evaluations occur only at stated intervals — usually quarterly for those on probation and annually for permanent employees. These written ratings become a permanent part of an employee's file, which grows in size over the years and becomes a case history which follows wherever the employee goes in the organization.

Supervisors develop their own personalized procedures for collecting data and evaluating personnel, but few enjoy the process. The process involves at least two people, the rater and the employee. After the supervisor has placed ratings on paper, the evaluation must be shown to and discussed with the employee, who also gets a copy. From this point, the specific procedures differ with the agencies. An employee does have the right to ask for a review by a higher authority and in some cases can appeal to a designated body outside the unit in which she or he is employed or file a grievance. Evaluation, then, is personal and not always pleasant.

Rating Factors. Each agency decides what factors are important and develops a form and procedure for eliciting the desired information from supervisors. In some cases, a supervisor simply checks the proper column with or without written comment, while others may be more "open-ended," requiring written, descriptive evaluations. There are basically three forms in use. One is a "trait" rating, in which theoretically desirable traits or employee characteristics — initiative, dependability, cooperativeness — are rated on some scale from unsatisfactory to outstanding. A second format, "performance rating," evaluates production rather than personality, with such items as "meets work norms," "fulfills assignments," "rate of errors" and other characteristics. A third form attempts to combine the key items from the above two.

Problems in Evaluation. The procedure of evaluation is complicated by the following:

1. There is a conflict between the theory of evaluation and the perceptions held by employees. The theory says that evaluations should be used as a basis for counseling employees to assist them in improving their performance and increasing their personal growth. Employees, on the other hand, do not usually view them in this positive way, but rather with some degree of apprehension, antagonism, and fear. They view ratings in terms of money, careers, and survival in the competitive personnel process.
2. The process is almost totally subjective rather than objective. The meaning of rating words is a good example. What is meant by "responsible," "cooperative," "satisfactory," and "superior"? Their meaning will depend upon the experience and value orientation of the rater.

3. The expectations of employees is also a hurdle. Since the selection and placement process theoretically demonstrated their competency, they not only do not expect an unsatisfactory rating, but also one of "satisfactory," "average," or "standard" is resented.
4. A supervisor is a human being with the same "hang-ups" as other humans. He or she understands the expectations of the employees and the career impact of the ratings, does not really enjoy explaining and justifying low ratings in face-to-face meetings with employees, is reluctant to get involved in the complex time-consuming grievance and appeals process, is conscious of the difficulty of defending against the charge of "racial bias" in the case of minority employees, and has a normal preference to be viewed as a "decent" person who is liked.

When an employee is clearly outstanding or unsatisfactory beyond a doubt, the rating process is comparatively simple. But what about the nice, cooperative individual who is not a visible "disaster" on the job, but whose performance borders on unsatisfactory? In general, and even during the probationary period when an employee theoretically has none of the protections, ratings tend to be on the high rather than the low side, because of the problems discussed in the preceding list. After the probationary period, it becomes even more difficult to rate a permanent employee "unsatisfactory," unless there is a solid case supported by evidence to prove the reason for the rating. In practice, the evaluation process usually removes few people from the career service. However, ratings do have an important impact on careers. Employees with average or standard ratings may find it difficult to go up the promotion ladder.

Promotion

Any public or private employee wants some idea of the potential of a position when accepting employment. Career chains or ladders are important incentives in attracting and retaining quality employees. But establishing the criteria for promotion is a difficult problem. The simplest and most completely objective way is to promote strictly on the basis of the length of service. Such a procedure assumes that an employee continues to learn on the job and becomes more competent and valuable in direct relation to seniority, which is not necessarily true. An employee may actually be a rather mediocre individual who "kept his nose clean," assumed the expected roles, didn't "rock the boat," and quietly accumulated years of service. When a vacancy occurs, this person would automatically move into the position. As can be seen, this system does not necessarily promote the best-qualified candidate, but it also may create a couple of other characteristics in the organization.

First, it favors conservatism. After a number of years in an organization, an individual becomes organizationally socialized. The employee has internalized the values of the organization, often has lost contact with the outside world, has a tremendous time investment in the organization, and has learned the fine art of compromising and "getting along." With such a background, these senior individuals cannot be expected to be active innovators challenging an organization and its procedures which have developed over the years. The second aspect of a strict seniority system is the possibility of an age conflict, a serious obstacle to organizational effectiveness. Young, sharp, and often idealistic employees not only cannot understand the reluctance to experiment and innovate among senior employees but also see their promotion path clogged with these more senior people. On the other hand, the more senior leaders, responsible for the welfare and survival of the organization, often resent the young activists for a variety of logical and illogical reasons. This resentment may be due to an emotional threat that the younger employees represent; honest differences in orientation, opinion, and background; sensitivity to the fact that seniority and age are often equated automatically with obsolescence and mediocrity; and a belief that the younger employees often push too hard for too much without understanding the political process or the tender art of compromise and the trade-offs necessary to accomplish what is possible under the conditions that exist at any given time.

If seniority is not the basis for promotion, what is the alternative? The one most frequently advanced is merit, a wonderful word which is acceptable to most people. A system for objectively defining and measuring this commodity among candidates is not so easily agreed upon. One possible approach is a competitive examination administered to all those who meet the minimum qualifications. The names of successful candidates can be placed on an eligible register for screening and appointment as positions open. However, there are the problems of constructing a suitable test and deciding whether to assign government experience any weight in compiling the final score.

The federal government, struggling with the criteria problem, has been operating under a new system, or systems, since 1969. Each agency, within guidelines issued by the Civil Service Commission, is required to develop its own promotion plan. The general standards are designed to insure as wide a pool of talent as possible. Seniority is to be used as a ranking factor only where it is of demonstrated validity and written promotion exams are to be used only with the advance approval of the Civil Service Commission. However, for the so-called super grades (GS 16–18), the Executive Assignment System has been created. Under this system, the Bureau of Executive Manpower of the Civil Service Commission has compiled a list of names of employees in these grades plus qualified people outside the government. As top positions open in the various agencies, this is the qualified list from which appointments are made.

Discipline

Every organization has a right to discipline employees for unacceptable conduct. Discipline may range from an informal, parental conversation to dismissal. Any formal action — suspension, demotion, or dismissal — which affects the rights or status of a permanent career employee is regulated. Laws, civil service rules and regulations, and in some cases union contracts carefully prescribe the legitimate reasons for formal action, the procedures that must be followed, and the rights of the employees.

The question of dismissal is an especially difficult problem. How to balance the need of an organization to rid itself of incompetent employees and at the same time protect "merit" employees from the capricious whims of supervisors is a touchy area. At most levels of government—especially the federal level — there is a whole complex series of hearings and appeals an employee may use.[17] Such appellate provisions serve as a deterrent to hasty administrative action. The administrative time involved in preparing for an appearing at the hearings, when combined with the difficulty of documenting valid reasons for dismissal, forces a supervisor to think seriously before initiating the process. In fact, the protections make dismissals less frequent than they probably should be for the good of the public service. In the case of the out-and-out demonstrably incompetent, there is usually no problem. In the much more common cases of the marginally effective person, most supervisors will tolerate such individuals rather than activate the protection machinery available to the employee.

Unplanned Events

While most of the personnel management activities we have talked about are difficult, they are comparatively formalized, with prescribed and accepted procedures. The topic of this section is those events which are not scheduled nor covered by regulations, procedures, and manuals. They are spontaneous occurrences that supervisors face daily. Some examples of these activties are:

1. The reclassification problem: An employee is hired into a position as a Clerk-Typist I. Over the course of two years, new duties and responsibilities accrue to the position. The employee asks that the position be reclassified to a Clerk-Typist II level. This involves studying the job to see if the duties have indeed expanded sufficiently to meet the higher class standards prescribed by the personnel agency. If it does not, the employee is unhappy. If it does, it not only creates problems on how to fund the salary increase but also creates demands for reclassification by many other employees.

2. The space problem: Few government agencies have adequate, let alone desirable, space in which to work. They are usually overcrowded and often squeezed into dilapidated buildings constructed as temporary facilities during World War II. Under such conditions, simply squeezing people closer together in an already inadequate space to make room for new employees disturbs the physical scene and can create headaches for an administrator. In addition to just the logistics of "shoe horning" people in, there may be much importance attached to location in the general work area, alignment of desks, nearness to a window, proximity to an individual's assistant, the need to have a window in an office, and the status of a private office.

3. Interpersonal conflicts can make for interesting situations. Most large organizations have a cross section of personalities and styles. Working in close proximity, this heterogeneous mass is certain to generate conflicts between individuals and sometimes among groups. These conflicts are

often triggered by incidents which might seem trivial, but the administrator may be forced to become a referee or broker. Consider, for example, the problem of a highly skilled, permanent employee who has the office in a turmoil because of chronic "griping."

4. The grievance procedure can also be an unanticipated demand. In spite of how good an operation is, there will always be formal grievances. The procedures are specified but processing each one is a time-consuming and delicate process.

5. Motivation, counseling, and guidance are other duties. Many books have been written on each of these topics. Every supervisor is destined to spend a considerable amount of time in these activities.

Conclusions

This chapter has discussed the "human fuel" of an organization. It presents an overview of the people and the personnel process, all the while recognizing that there is not a single system, but only some general concepts which different governmental units adapt to fit their particular needs. The professional personnel administrators will be found in the central personnel offices which provide varying degrees of service to the operating units. However, in actual practice, the bulk of personnel management is done by on-the-job supervisors, most of whom have had no formal personnel training. In the final analysis, few employees have much, if any, contact with the personnel office after testing and selection. An employee's personnel manager is his or her supervisor. Supervisors or managers are often surprised at the amount of time consumed in dealing with the human needs, emotions, and problems of individuals, as well as the tension and conflicts created by individual personalities in the organization. There is often a tendency to resent this time, but it is an important part of the management process.

NOTES

1. Figures in this section are taken from *Monthly Labor Review* 98, no. 4 (April 1975): 97.

2. Gerald E. Caiden, *The Dynamics of Public Administration: Guidelines to Current Transformations in Theory and Practice* (New York: Holt, Rinehart, & Winston, 1971), p. 211.

3. For a succinct description of the purposes and techniques of job analysis, see U.S. Civil Service Commission, Bureau of Intergovernmental Personnel Programs, *Job Analysis, Key to Better Management* (Washington, D.C.: Government Printing Office, September 1973).

4. Such standards are usually dated and published in a loose-leaf format so that new or revised standards can be easily inserted in a ring binder. For a detailed description of position classification and standards at the federal level, see U.S. Civil Service Commission, Bureau of Policies and Procedures, *Position Classification Standards for the General Schedule (GS)* (Washington, D.C.: Government Printing Office, 1970). For a suggested simplified method of keeping descriptions current, see Carl F. Lutz, "Efficient Maintenance of the Classification Plan," *Public Personnel Management* 2, no. 4 (July–August 1973): 232–41.

5. Herbert A. Simon, Donald W. Smithburg, and Victor A. Thompson, *Public Administration* (New York: Alfred A. Knopf 1950), p. 78. Used by permission.

6. For a discussion of Executive Development, see U.S. Civil Service Commission, Bureau of Executive Manpower, *Executive Manpower in the Federal Service,* March 1973 (Washington: Government Printing Office, 1973). Also, Raymond Pomerleau, "Management Development in the Federal Service," *Public Personnel Management* 3, no. 1 (January-February 1974): 23–27.

7. For a description of the concept, direction, and offering for fiscal year 1975 by the Institute director, see Chester A. Newland, "The Federal Executive Institute," *Civil Service Journal* 14, no. 3 (January-March 1974): 10–15.

8. Much of this activity was generated as a result of the report of the Task Force on Career Advancement. For the report, see *Investment for Tomorrow: A Report of the President's Task Force on Career Advancement* (Washington, D.C.: Government Printing Office, 1967). The recommendations were implemented by President Johnson's Executive Order 11348 of April 20, 1967.

9. For a list of the courses available to federal, state, and local officials under the Intergovernmental Personnel Act, see U.S. Civil Service Commission, Bureau of Training, *Interagency Training, Catalog of Coures, 1973–1975* (Washington, D.C.: Government Printing Office, Pamphlet T–9, July 1973).

10. Reprinted by special permission from *ORGANIZATION DEVELOPMENT: Its Nature, Origins, and Prospects* by Warren G. Bennis, Addison-Wesley Publishing Company, Inc. Copyright ©1969. All rights reserved.

11. For a summary of other intervention strategies, such as team building, multi-team building, trans-team building, organizational mirror, deep sensing, force field analysis, and others, see Larry Kirkhart and Orion F. White, Jr., "The Future of Organization Development," *Public Administration Review* 34, no. 2 (March-April 1974): 129–40; and for a more detailed discussion, see Richard Beckhard, *Organization Development: Strategies and Models* (Reading, Mass.: Addison-Wesley, 1970).

12. For the history of T-Groups, see Leland P. Bradford, "Biography of an Institution," *Journal of Applied Behavioral Science* 3, no. 2 (1967): 127–43; and Leland Bradford, Jack R. Gibb, and Kenneth D. Beene, eds., *T-Group Theory and Laboratory Method: Innovation and Reeducation* (New York: John Wiley, 1964).

13. For background on the National Training Laboratory, see Alfred J. Marrow, "Events Leading to the Establishment of the National Training Laboratories," *Journal of Applied Behavioral Science* 3, no. 2 (1967): 144–50.

14. Reprinted by special permission from *ORGANIZATION DEVELOPMENT: Its Nature, Origins, and Prospects* by Warren G. Bennis, Addison-Wesley Publishing Company, Inc. Copyright ©1969. All rights reserved.

15. For a description of one method, see Neely Gardner, "Action Training and Research: Something Old and Something New," *Public Administration Review* 34, no. 2 (March-April 1974): 106–15.

16. For some of the problems, see Robert T. Golembiewski, "The Laboratory Approach to Organization Change: Schema of a Method," *Public Administration Review* 27, no. 3 (September 1967): 211–21; Bennis, *Organization Development;* Larry Kirkhart and Orin F. White, Jr., "The Future of Organization Development," *Public Administration Review* 34, no. 2 (March-April 1974): 129–40.

17. For a diagram and discussion of the present and proposed modifications in the federal appeals procedure, see *Civil Service Journal* 13, no. 4 (April-June 1973): 4–9.

16

Unionization and Collective Bargaining

In the preceding chapters, we discussed the history and basic ingredients of a personnel system. In the 1970s, the traditional methods of managing human resources are changing rapidly. People do not fit the traditional stereotype of the satisfied and docile public bureaucrat any longer. Their thought processes, expectations, and reactions have changed. Public employees, including white-collar and professional employees, have become disenchanted, alienated, and unhappy with the system of public personnel administration and feel discriminated against. While this is not necessarily new, the extent of their militancy, belligerency, and techniques for expressing displeasure is a recent development.

Personnel management is no longer a simple process in which personnel agencies, professional personnel people, and supervisors apply unilaterally determined policies and procedures with every expectation that they will be accepted by employees and the public with little, if any, comment and no organized opposition. The merit system — philosophy, organization, objectives, procedures, and results — is being challenged by forces and groups from inside and outside the government.

This change, however, should not have come as a surprise. The environment in which government and administration function (discussed in chapter 3) has changed drastically. The concept of bureaucratic organizations with all their dehumanizing aspects is being challenged; the worth, personal growth, and importance of individuals have achieved new importance; and

241

laws, police, traditions, and all other forms of authority — including bureaucratic — are being challenged. The public employee, the bureaucrat, is a part
of that culture and has reacted accordingly.

The most readily visible manifestation of these changes is unionization,
which represents a challenge to the personnel system, decision-making process, and authority structure from inside the organization.

History of Unionization

Gus Tyler, assistant president of the International Ladies' Garment Workers
and a labor authority, divided the labor movement into three segments. "The
first period, from 1900 to the mid-1930's, reflected the unionization of the
skilled craftsmen; the second, from the mid-1950's saw the rise of the semi
and unskilled in mass manufacture; the third, which started with the mid-
1960's, voices the aspirations of the white-collar and service-economy employee very heavily engaged in public employment."[1]

The union movement in the private sector has had a turbulent history in
the United States. In the 1930s, the right of private employees to unionize and
bargain collectively was recognized and legitimized by law.[2] Since then, the
process has undergone rather constant refinement and modification, but
unions and collective bargaining are accepted and powerful components of
the private sector.

It has been a different story for public employees. Although public employee unions have existed for years, especially at the federal level in ship-
yards, arsenals, and other industrial type enterprises, government resisted
the legalization of unions and collective bargaining for other types of employees. The primary basis used to justify this opposition was a broad interpretation of the concept of sovereignty. This doctrine historically meant that
government could do no wrong, unilaterally decided on any commitments
it would make, could not be sued without its consent, and possessed a
variety of other privileges. If workers were permitted to share in the decision-
making process through collective bargaining, the freedom and discretion of
government to legislate on all personnel matters would be reduced and its
sovereignty compromised. Therefore, public unions with the right to bargain
collectively were either prohibited by law or ruled against in the courts,
at all levels of government. This legal barrier was made possible and reinforced by public and employee attitudes, which can be summarized as
follows:

1. Unionization was against the popular ethic. When an individual accepted
   a government position, he or she accepted the role of the "public servant,"
   which dictated that the person become a dedicated, loyal, anonymous
   individual willing to accept the salary and working conditions imposed
   by government. Public employment was a privilege, not a right. The public
   attitude was that employees, who were probably overpaid anyway, were
   ungrateful if they wanted to unionize.
2. Public employees, in general, accepted this master-servant relationship.
   Emotionally and psychologically they were reluctant to challenge their
   government. This was especially true of white-collar and professional em-

ployees, who comprised a major portion of the labor force. Professionals, historic joiners of their respective professional societies and associations, thought it was unprofessional, unethical, and degrading to join a true union that frankly subscribed to traditional union objectives. Joining a union was for expendable "blue-collar" workers who had no other job opportunities and needed such group leverage.

3. The advent of "employee associations" created obstacles in some cases. These associations, formed by a particular group of employees at a specific level, were not affiliated with any of the nationwide industrial-type unions. While some of them had sufficient members to have some "clout," associations in many organizations were small, isolated, and essentially "in-house," company-type organizations with no "muscle." Government, by dealing with them, delayed attempts to unionize the labor force.

As a result of these legal and attitudinal obstacles, the unionization of public employees sputtered along with spotty success. Although activities were intensified during and immediately after World War II, unionization made little progress during the 1950s at the federal level and even less at the state and local levels.

Current Legal Status

Due to pressures from employees and the changing environment, governments have been forced to modify their opposition to the unionization of their labor force. Like other changes within the federal system, there are great differences among the various levels of government.

Federal Level. Although unionization had been debated and studied by previous commissions, the major turning point came with the election of John F. Kennedy as president. Soon after his election, he appointed the President's Task Force on Employee-Management Relations in the Federal Service.[3] Based upon the committee report, President Kennedy issued Executive Order 10988 in January, 1962. This order officially recognized all unions as legitimate for the first time, provided machinery for voting on exclusive bargaining units, authorized negotiated written agreements or letters of understanding and other provisions. This "foot in the legal door," which unions had been seeking for years, was used as a basis for extensive unionization effort.

The experience under the order was reevaluated during the Johnson and Nixon administrations. Although no basic changes were made by President Johnson, President Nixon issued Executive Order 11491.[4] This order was again amended by Executive Order 11616 in 1969.[5] The resultant policies, which apply to most employees, are as follows:

1. The activity is frankly designated as labor-management relations rather than the earlier title of employee-management cooperation.
2. Organizations are frankly called labor organizations rather than employee organizations.
3. Employees may voluntarily have union dues automatically deducted from their checks, with the written consent of the employer; but union mem-

bership cannot be a condition of employment.

4. A labor organization which receives a majority of the employee vote in a unit becomes the exclusive employee representative in the negotiation process.

5. Government and labor representatives are required to "meet and confer" in good faith on personnel policies and working conditions (within limits discussed below) and execute negotiated written agreements or memoranda of understanding.

6. Accepted conduct for labor and management is prescribed with certain unfair practices prohibited to both sides.[6]

7. The position of Assistant Secretary of Labor for Labor-Management Relations was created.

8. The Labor Relations Council, which will develop major policy guidelines and procedures and hear appeals from the Assistant Secretary of Labor for Labor-Management Relations, was established.

9. Machinery and procedures to process negotiations and appeals and to resolve negotiation impasses now exist.[7]

What does it mean? It means fundamental changes in federal personnel administration in two ways. First, personnel policies and decisions are no longer handed down by edict. The management of human resources is now a bilateral process with meaningful participation by employees or their representative as an established right. Second, the concept of "third party" has been inserted into the process. If negotiated agreements cannot be reached, employees no longer have ultimately to give in to the weight of management but may utilize arbitration, mediation, and fact finding by someone outside of their agency to settle the impasse.[8]

However, unions of federal employees are still less powerful than their counterparts in the private sector for three major reasons. First, the authority for public unions is based on Executive Orders, and not on federal laws, which limits access to the courts as a final decision maker. Second, many areas, such as salaries, budgets, fringe benefits, and some aspects of working conditions, are not subject to negotiation.[9] However, employee organizations do make inputs on salary decisions through membership on the Federal Employee Pay Council and the Prevailing Rate Advisory Committee, discussed in the preceding chapter. Finally, public employees are denied the ultimate weapon, the right to strike.

State Level. In contrast to the federal level, the state labor scene is characterized by confusion and wide diversity. As would be expected, each of the fifty states has responded to the attitudes and conditions in its environment. Although many study groups and task forces, including the Federal Advisory Commission on Intergovernmental Relations and the task force on State and Local Labor Relations of the Governor's Conference, have recommended that states legislate to formalize labor-management relations, the states have been slow to respond. At the end of 1970, forty states had authorized some form of union organization, eight had no legislation, and two prohibited unions.[10] Of the forty, some had comprehensive legislation covering most state or local employees or both, but others covered only selected groups of employees; some require or authorize collective bargaining, others specify a "meet and confer" situation; and some have created machinery for regularizing labor-management relations, while others have not. Since 1970, additional states have legislated either comprehensive plans or covered specific groups such as police, firefighters, and teachers.[11] However, some states have gone farther than the federal government in granting public unions comparability with those in the private sector, including the right to strike for most groups, excluding police and firefighters.

Local Level.   Local policy makers — city councils, boards of supervisors, school boards, boards of special districts — have been more reluctant than state legislatures to make provisions for negotiating with representatives of unions. The reasons for this posture include both local and statewide factors.

First, on the local scene, in some cases there seems to be a feeling of disbelief that unionization of public employees is really occurring, that it is here to stay, and that it will make any significant changes in the way things have been done in the past.[12] Second, many have had experience in dealing with the older style, and as yet semi-cooperative, employee associations. This experience has given some a sense of security, which might prove to be an illusion in future negotiations with militant groups represented by professional, experienced, and highly skilled negotiators. Third, although some local units are fortunate to have experienced negotiators on their staffs, many have none, which could create some hesitancy to move actively into the labor-management relations area. Local units which have entered the area have handled the problem in a variety of ways. In some cases, negotiations have been assigned to the personnel director or assistant director, who may or may not be prepared for the job. In other cases, labor-management relations is simply assigned as an additional duty to some "lucky" individual, who knows little or nothing about it, but most agencies contract the negotiating work out to experienced and skilled people on a consulting basis.[13]

However, this lack of action is often not the choice of local officials but rather is dictated by the state. In some cases, certain groups may lobby legislation through the legislature to provide statewide coverage of items normally covered by bargaining — wages, professional qualifications, fringe benefits, work week. These topics then are not subject to local bargaining. In other states, laws permit unionization only by specified groups. In addition, sometimes there is ambiguity in procedures which creates "gray areas" where local units do not know what is expected or legal.

Union Reaction to Current Status.   Unions have two basic concerns — the refusal of some states to legalize unionization, including collective bargaining or "meet and confer," and the lack of uniformity among the existing state and local legislation. Such conditions create problems for nationwide unions. They are unable to develop a standard package but have to tailor each action to fit the peculiarities of a variety of laws, which adds to the cost and complexity of the negotiating process.

To surmount these obstacles, different groups have proposed different solutions. Some organizations, like the Advisory Commission on Intergovernmental Relations, have proposed a uniform model law that should be adopted by each state. Some unions insist that the only solution is federal legislation which would impose a uniform system of unionization and bargaining on state and local governments. Unions have been successful in getting such legislation introduced into Congress. In 1973 and 1974, three bills were given major attention. H. R. 9730 was proposed to amend the National Labor Relations Act, which governs labor relations in the private sector, to include the previously excluded state and local employees. Two other bills (H.R. 8677 and S 3294: The National Public Employment Relations Act) were sponsored by the newly formed Confederation of American Public Employees, a coalition of the American Federation of State, County, and Municipal Employees (700,000 members), the National Education Association (1,100,000 members), and the U.S. Treasury Union (40,000 members). The Public Employment Relations Act would have imposed nationwide standards for collective bargaining, granted other union goals including the right to strike, set up national enforcement machinery, and superseded state and local laws, except those that were substantially equivalent to the federal law.

Such proposed legislation, of course, immediately becomes an intense political issue, involving contests for power as well as constitutional issues. Some unions and employee associations, established at the state and local level and not affiliated with a national union, saw the proposed laws as threats to their power, influence, and existence. State and local governments see such proposals as an invasion of areas reserved to them under the federal form of government. A variety of groups who oppose such laws, including some unions and subnational governments, argued that it would destroy the merit system by making some rights now protected by civil service regulations subject to negotiation.

What was the outcome? In 1974, Congress did not enact either bill into law. It did, however, succeed in amending the Fair Labor Standards Act, initially passed in 1938, to include state and local employees. While this law, which applies mainly to wages, hours and working conditions, was much less than some unions hoped for, state and local governments see it as the forerunner of more detailed control in the future. Because of this perceived threat, organizations such as the National League of Cities, leagues of cities in the various states, the U.S. Conference of Mayors, as well as associations of state governments, state attorney generals, supervisors, and other interested groups are resisting the change. In late 1974, a court case challenging the constitutionality of the legislation was filed.[14] If the challenge is successful, it will preclude or at least delay the passage of more comprehensive legislation such as the proposed National Public Employment Relations Act.

Union Membership

The changing labor scene — legitimization of unions and the changing attitudes of public employees — caused the number joining unions to skyrocket. In 1956, when the U.S. Bureau of Labor Statistics started indicating union membership by industry, a total of 915,000 public employees at all levels belonged to unions. The number had increased to 1.2 million by 1962 and 2.2 million by 1968. The trend is even more startling if the figures are compared with those in the private sector. As a percentage of the total union membership, public employees increased from 5.1 percent in 1956 to 10.7 percent in 1968. During this 1956–68 period, union membership in the private sector increased approximately 5 percent while public unions increased by a startling 135.5 percent. However, to provide perspective, it should be pointed out that the number of public employees increased 45 percent over the period — from 8.4 million in 1960 to 12.2 in 1969.

At the federal level, the liberalized policy encouraged unions to launch an intensive organizing effort, which produced impressive membership results during the 1960s. By 1968, 1.4 million federal employees had joined unions. However, the rapid pace could not be maintained. The latest report, for November, 1973, indicates that a continued leveling off in organizing activity and step-up in the number and coverage of negotiated agreements were the major trends in federal employee labor relations for 1973.[15] The slowdown in the rate of growth was probably due to the smaller numbers of employees left to organize (and they are the ones less interested in unionization), plus the desire of the unions to consolidate their gains before expanding their membership.

The shift in union emphasis from organizing to consolidation in 1973 is indicated by two factors — the number of exclusive bargaining units and the number of negotiated agreements.[16] The number of exclusive units (a majority of the workers voted for a specific union to represent them) in the nonpostal service increased by 94 to 3,486 as of November, 1973. But the "dramatic gains in 1973 came in number and coverage of negotiated agreements. Bargaining activity produced 210 new agreements bringing the total up 12 percent to 1,904 (compared with a 3 percent rise in 1972)."[17] In 1973, such negotiated exclusive union agreements covered 1,086,361 nonpostal employees, compared with 1,082,587 in 1972, and 614,554 postal employees, up from 604,660 in 1972. In percentages of the work force, these figures represent an increase from 54 percent of the nonpostal workers in 1972 to 56 percent in 1973; for postal workers, although the numbers increased, the percentage covered dropped from 91 to 89 percent, due to an increase in the number of workers.

Total and accurate membership figures for unions at the state and local levels, unlike the federal level, are not compiled. However, based on a sample survey, the U.S. Bureau of Labor Statistics estimated that a majority of the workers in the 2,064 cities of over 10,000 populations were union members in 1972. In total numbers, the U.S. Bureau of Labor Statistics estimated that more than three million state and local employees belonged to unions or employee associations in 1973.[18] In addition to this, many cities apparently bargain but issue the results in the form of personnel regulations, executive orders, and ordinances without any indication that employee representatives participated in the decisions.

Actual union membership is only part of the picture, for two major reasons. In the first place, additional thousands of public employees are members of a wide variety of professional associations which, although they may have the same general objectives as unions, are not technically unions and are not included in the above figures. While no accurate membership figure is available, estimates for professional associations alone range from 2 to 2.5 million.

A second factor is that a simple head count does not tell the whole story. Although employees are not forced to join a union to retain their positions, a union recognized as the representative for a unit bargains for all workers, both union and nonunion. A specific union, then, often represents a much larger number and its bargaining strength is far greater than its actual paid membership.

Who joins unions? Historically unions depended on the blue-collar workers for their support. One of the more significant aspects of the recent union movement has been the changed attitude of the white-collar worker. In the 1960s, the general disenchantment with conditions induced these formerly individualistic employees to seek redress through group activity. They joined unions by the thousands and became the major source of new members. In November, 1973, of the nonpostal workers, 47 percent (681,406) of all white-collar federal workers were in exclusive units, compared with 84 percent (404,955) of the blue-collar workers. The same phenomenon has occurred at the subnational levels where the white-collar workers, such as teachers, social workers, paramilitary, and others, have been the major source of new recruits.

Reasons for Unionization

Why would public servants, historically a comparatively docile, conforming, and nonaggressive group, embrace unions and their traditional methodology?[19] The reasons are complex, but they include:

1. Unions in the private sector have produced and are producing visible, impressive gains for employees. So why should public employees refrain from unionizing, take what government wants to give them, and go lower on the comparative economic ladder?
2. It could be a part of the national mood in which militancy, although not encouraged, is condoned and gets government action.
3. A dissatisfaction with the system which employees feel cannot be corrected by individuals. A limited number of dissenters or "boat rockers" can be isolated and dealt with individually, but the personnel of an entire organization provides safety in numbers.
4. The changing attitude of personnel, especially professionals, has moved them to express their desire to participate in decision making. Since blue-collar workers had been organized earlier, much of the new thrust came from this group.
5. The increased number of government employees and the recognition that public servants comprise a major segment of the total labor force may have fueled the militancy.
6. The increasing number of public employees, combined with the few pools of unorganized groups left in the private sector, induced union organizers to focus their efforts on this essentially untapped pool of potential members.

Objectives of Unions

While the specific objectives of unions are varied, the fundamental goal is to force modifications in the unilateral paternalism of the traditional personnel system. The system, historically, provided no role for the employee, but was paternalistic and dictated everything — position descriptions, qualification requirements, promotion policy, salaries, dismissal procedures, working conditions, protections, and all other policies. Unilateral action is no longer acceptable. Employees want some voice in making the decisions that affect them.

One of the problems for the government in responding to this change is that different organized groups may have different objectives. In general, the nonprofessionals are primarily interested in salary, hours, working conditions, job security, and other items traditionally included as topics for bargaining in the private sector. Professional groups, on the other hand, want to expand this basic list to include items such as career ladders and professional development, participation in policy making, instituting professional norms in their relationship with the clients they serve, and control over work loads, to name a few. For example, in the world of higher education, professors, in addition to concerns over economic questions, want a voice in determining faculty-student ratios, teaching loads, leave policy, procedures for making faculty input into university decision making, tenure, and other personnel policies.

Where bargaining is legal, the traditional economic issues are normally legitimate topics. The additional topics professionals want to include as bargainable items are often considered to be the prerogatives of legislative bodies or management and are resisted.

Tactics of Unions

Although individual public employees are usually prohibited from actively engaging in partisan politics, their unions are very active. They have adopted and refined the techniques which proved successful for private unions and other pressure groups. The techniques include hiring full-time professional lobbyists, creating political action committees, accumulating and using large sums of money for political activities, publicizing the voting records of legislators, endorsing candidates, making campaign contributions, using public relations firms to present their case to the public, mounting letter-writing campaigns, conducting classes to educate employees on the political process and how to become an activist in the system, and a variety of other techniques.[20]

As a result of these political tactics, public employee unions are an important force in the political process. The key elements in a successful political campaign are money and votes, both of which the unions have in abundance. By using this leverage they can help to elect legislators and executives sympathetic to their cause and defeat opponents. Under our political system, those whom employees helped to elect are expected to vote for the programs that will benefit employees — wages, fringe benefits, working conditions, legalization of collective bargaining where it does not exist, and legitimating the right to strike. Incumbent politicians, knowing that employees, especially at the state and local levels, represent an important voting block, are inclined to listen to their demands.

However, elected legislators and executives are not the only ones involved in the labor-management process. While the legislative bodies usually establish the general framework and may have to approve the final settlement, the face-to-face negotiations occur between union representatives and the bureaucrats, such as city managers, personnel directors, directors of employee relations, and others assigned by the organization.

Negotiating Techniques

Over the years, a variety of techniques have been developed for reaching labor-management agreements. The major ones, excluding strikes which indicate that negotiations have failed, are bargaining, mediation, fact finding and compulsory arbitration.

Bargaining is the normal starting, and often ending point, in negotiations. In the bargaining process, representatives of labor and management meet face-to-face across a bargaining table to attempt to arrive at an agreement. This is not an ad hoc procedure, but rather a formalized process. Usually the first issues put on the bargaining table are the rules and regulations which spell out in detail the membership of the bargaining teams and the procedures which will be used. This initial item can be a very controversial issue. After procedures have been agreed to, the bargaining on issues begins. The tactics are fairly predictable. Each side will present its initial package — demands by labor and offers by management — which each knows is simply the unrealistic opening ploy which will be unacceptable to the other. Each initial package will contain "trade goods" which can be sacrificed either as concessions to show good faith or in return for something from the other side. In many succeeding meetings, each of the contestants will modify their positions until a compromise solution can be reached. In the process, neither side can be destroyed; each must have won some concessions. This is important because the representatives of the respective sides have to answer to their groups who have certain expectations. A representative who does not secure a solution close to the group's expectations will be replaced; and the acceptability of the bargaining process will suffer.

Although many agreements are reached through bargaining, somtimes an impasse — the inability to reach an agreement — develops. Settling an impasse requires that a "third party" be injected into the negotiations to break the deadlock. There are three commonly used procedures — mediation, fact finding, and compulsory or binding arbitration.

In mediation, a skilled, impartial third party (the mediator) analyzes the issues, problems, and positions of the parties and suggests ways to come to a compromise agreement. The mediator, however, serves as a broker to find some middle ground acceptable to both sides but has no authority to impose a settlement. Many states and the federal government authorize this technique and often create a special mediation service to provide assistance — the Mediation and Conciliation Service at the federal level is an example.

Fact finding, like mediation, is still a part of the bargaining process, but is a little more public. The usual procedure is to appoint a fact-finding panel consisting of one member chosen by labor, one by management, and the third chosen by the other two. After evaluating all of the data, and possibly holding public hearings, the panel makes written recommendations which do not have to be accepted. However, since the recommendations are made public by the fact-finding panel, the parties to the dispute are under some public pressure to accept the recommended solution.

Compulsory (or binding) arbitration, unlike those above, is not a recommendation but a dictated settlement.[21] The negotiation deadlock or impasse is submitted to an outside arbitrator or panel whose decision must be accepted by labor and management. Two types of arbitration may be used. In the older type, the arbitrator is free to negotiate with both sides in an attempt to secure concessions which will lead to a compromise settlement acceptable to both sides. In the newer form, called final-offer arbitration, the compromise procedure is not acceptable. The arbitrator is required to analyze the final offer made by each of the contestants and accept one of them as the recommended solution, without modifying it in any way. The theory is that each side, knowing that negotiations are prohibited and that unrealistic proposals will be rejected, will encourage management to propose more acceptable offers and labor more reasonable demands.

In the future, the accepted negotiating techniques will continue. Arbitration, in some form, will probably be required as a substitute for the strike as a method of resolving impasses in the public sector. The ultimate weapon, when all other techniques fail, is the strike.

The Strike Question

The ultimate union weapon in collective bargaining is the power to shut the operation down by pulling the labor force out on strike. Such an action, with its attendant loss of income and risks, is not taken lightly, but the knowledge that a strike is a possibility has an important influence on the decision-making process of managers in the collective bargaining process. In the private sector, unions, after many years of struggle and some bloody confrontations, won the right to strike, which is legally guaranteed, defined, and regulated. Public employees, however, are in a different category and many are not happy about it.

Legality of Strikes

Historically, the public strike question was rarely addressed by laws, but the courts had applied the common law concepts and declared them illegal. After the war-time measures imposed on labor were lifted at the end of World War II, labor unrest, strikes, and work stoppages by public employees triggered the passage of a whole series of antistrike legislation at all levels of government.

The antistrike movement at the federal level was reflected in 1947 by a provision in the Taft-Hartley Act which punished strikers by immediate dismissal, forfeiture of all civil service rights, and a prohibition against rehiring for three years. In 1955, this was thought to be too soft and was

replaced by a law (84—330) which made it a felony — not misdemeanor —
to strike or advocate the right to do so. The penalty was no longer simply
dismissal, but a criminal prosecution with a maximum potential penalty of
a fine of $1,000 or prison for one year and a day, or both.

Many states also added antistrike laws after World War II. While there
is no uniform pattern, most of them prohibit strikes not only by state employees, but by workers in the local governmental subdivisions as well.
However, these laws were not as severe as the federal statute. Threat of dismissal, rather than criminal prosecution, was the usual sanction relied upon
to force compliance by individual workers. In some cases, fines may be
levied against the union treasury for each day a strike continues and fines
and jail terms may be imposed on union officers.

In 1974 strikes by public employees were still illegal in most governmental
jurisdictions in the United States, except in a few states where a limited
right to strike has been authorized.

Reasons for Antistrike Laws

There are some basic arguments which are often used to justify prohibiting
strikes, but the unions have a response to each. The arguments go as follows:

1. *Government* — a strike violates the concept of sovereignty. Since government is a banding together of people to serve mankind, a strike against
   government is a strike against the people. Hence it is immoral, a breach of
   faith, unacceptable and un-American.
   Union — this is nonsense. Strikes would not encroach upon a reasonable
   interpretation of sovereignty. Also, the word "freedom," which is an
   equally important word, would guarantee the public workers the same
   freedom in employment as employees in the private sector.
2. *Government* — public employment is different from private employment.
   It is essential, more crucial, and cannot be discontinued.
   Union — this is some form of fictional nonsense used to create an artificial
   barrier. With the exception of police and fire employees, which are in a
   different category, how do government jobs differ in importance from
   those in the private sector? Which is more important, a city worker collecting rubbish or an employee of a private company collecting the same
   rubbish on contract, a Streets Department employee laying concrete or a
   worker doing the same work for a private contractor, a city or private
   public utility worker, and so on?
3. *Government* — public agencies do not operate within the same economic
   framework as the private sector. In the private sector, the cost of increases
   in salaries and fringe benefits can be passed on to the consumer, but governments lack this flexibility.
   Union — there are practical limitations, such as available income, limitations on the taxes people should be asked to pay, differing claims on
   limited resources, and political factors, which realistic people will accept.
   But the public should be expected to pay for the product, which is service,
   in the same way that they pay for all products delivered by the private
   sector. In the allocation of limited resources, public employees should
   not receive what is left after all other demands have been met.

In summary, public employees can see no reason why the right to strike — the ultimate weapon — has been guaranteed to private employees for years but denied to public employees. The situation is that one side says, "strikes against the public cannot be tolerated!" and the other side replies, "why not?"[22]

Results of Antistrike Laws

The results of antistrike laws are difficult to evaluate. Their existence may have served as a deterrent to some groups that were tempted to strike. The threat of imposing sanctions may also have shortened some strikes. Nevertheless, it is clear that antistrike laws have not prevented strikes even where severe sanctions such as loss of job, fines, and jail terms were possible. While the federal employees, with a few exceptions, have honored the strike ban, the same is not true at the state and local levels.[23] Nationwide there has been work stoppages by a variety of groups including police officers, firefighters, social workers, refuse collectors, public works employees, and teachers. Strikes are no longer reserved for blue-collar workers and lower echelons, but para-military and professional employees have joined the ranks.

In addition to the frank strike, other groups, either in an attempt to avoid sanctions or because of a moral question associated with the word "strike," have used a variety of "nonstrike" techniques to reinforce their demands or to indicate their displeasure. Some of the techniques have been rather innovative. The so-called blue flu, where most or many members of an organization call in sick, has been used. Police officers in some cities, suddenly tiring of being the "heavy," refuse to issue traffic tickets, which not only creates shock among the populace, but also considerably reduces the municipal revenue. The medical staffs of some public hospitals have conducted "heal-ins" by retaining patients longer than normal in the interest of good medicine, but which effectively packed the medical facilities and jammed the admission channels. "Slowdowns," following all of the time-consuming procedures to the letter, and a variety of other tactics have been used.

Are Strikes Successful?

In general, most strikes by public employees, even though illegal, have been effective. In addition to the economic and other demands, strikers usually insist as a part of the settlement that no punitive action be taken against the strikers. In most cases where a strike involves the mass of a labor force, and not just a few dissidents, the unions have achieved part or all of their demands. In some cases, union leaders have been fined or jailed in an attempt to force them to order their members back to work, but the general union membership has benefitted.

The Failure of Antistrike Laws

Rigid enforcement of the antistrike laws is difficult for a variety of reasons. The first obstacle is the numbers involved. Any law is made for the few who will not voluntarily conform to the accepted rules of the game. If a law is considered unfair by a large segment of the population, enforcement becomes extremely difficult. In dealing with 1,000 striking police officers, thousands of teachers or postal workers, prosecution would create fantastic mechanical problems for the already overloaded courts, as well as tarnishing the image of government as a model employer.

A second problem is that of finding qualified replacements, if the law requires the dismissal of all strikers. Qualified staff in large numbers cannot be recruited quickly, if at all, and the agency experience cannot be replaced. For example, if a county discharges all of its nurses or social welfare workers, what happens to the immediate and future programs of the organization? Or, how does a school system replace 3,000 secondary teachers who strike on the opening day of school in September?

A third factor, which will probably become more important as unionization progresses, is the danger of a corollary or supportive strike. In these early phases of the unionization effort, only a segment or portion of the membership of a union may strike and sometimes in defiance of the union leadership. If government retaliates against the strikers, it may run the risk of the whole union "going out" in support of its endangered members. A companion aspect is that other unions, including those in the private sector, may come to the support of their brethren by refusing to cross a picket line to provide services.

Future Strike Questions

Unless things change drastically, the strike question will undoubtedly be a central issue in labor-management relations for quite some time to come.

Unions, reflecting the changed attitude of their membership and the positive results of strikes, will intensify their efforts to secure the legalization of strikes, or "withdrawal of service" as some groups still prefer to label it. A good indication of this mood is the growing list of unions that publicly claim the right to strike, who have removed the no-strike pledge from their constitutions, and who have increased dues to create a special political fund to be used in an effort to secure legislation legalizing strikes.

Faced with this rather belligerent attitude some state governments have legalized strikes for some employees and under certain conditions. However, the federal government and most states will probably continue their resistance to sanctioning strikes.[24] If they do continue to make strikes illegal, past experience indicates that strikes will continue and possibly increase in number. The chairman of the U.S. Civil Service Commission summarized the problem when he said, "I acknowledge the claim of unions for a better balance of power with public employers, because otherwise they are, as they rightfully claim, limited in impact at the bargaining table. There has to be developed an acceptable substitute for the strike."[25]

Implications of Unionization

Unionization will have a very important impact on the merit system, personnel procedures, and public administration in general.[26] A more central issue raised by unionization is the problem of balancing the rights and wishes of the tax-paying public, as expressed through its elected representatives, with the rights of employees. Within this general issue, there are some specific problems raised by unionization.

One problem is the combination of economic and political bargaining which creates a situation quite different from collective bargaining in the private sector. In the private sector, bargaining is between labor and representatives of the board of directors, who are elected by the stockholders and not the workers. In the public sector, labor not only helps choose the policy-making groups — Congress, legislature, city council, and so on — but also is a potent political force in elections, especially at the state and local level. As a result, unions have no qualms about using both economic and political leverage. As a result, while union negotiators are bargaining with management, they may also be attempting to subvert the process by going directly to the legislative body for action. For management, this is not a comfortable situation.

The financial implications of unionization are important. There is concern that public unions, as has often happened in the private sector, will push for their own financial objectives with little or inadequate concern for the public interest. The tax burden could increase drastically.[27]

Budgetary procedures would be modified. Since salary levels would no longer be what the system dictates, any negotiated increases would have to be included in the budgetary requests submitted by the managers. Because of this, liaison between managers and the legislative bodies would also have to be close.[28] The legislative body must be willing to appropriate the money needed to fund a salary increase negotiated and agreed to between management and labor.

The Effect of Unionization on the Merit System

There is considerable disagreement as to the impact unionization will have on the merit system. Some argue that it will destroy it, while others say that this is nonsense. Part of the disagreement is due to the loose usage of the terms "merit" and "merit system." As David T. Stanley points out, there are basic differences between the concepts. He says that the merit principle means that "public employees are recruited, selected and advanced under conditions of political neutrality, equal opportunity and competition on the basis of merit and competence."[29] On the other hand, the merit system refers to the rather elaborate personnel management procedures which have developed to implement personnel concepts, including merit.

Those who argue that unionization and bargaining will be detrimental usually combine the two concepts. They see unions, through collective bargaining, being in a position to insist on modifications not only in the definition of merit, but also in the techniques of measuring and evaluating it. They fear that, in the process, the historic practice of hiring, advancing, and retaining the most qualified will be compromised. These opponents also worry that most of the personnel procedures, now determined by management, will become subject to negotiations with labor.

Unions, on the other hand, say they have no quarrel with the merit principle. In fact, they argue that they have been one group resisting the extension of patronage appointments. The merit system — the mechanism — is a different matter. As Jerry Wurf, president of the American Federation of State, County, and Municipal Employees Union says, "the civil service or merit system is first, second, and finally, management's personnel tool."[30] He continues by saying that "however well-intentioned public management may be, it cannot unilaterally devise a merit system that will provide objective, third party treatment for public employees."[31]

Unionization and collective bargaining will bring modification in four principle areas. First, although unions believe in the principle of merit, they want some voice in how merit is defined and measured. They will be interested in looking at the requirements used to determine merit — education, experience, height, strength — to insure that they are legitimate. Second, collective bargaining will replace the historic unilateral setting of salaries, fringe benefits, and working conditions by laws and civil service commission regulations. Decision making in these areas will become a cooperative process, with authoritative participation by employee representatives, and the list of items subject to bargaining will probably be expanded. Third, the uniformity, neatness, and standardized treatment of personnel is endangered. The distinguishing characteristic of civil service policies has been standardized selection, promotion, transfer, pay grades, and protections that apply uniformly to most classes of employees regardless of their specialty, agency, or place of employment. In the competitive bargaining process, each union will be attempting to get the best possible deal for its members in order to justify its existence and to recruit new members. Due to differences in size, power, importance, and prestige of unions, it will be extremely difficult to maintain uniform treatment for personnel. Fourth, the role, functions, and importance of Civil Service Commissions will probably decrease. As more topics become legitimate for bargaining and as special machinery is created to handle labor-management problems, as has been done at the federal level, these functions will be removed from Commission control.

Conclusions

The changing expectations and attitudes of public employees have been one of the important changes in the environment of public administration. This attitudinal change is most visibly expressed by the unionization movement, which came as a shock to many legislative bodies and public managers. Unionization and collective bargaining in themselves are extremely controversial issues in public administration. When the topic of the right to strike is added, the battle is joined. While many jurisdictions have legalized collective bargaining, and a few the limited right to strike, most governments are resisting legitimizing the general right to strike in every political and legal way possible. On the other hand, unions can be expected to continue their drive to get collective bargaining and the right to strike legalized, preferably through federal legislation on a nationwide basis.

Regardless of the long-range outcome, unions have forced significant changes in personnel management at all levels of government. Even where unions are not recognized, the possibility of unionization may have had some impact on the attitudes of managers in the personnel process. Also, unions of public employees are here to stay. Learning to live with them and to accommodate them in the public administration system will be a continuing challenge. In the next few years, this process of accommodation will be characterized by tension, experimentation, trial and error, and fundamental changes in the historic roles assigned to policy makers, executives, managers, supervisors, and workers in our system of public management.

NOTES

1. Gus Tyler, "Why They Organize," *Public Administration Review* 33, no. 2 (March-April 1972): 98.

2. At the federal level the major legislation which specifically exempted public employees was the National Labor Relations Act (Wagner Act) of 1935.

3. For the product of this task force, see *A Policy for Employee-Management Cooperation in the Public Service* (Washington, D.C.: Government Printing Office, November 1961).

4. The order was based on recommendations of a study committee appointed in 1969 and chaired by Robert E. Hampton, chairman of the U.S. Civil Service Commission. *Report, and Recommendations on Labor-Management Relations in the Federal Service* (Washington, D.C.: U.S. Civil Service Commission, October 1969).

5. For details of the order, see U.S. Civil Service Commission, Office of Labor-Management Relations, *Labor-Management Relations in the Public Service, Executive Order 11491 as Amended* (Washington, D.C.: Government Printing Office, 1972).

6. For the code of conduct, see *Guide to Standards of Conduct for Federal Employee Unions under Executive Order 11491* (Washington, D.C.: U.S. Department of Labor, 1973).

7. For a report of the activities, see *Decisions and Reports of the Assistant Secretary for Labor-Management Relations* (Washington, D.C.: Department of Labor, 1972).

8. For a discussion of some of the procedures, see William J. Kilberg, Thomas Angelo and Lawrence Lorber, "Grievance and Arbitration Patterns in the Federal Service," *Monthly Labor Review* (November 1972), pp. 23–30. For a larger discussion of the roles and procedures at the federal level, see Paul Prason and others, *Scope of Bargaining in the Public Sector* (Washington, D.C.: Government Printing Office, 1972).

9. For some of the logic for these limitations as well as the need for some reevaluation by the chairman of the U.S. Civil Service Commission, see Robert E. Hampton, "Unionism and the Public Employee," *Civil Service Journal* 14, no. 3 (January–March 1974): 5–9.

10. For a discussion of the status in the states, see *Monthly Labor Review,* January 1971; also the January issue of the *Monthly Labor Review* reviews all labor legislation for the preceding year.

11. For a listing of agencies, see U.S. Department of Labor, Labor Relations Information Exchange, *A Directory of Public Employment Relations Boards and Agencies, A Guide to the Administrative Machinery for the Conduct of Public Employee-Management Relations Within the States* (Washington, D.C.: Government Printing Office, November 1971).

12. For the union impact on local government see David T. Stanley, *Managing Local Government Under Union Pressure* (Washington, D.C.: Brookings Institution, 1972). Also, Harry H. Wellington and Ralph K. Winter, *The Unions and the Cities* (Washington, D.C.: Brookings Institution, 1971); Robert H. Connery and William V. Farr, eds., *Unionization of Municipal Employees,* Proceedings of the Academy of Political Science, 30, no. 2 (December 1970); and Felix A. Nigro, "Labor Relations in State and Local Governments," *Personnel Administration* 33, no. 6 (November-December 1970): 34–38.

13. For some of the city experience, see Richard R. Nelson and James L. Doster, "City Employee Representation and Bargaining Policies," *Monthly Labor Review* (November 1972): 43–50.

14. During World War II, the War Labor Board ruled against extending the act to cover public employees, but at a later date in *Maryland* v. *Wirtz*, 20 L. Bd. 2d. 1020, the U.S. Supreme Court ruled that extending it to schools, hospitals, and other narrowly defined enterprises was valid.

15. Kathryn Ryder Hobbie, "Spotlight on Labor Relations," *U.S. Civil Service Journal* 14, no. 4 (April–June 1974): 13. Data for this section taken from same source.

16. For a discussion of exclusive agreements, see Anthony F. Ingrassia, "The Maturing Federal Labor-Management Relationship," *Civil Service Journal* 12, no. 4 (April–June 1973): 6–10; also for a listing of the agencies, see U.S. Civil Service Commission, Office of Labor-Management Relations, *Union Recognition in the Federal Government*, November 1973 (Washington, D.C.: Government Printing Office, 1974).

17. Hobbie, "Spotlight on Labor Relations," p. 13.

18. The fastest growing union is the American Federation of State, County, and Municipal Employees (AFSCME), an AFL-CIO affiliate, which claimed a membership of 700,000 in late 1974.

19. For a discussion on the reasons, see Louis V. Imundo, Jr., "Why Federal Government Employees Join Unions: A Study of AFGE Local 916," *Public Personnel Management* 2, no. 1 (January–February 1973): 23–28.

20. A good example of the educational program is the Public Employees Organized to Promote Legislative Equality (PEOPLE) program of AFSCME.

21. For a discussion of the problems, variations, and experiences under compulsory arbitration, see Karl A. Van Asselt, "Impasse Resolution," *Public Administration Review* 32, no. 2 (March–April 1972): 114–19. For a case study, see Fred Whitney, "Final Offer Arbitration: The Indianapolis Experience," *Monthly Labor Review* 96, no. 5 (May 1973): 20–25; and for another experience, see James L. Stern, "Final Offer Arbitration — Initial Experience in Wisconsin," *Monthly Labor Review* 97, no. 9 (September 1974): 39–43.

22. For an analysis of the disputed points, see Robert Booth Fowler, "Normative Aspects of Public Employee Strikes," *Public Personnel Management* 30, no. 2 (March–April 1974): 129–37.

23. A good example of the exception is the 1970 strike of the employees of the U.S. Postal Service. One of the results was that the postal service was converted from an executive department to a government corporation and the employees were placed under the National Labor Relations Board like private employees.

24. For a discussion of some changes, see Jerome T. Barrett and Ira B. Lobel, "Public Sector Strikes — Legislative and Court Treatment," *Monthly Labor Review* 97, no. 9 (September 1974): 19–22.

25. Robert E. Hampton, "Unionism and the Public Employee: A Living Testing Ground for Public Service," *Civil Service Journal* 14, no. 3 (January–March 1974): 5–9.

26. For a discussion of the implications over a time span, see two articles by Felix A. Nigro, "Implications for Public Administration," *Public Administration Review* 28, no. 2 (March–April 1968): 137–47; and *Public Administration Review* 32, no. 2 (March–April 1972): 120–25.

27. For a discussion of this problem, see Arnold M. Zack, "Meeting the Rising Costs of Public Sector Settlements," *Monthly Labor Review* 96, no. 5 (May 1973): 38–40.

28. The state of Wisconsin now includes representatives of the legislature on negotiating teams dealing with state employees.

29. David T. Stanley, "What are Unions Doing to the Merit System?" *Public Personnel Review* 31, no. 2 (April 1970): 109. Reprinted by permission of the International Personnel Management Association, 1313 East 60th Street, Chicago, Illinois 60637.

30. Jerry Wurf, "Merit: A Union View," *Public Administration Review* 34, no. 5 (September–October 1974): 431.

31. Ibid.

17

The Search for Equal Employment Opportunity

Since government is such a pervasive influence in American life, it has tremendous power to effect social change by legislation. In the area of employment, it should lead by demonstrating nondiscriminatory practices in the public service. However, discrimination because of racial and ethnic background, sex, age, and physical disability has been practiced by all levels of government. This chapter will review the history of discrimination, look at its present status and comment on the implications for public administration.

History of Ethnic and Sex Discrimination

Discrimination in many areas, including employment, is not unique to the United States. Overtly or covertly it has been and is being practiced in varying degrees of intensity around the world. Discrimination may be based on birth, religion, education, skin color, tribe, family, sex, country of origin, or a variety of other factors. Few, if any countries, are without some form of discrimination. In the United States, the reasons for discrimination have varied with the geographic regions and historical periods; but the principal reasons have been color and sex.

To provide some background, we will review the history of discrimination in public personnel procedures. The chapter emphasizes recent changes, current status, and what that status means for public administrators.

History Prior to the 1960s

Like all other areas, discrimination in public employment has evolved over the years and is still an area of conflict. Since the public employment process was historically considered to be under the control of the respective governments, the evolution has varied with the levels of government.

Federal Level.   Studies have indicated that public employment practices at all levels have discriminated against women and minorities, either as a conscious, planned program or as a product of the procedures, throughout much of our history. At the federal level, the passage of the Civil Service Act of 1883, which established the basis for the merit system, should have but did not eliminate discrimination as an accepted practice. The procedures adopted to implement the merit concept made it possible to continue racial discrimination openly. In 1940, the Ramspeck Act and President Franklin D. Roosevelt's Executive Order 8587 provided for equal employment opportunity by specifically prohibiting racial discrimination in federal employment. Enforcement of the policy, however, was almost nonexistent.[1]

Although succeeding Presidents Truman and Eisenhower continued to issue Executive Orders and directives designed to insure minorities equal opportunities for federal employment, racial discrimination in hiring, promotions, and other personnel areas continued to be a way of life. As John W. Macy, Jr., the distinguished chairman of the U.S. Civil Service Commission said, "whereas the rhetoric of the policy statements usually sounded noble and clear, the application of those words in government offices, plants and installations was frequently slow and confused."[2] Minorities were discriminated against in a variety of ways. Some of the more important problems were:

1. Equal employment opportunity essentially meant that minorities could not be denied the right to compete for federal jobs. For the better positions, this meant taking a standardized written examination administered to all competitors. Many minority applicants, due to inferior education opportunities, language barriers, and life experiences were not competitive in taking the examination constructed to select from among white university graduates from essentially the same economic, social, and cultural background. An illustration of the problem is the results of the Federal Service Entrance Examination, the entry gateway for university graduates, "where the percentage of competitors passing the nation-wide test was 45; it was a rare Negro institution whose graduates could reach a 4 to 6 percent passing rate."[3]
2. If a supervisor was determined to discriminate, minority applicants who survived any written test could be screened out in the oral interview. Since evaluation is a subjective process, it was difficult to prove that the selection had been on the basis of race rather than competency, organization need, differences in quality and other legitimate "merit" considerations.
3. The U.S. Civil Service Commission resisted the creation of any special training programs or other advantages for minorities as a violation of the principle of nondiscrimination and as a threat to the open competition orientation of the merit system.

4. The machinery to investigate charges of discrimination was hopelessly inadequate. There was no process for monitoring hiring practices consistently. The enforcement machinery was activated only on the basis of individual complaints which were investigated, by an understaffed enforcement agency, on a case-by-case basis.

The whole inadequate process created a fantastic backlog of cases which usually meant that an applicant could not wait the months or years for a decision but had to take another job. Also, there were few sanctions that could be applied against an agency, even if it was found that discrimination had occurred.

State and Local Level.   At the state and local level, the situation was even worse. Although some states had created fair employment practices commissions and similar agencies in the 1950s, many had not expressed any concern through legislation, executive or other official action. In the absence of any top-level direction, those doing the hiring felt no pressure against discriminating. Even in jurisdictions where regulations existed, objectives usually were not defined, enforcement responsibility was not fixed, monitoring and enforcement mechanisms were inadequate, and the regulations were often observed only when is was convenient.

Personnel policies which were discriminatory were very prevalent at all levels of government as the 1950s came to a close, but the practice was to be dramatically challenged in the 1960s.

Developments in the 1960s and 70s

In the decade of the 1960s, ethnic minorities and women, but especially minorities, violently challenged the practices of discrimination both in the private and public sectors. In the 1970s, the social, economic, political, and administrative systems are still being challenged. The purpose now is to define, consolidate, and expand the fundamental gains which have been achieved; and the groups now work within the system to achieve their objectives through the political process.

Civil Rights Movement.   The civil rights movement was a complex event — not a single movement, but a series of movements. Individual segments, even within the same ethnic group, had different leaders, objectives, and tactics. The competition for power, dominance, and recognized leadership among the groups was intense.

Ethnic minorities ceased to be passive about their plight in the 1960s. Blacks, who initiated the movement, used a variety of tactics to focus attention on their demands. The tactics ranged from peaceful, nonviolent marches to bloody riots and the burning of cities. The serious rioting and "torching," which started with the Watts riots in 1965, soon spread to other cities across the country. Although the initial deadly demonstrations were later replaced by marches, rallies, and other nonviolent forms of protest, the movement had seen the murder and martyrdom of some of its leaders — notably Reverend Martin Luther King and Medgar Evers. The process focused worldwide attention on the treatment accorded blacks in our democracy; the social consciousness of the nation was aroused; and race became a political issue. Blacks found a new identity which included an insistence that they be referred to as "black" rather than "Negro"; slogans such as "Black is Beautiful" were developed; and a sense of hope and power were felt. Blacks, as an organized, activist group, had forcefully and dramatically made the point that concrete action rather than promises was the the only acceptable product.

Objectives of the Civil Rights Movement. The objectives of the ethnic movement, born of utter frustration and a sense of total disenchantment with the political, social, and economic system, were complex and often ill-defined in the initial stages. They revolved around the abolition of discrimination and guarantees of equality in voting, housing, education, transportation, economic opportunity, and other rights enjoyed by other Americans. But a basic concern was economic — the abolition of discrimination in private and public hiring. Because of this economic concern, the leaders of the movement looked for relief to the federal government for several reasons. First, the federal government had the constitutional power to outlaw discrimination in hiring in some sectors of the private economy over which it had control — businesses engaged in interstate commerce, those holding government contracts, and federally funded projects, for example. Second, federal agencies are a major user of labor. Third, the federal government is expected to be a model employer, setting an example for others to follow. For these reasons, the personnel policies, procedures, and merit systems of public agencies, especially the federal, came under severe, concerted attack by the minority groups in the 1960s; criticism continues to this day.

Extension of the Rights Movement. The attention and success of the black movement encouraged other ethnic minorities such as the browns — variously labeled Chicano, Mexican-American, and Spanish-surnamed — and Native Americans (Indians) to organize to secure their rights. While their tactics were less violent than blacks, their efforts focused public attention on their concerns.

Women also became very active in the 1960s. Although the campaign for women's rights was not new, women added a vigorous woman's liberation movement to the campaign for equality.[4] Organizations, such as the National Organization for Women (NOW), launched a major feminist movement which adopted a vocal militant stance to secure their goals. While their overall objectives included the advancement of the status and equality of women in all areas, a major thrust was the removal of artificial barriers and discrimination in employment, promotion, salary, and other economic matters in both private and public employment.

Women had a steep, uphill battle to secure equality. In the private sector, their role in society had been stereotyped; they had been excluded from many professions and careers; they were not expected to occupy executive and supervisory positions; they were not expected to seek elective office; they were paid less than men for comparable work; and men were usually given preference in hiring and in promotion.[5]

In public employment, women were also discriminated against, but less so than in the private sector.[6] Historically, women had a right to take examinations and compete for positions, but they were discriminated against in a variety of ways: hiring authorities would request names of men only for most of the better positions; women employees were concentrated in the lower positions; women with education comparable to men were normally at a lower grade on the career ladders; and promotion into supervisory positions was difficult.[7] In fact, in 1864 a federal law had legalized a lower pay scale for women doing comparable work.

Results of Pressure by Women and Minorities

Since the early 1960s, the script on discrimination in hiring minorities and women has been drastically revised under the leadership of Presidents Kennedy, Johnson, and Nixon. Without tracing the whole history of change, some of the major landmarks should be mentioned.[8]

Federal Reaction

Executive Order 10925.   The new direction began when President Kennedy in keeping with his campaign commitment against discrimination, issued Executive Order 10925 on March 6, 1961, which created the President's Committee on Equal Employment Opportunity.[9] Although the order restated the earlier and historic prohibitions against discrimination, which presidents since Franklin D. Roosevelt had expressed, its major contribution was the introduction of the concept of affirmative action in federal hiring, which was significantly different from the connotation given to the older philosophy of equal opportunity. The equal employment opportunity label, by simply prohibiting discrimination, was a negative concept. Affirmative action, on the other hand, was a positive program requiring governmental agencies and private employers doing contract work for the government, to review employment and other personnel practices, to make a determined effort to recruit minorities, to adopt measures to seek out minorities, and to adopt personnel procedures that would eliminate racial discrimination in hiring, retention, promotion, and all other aspects of the personnel process. The responsibility for implementation under this order was not defined nor clearly assigned, and the enforcement machinery was inadequate. The employment opportunities for minorities were not significantly expanded.[10]

Civil Rights Act.   In 1964, with the passage of the comprehensive Civil Rights Act, civil rights leaders saw many of their objectives come to fruition on paper. In addition to the other rights guaranteed by the act, the federal government recognized a fair chance at employment as a "right" and acknowledged that discrimination in hiring was a major problem. Title VII of the law made it illegal for employers, employment agencies, and labor organizations in the private sector to discriminate on the basis of race, religion, sex, or national origin. The Equal Employment Opportunity Commission (EEOC) was created to enforce the law.[11] The law had a tremendous impact on private employers, but significantly the law exempted the federal

government and other public employers. The national government chose
to continue to rely on executive orders to put its own house in order.

Executive Order 11478.   In 1969, President Nixon issued Executive Order
11478 which further defined the intent of the program and, unlike earlier
orders, specified the steps that had to be taken by federal departments and
assigned department and agency heads responsibility for developing and
monitoring a program to meet the stated objectives. Although this order
was precise and assigned responsibility, the major change in public employment came with the passage of the Equal Employment Opportunity Act.

Equal Employment Opportunity Act.   In 1972, the Equal Employment Opportunity Act (PL 92–261) was passed. This law extended most of the equal
opportunity provisions found in Title VII of the 1964 Civil Rights Act to
cover career employees of the federal, state, and local governments, including public educational institutions.[12] Discrimination on the basis of race,
religion, or sex in all public personnel procedures now violates the law of
the land and not executive orders.[13] The difference is very significant. An
applicant or employee who files a complaint of discrimination now not only
has elaborate administrative machinery as a protection but also can, under
certain conditions, take the case into the courts to force compliance or a
redress of the grievance.

As Earl J. Reeves said, "the employment practices of the federal government have evolved gradually from positive discrimination to active commitment to equal opportunity. A concerted effort to hire women and minorities
is an integral and serious part of the personnel program."[14] These federal
changes have affected all public personnel systems.

State and Local Situation

Even before passage of the Equal Employment Opportunity Act and prior
legislation, which required action by subnational governments, many state
and local governments passed laws prohibiting discrimination in public employment and created new or expanded existing enforcement agencies, such
as civil rights commissions, human relations commissions and equal employment agencies. Now that federal legislation is applicable, state and local
programs, procedures, and requirements are being redefined.

The Present Affirmative Action Program

Affirmative action programs now cover employment in both the private and
public sector. As Krislov points out, the symbolic importance of governmental action is that "if elimination of prejudice cannot be achieved in the
public sector bureaucracy, it is unlikely that it will be achieved anywhere."[15]

The Problem of Definition

Equal employment opportunity and affirmative action mean different things
to different people. There are essentially three connotations which have
been given to the terms. First, some argue that simple nondiscrimination
in hiring is inadequate to correct the racial imbalance in the public labor

force created by the historic discrimination policy. What is needed is a system variously referred to as "preferential treatment," "reverse quotas" or "compensatory employment" for minorities, which is actually discrimination in reverse.[16] These practices, which would ignore comparative qualifications between caucasian and minority applicants, should be followed until the ethnic composition of the labor force reflects that of the general population. This proposal has been resisted as a complete reversal of the basic tenets of the merit system. A second proposal, similar to the first but more restricted, gives preference to a qualified minority applicant for a position even though the candidate was not the most qualified for the position. A final interpretation is that the personnel procedures should be reevaluated to remove any illogical requirements and procedures which create artificial barriers that penalize minorities and women.

Program Requirements

The federal government, in addition to dictating the procedures for enforcing the affirmative action goals in the federal personnel process, has issued a series of guidelines, directives, policy statements, and orders which apply to state and local governments and educational institutions. Although these controlling documents, which are revised periodically, differ somewhat with the type of organization concerned, they require essentially the same procedures. In general, each agency covered by the laws and executive orders must develop an affirmative action plan which contains the required information in the format prescribed by the responsible federal compliance agency. The plan, which must be submitted for approval, includes a detailed statistical analysis of the work force which indicates the total number of minorities and women, a numerical breakdown in each category of employment and salary level, a goal statement as to the ethnic and sexual ratio the agency plans to achieve in the short and long run, and procedures for achieving these goals.

Development of a Program

Some of the problems and uncertainties encountered in developing an affirmative action program are:

1. The language of the laws and regulations, which are not and cannot be precise, are subject to many interpretations. What is a "goal" for the employment of minorities and women? It is not the same as a "quota," because that has bad connotations when it was used to limit the number admitted to employment, professional schools, and other areas.
2. What should be used as a basis for determining a realistic comparison to establish a goal? Should the labor force reflect the ethnic composition of the country, the state, the population in the geographic area served or some other standard?
3. Developing guidelines and procedures, especially in a university environment, is difficult and time consuming, because students, faculty, staff, administrators, community groups, each minority group, and women want to have input and influence the product. The input from ethnic minority

groups is complicated by their fragmentation into factions and lack of common objectives, leadership, or spokespeople. Also, each group — black, brown, native American, oriental, women — is competing to secure an advantage or at least to protect its own economic interests.

4. Agreeing on procedures for recruiting, appointing, and other personnel procedures is difficult.
5. The process of hiring an affirmative action coordinator, a step usually taken by most agencies, can be very trying for the interview panel and the appointing authority. Each group or faction, very much interested in placing one of its members in the position, will bring whatever pressure it can muster from its own group as well as from support groups outside the organization.
6. Questions of the reporting level of the coordinator as well as the location of the coordinator's office may become issues. Should the coordinator report to the top administrator or to someone lower in the hierarchy? Should the office be with the management group or in a department? Since these points are indicators of both the status assigned to the program as well as the coordinator's access to the decision makers, they are important to the groups.

Program Implementation

Even after an overall plan for an agency has been developed, monitoring the recruiting, hiring, promotion, and other aspects of personnel administration, as well as maintaining personnel statistics, is a continuous process. Some of the problems encountered in meeting the stated goals of hiring minorities are:

1. It is difficult to identify minority applicants from written application forms. Historically, to make it more difficult to discriminate, laws were passed making it illegal to ask for racial information or a picture on a written application form. Consequently, unless the administrator personally interviews all applicants, often an impossibility with limited recruiting budgets, it is difficult to determine which are minorities. Although applicants often let it be known that they are from a minority group, agencies often use such things as name, high schools and universities attended, and residence as a basis for guessing ethnic background. This, of course, is far from scientific and can produce surprises. A good example is a woman who may be from any country in the world, who has acquired a Spanish surname through marriage.
2. There is a shortage of minority talent in the professions and skilled trades. This is because many minorities historically have not entered the universities or trades in large numbers for a variety of reasons, including discrimination. This shortage is improving but history cannot be reversed quickly.
3. A corollary problem is the intense competition for the talent available. Since private industry, educational institutions, private foundations, and every level of government are under the affirmative action program, everyone is attempting to recruit from the same limited pool of talent. Above the entry level, the result is what amounts to competitive bidding for new minority talent entering the labor market and raiding each other and buy-

ing away qualified, experienced employees. If an organization's salary schedule and fringe benefit package are not competitive, it will not be able to hire or retain many minorities.

Enforcement of Equal Employment Opportunity

Enforcement has three aspects — a basis for evaluation, the machinery for compliance, and sanctions which can be imposed for noncompliance.

Basis for Evaluation. Before a program may be evaluated, there must be something with which to compare it. The base for enforcement of equal employment opportunity is the detailed historical data and goal statement filed with the compliance unit. Each required annual report is then compared with the preceding one and with the original plan to gauge progress, or lack of it, toward the stated objective. The criteria for progress is that the agency must be "making a good faith effort" to achieve the objectives. What does this subjective statement mean? Essentially it means that if one has not made significant progress in achieving a racially and sexually balanced labor force, he or she should be prepared to document that an honest and positive effort to do so has been made and that there are no artificial barriers in the personnel procedures.

The Machinery. At the federal level, the national government has established machinery to monitor compliance and to hear complaints of discrimination by federal employees. Those that cannot be settled within the agencies may be appealed to the U.S. Civil Service Commission and then to the federal courts.

At other levels of government, compliance is usually through three channels — within the agency, by a specialized compliance agency, and finally through the Equal Employment Opportunity Commission (EEOC).

If they choose, employees may use the "in-house" procedures established to process personnel grievances. However, since such procedures are often geared to hearing the more traditional employment complaints, an employee often elects not to file a discrimination case at this level.

The second level of enforcement is through a variety of mechanisms. The federal government has assigned responsibility for monitoring the employment practices of states in some programs to the U.S. Civil Service Commission. For other groups, a variety of civil rights compliance agencies have been created in many federal executive departments. However, day-to-day enforcement is often delegated by the central department in Washington to one of their regional offices. For example, the Office of Civil Rights in the Department of Health, Education, and Welfare, which is the compliance unit for higher education, has assigned enforcement responsibilities to each of its ten regional offices. At this level, the usual sanction is economic. The penalty for noncompliance can be the suspension or loss of grants, subsidies, and all other types of federal assistance. Since such funds are an important revenue source for universities and subnational governments, this threat is an effective sanction.

The third level is to file a complaint with the Equal Employment Opportunity Commission (EEOC). The EEOC will investigate complaints and attempt a solution through conciliation.[17] If this fails, the Justice Department can file a suit against the public employer. If the employee wins the case in the court, an agency may be ordered to reinstate an employee, pay back salaries, validate employment tests, give preference in hiring to those who can prove past discrimination in hiring, modify any offending aspect of the whole personnel process, develop and implement an acceptable affirmative action program, and alter any procedures or practices which do not conform to the intent of the law.

Affirmative Action Impact on Public Administration

The impact of affirmative action has been reflected by changes in three principal areas — modifications in personnel practices and procedures, alterations in the organizational environment, and increased numbers of minority and women employees at all levels of government.

Modifications in Personnel Procedures

The traditional methods of performing the basic personnel functions have been and are being altered. The more important changes are:

1. There is an acceptance, arrived at willingly or reluctantly to avoid sanctions, that minorities and women must be hired to achieve the goals stated for the organization.
2. Position announcements carry a label such as "An Affirmative Action Employer" or similar statements to indicate a policy of nondiscrimination.
3. The recruiting techniques and sources have changed. For lower echelon positions, in addition to the regular sources, job announcements are usually sent to an extensive list of all minority organizations, leaders, associations, and community groups from which the organization hiring could conceivably draw minority applicants. For higher echelon and professional jobs, recruiters contact every black university, universities in the Southwest, and attend the annual meetings of the professional associations.
4. Raiding has become a common practice. By offering higher salaries, some organizations lure minority employees away from their current employer. In the academic world, presidents of black universities almost plead with other, more affluent, prestigious universities not to "buy" away their faculty members.
5. Testing procedures have been modified. In some cases, written tests are no longer required for certain jobs. Where they are used, they have been analyzed and often rewritten to remove language that would build in a cultural bias.
6. Tests must be validated to prove that they are valid predictors of success on the job.
7. The appointment process has been affected. The department head, responsible for operating an efficient operation and delivering a product, is interested in hiring the most competent people available. But, if there are minority candidates in the final group, there is pressure introduced

into the system. If the minority candidate is as qualified or more qualified than the nonminority candidates, there is no problem in selection. But, if a minority candidate is evaluated as the second, third, or fourth most qualified, the decision is more difficult. In any case, if the nonminority candidate is selected, the hiring authority must be able to document the qualifications and basis on which the selection was made.

8. The process of evaluation is closely scrutinized. In evaluating an employee during the probationary period to decide whether to retain or release the employee, or in disciplinary cases, in promotions, or in dismissals, the process is very "touchy" where minorities or women are involved. Supervisors have to be very cautious to avoid a charge of discrimination. In some cases, there is a temptation to employ a double standard and tolerate substandard or marginal behavior rather than spend the time and effort needed to defend against an investigation, if a charge of discrimination is filed with the civil rights compliance agency.

9. Personnel documentation procedures have been altered. Records are now kept on where position announcements are sent, the number of applicants who met minimum qualifications, the number and ethnic composition of those interviewed, the positions offered to minorities and women that were refused, and other detailed information. Such statistical information is needed for reports and compliance reviews in case a discrimination claim is filed.

10. The required qualifications for positions are being reevaluated to see if indeed they are relevant to successful performance on the job. Is graduation from high school or a university degree required for success on the job?

Changes in Organizational Environment

In addition to the above specific procedural changes in personnel procedures, there has been a change in the organizational atmosphere in two basic ways. First, the program has created a sensitivity or mental attitude among personnel people and supervisors from the first line to the top echelon. The intent of the legislation, the availability of employee protective mechanisms and the threat of sanctions influence the decision-making process. Supervisors, always conscious of the possibilities for charges of discrimination, are cautious in their supervisory methods as well as in their role in the personnel process. Even such things as job and shift assignments may have discriminatory overtones. A second and somewhat corollary product is that a degree of tension has been injected into organizations. Agencies that are honestly attempting to increase their minority representation resent some of the tactics used by some of the more militant groups. Some supervisors, including minority members, resent the necessity of being constantly cognizant of the sensitivities of minority employees. Finally, the attitudes of white applicants and employees adds to the tension. Some caucasians feel that the minority program is a form of "compensatory employment" where minorities are given preference to compensate quickly for all of the years of discrimination. If there is a feeling that such "reverse discrimination" is occurring, an agency may have a "mixed" work force, but it will in no sense be an integrated, smoothly operating unit.

Employment of Minorities and Women

The procedure has changed from hiring a few minorities and placing them in readily visible work stations to a concerted effort to meet the hiring goals established in the goal statement of the agency. The gross number of minorities and women on the federal payroll has increased significantly in recent years. "As of May 31, 1973, Negroes, Spanish Surnamed Americans, American Indians and Oriental Americans held 515,129 government jobs, up from 505,468 in the preceding year, and comprised 20.4 percent of the Federal civilian work force, compared with 19.6 percent the year before."[18] However, gross numbers do not tell the complete story. The agency must also consider how representative the bureaucracy should be of the total ethnic composition of the society.

Representative Bureaucracy

Since the bureaucracy at all levels of government plays an important role in policy making, the composition of the labor force is important in a democratic society.[19] An important issue raised as a consequence is whether the bureaucracy should reflect the social and ethnic composition of the society. This is a controversial question. Some say it is not desirable and not possible. Gerald Caiden says, "while there is no dispute with the idea that somewhere within the public bureaucracy diverse views and unpopular opinions should be aired and considered, it does not follow that the public bureaucracy could or should be a mirror of the social structure."[20] Others insist that representativeness is important. Frederick Mosher points out that "a broadly representative public service, especially at the level of leadership, suggests an open service in which access is available to most people, whatever their station in life, and in which there is equality of opportunity. These are values which Americans have honored — in speech if not always in deed — for more than a century."[21] He, like Caiden and other writers, points out, however, that employees from certain groups and with certain backgrounds will not necessarily reflect the thinking and desires of similar groups.[22]

Although representativeness has been subject to numerous studies, many of them have concentrated on selected groups — blacks, Spanish-surnamed, women — and have been confined to the federal level due to the unavailability of comprehensive state and local data.[23]

The studies have also yielded conflicting conclusions. One study concluded ". . . that the federal bureaucracy — in the aggregate — is highly reflective of its nonfederal working counterpart" and is similar in composition to the social structure in the United States.[24] A later study concluded that in the federal government, "we can generalize that in the aggregate, women and the Spanish surnamed are underrepresented, while Negroes, Indians and Orientals have overall quantitative representation."[25] It also points out that all minorities and women are underrepresented in the higher level positions.

Minorities and women agree that there have been significant gains in the numbers employed. However, they correctly point out that most are concentrated in the lower-paying positions. They are insisting that the concept of a representative bureaucracy requires proportionate representation in the executive levels of public employment.

Combating Other Forms of Discrimination

Although ethnic and sexual discrimination have received the most attention, two other bases for discrimination — age and physical disability — are being given increasing attention.

Age

Another form of discrimination, especially in the private sector, has been age. The age of forty, for all practical purposes, has become the maximum age for initial employment in the private sector. While public agencies do impose age ceilings for initial employment in certain positions, there are no stated ceilings for most jobs. However, often there has been a bias against hiring an older person. The rationale is that the shorter potential working time does not justify investing time and money in training; health problems and absenteeism will be more common; work habits and behavioral patterns have been formed and are difficult to change; and older workers are less efficient than younger people.

Concern over the problem of age discrimination resulted in the Age Discrimination in Employment Act of 1967. The federal act, as amended in May of 1974, covers most private employers, the federal government and state and local agencies (including educational institutions) who receive federal monies (which includes almost all subnational governments). The law, designed to protect the forty to sixty-five age group, makes it unlawful for an employer to refuse to hire, discharge, or otherwise discriminate against an individual with respect to compensation, terms, conditions, or privileges of employment because of age.

What does it mean? It does not mean that employers have to hire unqualified or less qualified people just because they are in the indicated age bracket. Instead, the employer must be able to demonstrate that the younger person was selected because he or she was either more qualified or that age had a direct bearing on success in the position. If the hiring authority cannot demonstrate these factors or possibly indicates a bias by asking a person's age in the interview or in other ways conveys the attitude that age was a factor, the applicant has an appeal mechanism through the U.S. Department of Labor.

Disability

Historically, the physically handicapped person was passed over in the hiring process. Public and private employers were concerned over their efficiency, potential health problems, and the need for special facilities. Now, the federal government as well as many state and local units have legislation to encourage the hiring of the physically handicapped. Others make discrimination illegal, unless the handicap would make it impossible to fulfill the duties of the position. Special programs have been created, facilities are being modified to accommodate such employees, and they are being actively recruited.

At the federal level, the practice of employing the handicapped was given added emphasis with the passage of the Rehabilitation Act of 1973. This law created an Interagency Committee on Handicapped Employees and required each federal agency to develop an affirmative action plan for the hiring, placement, and advancement of handicapped individuals.[26] The plans are to be reviewed annually by the Civil Service Commission and the Interagency Committee.

Conclusions

The target for much of the attack by women and minorities has been the merit system, which ironically is the foundation on which all career systems are based. Many groups, and not only minorities, argue that the merit system is one of the most effective discriminatory devices ever invented. They ask a variety of questions to illustrate the point. Why do so many positions require a college degree which is not really essential for success on the job? Why does the language and style of written examinations favor applicants coming from a certain educational, cultural, and experiential background? Why do many police agencies require a height of 5'10" or 5'11"? Why do more minorities not seek public employment? Why do minorities and women occupy only the lower-paying positions? Why do certain positions exclude women? and so on. As the executive director of the U.S. Civil Service Commission says, "Demands for change and improvements have been voiced by many segments of society — minorities, women, youth, labor and others. Government response has not always been successful or timely. Many citizens feel the system is not working effectively — and some say that it can't work."[27]

The impact which the affirmative action program has had on the merit system is a debatable question. Some argue that the challenges from minorities have yielded only positive results. Those who take this point of view base their arguments on three principal factors. The first result is moving toward realization of the concept of a representative bureaucracy. In a democratic society, the mix of public employees should reflect the ethnic composition of the society. The affirmative action program has made progress toward that democratic goal. Second, it is morally correct. Third, it has forced a reanalysis of the whole personnel system which has updated personnel practices to meet modern conditions.

Others argue that the merit concept of employing the most qualified individuals through the competitive process is being destroyed. The quality of personnel, they insist, is declining due to an actual lowering of standards, compensatory employment, reverse favoritism in promotion, and a reluctance to dismiss below-standard minority and female employees — in short, practices which violate the traditional concept of merit.

Despite the disagreement on outcomes, the challenges have forced drastic modifications in the historic personnel systems. Even the basic foundations of the system — quality, which has been difficult to measure and usually is based on education, and efficiency — are being challenged by a new philosophy of equity and equality.[28]

Affirmative action will continue to be a very controversial issue in both the private and public sectors. Since the program is attempting to alter historic concepts and behavioral patterns, it is an emotional issue. Some say that we are moving too rapidly and actually practicing reverse discrimination. On the other hand, minorities and women think that progress is too slow. It is a situation loaded with tension and potential problems.

Administrators, regardless of their personal feelings, are in the middle of the problem. They must be conscious of the laws, aware of the incompatible expectations of the various groups, and capable of handling controversy. This process adds another interesting dimension to being an administrator.

NOTES

1. For the history and operation of the federal Equal Employment Opportunity Program, as well as the role of the Civil Service Commission, see S. Krislov, *The Negro in Federal Employment* (Minneapolis: University of Minnesota Press, 1967); David Rosenbloom, *The U.S. Civil Service Commission's Role in the Federal Equal Employment Opportunity Program,* Civil Service Commission, administrative study (December 1970); and David Rosenbloom, "The Civil Service Commission's Decision to Authorize the Use of Goals and Timetables in the Federal Equal Employment Opportunity Program," *The Western Political Quarterly* 26, no. 2 (June 1973): 236–51.

2. John W. Macy, *Public Service: The Human Side of Government* (New York: Harper & Row, 1971), p. 66. Used by permission.

3. Ibid., p. 74. Used by permission.

4. For a description of the women's movement, see Jayne B. Spain, "The Best is Yet to Come," *Civil Service Journal* 13, no. 3 (January-March 1973): 8–11.

5. Since passage of the Equal Pay Act of 1963, as amended in 1966 and 1972, a woman doing work comparable to that of her male counterpart must receive equal pay. But for statistics which indicate that women in the private labor market earn approximately 50 percent less than their male counterparts of equivalent age and education, see *Monthly Labor Review* 96, no. 5 (May 1973): 65.

6. For a description of the problem and changes in the public sector see "Every Day is Ladies Day" in Macy, *Public Service*, pp. 83–93.

7. An analysis of the situation in federal employment is contained in the U. S. Civil Service Commission, *Study of Employment of Women in the Federal Government* (Washington, D.C.: Government Printing Office, 1968).

8. For more detailed discussion of the historical development and phases of Equal Employment Opportunity, see Don Hellriegel and Larry Short, "Equal Employment Opportunity in the Federal Government: A Comparative Analysis," *Public Administration Review* 32, no. 6 (November-December 1972): 851–58; and "Making Equal Opportunity a Reality" in Macy, *Public Service*, pp. 65–81.

9. In 1963, the committee became known as the Plans for Progress, to indicate the alliance between industry and government to eliminate discriminatory practices.

10. Later, President Johnson issued two Executive Orders: 11246, which reinforced the affirmative action policy, and 11375, which prohibited discrimination because of sex; but the impact on federal personnel practices was negligible.

11. For a discussion of the techniques and success of compliance, see Arvil V. Adams, "Evaluating the Success of the EEOC Compliance Process," *Monthly Labor Review* 96, no. 5 (May 1973): 26–29. For a 425-page discussion of the larger civil rights effort, see *The Federal Civil Rights Enforcement Effort: A Reassessment, A Report of the United States Commission on Civil Rights* (Washington, D.C.: U.S. Commission on Civil Rights, 1973). The Commission also publishes a quarterly *Civil Rights Digest.*

12. For a concise chronicle of equal employment opportunity, see Irving Kator, "Third Generation Equal Employment Opportunity," *Civil Service Journal* 13, no. 1 (July-September 1972): 1–5.

13. To further focus on the economic status of women, in September 1972, President Nixon created the Advisory Committee on the Economic Role of Women. The committee, organized in January 1973, works with the chairman of the Council of Economic Advisors. President Ford declared August 26, 1974, as Women's Equality Day.

14. Earl J. Reeves, "Making Equality of Opportunity a Reality in the Federal Service," *Public Administration Review* 30, no. 1 (January-February 1970): 43–49.

15. S. Krislov, *Monthly Labor Review* 96, no. 2 (February 1973): 66.

16. For discussions on the concept of compensatory employment, see Krislov, *The Negro in Federal Employment;* and R. Lichtman, "The Ethics of Compensatory Employment," *Law in Transition Quarterly* 1 (1964): 76–103.

17. For the actions by this agency, see the Annual Reports of the Equal Employment Opportunity Commission.

18. *Civil Service Journal* 14, no. 4 (April-June 1974): inside back cover.

19. For an extensive discussion of this aspect, see Frederick C. Mosher, *Democracy in the Public Service* (New York: Oxford University Press, 1968); and Emmett S. Redford, *Democracy in the Administrative State* (New York: Oxford University Press, 1968).

20. Gerald E. Caiden, *The Dynamics of Public Administration: Guidelines to Current Transformations in Theory and Practice* (New York: Holt, Rinehart and Winston 1971), p. 206.

21. Mosher, *Democracy in the Public Service,* pp. 13–14. Used by permission.

22. For other reasons for representativeness, see Harry Kranz, "Are Merit and Equity Compatible?" *Public Administration Review* 34, no. 5 (September-October 1974): 434–39.

23. For some discussion of the state and local situation and references to sources, see Harry Kranz, "How Representative is the Public Service," *Public Personnel Management* 2, no. 4 (July-August 1973): 242–55.

24. Milton C. Cummings, Jr., M. Kent Jennings, and Franklin P. Kilpatrick, "Federal and Nonfederal Employees: A Comparative Social-Occupational Analysis," *Public Administration Review* 27, no. 5 (December 1967): 402.

25. Kranz, "How Representative is the Public Service," pp. 242–55. Reprinted by permission of the International Personnel Management Association, 1313 East 60th Street, Chicago, Illinois 60637. For the status of Chicanos, see Maria Dolores Dias de Krofcheck and Carlos Jackson, "The Chicano Experience with Nativism in Public Administration," in Symposium, Minorities in Public Administration, *Public Administration Review* 34, no. 6 (November-December 1974): 534–39.

26. The law designated the secretary of Health, Education and Welfare and the chairman of the Civil Service Commission as cochairpersons of the Interagency Committee. For a discussion of past practice and the new law, see Jayne B. Spain, "Equal Employment Opportunity for the Handicapped," *Civil Service Journal* 14, no. 4 (April-June 1974): 1–8.

27. Bernard Rosen, "The Changing Civil Service," *The Civil Service Journal* 13, no. 2 (October-December 1972): 1.

28. For a number of articles on the question of social equity, see the section Symposium on Social Equity and Public Administration in the *Public Administration Review* 34, no. 1 (January-February 1974): 1–51.

18

The
Cost
of
Government

From the earliest of times, money — we should say the *shortage* of it — has 'been a root cause of difficulties faced by governments and regimes. England's King Charles I and France's Louis XVI lost their heads partly over political conflict concerning the raising and spending of public funds. It was a shortage of money that almost defeated General George Washington in the U.S. War of Independence. The same shortage which exists today can be expected to escalate in the future due to an increasing demand for services, inflation, and the competition for resources. With this trend will come a deeper and more intense political give-and-take.

Every society, from tribal to the most complex, develops some form of government to provide selected services to the population as a whole. Consequently, there are always economic costs associated with government, regardless of the political, economic, and social framework within which it operates. In a complex, industrialized society like the United States, the costs are high. In this chapter we will examine total expenditures, who spends the money, what it is spent for, and sources of revenue.

Total Expenditures

In the United States, the total amount spent by all public agencies has been increasing at a steady rate. To illustrate the expenditure pattern, we will use figures from two sources — the *United States Budget in Brief, Fiscal Year 1976* and *Trends in Fiscal Federalism 1954–1974* published by the Advisory

Table 2 Budget Receipts by Source and Outlays by Function, 1966–76 (in billions of dollars)

Description	Actual									Estimate	
	1966	1967	1968	1969	1970	1971	1972	1973	1974	1975	1976
Receipts by Source											
Individual income taxes	$55.4	$61.5	$68.7	$87.2	$90.4	$86.2	$94.7	$103.2	$119.0	$117.7	$106.3
Corporation income taxes	30.1	34.0	28.7	36.7	32.8	26.8	32.2	36.2	38.6	38.5	47.7
Social insurance taxes and contributions	25.6	33.3	34.6	39.9	45.3	48.6	53.9	64.5	76.8	86.2	91.6
Excise taxes	13.1	13.7	14.1	15.2	15.7	16.6	15.5	16.3	16.8	19.9	32.1
Estate and gift taxes	3.1	3.0	3.1	3.5	3.6	3.7	5.4	4.9	5.0	4.8	4.6
Customs duties	1.8	1.9	2.0	2.3	2.4	2.6	3.3	3.2	3.3	3.9	4.3
Miscellaneous receipts	1.9	2.1	2.5	2.9	3.4	3.9	3.6	3.9	5.4	7.7	10.9
Total receipts	130.9	149.6	153.7	187.8	193.7	188.4	208.6	232.2	264.9	278.8	297.5
Outlays by Function											
National defense[1]	55.9	69.1	79.4	80.2	79.3	76.8	77.4	75.1	78.6	85.3	94.0
International affairs	4.6	4.7	4.6	3.8	3.6	3.1	3.7	3.0	3.6	4.9	6.3
General science, space, and technology	6.8	6.3	5.6	5.1	4.6	4.3	4.3	4.2	4.2	4.2	4.6
Natural resources, environment, and energy	3.1	3.4	3.6	3.5	3.6	4.4	5.0	5.5	6.4	9.4	10.0
Agriculture	2.4	3.0	4.5	5.8	5.2	4.3	5.3	4.9	2.2	1.8	1.8
Commerce and transportation	9.0	9.2	10.6	7.1	9.1	10.4	10.6	9.9	13.1	11.8	13.7
Community and regional development	1.5	1.7	2.2	2.5	3.5	4.0	4.7	5.9	4.9	4.9	5.9
Education, manpower, and social services	4.1	6.0	7.0	6.9	7.9	9.0	11.7	11.9	11.6	14.7	14.6
Health	2.6	6.8	9.7	11.8	13.1	14.7	17.5	18.8	22.1	26.5	28.0
Income security	28.9	30.8	33.7	37.3	43.1	55.4	63.9	73.0	84.4	106.7	118.7
Veterans benefits and services	5.9	6.9	6.9	7.6	8.7	9.8	10.7	12.0	13.4	15.5	15.6
Law enforcement and justice	.6	.6	.6	.8	1.0	1.3	1.6	2.1	2.5	3.0	3.3
General government	1.4	1.6	1.7	1.6	1.9	2.2	2.5	2.7	3.3	2.6	3.2
Revenue sharing and general purpose fiscal assistance	.2	.3	.3	.4	.5	.5	.5	7.2	6.7	7.0	7.2
Interest	11.3	12.5	13.8	15.8	18.3	19.6	20.6	22.8	28.1	31.3	34.4
Allowances[2]										.7	8.0
Undistributed offsetting receipts	−3.6	−4.6	−5.5	−5.5	−6.6	−8.4	−8.1	−12.3	−16.7	−16.8	−20.2
Total outlays	134.7	158.3	178.8	184.5	196.6	211.4	231.9	246.5	268.4	313.4	349.4

[1]Includes civilian and military pay raises for Department of Defense.
[2]Includes energy tax equalization payments, civilian agency pay raises, and contingencies.

Source: The United States Budget in Brief, Fiscal Year 1976, p. 49.

Commission on Intergovernmental Relations in February, 1975. Both sets of figures are revealing, but since the first source compiled data by fiscal year and the second by calendar year, the figures cannot be compared.[1]

Budget Figures

From an analysis of table 2, the constant upward spiral of federal expenditures in recent years is evident — $134.7 billion in 1966 to an estimated $349.4 billion for fiscal 1976. For comparative purposes and to further illustrate the progression, federal expenditures were $92 billion in fiscal 1960 and 112 billion in 1963.

To put it another way (table 3), federal expenditures consistently represent a considerable portion of the gross national product — the value of all goods and services produced in the nation. Since 1954, the federal budget has ranged from a low of 17.2 percent of the gross national product to a high estimated at 21.9 percent in fiscal 1976. The latter percentage will undoubtedly be higher due to the declining value of the gross national product caused by the 1975–76 economic recession. Nevertheless, the budget of the federal government represents only a portion of the total spent by public agencies. To this amount must be added the billions spent by the states and over 80,000 units of local government.

Table 3   Federal Finances and the Gross National Product, 1954–76 (dollar amounts in billions)

| Fiscal year | Gross National Product | Budget Receipts | | Budget Outlays | | Federal Debt, End of Year | | | |
| | | | | | | Total | | Held by the Public | |
		Amount	Percent of GNP	Amount	Percent of GNP	Amount	Percent of GNP	Amount	Percent of GNP
1954	$ 362.1	$ 69.7	19.3	$ 70.9	19.6	$270.8	74.8	$224.5	62.0
1955	378.6	65.5	17.3	68.5	18.1	274.4	72.5	226.6	59.9
1956	409.4	74.5	18.2	70.5	17.2	272.8	66.6	222.2	54.3
1957	431.3	80.0	18.5	76.7	17.8	272.4	63.1	219.4	50.9
1958	440.3	79.6	18.1	82.6	18.8	279.7	63.5	226.4	51.4
1959	469.1	79.2	16.9	92.1	19.6	287.8	61.3	235.0	50.1
1960	495.2	92.5	18.7	92.2	18.6	290.9	58.7	237.2	47.9
1961	506.5	94.4	18.6	97.8	19.3	292.9	57.8	238.6	47.1
1962	542.1	99.7	18.4	106.8	19.7	303.3	55.9	248.4	45.8
1963	573.4	106.6	18.6	111.3	19.4	310.8	54.2	254.5	44.4
1964	612.2	112.7	18.4	118.6	19.4	316.8	51.7	257.6	42.1
1965	654.2	116.8	17.9	118.4	18.1	323.2	49.4	261.6	40.0
1966	721.2	130.9	18.1	134.7	18.7	329.5	45.7	264.7	36.7
1967	769.8	149.6	19.4	158.3	20.6	341.3	44.3	267.5	34.8
1968	826.0	153.7	18.6	178.8	21.6	369.8	44.8	290.6	35.2
1969	898.3	187.8	20.9	184.5	20.5	367.1	40.9	279.5	31.1
1970	954.6	193.7	20.3	196.6	20.6	382.6	40.1	284.9	29.8
1971	1,012.1	188.4	18.6	211.4	20.9	409.5	40.5	304.3	30.1
1972	1,101.6	208.6	18.9	231.9	21.0	437.3	39.7	323.8	29.4
1973	1,224.1	232.2	19.0	246.5	20.1	468.4	38.3	343.0	28.0
1974	1,348.9	264.9	19.6	268.4	19.9	486.2	36.0	346.1	25.7
1975 estimate	1,434.0	278.8	19.4	313.4	21.9	538.5	37.6	389.6	27.2
1976 estimate	1,596.0	297.5	18.6	349.4	21.9	605.9	38.0	453.1	28.4

SOURCE: *The United States Budget in Brief, Fiscal Year 1976*, p. 59.

Advisory Commission Data

Figures from *Trends in Fiscal Federalism 1954–1974*, which are on a calendar year basis, provide excellent data on total expenditures as well as the amounts spent by the different levels of governments.

The figures in table 4 indicate that the total expenditures by all levels of government has increased rapidly — from $96.7 billion in 1954 to $458.0 billion in 1974, that expenditures consistently consume a high percentage of the gross national product; that although expenditures for national defense have more than doubled since 1954, the amount represents a decreasing percentage of the total expenditures — 51.5 percent in 1954 to 22.7 percent in 1974 — as well as a declining percentage of the gross national product.

Table 4   The Growing Public Sector[1]: 1954, 1964, and 1969 through 1974
(Government Expenditure)

Calendar Year	Total Public Sector	Domestic (Federal, State, and Local)	Defense[2] (Federal)	Total Public Sector	Domestic (Federal, State, and Local)	Defense[2] (Federal)
	Amount (in billions)			As a Percent of GNP		
1954	$ 96.7	$ 46.9	$ 49.8	26.5	12.9	13.7
1964	175.6	110.8	64.8	27.8	17.5	10.3
1969	290.0	191.6	98.4	31.1	20.6	10.6
1970	312.7	215.8	96.9	32.0	22.1	9.9
1971	340.1	245.2	94.9	32.2	23.2	9.0
1972	372.2	278.2	94.0	32.1	24.0	8.1
1973[3]	408.1	310.8	97.3	31.5	24.0	7.5
1974 est.	458.0	354.0	104.0	32.8	25.4	7.4
	Percentage Distribution			Annual Percent Change		
1954	100.0	48.5	51.5	—	—	—
1964	100.0	63.1	36.9	6.1[4]	9.0[4]	2.7[4]
1969	100.0	66.1	33.9	10.6[5]	11.6[5]	8.9[5]
1970	100.0	69.0	31.0	7.8	12.6	—1.5
1971	100.0	72.1	27.9	8.8	13.6	—2.1
1972	100.0	74.7	25.3	9.4	13.5	—0.9
1973	100.0	76.2	23.8	9.6	11.7	3.5
1974	100.0	77.3	22.7	12.2	13.9	6.9

[1]National Income and Product Accounts.
[2]National defense, international affairs and finance, and space research and technology. Also includes the estimated portion of net interest attributable to these functions.
[3]Partially estimated.
[4]Annual average increase 1954 to 1964.
[5]Annual average increase 1964 to 1969.

SOURCE: Advisory Commission on Intergovernmental Relations (ACIR), *Trends in Fiscal Federalism, 1954-1974,* February 1975, p. 9; from ACIR staff compilation based on U.S. Department of Commerce, Office of Business Economics, *Survey of Current Business,* various years; *Budget of the United States Government,* various years; and ACIR staff estimates.

Table 5, which deals only with domestic (nondefense) expenditures, indicates the relative amounts spent by the federal and subnational governments from their own funds — excluding state and local expenditures received from outside sources such as grants, subsidies, and shared revenue received from higher levels of government. The data clearly show that although state and local expenditures have increased dramatically, the federal expenditures have increased even more rapidly. As a result, the amount spent by subnational governments represents a declining percentage of the total public expenditures — 57.6 percent in 1954 to 45.5 percent in 1974.

To illustrate the expenditure pattern a bit further, an analysis of the expenditures of state and local governments from their own funds (table 6) shows an important trend. The data show that the state's percentage of all subnational expenditures, including school districts, has increased in every

Table 5   The Growing Domestic Public Sector[1]:
1954, 1964, and 1969 through 1974
(Government Domestic Expenditure, *From Own Funds*)

Calendar Year	Total Domestic Expenditure (Federal-State-Local)	Federal Domestic Expenditure[2]	State-Local Total Expenditure	Total Domestic Expenditure (Federal-State-Local)	Federal Domestic Expenditure[2]	State-Local Expenditure
	Amount (in billions)			As a Percent of GNP		
1954	$ 46.9	$ 19.9	$ 27.0	12.9	5.5	7.4
1964	110.8	53.3	57.5	17.5	8.4	9.1
1969	191.6	92.9	98.7	20.6	10.0	10.6
1970	215.8	107.0	108.8	22.1	11.0	11.1
1971	245.2	125.4	119.8	23.2	11.9	11.4
1972	278.2	150.7	127.5	24.0	13.0	11.0
1973[3]	310.8	166.9	143.9	24.0	12.9	11.1
1974 est.	354.0	193.0	161.0	25.4	13.8	11.6
	Percentage Distribution			Annual Percent Change		
1954	100.0	42.4	57.6	—	—	—
1964	100.0	48.1	51.9	9.0[4]	10.3[4]	7.9[4]
1969	100.0	48.5	51.5	11.6[5]	11.8[5]	11.4[5]
1970	100.0	49.6	50.4	12.6	15.2	10.2
1971	100.0	51.1	48.9	13.6	17.2	10.1
1972	100.0	54.2	45.8	13.5	20.2	6.4
1973	100.0	53.7	46.3	11.7	10.7	12.9
1974	100.0	54.5	45.5	13.9	15.6	11.9

[1]National Income and Product Accounts.

[2]Excludes federal expenditure for national defense, international affairs and finance, space research and technology, and the estimated portion of net interest attributable to these functions. Includes Social Security (OHSDHI) and all federal aid to state and local governments including general revenue sharing payments.

[3]Partially estimated.

[4]Annual average increase 1954 to 1964.

[5]Annual average increase 1964 to 1969.

SOURCE: *ACIR, Trends in Fiscal Federalism, 1954–1974*, February 1975, p. 11; from ACIR staff compilation based on U.S. Department of Commerce, Office of Business Economics, *Survey of Current Business*, various years; *Budget of the United States Government*, various years; and ACIR staff estimates.

year except 1972. The data also demonstrate the relatively high percentage of local expenditures devoted to local school districts.

Who Spends the Money

Money included in the budget of a particular level of government does not necessarily mean money actually spent at that level. Due to the systems of revenue sharing, grants, and other forms of subsidies, a portion of the money included in the federal budget is allocated to state and local governments and monies appearing in state budgets are disbursed by local units. To illustrate this point, for fiscal 1976, approximately $56 billion of the estimated $349.4 billion federal budget is destined for aid to state and local government. This federal aid is approximately 15.9 percent of the total federal expenditures or 22.3 percent of the money spent on domestic programs.

Table 7 shows the actual expenditure patterns for the federal and subnational governments in the past. Since these figures indicate amounts from all sources, they illustrate who actually spent the funds as well as the importance of federal financial assistance to subnational units, which is dis-

Table 6   The Increasing State Share of the State-Local Sector:
1954, 1964 and 1969 through 1974
(State and Local Expenditures, *From Own Funds*)

Fiscal Year	Expenditure From Own Funds[1]			Expenditure From Own Funds[1]		
		Local Governments			Local Governments	
	State Governments	Other Than School Districts	School Districts	State Governments	Other Than School Districts	School Districts
	Amount (in billions)			As a Percent of GNP		
1954	$12,861	$10,561	$ 4,314	3.6	2.9	1.2
1964	27,685	21,283	10,332	4.5	3.5	1.7
1969	49,306	32,471	15,798	5.5	3.6	1.8
1970	55,437	36,955	17,082	5.8	3.9	1.8
1971	63,750	42,119	18,659	6.3	4.2	1.8
1972	68,624	46,415	20,581	6.2	4.2	1.9
1973	74,535	45,483	21,812	6.1	3.7	1.8
1974 est.	81,000	49,000	23,500	6.0	3.7	1.8
	Percentage Distribution			Annual Percent Change		
1954	46.4	38.1	15.6	—	—	—
1964	46.7	35.9	17.4	7.9[2]	7.3[2]	9.1[2]
1969	50.5	33.3	16.2	12.2[3]	8.8[3]	8.9[3]
1970	50.6	33.8	15.6	12.4	13.8	8.1
1971	51.2	33.8	15.0	15.0	14.0	9.2
1972	50.6	34.2	15.2	7.6	10.2	10.3
1973	52.6	32.1	15.4	8.6	−2.0	6.0
1974	52.8	31.9	15.3	8.7	7.7	7.7

Note: The National Income and Product Accounts series, used in the previous tables, does not provide a breakdown between state and local governments. This table is based on data from the U.S. Bureau of the Census series, and is on a fiscal year basis.

[1] Excludes federal aid, and utility, liquor store, and insurance trust expenditures. Insurance trust systems are government-administered programs for employee retirement and social insurance protection relating to unemployment compensation, workmen's compensation, old age survivors disability, and health insurance, and the like.

[2] Annual average increase 1954 to 1964.

[3] Annual average increase 1964 to 1969.

Source: ACIR, *Trends in Fiscal Federalism, 1954–1974*, February, 1975, p. 17; from ACIR staff compilation based on U.S. Bureau of the Census, *Governmental Finances*, various years; and ACIR staff estimates.

cussed in detail under fiscal federalism in chapter 6. A comparison of table 5 with table 7 will illustrate. For example, of the $193 billion federal budget in calendar 1974 (table 5), only $149.5 billion (table 7) was spent at that level. Correspondingly, although state and local governments spent $161 billion of their own funds (table 5), they actually spent $204.5 billion (table 7) on their own programs. The $43.5 billion difference in both expenditure figures represents the amount of federal money transferred to subnational governments. In practice then, the amount spent directly to fund federal domestic programs was not 54.5 percent of total domestic expenditure, but 42.2 percent; and it represented only 10.7 percent of the gross national product rather than 13.8 percent.

Purposes of Expenditures

Money is spent to provide benefits and services for consumption by either the general population or selected groups, such as veterans, farmers, businesspeople, economically disadvantaged, and others. At the federal level, the major expenditure is for wars — past, present and future. As indicated in

Table 7 The Growing Domestic Public Sector[1]:
1954, 1964, and 1969 through 1974
(Government Domestic Expenditure, *After Intergovernmental Transfers*)

Calendar Year	Total Domestic Expenditure (Federal-State-Local)	Federal Domestic Expenditure[2]	State-Local Total Expenditure	Total Domestic Expenditure (Federal-State-Local)	Federal Domestic Expenditure[2]	State-Local Expenditure
	Amount (in billions)			Annual Percent Change		
1954	$ 46.9	$ 17.0	$ 29.9	12.9	4.7	8.2
1964	110.8	42.9	67.9	17.5	6.8	10.7
1969	191.6	72.6	119.0	20.6	7.8	12.8
1970	215.8	82.6	133.2	22.1	8.5	13.6
1971	245.2	96.4	148.8	23.2	9.1	14.1
1972	278.2	113.3	164.9	24.0	9.8	14.2
1973[3]	310.8	126.4	184.4	24.0	9.8	14.2
1974 est.	354.0	149.5	204.5	25.4	10.7	14.7
	Percentage Distribution			As a Percent of GNP		
1954	100.0	36.2	63.8	—	—	—
1964	100.0	38.7	61.3	9.0[4]	9.7[4]	8.5[4]
1969	100.0	37.9	62.1	11.6[5]	11.1[5]	11.9[5]
1970	100.0	38.3	61.7	12.6	13.8	11.9
1971	100.0	39.3	60.7	13.6	16.7	11.7
1972	100.0	40.7	59.3	13.5	17.5	10.8
1973	100.0	40.7	59.3	11.7	11.6	11.8
1974	100.0	42.2	57.8	13.9	18.3	10.9

Note: All federal aid to state and local governments, including general revenue sharing payments is included as state-local expenditure and excluded from federal domestic expenditures.

[1] National Income and Product Accounts.

[2] Excludes Federal expenditure for national defense, international affairs and finance, space research and technology, and the estimated portion of net interest attributable to these functions. Includes Social Security (OASDHI).

[3] Partially estimated.

[4] Annual average increase 1954 to 1964.

[5] Annual average increase 1964 to 1969.

SOURCE: ACIR, *Trends in Fiscal Federalism, 1954–1974,* February, 1975, p. 12; ACIR staff compilation based on U.S. Department of Commerce, Office of Business Economics, *Survey of Current Business,* various years; *Budget of the United States Government,* various years; and ACIR staff estimates.

table 2, the president requested $94.0 billion for national defense in his fiscal 1976 budget. If the $15.6 billion in veterans benefits is added to the $6.3 billion for international affairs, defense and defense-related activities will consume approximately one-third of the budget. When the $34.4 billion interest on the national debt is added, some of which is war related, only about 55 percent of the money is left to fund all other programs and activities of the federal government, including providing financial assistance to state and local government.

At the state level, the objects of expenditure include university-level education, highways, public welfare, correctional institutions, police, subsidies to local government, parks and recreation, and a variety of other services provided on a statewide basis. Locally the services become more immediate. They include elementary and secondary education, streets, police and fire protection, sewage disposal, health, water, and other services which are minimally available in many countries, but which are expected as a matter of course in the United States.[2]

Reasons for Increased Expenditures

There are a variety of reasons why public expenditures for nonmilitary programs constantly escalate. In the first place, inflation has an important impact. A considerable portion of the increased expenditures has been consumed by the inflationary trend which increases the cost of goods and services purchased by all levels of government. Under such economic conditions, government has to spend more each year just to maintain the same level of services provided the previous year. If total expenditures are converted to fixed-dollar prices, which indicates purchasing power, the comparative expenditures become more realistic. Comparing federal figures in table 8, where all amounts have been converted to 1969 prices, with those

Table 8 Composition of Budget Outlays in Constant (Fiscal Year 1969) Prices: 1955–76

(in billions of dollars)

Fiscal Year	Total Outlays	National Defense	Nondefense				Addendum: Composition of Payments for Individuals			
			Total Non-defense	Payments for Indi-viduals	Net Interest	All Other	Total	Direct		Indirect (through State and Local Gov-ernments)
								National Defense	Non-defense	
1955	109.1	60.7	48.4	17.2	14.3	16.9	17.7	.6	14.9	2.2
1956	107.5	57.9	49.6	18.2	13.7	17.7	18.9	.6	15.9	2.3
1957	110.2	58.1	52.1	20.0	13.0	19.1	20.7	.7	17.6	2.4
1958	114.0	58.0	56.0	24.1	13.0	18.9	24.8	.7	21.3	2.7
1959	122.9	58.4	64.5	26.4	13.2	25.0	27.1	.8	23.4	2.9
1960	120.3	56.9	63.4	27.5	13.1	22.8	28.3	.8	24.5	3.0
1961	124.8	57.2	67.6	30.7	13.0	23.9	31.6	.9	27.5	3.2
1962	135.8	62.0	73.8	31.8	13.4	28.5	32.9	1.1	28.2	3.6
1963	138.7	62.7	76.0	33.8	13.6	28.6	35.0	1.2	30.0	3.8
1964	143.4	62.1	81.4	34.4	13.5	33.4	35.8	1.4	30.3	4.1
1965	139.2	55.3	84.0	34.7	13.5	35.8	36.3	1.6	30.5	4.2
1966	152.8	61.7	91.2	38.0	13.4	39.7	39.8	1.8	33.3	4.8
1967	173.4	74.5	98.9	43.3	13.1	42.4	45.3	2.0	38.2	5.2
1968	189.6	83.1	106.5	47.7	13.8	45.0	49.9	2.2	41.4	6.3
1969	184.5	80.2	104.3	52.5	12.7	39.2	54.9	2.4	45.4	7.1
1970	180.8	72.3	108.5	56.1	12.3	40.1	58.8	2.7	48.1	8.0
1971	181.6	63.8	117.7	66.4	12.5	38.9	69.4	3.0	55.9	10.5
1972	191.2	61.2	130.0	73.3	12.8	43.9	76.6	3.4	60.7	12.6
1973	191.7	54.9	136.9	79.3	13.0	44.5	83.0	3.7	67.2	12.1
1974	189.7	52.7	137.0	84.3	12.1	40.7	88.2	3.9	72.1	12.2
1975 estimate	199.1	50.9	148.2	93.8	12.2	42.1	98.1	4.3	82.0	11.9
1976 estimate	202.7	51.0	151.7	95.3	13.0	43.4	99.6	4.3	84.0	11.3

SOURCE: *The United States Budget in Brief, Fiscal Year 1976*, p. 58.

in table 1, we can see the impact of inflation. Such a comparison shows that on this basis the pre-1969 expenditures would increase while those in the post-1969 period would decrease. For example, the 1966 figure would increase from $134.7 to $152.8 billion — while the amount estimated for 1976 would decrease from $349.4 to $202.7 billion.

Second, citizens are placing increasing demands upon their governments. In recent years, many programs designed to achieve social objectives in areas such as welfare, housing, equal educational opportunity, care of the aging, and control of all forms of pollution have been added to the functions of government. Third, most programs extend over many years, expand in scope, and increase in cost. A good example of this (table 2) is income security (social security) which jumped from actual expenditures of $9.1 billion in

1955 to $28.9 billion in 1966 to an estimated $118.7 billion for 1976. Finally, programs — once included in the budget — normally perpetuate themselves, sometimes long after the need has passed. Pressure by organized recipients of the benefits, as discussed in chapter 19 under politics of budgeting, has been very successful in insuring the survival of their pet programs.

Sources of Revenue

The possible sources from which these great sums of money come, excluding the uncontrolled printing of money which creates a variety of inflationary and other problems, could be grouped into two categories — taxes and levies and other sources. The source or sources selected for emphasis and how they are manipulated can have a significant impact on the social and economic structure of a nation. What should be taxed and at what rate? On which group should the heaviest burden fall? What type of tax incentives should be used to encourage or discourage selected activities? Should inheritance and income taxes be used to reduce economic differences and essentially redistribute the wealth? From these and a variety of other alternatives, the political leadership will choose the policy that will be followed at any given time.

Taxes and Levies

As indicated in table 2, the most important single source of federal revenue is the individual income tax, followed by the social insurance taxes and contributions, which consist largely of payroll taxes. However, the latter funds are trust accounts designed to fund retirement and pension programs.[3]

At the state and local levels, income and corporate taxes play a much less significant role.[4] Of the revenue generated from state sources in 1971–72, the sales and gross receipts taxes levied on the sale of commodities, alcoholic beverages, tobacco, and services produced approximately 40 percent of the revenue. The most important single source of locally generated revenue is the property tax, which is not used by the federal government and is only slightly used by the states. This tax, on a nationwide basis, produced approximately 54 percent of the locally generated income in 1971–72. In addition to this, local governments use a variety of other taxes, levies and fees, special assessments, and service charges.[5]

An analysis of the combined sources of revenue for state and local government (table 9), undifferentiated as to the level of government, indicates that in 1974 the most important producers of tax revenue in order of priority were property taxes, sales and gross receipts, and income. But, it should be pointed out that while the importance of the property tax is declining, the percentage of revenue produced by income taxes is increasing.

Other Sources

Other major sources of funds include public enterprises, intergovernmental transfers, and borrowing. Public enterprises, designed as profit-making entities, are owned and operated by all levels of government. These facilities may be found in areas such as power generation and distribution, transportation, recreation, harbors, research, and a variety of other areas. This is

Administration as Management

Table 9 The State and Local Revenue System Becomes More Diversified with Relative Decline in Property Taxes and Relative Increase in State Income Taxes and Federal Aid: 1954, 1964, and 1969 through 1974

| Fiscal Year | Total State-Local Revenue | General Revenue | | Tax Revenue | | | | Charges and Miscellaneous General Revenue | Utility, Liquor Store, and Insurance Trust Revenue |
		Total	Federal Aid	Total¹	Property	Sales, and Gross Receipts	Income		
				Amount (in billions)					
1954	$ 35.4	$ 29.0	$ 3.0	$ 22.1	$ 10.0	$ 7.3	$ 1.9	$ 4.0	$ 6.4
1964	81.5	68.4	10.0	47.8	21.2	15.8	5.5	10.7	13.0
1969	132.2	114.5	19.2	76.7	30.7	26.5	12.1	18.7	17.6
1970	150.1	130.8	21.9	86.8	34.1	30.3	14.6	22.1	19.4
1971	166.1	144.9	26.1	95.0	37.9	33.2	15.3	23.8	21.2
1972	189.7	166.4	31.3	108.8	42.1	37.5	19.7	26.3	23.4
1973	217.6	190.2	39.3	121.1	45.3	42.0	23.4	29.8	27.4
1974²	234.3	204.8	41.0	131.8	48.8	47.2	25.6³	32.0	29.5
				Annual Percent Change					
1954	—	—	—	—	—	—	—	—	—
1964	8.7⁴	9.0⁴	12.8⁴	8.0⁴	7.8⁴	8.0⁴	11.2⁴	10.3⁴	7.3⁴
1969	10.2⁵	10.9⁵	13.9⁵	9.9⁵	7.7⁵	10.9⁵	17.1⁵	11.8⁵	6.2⁵
1970	13.5	14.2	14.1	13.2	11.1	14.3	20.7	18.2	10.2
1971	10.7	10.8	19.2	9.4	11.1	9.6	4.8	7.7	9.3
1972	14.2	14.8	19.9	14.5	11.1	13.0	28.8	10.5	10.4
1973	14.7	14.3	25.6	11.3	7.6	12.0	18.8	13.3	17.1
1974	7.6	7.7	4.3	8.8	7.7	12.4	9.4	7.4	7.7
				Percentage Distribution					
1954	100.0	81.9	8.5	62.4	28.2	20.6	5.4	11.3	18.1
1964	100.0	83.9	12.3	58.7	26.0	19.4	6.7	13.1	16.0
1974	100.0	87.4	17.5	56.3	20.8	20.1	10.9³	13.7	12.6

¹Including amounts for categories not shown separately.
²Partially estimated.
³Receipts from individual taxes in 1974 were $19.6-billion (8.4 percent of total revenue).
⁴Annual average increase 1954 to 1964.
⁵Annual average increase 1964 to 1969.

SOURCE: ACIR, *Trends in Fiscal Federalism, 1954–1974,* February, 1975, p. 21; from ACIR staff compilation based on U.S. Bureau of the Census, *Governmental Finances,* various years; and ACIR staff estimates.

not a major source of revenue for most governments, but it is important to some.

Intergovernmental transfers — grants, revenue sharing, and subsidiaries — are an important source of state and local revenue. The federal input to state and local governments, discussed previously in this chapter, is further illustrated by the data in table 9, which show that 17.5 percent of the income of subnational governments in 1974 came from federal grants. For local governments, an additional important source of money is state government.

On a nationwide basis, subventions from the states now more than equal the amounts generated from purely local sources (table 10). The table also indicates that over one-half of this state money goes to support education. Without this source, as well as federal money, local governments could not function.

Table 10 State Aid Registers Steady Increase in Relation to Local Own Source Revenue: 1954, 1964, and 1969 through 1974

Fiscal Year	Total State Aid		General Local Government Support	Education	Highways	Public Welfare	All Other
	Amount	As a Percent of Local General Revenue From Own Sources					
Amount (in millions)							
1954	$ 5,679	41.7	$ 600	$ 2,930	$ 871	$1,004	$ 274
1964	12,968	42.9	1,053	7,664	1,524	2,108	619
1969	24,779	54.0	2,135	14,858	2,109	4,402	1,275
1970	28,892	56.2	2,958	17,085	2,439	5,003	1,408
1971	32,640	57.3	3,258	19,292	2,507	5,760	1,823
1972	36,759	57.0	3,752	21,195	2,633	6,944	2,235
1973	40,822	57,9	4,280	23,316	2,953	7,532	2,742
1974 est.	45,000	57.5	4,700	25,800	3,200	8,400	2,900
Annual Percent Change							
1954	—	—	—	—	—	—	—
1964	8.6[1]	—	5.8[1]	10.1[1]	5.8[1]	7.7[1]	8.5[1]
1969	13.8[2]	—	15.2[2]	14.2[2]	6.7[2]	15.9[2]	15.6[2]
1970	16.6	—	38.5	15.0	15.6	13.7	10.4
1971	13.0	—	10.1	12.9	2.8	15.1	29.5
1972	12.6	—	15.2	9.9	5.0	20.6	22.6
1973	11.1	—	14.1	10.0	12.2	8.5	22.7
1974	10.2	—	9.8	10.7	8.4	11.5	5.8
Percentage Distribution							
1954	100.0	—	10.6	51.6	15.3	17.7	4.8
1964	100.0	—	8.1	59.1	11.8	16.3	4.8
1974	100.0	—	10.4	57.3	7.1	18.7	6.4

[1]Annual average increase 1954 to 1964.
[2]Annual average increase 1964 to 1969.

SOURCE: ACIR, *Trends in Fiscal Federalism, 1954–1974,* February, 1975, p. 29; from ACIR staff compilation based on U.S. Bureau of the Census, *Governmental Finances,* various years; and ACIR staff estimates.

Borrowing, when revenue is less than expenditures, is a common practice. There is, however, great variation in the acceptability of borrowing among the units of government in the United States. At the federal level, where extensive borrowing has been practiced for years, the national debt projected to reach $605.9 billion by June, 1976 (see table 3), will be increased by approximately $30 billion due to tax cuts made to stimulate the economy in March, 1975. At the state and local levels, and especially the local, there are more limitations on borrowing.[6] In many cases, money may be borrowed only to fund projects which will generate income to retire the debt and then only after a public vote on the issue. However, at the end of the 1972 fiscal year, state and local governments had an accumulated debt of approximately $175 billion, of which $120 billion was owed by the states.[7]

Conclusions

From the above, it is quite evident that modern government has a voracious appetite for money. These costs, which consume a significant percentage of the gross national product, have been a controversial issue. Many people, who argue that government has become too large, provides too many services, and plays too big a role in society, urge a reduction in government which would reduce costs. Others insist that public monies should be used to provide the full range of services.

A companion issue has been the sources of money — principally tax policy and the debt. Tax policy, of course, may be manipulated to achieve a variety of purposes. Some are saying that the income tax structure places an excessive burden on the wealthy and middle class in order to fund extensive programs for the economically disadvantaged. Debt policy and deficit financing as a source of revenue are criticized as unsound by some and necessary by others.

However, if one looks at the federal budget, most of the money is spent for defense and security-related measures, leaving only a portion to fund all other programs. At all levels, governments are faced with two problems — inflation, which means it costs more each year just to maintain the level of service of the previous year, and increasing demands for the addition of new services and improvement in the service levels. As long as these conditions remain, the cost of government will not decrease.

However, there is some limit, which will be expressed by the voting population. The citizens, when they have direct control, have expressed their displeasure by failing to pass state and local bond issues. If this so-called taxpayers revolt becomes intense and organized, it may become a major political issue and may force change through the electoral process.

The topic of public finance is concerned with where vast sums of money come from, the purposes for which it is spent and how it is managed and accounted for. Broadly defined, it includes taxation and tax policies, treasury operations, debt management, the budget process, accounting, auditing, and purchasing. All of these functions must be provided by the governmental system of any nation. Their role and the specific techniques used will be dictated by the political and economic framework of the country. However, since a detailed discussion of the whole finance field is beyond the scope of this book, we have been forced to be selective as we present this topic in the next chapter. We shall not attempt to discuss the innumerable systems used at the various levels of government but shall discuss some general concepts. Second, we will exclude a discussion of the highly technical areas of taxation, monetary and fiscal policies, and debt management, with which few people have much contact. We will focus on the budgeting, accounting, and auditing functions, with special emphasis on the budgetary process.

NOTES

1. The fiscal year of the federal government, which runs from July 1 of one year to June 30 of the following year, is designated by the year in which it ends — July 1, 1974 – June 30, 1975 is fiscal 1975. However, the Budget and Impoundment Control Act of 1974 will alter this time frame. The 1976 budget covers the period of July 1, 1975 – June 30, 1976. Subsequent fiscal years, however, will begin on October 1 and end of September 30. To make the change, there will be a "mini" budget covering the three months — July, August, and September, 1976 — the transition period.

2. For the figures and a discussion of state and local revenue and expenditures, see Advisory Commission on Intergovernmental Relations (ACIR), *Federal-State-Local Finances: Significant Features of Fiscal Federalism*, Report M–79 (Washington, D.C.: Government Printing Office, 1974) and ACIR, *Trends in Fiscal Federalism, 1954–1974,* (Washington, D.C.: Government Printing Office, February 1975).

3. For a discussion of trust funds, see *Federal Trust Funds: Budgetary and Other Implications* (New York: Tax Foundation, 1970).

4. For detailed data on all state and local sources, see ACIR, 1973–74 edition of *Federal-State-Local Finances*, pp. 2–52.

5. Ibid.

6. For the details on borrowing limitations, see ACIR, 1973–74 edition of *Federal-State-Local Finances*, pp. 139–58.

7. For the data on borrowing, see ibid., pp. 133–38.

19

Financial Management

The topic of public finance is concerned with where vast sums of money come from, the purposes for which they are spent, how they are managed and accounted for. Broadly defined, it includes taxation and tax policy, treasury operations, debt management, budgeting, accounting and auditing, as well as some of the functions of the Federal Reserve Board.

All of these functions must be provided by the governmental system of any nation, as well as by states and other subunits. But their role, relationship with other systems — economic, social, and political — and the specific techniques used will depend upon the political and economic framework within which the government functions. In the United States, accounting and auditing follow technical and prescribed procedures, but decisions on the remainder of the functions, which are value laden, are made through the democratic political process.

Since a detailed discussion of the whole field of finance is beyond the scope of this book, we have been forced to be selective. First, general concepts will be discussed, but no attempt will be made to cover the different systems at the various governmental levels. Second, we will exclude a discussion of the technical areas of taxation, monetary and fiscal policies, and debt management, which are rather specialized fields.

Public administrators are generally (1) involved in preparing the budget, guiding it through the enactment process and spending the money, (2) responsible for the accounting process which shows how the money was spent, and (3) interested in the results of an audit of the books by an outside agency. Therefore, the focus of this chapter will be on budgeting, accounting and auditing.

Budgeting

Budgeting is a complex, time-consuming process that involves both the executive and legislative branches. We will look at the purposes of a budget, some of the forms it has taken, and the budgeting process itself.

Purposes of a Budget

Someone once said that, "A budget is a method of worrying before you spend instead of afterward." In a world of big government and gigantic expenditures, however, legislators, financial managers, top executives — in fact, all managers — have to worry before, during and after the spending of the public's money. Actually, a public budget serves many purposes:

1. It is the basic planning document by which government decides what its objectives are and what they will cost.
2. A budget is a decision instrument by which a limited amount of money is allocated among unlimited competing programs costing more than the available resources.
3. It could be considered a value indicator. The programs included and their comparative levels of funding indicate the system of priorities and relative importance assigned to the competing claims for funds.
4. Since governmental receipts and expenditures have such a tremendous impact on the American economy, the federal budget must be considered a statement of economic policy.
5. It is a policy statement indicating the direction government plans to take and how it intends to get there.[1]

A budget may be tailored to fit many purposes, including retaliation and discipline, which can be achieved by reducing the requests for specific functions, failing to include money for salary increases, and not including any amount to fund the unit, which effectively kills the agency.

However, the budget is not a totally honest document. To be sure, it is public information, but it is impossible by reading the federal budget to know exactly the purposes for which money was actually spent. Some money for defense and the Central Intelligence Agency, for example, are hidden in the budgets of other units, intergovernmental financial transfers are not clearly defined, operating budgets of public and mixed enterprises are difficult or impossible to identify, and other monies are not clearly labeled.

The Dilemma

In budgeting, government is faced with the insoluble dilemma of reconciling two opposing citizen inputs into the political process. One input is the unlimited and increasing demand for government to provide new services, to intensify traditional ones, and to assume new responsibilities. The opposing and increasingly insistent demand is for government to limit or reduce the variety and level of taxes. The dilemma is that no government can reduce the financial demands it places on its citizens and at the same time respond to their clamor for an increasing variety and level of services. As a result the money available is always insufficient to fund all of the legitimate and worthwhile programs. Difficult choices, decisions, and compromises have to be made. As we discuss later in the chapter, the decision-making process is a political one.

The History of Budgeting

The purposes of budgets, as well as the forms and procedures, like most aspects of administration, have evolved through a series of stages that were influenced, if not dictated, by the political, social, and economic environment of the times. As a particular form or procedure produced results below those expected by or acceptable to the environment, a reform movement would begin and force the desired modifications. Although this is not a history book, a synopsis of the past experience will establish the background of the present system, which can be discussed under two headings — pre-executive budget and executive budget.

Pre-Executive Budget Period

In the early history of the United States, government at all levels was reluctantly accepted as a necessary evil. It provided limited services to the people and procedures were influenced by the laissez-faire economic system. Budgets and control systems as we know them today were thought to be undesirable and unnecessary. In budget preparation, each organizational unit in the executive branch went directly to the legislative body to present, defend, and fight for its request for funds. No one person or agency in the executive branch had authority to reduce the amounts requested or to consolidate them into a single budget which reflected the total amount requested. In budget enactment, the requests of each department were manipulated by the legislatures and appropriations bills were passed separately without a budgetary master plan. When the action was over, the total amount authorized and its distribution among programs often came as a shock and was not necessarily rational. After the money was appropriated, it was spent by each unit with few, if any, outside restraints, controls, or supervision. Because of the resulting chaos, including graft and corruption, a new system emerged.

The system took the form of a legislative budget. Budget preparation was not centralized and few changes were made in this phase of the budgetary process. All of the requests originating in the executive units were consolidated into one document and processed through the legislative committee structure. This system still did not fix responsibility and accountability, but at least there was a document which reflected the totals. Due to its defects and inadequacies, a serious reform movement started around 1900. The major product was the executive budget.

Executive Budget

In the 1920s, the federal government adopted the concept of the executive budget and created the Bureau of the Budget and the General Accounting Office. The executive budget system centralizes responsibility for budget preparation in the executive office, based on the theory that the executive — president, governor, manager, school superintendent — is the one in a position to know the needs of the whole organization. Although the actual preparation will be done by a staff agency, it is prepared within guidelines laid down by the executive; she or he consults in its preparation and makes the final decision on how much money the executive branch will ask for and how it will be allocated among the various programs. The legislature has one package to process rather than a series of separate, uncoordinated, and untotaled requests from individual executive departments.

However, the intent and uses of the executive budget have evolved in three phases, each of which made modifications in the system and procedures.[2]

First Phase. During the initial phase, from approximately 1920 to 1935, the emphasis was on creating a system to control expenditures to correct previous abuses. The planning and management aspects of budgeting were of secondary importance. One of the fundamental control techniques was the adoption of the line item or object of expenditure format for the budget. In this format, the purposes of expenditures are either indicated by specific items — such as each individual position by class and salary level — or a lump sum is provided for personnel, supplies, communications, capital improvements, and each of the other functions. As an added control, the executive departmental managers normally have no authority to transfer funds between categories without prior approval of the central fiscal control unit, such as the Bureau of the Budget or Department of Finance. With this emphasis on control, budgets were essentially a collection of detailed figures with no indication of work programs, objectives, standards, and other components for measuring effectiveness.

Second Phase. In the second period, the emphasis shifted from control to management. The control orientation, criticized for years, became totally inappropriate to process the demands placed on the federal government by the economic depression of the 1930s. Government now was not viewed as a necessary evil delivering limited services, but as the only agency that could provide needed massive social and economic benefits to the residents. Under the New Deal slogan of President Franklin D. Roosevelt, federal programs and expenditures expanded dramatically. Management of these resources in order to provide the desired benefits, rather than fiscal control, now became the need.

In 1937, the President's Committee on Administrative Management criticized using the budget as an instrument of control and recommended that it be made a management tool by which the president could manage and coordinate the extensive and complex programs. As a result, the Bureau of the Budget was transferred from the Treasury Department to the newly created Executive Office of the President in 1939. In addition to this, a series of modifications were made in the budgeting format and procedures.

The culmination of this phase was the introduction of Performance Budgeting as recommended by the Hoover Commission.[3] This system introduced such concepts as budgeting on the basis of major functions and activities — public safety, welfare — rather than on a line item basis (including a description of each activity and its objectives in the budget document) and measuring efficiency through work measurement, cost effectiveness, and other techniques.

PPB Phase.   In the third phase, a budget was viewed not as a control or management tool, but as a planning document and the Planning, Programming, Budgeting System replaced Performance Budgeting as the model. The system, introduced into the Department of Defense in 1961, was extended to all major federal agencies in August, 1965, and was adopted by some state and local governments. As Dwight Waldo said, "in terms of amount of interest and professional attention, PPBS is probably the happening of the decade in public administration."[4] Few things in public administration have generated such intense controversy. The most ardent proponents have sold it as a semi-miracle cure for a variety of ills, while opponents have been equally vocal.[5]

What Is PPB?   The PPB system, designed to permit managers and legislators to make logical choices among alternate ways of allocating scarce resources, creates a different environment for choice. As Allen Schick points out, "traditionally, budgeting has defined its mission in terms of identifying the existing base and proposed departures from it — 'This is where we are; where do we go from here?' PPB defines its mission in terms of budgetary objectives and purposes — 'Where do we want to go? What do we do to get there?' "[6]

The two philosophies produce different responsibilities, procedures and products. Under the traditional format, it is an incremental process when each administrative organization prepares its budget by simply adding to last year's budget to cover new programs and new costs with no evaluation of its program. In the PPB system, goals and objectives established by top management become the framework within which each unit prepares its budget estimates. Rather than being incremental it is a process in which each unit has to justify its programs in competition with those of other units. Choices are made between program alternatives.

Components.   The individual components or techniques associated with the system include planning, programming, budgeting, cost-benefit analysis, marginal analysis and work measurement. There is, however, no single system, nor is there universal agreement that it is worth the effort. Consequently, the system is modified to fit the particular needs and environment of the specific level of government adopting it and differs in complexity.

The major components of any such program are as follows:

1. Rather than listing each administrative department, the budget is divided into several broad program areas — public safety, health, education, and so on.
2. All governmental services are analyzed and placed in one of these program categories, regardless of which organizational unit provides the

service. As a result, a unit which provides services to more than one program will be listed in more than one place. This procedure is called "crosswalking."

3. The cost of the service provided by each unit to each program is listed on the program category sheet, which gives a composite total of how much it costs to provide public safety, education, and each other service.

4. In addition to the annual budget, there is a long-range budget covering a period of time, usually five years, to project needs and allow for planning.

5. Both capital and current expenditures are included.

6. There is a continuous system of computer-assisted program analysis to generate and evaluate alternate purposes of expenditures, as well as to update the spending plan.

7. A series of three basic documents are usually used. One is the program memorandum, which outlines the general objectives, choices available, basic approaches, and some tentative recommendations for each of the program categories. The multiyear program and financial plan shows the expected impact this year's financial decisions will have on present and future budgetary requirements. Special studies furnish the data for making, reevaluating and modifying program decisions included in the program memorandum.

The Status of PPB.   In 1975, the status as well as the future of the PPB system was confused. There was no clear agreement as to its essential components, but many diverse procedures were being practiced under its name. There was rather common agreement that it had been oversold as the model for financial decision making to the exclusion of traditional techniques. There was also almost unanimous consensus that introduction and full implementation of the theoretical model is politically impossible in many cases, and difficult at best. Nevertheless, some governmental agencies are using the system exclusively, others use it but also prepare a traditional budget, and some have reverted completely to the traditional system of budgeting.

The implementation success of the system at the federal level, where it was the most highly developed, is indicated by a 1968 study.[7] The Office of Management and Budget, after analyzing sixteen federal agencies to determine the extent to which PPB was being utilized in decision making, concluded that the traditional process of making planning, programming, and budgetary decisions in most agencies had not been significantly changed by the introduction of PPBS. On June 21, 1971, the system, for all intents and purposes, was abandoned by the federal government. The Office of Management and Budget issued a memorandum stating that agencies no longer had to submit multiyear financing plans, program memoranda, and other elements which had been required under the PPB system.[8]

The Budgetary Process

The budgetary process in the executive budget system, regardless of the internal format of the budget, consists of budget preparation, budget enactment, and budget execution. Responsibility for each phase shifts between the executive and legislative branches: executive prepares budget, legislature appropriates money, executive supervises expenditures. As mentioned earlier in the chapter, the preparation, enactment, and execution phases of the process are highly political. We will briefly describe the steps in the total process and then turn to these human behavioral aspects.

Budget Preparation

Budget preparation involves specific, detailed techniques, forms, time schedules, and procedures that vary with the different governments. All of these are prescribed by constitutions, charters, laws, or ordinances and further defined by agency procedures and manuals. Hence, this section concentrates on only some general concepts.

Responsibility and Limitations.   In the executive budget system, regardless of the format, the chief executive officer does not have total freedom. He or she is limited principally by three factors. First, the legislative body often passes the word as to what it expects. Since some legislators may have been elected on the basis of a pledge not to increase taxes or to actually reduce them, the legislative body may inform the executive that the proposed budget ceiling should be what the current tax levy will produce. A second limiting factor is an executive sensitivity to political realities or what can realistically be passed by the legislative body. Finally, the executive must consider the expectations, hopes, and demands expressed by the groups served by the particular government.

Procedures.   Although procedures vary with the budget format, the process normally starts with the chief executive issuing budget ceilings or guidelines to assist units in preparing their budget requests. Budget preparation starts with the lowest unit of each executive department completing the required forms in which it requests and attempts to justify the amounts needed to perform its functions for the next year. These estimates then progress through each echelon of the department where the requests are consolidated, discussed, and possibly revised. The proposed budget from each department then goes to the Office of Management and Budget at the federal level, to a department of finance or similar specialized staff agency in the states and larger units of local government, and to the managers or other chief executive officer in smaller jurisdictions. At this stage, the requests are consolidated into a budget, which always exceeds the money available. Then, hearings in which administrative departments attempt to justify their requests are usually conducted. As a result, the requests are normally reduced and some reallocations are made, either through negotiations, by arbitrary action of the staff agency, or as a result of a department's reanalysis of its request to conform with a reduction (usually specified by a percentage or dollar amount of the original request). After the modifications have been made, requests from units not controlled by the executive — the legislative body, courts, and independent administrative agencies — are combined with those from the administrative units to make the final executive budget. This spending plan will normally have a companion revenue section which indicates the sources of revenue to fund the program.

The Document.   The budget documents published by the various levels of government are not standardized in format or content and vary greatly in complexity. The federal budget document is the most detailed. The federal government, after experimenting with three specialized budgets — administrative budget, consolidated cash budget, and national income accounts budget — adopted a unified budget in 1969 which reflects all financial transactions. The present budget, which is not a "best seller" except among researchers and the agencies concerned, is not a single document. The actual budget, prepared by the Office of Management and Budget in the Executive Office of the President, consists of two parts. The first is the *Budget of the United States Government,* which is a rather small volume containing the president's budget message and other facts, figures, data, and comments by which he attempts to explain and justify the major programs, direction, policies, and intent of the administration to Congress. The second part is the much larger *Appendix,* containing the detailed, specific data and the text of proposed appropriations bills for congressional consideration. Two other useful corollary documents should be mentioned. One is the *Budget in Brief,* which consolidates and presents the financial picture in a very concise nontechnical form. The second, the *Special Analyses, Budget of the United States,* contains analyses of most program areas and budget data.

Time Concepts.   Budget preparation is usually a hectic, time-consuming, and essentially continuous process. The preliminary work, which begins a year or more in advance of submission to the legislative body, starts at a rather relaxed pace and apparently with sufficient lead time.[9] As time disappears, the completion date sneaks up, and the pressure intensifies. The final tough decisions, which are the time-consuming key to the process, writing justifications, preparing the final budget document, and other finishing details are normally made under intense time pressures. The process is no longer leisurely but becomes an all-consuming, energy-draining process bordering on panic for those involved. In the process, nerves can become frayed, and most people involved would agree that "it isn't any way to live." Although many think that a particular budget will never be completed on time, deadlines are met, people survive the process and everyone breathes a sigh of relief when it is completed.

The relief, however, is only temporary. Soon after the budget is completed, preliminary work for next year's budget begins. The budgetary process, a fact of life in any type of organization, really never ends; it only varies in intensity. For top administrators, department heads and others most deeply involved, it is accepted as essential, but not anticipated with any great pleasure.

Budget Enactment

Once the budget is prepared, it is sent to the legislative body — Congress, state legislature, city council, county board of supervisors, school board, or other policy-making body. The document is processed through a committee structure or however the rules provide.[10] Since no money can be spent without legislative authorization, the legislatures, within whatever constitutional or legal limitations have been placed upon them, have the authority to make the final decisions on the allocation of resources. In the process, the budget is used as a starting point, but it is far from a sacred document. With luck, the executive may get essentially what was requested. The finished product may also resemble a very distant, but hopefully recognizable, relative of the document so painfully prepared and submitted.

What can an executive do if the legislative product is unsatisfactory? The options depend on the system. At the federal level and in some states, the chief executive must either accept or veto the whole appropriations package. To veto has many obvious risks. In many states, where the item veto is constitutional, the governor may reach in and veto or reduce certain expenditure items but accept the remainder. At the local level, elected mayors in a strong mayor-council form of government may also have some veto power, but a general or item veto at any level may be overridden by the legislative body.

However, administrators such as city managers, county administrative officers, school superintendents and others appointed by and responsible to an elected body are in a different position. Since they are nonpartisan professionals with no political responsibility to the voters, they do not have veto power. Their role is to make and quietly try to sell their financial recommendations to the policy-making body before and during budget preparation. The final budget submitted should be within the expectations of the politicians. If it comes as a surprise or has to be drastically modified, something is wrong. Such an error could be explained by a sudden drop in the revenue which could not have been anticipated: the signals were changed on the administrator due to the election or appointment of new personnel to the policy-making body; failure of the administrator to work within the guidelines established by the policy group; or administrative insensitivity to the group's intentions and wishes. In the latter two cases, the administrator may soon be looking for another agency that can use his or her talents.

Budget Execution

Once the money has been appropriated for a particular unit or program, the agency does not have an unlimited license to spend. Although monitoring expenditures is normally assigned to a central staff agency, the chief executive is in control of the process. Three major control devices are used. One is the allotment system, where a spending unit is given its appropriated funds in quarterly allotments, which may or may not be in equal installments to insure a rational rate of expenditure and to protect against a depletion of funds prior to the end of the fiscal year. A second method is a system of preaudits. A preaudit, unlike a post audit, is a device to control expenditures before obligations are incurred. The paperwork on every proposed transaction which commits funds must be submitted to the staff agency for advance approval. The proposed transaction is evaluated for legality, compliance with established policies and procedures, availability of funds, and other factors indicated by the executive. Only after it has survived this screening process is the paperwork released and the financial commitment made. A final control, used at the federal level and in some states, is the controversial practice by which the executive impounds (refuses to spend) funds appropriated by the legislature.[11]

General Characteristics of the Budgetary Process

The budgetary process exhibits various characteristics during the various phases. We will focus on three characteristics — the political aspects, roles people play, and incrementalism.

The Political Aspects of Budgeting

The process of budget preparation, enactment, and — to some degree — the execution is political in nature.[12] Even where the PPB system is in operation, the decisions allocating scarce resources cannot be made on a strictly logical, objective basis divorced from political reality. The whole process is value-laden. Within the total scheme of governmental activities, what relative priority and value should be placed on programs for minorities, social welfare, education, highways, parks and recreation, ecology and environmental quality, as well as all the other services provided by government? Which existing programs should be expanded, reduced, abolished and what new ones, if any, should be added? Since there is no empirical, objective yardstick or computer program for automatically making the "right" decisions, they have to be made by people working through the political process in which interested individuals and groups compete to secure their share of the limited amount of money available.

Who are the actors in this process? There is a very large cast playing both major and supporting roles, but roles change depending upon the issues, times, political conditions, and other environmental factors. The actors include elected executives, political party leaders, elected policy makers, appointed administrators, career bureaucrats, major contributors to political campaigns, politically powerful individuals, and organized pressure groups. All of these elements make inputs into the decision process at one or more of the phases of budgeting.

Although the importance of these inputs will vary with conditions, issues and levels of government, one of the consistently important inputs comes from outside pressure groups. Such groups, who represent the organized portion of society, usually have a budget to fund their activities, a headquarters office and staff, a paid lobbyist, and varying degrees of political muscle.

A second input is the political considerations of individual elected legislators. In addition to their own value systems, politicians must be concerned with the implications their decisions will have on their reelection or hopes for higher office. In this regard, a politician must actually be sensitive to two groups. The first is the organized group or groups on which his political support may be based. To offend this segment of the electorate is to invite retaliation. The second group is his total constituency, which tends to rate a politician on the basis of what he "has done" for his area. Has he secured a military base, a national park, a subsidy program, a state university, a state park, a municipal recreation area and other "goodies" from public funds?

The career bureaucrats also play a political role. They could often be called an "inside pressure group." They are concerned with the program of their agencies as well as career interests, such as working conditions, salary levels, staffing formulae, retirement benefits, and other factors. The political power of public employees, historically based on their importance as a significant segment of the voting population, has been increased due to their unionization at many levels of government. (For the significance of unionization, see chapter 16.)

These actors, in competing for public money, will use whatever support can be enlisted. Each administrative department attempts to elicit the support of the client group served by its program. Legislators call for support from interested groups and influential people from the areas they represent. Groups whose interests are similar or whose interests at least do not conflict on a particular issue often form floating coalitions to support each other. Units within the executive branch can also be expected to stop fighting each other and close ranks to present a united front in some issues.

The strategies, tactics, and methods of attempting to influence the process are almost endless. The general process can be summarized, however, by saying that it is a system of negotiations and bargaining between the government and interest groups in our pluralistic society. In the absence of any objectively measurable standards, we rely on the concept of "balance of forces" among these groups and political considerations to provide the "proper" allocation of resources.

The budget is the most contested document in the political arena. The final budget, which is always a compromise document, rarely provides any group or segment of society with all the money it could legitimately spend on its program, and some feel absolutely discriminated against. As Wildavsky says, "the victories and defeats, the compromises and the bargains, the realms of agreement and the spheres of conflict in regard to the role of national government in our society all appear in the budget."[13]

The Roles People Play

In budget preparation and legislative enactment, people play games and assume roles. In the preparation phase, one can assume that the director of a unit honestly thinks that the program is important, is understaffed, improperly housed, and needs more money to accomplish its mission. The process requires gamesmanship among competitors struggling for funds that are always insufficient to provide for all worthwhile programs at the desired levels. Those responsible for preparing an agency budget must be strategists in answering a number of questions: How much increase can I ask for without violating any general guidelines, inviting close scrutiny, asking for trouble, or looking ridiculous? Shall I go for the big increase in one year or phase it in over a longer term? How can I best and most logically justify the increase? What sort of support or opposition will I receive from other units? These become crucial decisions. If he or she requests too little, the program will be in trouble. If too much is requested too often, the reviewing agency and legislative body loses confidence in the validity of such requests, automatically cutting them drastically.

In walking this fine line, there are no textbook answers. Decisions are made on the basis of experience and intuition, accompanied by the expenditure of some nervous energy. Budget planners must be politically literate — capable of reading the political and economic environment around them. At the operating level, most unit directors are expected to be advocates. Such advocacy means that they not only sincerely believe in the program but also attempt to expand the role, budget, and importance of the unit, defend the program and its personnel and look after its interests in general.

Moving up the organizational hierarchy in budget preparation, the roles change. The individual or executive agency responsible for consolidating all of the unit requests into a final executive budget has a different responsibility. It is a difficult role due to the variety of concerns and inputs into the decision making. The responsibility now becomes one of assembling a budget which provides for the total administrative organization. The preparer must be concerned with the impact on the tax rate, orientation of the legislative body toward increasing taxes, the political power and influence of organized special-interest groups, and a variety of other factors. In most cases, it is still an advocacy role, but it is now focused on the total package, rather than on individual programs.

At the legislative level — Congress, board of supervisors, governing board, city council — games are also played in evaluating the budget and appropriating the money. However, here the accepted role changes from that of an advocate or seller of expenditures to one of protecting the taxpayer's money.

Wildavsky, in describing the attitude of the Congressional Appropriations Committee, "As guardians of the public purse, committee members are expected to cast a skeptical eye on the blandishments of a bureaucracy ever anxious to increase its dominion by increasing its appropriations," described the attitude of most legislative bodies.[14] The overall thrust here is to reduce the amounts requested by the executive branch. Certain individuals may resist reducing the requests of specific agencies or programs with which they identify closely, either for political or personal reasons. As a general rule, members also struggle to defend funds that will affect programs in the geographic area from which they are elected. A member of the Appropriations Committee may agree that the reduction of defense expenditures is a great idea, so long as it does not mean closing a military facility in her or his district, which could have an impact on reelection.

Incrementalism

Annual budgets are not prepared, evaluated, or accepted as wholly new packages, but rather they are accepted on an incremental basis.[15] In preparing its budget, each agency uses the budget from the previous year as a starting point and adds new programs or increments to it. As a result, the basic program built up over the years dictates much of the content, which leaves little flexibility in the allocation of total resources. To illustrate this, over $223 billion, or approximately three-quarters of the federal budget for fiscal 1975, were not susceptible to meaningful modification. This amount is consumed by fixed charges and commitments made in the previous year — social insurance, interest on the debt, mandatory grants to state and local governments, increasing costs of open-ended programs from prior years, and outlays from previous contracts. Thus, only comparatively small sums of money are available to be manipulated each year.

The executive agency responsible for evaluating these departmental requests — Office of Management and Budget, Department of Finance, etc. — uses the same incremental technique. It does not analyze the whole budget, but only the increments tacked onto last year's document. At the legislative level also, the emphasis is only upon the changes in the requests over the previous year. At no point in the budgetary process are all agency programs evaluated, compared, alternative allocations of money seriously considered, or the budget reviewed as a comprehensive, total package. What is dealt with are the "relatively small increments to an existing base."[16]

The incremental technique rather than a reevaluation of all budget items each year is a practical approach for a variety of reasons. In the first place, the previous year's budget was at least a satisfactory document — "satisfactory" in the sense that accommodations and compromises had been made, it reflected the balance of forces or power in the society, and no group was sufficiently agitated or strong to force major changes. Second, it avoids serious group conflict that could invite bitter battles with lasting scars, hatreds, and feelings that could do serious damage to the fabric of society. The budget for the previous year reflects the compromises which have resulted from these battles over the years. Third, since the budget is a political document, with no objective standards, there is no reason to believe that starting fresh each year would produce a "better" document. Fourth, changes are expensive — expensive in terms of negotiating time to affect the change, modification in agency personnel and procedures, and morale factors. Finally there is little need to alter existing programs which have been successful, unless societal conditions change.

Accounting

Accounting is essential to any organization and serves a variety of purposes. In the first place, it is used as a control device by both the administrative and legislative branch. The administrator uses the records to regulate the rate of expenditures and prevent overspending. The representative of the legislative body uses the accounts as a starting point for the post audit. While these control aspects are still vital, accounting as a management tool is now being emphasized. Especially where the PPB system is in operation, decision making requires a constant flow of financial data. The costs charged to each program category must be known and monitored; the rate of expenditures must be known; and cost data are constantly needed for the continuous cost-benefit analysis which generates the alternative proposals on resource allocations from which administrators may choose during the course of the fiscal year.

Accounting per se is a technical process regulated by law and internal procedures. However, there are variations in the location of responsibility for it and in the methodology. Responsibility at the federal level is retained by Congress, in spite of recommendations from numerous study commissions that it be transferred to the executive. The function is performed by the General Accounting Office (GAO) which is headed by the comptroller general, who is in a rather unique position. Although the individual is appointed for a fifteen-year term by the president (with Senate confirmation), the employee may not be removed by the president but only by congressional action through a joint resolution or impeachment. However, the GAO has delegated considerable authority which permits operating units to function within established guidelines. Such a structure indicates that Congress does not really accept the contention that accounting is a tool of management and has no intention of relinquishing control. Although a similar arrangement is found in some states, the more common practice at this and the local level is executive responsibility. The accounting work is done in a central department responsible to the executive, using the forms and procedures established by law.

The methodology of governmental accounting has been a subject for debate over the years. The choice is between the cash and accrual accounting systems, which have fundamental differences. The cash system and the newer accrual system can be summarized briefly. Under the cash system, entries are not made in the accounts until money is actually received or paid out. This means that the cost for both expendable items as well as nonexpendable items (buildings, equipment) are charged totally to the year in which they were purchased. Many of these items will be used in succeeding years, however, which gives a distorted picture. The apparent costs during the year these expenses were incurred will appear high. The expenditures of the following period will actually be higher than those reflected in the budget, because materials, supplies, and capital goods have already been charged to the previous period, although they are currently being used. In the accrual system, the respective accounts are posted when revenues are earned and expenditures committed rather than when the cash actually flows in and out. The cost of consumables are charged to the period when they are actually used rather than when they are purchased. Moreover, the cost of nonexpendable items is spread over their expected useful life rather than charged to the year of purchase. The accrual system, then, by reflecting the current income-commitment status provides a clearer picture and more accurate cost data essential to program planning.

Post Audit

The post audit, as the name implies, is completed after the money has been spent. Unlike preaudits, this is a legislative technique for verifying that the executive branch spent the money for the purposes intended, that it was spent legally and not embezzled, that proper procedures were followed and that it was spent efficiently. This audit, then, will be done by someone outside the executive branch of government who is responsible to the legislative body. At the federal level this is done by the General Accounting Office. However, the legislative bodies of many cities, counties, and other units of local government do not staff for it but contract with private accounting firms for the service.

The actual process of auditing is a technical, time-consuming, analytical process. The financial transactions of any organization, and not only government, are a real "paper mill." Each transaction, regardless of the amount, has to be supported by the required identifying documents, which usually include the requisition, purchase order, the invoice submitted by the vendor, and the cancelled voucher (check) with which it was paid.

What happens with this mountain of paper depends on the type of audit being used. If a comprehensive audit is in force, every transaction and its supporting documentation is analyzed and verified item by item. This is not only very expensive, but also extremely time-consuming. Few levels of government, including the federal, are staffed to accomplish such an audit without falling years behind in the process. Due to these problems, the federal government and many other levels have adopted a "business-type" or "management" audit. Under this system, auditors are more concerned with the overall picture, including the procedures used, internal checks and control devices, adequacy of the financial records, and possibly the effectiveness of programs. This general review will usually be accompanied by detailed "spot audits" or "sample audits" of transactions in selected areas, as a control device. A total review will only be made where the auditor senses there is something wrong.

Conclusions

In this chapter, we have attempted to present an overview of the area of public finance. As we pointed out, there are many systems other than that used in the United States. The process at any level of government could be described in one word — complex. This complexity is created by the absence of objective standards for allocating resources, competition for limited funds, long time lags, number of people involved, detailed procedures, activities of pressure groups, economic, political, and social implications, and a variety of other factors that are fluid, shifting, and in a rather constant state of flux. Regardless of these problems, budgets must be prepared and finances managed or the machinery of government runs out of fuel. Like so much else in government, there is nothing automatic in the managing of the public's money. Rather, decisions and judgments of a great many kinds must be made constantly, often with great difficulty and sometimes with agony. It is in the raising and spending of the public's money that the essence of the society and its government stands revealed.

Decisions in public finance, especially in nations like the United States where governmental expenditures represent a large percentage of the national income, have a direct impact in all aspects of national life. If a large percentage of the money is spent on wars and defense, fewer social programs can be funded. If the sources and rates of income taxation are manipulated, money can be drained from the wealthy to fund extensive programs for the economically disadvantaged. If the government reduces defense purchases, the decision has an immediate impact on the major suppliers and their sub-contractors. In short, almost any fiscal decision of government, especially the federal government, has economic implications for individuals, groups and the economy as a whole. This basic nature of money management was described over a century ago by Prime Minister William E. Gladstone who said, "budgets are not merely affairs of arithmetic, but in a thousand ways go to the root of prosperity of individuals, the relation of classes, and the strength of kingdoms."

Also, due to the present position of world leadership, fiscal decisions have international implications. The extent to which the United States will be involved in global defense, financial and technical assistance to developing nations and a host of other international programs depends on decisions made annually at the federal level. Other nations also worry about the impact our fiscal policies will have on the comparative value of the dollar, which has a basic impact on the economy of other nations.

Financial management — especially tax policy, debt management, and the budgetary process — is a part of the political process in all countries. In the democratic process of the United States, decisions are not based on some theoretical model but on value judgments made in the political arena, influenced by considerations of practical politics.

NOTES

1. For a discussion of the purposes, see John D. Millett, "Governmental Budgets and Economic Analysis," *Public Administration Review* 23, no. 3 (September 1963): 125–31; Aaron Wildavsky, *The Politics of the Budgetary Process,* 2d ed. (Boston: Little, Brown, 1974), chap. 1; and Jesse Burkhead, *Government Budgeting* (New York: John Wiley, 1956).

2. For a brief description, see Allen B. Schick, "The Road to PPB: The Stages of Budget Reform," *Public Administration Review* 26, no. 4 (December 1966): 243–58.

3. U.S. Commission on Organization of the Executive Branch of the Government, *Budgeting and Accounting* (Washington: Government Printing Office, 1949).

4. In the introduction to "A Symposium, Planning-Programming-Budgeting System Reexamined: Development, Analysis, and Criticism," *Public Administration Review* 29, no. 2 (March-April 1969): 111.

5. For an evaluation, see the articles contained in "Planning-Programming-Budgeting Symposium," *Public Administration Review* 26, no. 4 (December 1966): 243–310; and "Symposium on PPBS Reexamined," *Public Administration Review* 29 (March-April 1969): 111–202.

6. Allen Schick, "The Road to PPB: The Stages of Budget Reform," *Public Administration Review* 26, no. 4 (December 1966): 257.

7. This study is discussed in Edwin Harper, Fred Kramer, Andrew House, "Implementation and Use of PPB in Sixteen Federal Agencies," *Public Administration Review* 29 (November-December 1969): 623–32.

8. For a description of the reasons for the failure, see Allen Schick, "A Death in the Bureaucracy: The Demise of PPB," *Public Administration Review* 33, no. 2 (March-April 1973): 146–56.

9. At the national level, preparation of the 1976 budget for the fiscal year beginning July 1, 1975, and ending June 30, 1976, began in the spring of 1974.

10. At the federal level, the Congressional Budget and Impoundment Control Act of 1974 made procedural changes. It created a Congressional Budget Office similar to the Office of Management and Budget in the Executive Office of the President and a new budget committee in each House, as well as establishing a time frame for each step of the congressional action. For a discussion of the changes, see James J. Finley, "The 1974 Congressional Initiative in Budget Making," *Public Administration Review* 35, no. 3 (May-June 1975): 270–78.

11. At the federal level, the Congressional Budget and Impoundment Control Act of 1974 limits this practice. Deferrals (temporary withholding of money), which cannot extend beyond the end of the fiscal year, may be overturned by either house of Congress at any time. Rescissions (permanently cancelling budget authority) must be approved by Congress.

12. For a discussion of all aspects of this, see Wildavsky, *Politics of the Budgetary Process.*

13. Ibid., p. 5. Used by permission.

14. Ibid., p. 47. Used by permission.

15. For a discussion of incrementalism, see Wildavsky, *Politics of the Budgetary Process,* pp. 13–16; and Anthony Downs, *Inside Bureaucracy* (Boston: Little, Brown, 1967), pp. 249–52.

16. Wildavsky, *Politics of the Budgetary Process,* p. 15. Used by permission.

Challenge
of
Change

Responsibility and Ethics in the Public Service

As was pointed out in chapter 3, one of the more significant variables in modern public administration is social change. In Part Five, the implications of social change for public administration are explored. This chapter focuses on change and its impact on responsibility and ethics in the public service.

The modern bureaucracy at all levels of government has grown to be tremendously powerful. As has been shown in previous chapters, bureaucrats interpret laws, make policy, lead, make and enforce decisions, communicate, control, regulate, enforce, and engage in a variety of other activities that have a direct impact on the daily lives of citizens. As with any authority, administrative authority can be abused. There is no organizational system or program that will guarantee fairness, equity, rationality, sensitivity, responsiveness, honesty, and so on. The power is ultimately being exercised by ordinary human beings who may behave responsibly or irresponsibly, ethically or unethically.

Responsibility and ethics in politics and administration have been debated since political and administrative theory began. Attempting to define the terms as well as controlling behavior to achieve the desired ends has been difficult in all democratic nations, including the United States. In the following sections, responsibility and ethics are explored in some detail.

Responsibility

Political and administrative responsibility is a central theme in the democratic philosophy of "government by the consent of the governed."[1] Elected officials are held responsible through periodic elections; but bureaucrats, who are appointed, do not come under this control.

Administrative responsibility, however, was of little concern in the United States until comparatively recently. Historically, the accepted theory was that there was a separation between politics and administration. Under this dichotomy, goals and objectives which involved value judgments would be established by the people's elected representatives — the political branch — and administrators would simply decide the most effective means to implement these goals. This theoretical separation between politics and administration was discredited, however, in the 1930s and 1940s. It is now agreed that the historical dichotomy does not exist. Nonelected bureaucrats are not neutral executors of legislative policy and do in fact have enormous discretionary powers in decision making. Administrators who execute policies must interpret the statutes and fill in the detailed procedures. Such a broad grant of discretionary power not only throws a great deal of responsibility on administrators but also creates opportunities for irresponsible actions.

The search for administrative responsibility has thus become a basic concern. The search, however, has been handicapped by two obstacles — the difficulty of defining responsibility and developing techniques for monitoring and insuring responsible performance.

Defining Responsibility

"Responsible" and "irresponsible" are commonly used words, but they mean different things to different people and their meaning may shift with changing conditions. Mosher, in discussing responsibility, comments on the variety of definitions and pursues two in some detail. One he labels *objective responsibility* which "connotes the responsibility of a person or an organization to someone else, outside of self, for something or some kind of performance."[2] This is quite similar to accountability, in the sense that one who accepts and executes directives from those in a position of legitimate authority is acting responsibly and a refusal to do so is irresponsible action which exposes the individual to possible sanctions. The second meaning of responsibility is *subjective* or *psychological*. "Its focus is not upon to whom and for what one is responsible (according to the law and the organization chart) but to whom and for what one *feels* responsible and *behaves* responsibly."[3] This meaning is oriented toward loyalty and identification rather than accountability.

If the two meanings of responsibility are accepted, they may pull employees in two different directions. In the first, the employee looks upward and is accountable to the boss or to the policy-making groups. In the second, employees may be loyal to and identify with individuals and groups other than those in the hierarchy — outside pressure groups, professional groups of which they are a member, and peer groups. As a result of these two tendencies, there is the very real possibility that individuals will be faced with and have to choose between conflicting interpretations of responsibility. In modern administration, Mosher points out that professionalism has become so prevalent that the similar values and expectations held by the members of the same profession and the pressures exerted by these professionals on each other has become a dominant factor in determining how bureaucrats interpret their responsibility.

Criticisms of Bureaucratic Responsibility

The bureaucracy is under attack as being irresponsible on a number of grounds. Some of them include:

1. That bureaucrats, in their attempt to be neutral, have not been leaders in promoting human dignity and morality
2. That bureaucracy has become so overly centralized and huge that it is inefficient, isolated, and nonresponsive of the needs of the people
3. That the bureaucracy, interested in surviving and growing, resists change needed to meet social problems
4. That efficiency and economy, which guide bureaucratic action, give an improper orientation and product
5. That the bureaucracy has really become so large and powerful that it is not answerable to anyone
6. That the incidence of the misuse of funds and especially administrative power are far too prevalent
7. That often laws are enforced in a manner quite different from what the legislative body intended

The problem becomes one of how to redirect and control bureaucratic behavior.

Controlling the Bureaucracy

As was discussed in chapter 7, public administration functions within a complex legal framework. However, under the American constitutional system, bureaucrats were to be controlled principally by those elected by the people, and especially by the policy-making groups — Congress, legislatures, city councils, and boards.

Legislative Controls. Some of the major legislative control techniques with comments on their effectiveness follow:

1. Since administrative agencies are created by legislation, they may be abolished in the same way if their actions do not meet legislative expectations.

   This is a correct statement, but it is unrealistic. Once an agency has been created, it tends to develop a life of its own. It builds support with client groups, other administrative agencies and legislators, which makes abolishing it difficult.
2. Since no money can be spent without legislative authorization, the bureaucracy can be held responsible through financial controls.

   Again, this is true. Agency budgets may be increased, decreased, or abolished; but this is difficult because legislative bodies lack adequate data on which to make judgments, professional staff support to analyze budgets is inadequate, and the time pressures are great. Anything short of totally eliminating the budget usually takes the form of a gross reduction in the budget request, which indicates displeasure and reduces the program but is in no sense a mechanism of detailed program control.

3. The legislature can and does pass legislation to punish illegal and fraudulent acts by administrators.

It is true that there is a volume of legislation at all levels making the taking of bribes, gifts, and other favors to influence decisions an illegal act. The possibility of criminal prosecution probably offers some deterrent. This process, however, involves a lengthy and complex trial where the action has been flagrant and the case well documented. In other cases, an accused employee may resign rather than face prosecution. This type of control applies only in the exceptional cases and cannot be considered a device for frequent use.

4. The legislative bodies do have the authority and power to conduct hearings and investigations in administrative matters.

This control is used frequently. Legislative committees may investigate any administrative agency for any reason, but obstensibly as a basis for fact finding on which to base legislation. Nevertheless, this is a time-consuming process and often has partisan political overtones, which usually occur after something drastic has gone wrong. It is not an effective day-to-day control device.

Actually, all of the above controls may be and are used in an attempt to insure administrative responsibility to the policy-making body. However, in a large bureaucracy, such as the federal government, these are not effective control mechanisms. The federal bureaucracy is so large, so widely dispersed, and so protected by the merit system that any legislative control is exercised in a periodic and gross fashion. Legislators come and go, but the bureaucracy goes on. In some respects it has become a fourth branch of government.

Besides the problem of controlling bureaucrats — employees who are hired and work directly for government — the government must exercise some control over contracted employees — those who perform many services, operate facilities, and provide many products through contracts. These employees, although paid from public funds, are not government employees but work for a private organization. Control over such employees and employers is even more difficult. About the only control is through the language in the contracts, budgetary review, audits, and legislation protecting the rights of women and minorities in the employment process used by the private contractor. Because of the deficiencies of legislative control, other techniques have been proposed.

Other Control Techniques.   The list of suggestions for effecting some control is quite broad. One is that units should be made smaller, and government should be decentralized, the idea being that action would then be more readily visible and controllable by the people. Another is that legislative bodies should be reorganized and staffed so that control could be made more effective, a step which is being taken at the federal level. A further suggestion is to expand and tighten the laws on conflict of interest, fraud and other illegal activities of bureaucrats. A final one, which is used in a number of countries and is being suggested for adoption in the United States, is the office of ombudsman.

The office of ombudsman differs in the various countries where it functions, but the basic concept is the same. Although the method of selection may differ, the ombudsman is a nonpartisan official who is essentially independent of legislative, judicial, and political control. The individual has the power to launch an investigation against government employees either on his or her own initiative or on the basis of a citizen complaint. The investigation may be for illegal activities, trodding on the rights of residents, improper administrative conduct, or any other reason the ombudsman thinks would improve the conduct of government and its proper relationships with the citizens. Based upon the investigations, the ombudsman can either mediate a solution — if that is appropriate — or initiate a prosecution in the courts. The result is that a nonpartisan watchdog scrutinizes the actions of government on a continuous basis.

The ombudsman solution for the United States has some obvious problems. Due to the vast size of the country, such an office at the federal level would be comparatively useless. It has been suggested that they be created in each of the ten federal regions; but again, the geographic area would make it impossible for the individual to have any intimate knowledge of the cases or any close contact with the principals in the case. The same geographic problem would be encountered in the larger states. Probably the best hope of success would be at the local level, either in city halls or sub-city halls, which would permit accessibility to the citizens and a firsthand knowledge of the cases by the ombudsman.

Ethics

In the United States, ethics have been of interest since the nation was founded; however, the intensity of the interest has been cyclical. Each publicized case of unethical conduct or violation of the expected norms has brought on intensive investigations, study committees, and attempted corrective action. The most recent such event was the Watergate case, which has had major repercussions on and implications for public administration.

In an attempt to control unethical conduct, most levels of government have published Codes of Ethics for employees. At the federal level, Congress promulgated a Code of Ethics for Government Service in 1958; President Kennedy issued Executive Order 10939 which was a set of ethical standards; and many departments and agencies have drafted their own codes of conduct. Similar documents have also been adopted by many other levels of government. In addition, many professional societies, including the International City Managers Association, have published standards for their members.

In spite of this, unethical conduct by administrators has periodically rocked all levels of government. Most of these publicized incidents, such as the Watergate case, involved top-level, politically appointed (rather than career) bureaucrats. But such conduct is not confined to the top administrative echelons or to this type of public servant. There are untold numbers of other cases in which lower level officials have been reprimanded, transferred, demoted, suspended, and discharged for misconduct with little or no publicity. In addition to these known cases, there are others in which individuals crowd the legal line or perform unethical acts which are either never detected or never acted upon and reported.

Factors Contributing to Unethical Conduct

What encourages or at least permits such conduct to occur? There are numerous factors — some individual and some organizational — which contribute to the problem. Some of the more visible ones will be discussed.

Codes of Conduct Are Ineffective

It is extremely difficult, if not impossible, to construct a meaningful code of ethics. In the first place, if a code is written in general terms, it will be subject to much interpretation and leave a wide latitude for those under its guidance. On the other hand, if it is comprehensive, specific, and detailed, it may be so rigid that no flexibility is possible. This inflexibility makes it equally unenforceable, if the organization is to function, and such codes are rapidly made obsolete by changing conditions.

The Ethical World of the Administrator

Administrators, like all other employees, have their own system of goals, values, ethics, and morality in general. Since these are internalized and peculiar to each individual, there is no necessary homogeneity among the belief systems of administrators at the same or differing levels. These people must make decisions, many of which have ethical overtones, as a part of their daily administrative lives.

Ethical questions arise principally for two reasons. First, laws have to be interpreted. Since most laws are written in general terms, they must be interpreted and implemented by administrators. What is legal and what is proper is subject to various interpretations, which will be influenced by the value system of each interpreter, which means there will be disagreements. Second, most decisions are group rather than individual decisions. After inputs from various individuals are offered, the final decision will usually be a compromise solution acceptable to most people, but not exactly what any one individual would have preferred. As George A. Graham says, "an administrator learns, no matter where he is in the hierarchy, that he seldom can get his own way in the sense that the decision made or action taken is exactly what he personally thinks it should be."[4] Nevertheless, the members of the group are expected to abide by and execute the decisions.

Administrators then are faced with basic ethical questions as a part of their profession. There will be honest disagreements as to what is legal, what is in the public interest, and what is proper on many issues. How a person attempts to influence the group decisions, how he or she reacts once the group decision has been made, and how far that person compromises personal integrity have been subject to debate.[5] In the final analysis, individual administrators have to decide what is beyond their ethical or moral tolerance. When it passes that point they either must attempt to publicize what is going on, in the hope that outside pressure will force a reversal, and take the consequences for such action, ask to be transferred out of the activity (a difficult process), or resign.

Glorification of the Executive

One of the factors which has increased the possibility of improper conduct is the concentration of power in the hands of the chief executive. While this is true to some degree at the state level and in some local jurisdictions, it applies principally to the federal level. At this level, American writers in the fields of political science and public administration have advocated a strong executive. Numerous committees which have been created by law and executive order to study the executive branch and administrative process have also consistently recommended a concentration of power in the hands of the president.[6] Most reorganization plans, some of which resulted from study committees, have restructured the organization and created new mechanism to make presidential control easier. The creation of the Executive Office of the President, with its control over management, budgeting, resource allocation, reorganization plans and a host of other functions, was designed to provide a staff to increase the independence of the president.[7] The whole process was intended to provide an executive, who sat at the top of the hierarchy, with sufficient power to be the unchallenged single executive authority.

The result was the cult of the presidency. The office accrued a virtually unlimited reservoir of power, which could be used by the incumbent to achieve his desired purposes. Those purposes could be either beneficial or detrimental to the public, as well as ethical or unethical. This concentration of power and those who advocated it ignored Lord Acton's caution that "Power tends to corrupt, and absolute power corrupts absolutely."

Reasons for Glorification

Few democratic countries have concentrated such power as we do in the president and to a somewhat lesser degree in governors and some mayors. Why did we adopt this pattern? The principal reason was the system of checks and balances.

One of the basic concepts of the U.S. government is a balance of power among the three branches with a system of checks and balances designed to prevent domination by one branch. The checks on the power of the president include elections, legislative controls, judicial remedies, and administrative controls.

How effective are these mechanisms? James L. Sundquist views all of these historic safeguards as being ineffective as timely control devices. Elections he sees as being comparatively worthless. Under our presidential system, unlike the parliamentary system, the chief executive is elected for a fixed four-year term. If a chief executive loses the confidence of the people soon after an election, it is possible to have an ineffective leader for a considerable period of time, up to four years. Sundquist sums up by saying, "Elections as an ultimate check, yes. As a timely check when desperately needed to restore presidential leadership, no."[8]

The power of Congress to legislate programs and policies, to control the expenditure of money through appropriation acts, to confirm top-level appointments, to investigate executive actions, to declare war and to impeach the president are legislative checks in which we have placed great faith as a control mechanism. Nevertheless, they too are not effective if the president desires to be uncooperative. The problem arises in the responsibility assigned to the president by the Constitution to see that the laws are faithfully executed. Ultimately, most congressional controls are rather gross controls which are essentially negative — prevent executive action — and cannot force positive executive action. In addition, most actions, except appropriations, occur after the fact. On the balance side, the president can veto legislation, historically could impound (refuse to spend) money appropriated by Congress, invoke executive privilege to block legislative access to information, commit the military forces without a declaration of war, interpret laws and congressional intentions to his advantage, and a variety of other tactics.

The final control of the courts serves as a safeguard according to constitutional theory. In practice, Sundquist thinks this is inadequate for the same obvious reasons. First, the courts process cases only when laws have been violated, an after-the-fact action. Moreover, the activities of administrators which may be on the borderline of legality or detrimental to the public interest are not indictable acts subject to judicial action. Second, court proceedings are a slow, cumbersome process which may stretch out over a considerable period of time; the court system is not structured for quick action. Third, the judicial process does not prevent acts from occurring but attempts to punish individuals after the event has occurred. Despite these drawbacks, however, others, while acknowledging the difficult role of the courts, do see them as an effective ultimate control as was evidenced in the Watergate case.[9]

The external checks upon which we have relied have proven inadequate to control the strong presidency which we have created. This is not just true of the Nixon administration. Other presidents, especially since the 1930s, have been comparatively independent in their actions when they chose to be so. As Sundquist says, "the checks and balances, such as they are, operate either long *before* the fact, in the case of the confirmation power, or else *after* the fact — after the damage has been done. None of them operate during the fact, while the executive power is being used — and abused — which is the crucial time if the damage is to be prevented."[10]

There are no viable controls within the executive branch, that is, internal controls, either. Of the two possibilities—the cabinet and career bureaucrats—neither is effective. The cabinet, which is a control in some countries, is purely an advisory body in the United States. The president has no legal or political compulsion to accept their advice. Career bureaucrats may delay and resist certain actions, as they did in Watergate, but it is not their role to serve as a control mechanism. As Sundquist says, "bureaucratic foot-dragging may save the Republic from unwise or illegal conduct, now and then, but in the normal course the bureaucracy simply has to be effectively subordinated."[11] To function otherwise violates the whole concept of a neutral civil service executing the policies determined by the political leadership in control at any given time.

What Are the Solutions?

How may future betrayals of the public trust, such as Watergate, be guarded against? This question has generated much debate, controversy, and varied solutions. Some insist that the present system is adequate and should not be modified to any significant degree. They see the events of recent times as one-time occurrences which created such public shock that no future administration would dare use such tactics. However, few people seem to be ready to live with this concept. Most insist that modifications are needed. We will look at some of the suggestions.[12]

Parliamentary Executive

The most extreme modification suggests amendment of the Constitution to move from our present presidential form to a parliamentary format. The advocates of this solution argue that it is a much more responsive system, subject to more control, and capable of a quicker response in case of a loss of confidence in the executive.

Others, who insist that our basic system is sound, argue that such a fundamental change is unwarranted and unwise. The National Academy of Public Administration (NAPA) Panel is "unanimously opposed to basic changes in the American Constitution in the direction of parliamentary government."[13]

Easier Removal of the President

The suggestions under this heading include making provisions for recalling the president and vice-president through the electoral process initiated by a petition of the voters, broadening the reasons for impeachment, simplifying the impeachment process, and calling new elections by a two-thirds vote of both houses of Congress. A composite, suggested by Sundquist, would "empower Congress to act by a simple majority to remove the President and call a new election. But, to deter Congress from acting from trivial or fractious causes, require that the Congress, upon removing the President, itself be dissolved and all its members forced to face a new election."[14]

The NAPA study opposed such changes. This panel believed that the removal process should remain difficult as the framers of the Constitution intended, but that the high crimes and misdemeanors, which are the basis for impeachment, should be interpreted in the historical sense which included crimes against the state or society, as well as indictable crimes. Also, they suggested that impeachment should be extended to cover misconduct in political campaigns.

Fragment Presidential Powers

Some have suggested that presidential powers be greatly reduced by abolishing the Executive Office of the President, removing some agencies such as the Department of Justice, CIA, and Internal Revenue Service from presidential control, transferring a variety of powers to Congress, electing cabinet members, and so on.

Although there is consensus that the centralization of power has created an all-powerful presidency, few would agree that the executive powers should be shared, dispersed, or drastically reduced. Most agree that the concept of a strong single executive as a focus for coordination, control, and leadership is still essential, but there is also common agreement that modifications are necessary to correct the excessive concentration of power in the White House.

Other Modifications

The panel from the National Academy of Public Administration analyzed the problem of ethics within the framework of the Watergate case. In the publication, *Watergate: Implications for Responsible Government,* the group reviewed the American system of government and then made specific recommendations in eight areas. The categories and suggested modifications under each to permit more control and reduce the possibility for unethical conduct are as follows:

1. *The President, the White House and the Executive Office*
   Recommendations in this area are designed to limit the size of the White House staff, to prohibit injecting presidential assistants as a buffer between the president and department heads, to prohibit the heads of executive departments from serving as advisors to the president, to remove agencies not providing direct staff assistance to the president from the Executive Office, and other recommendations. In the final analysis, the "functions of the Executive Office of the President should be to assist the President, not to be the general manager of the Executive Branch."[15]

2. *Chief Executive and the Executive Branch*
   The panel, after commenting on the historic problems of defining the proper relationship between the president and the units comprising the executive branch, criticized the philosophy of operating the U.S. government like a corporation "with all powers concentrated at the top and exercised through appointees in the President's Office and loyal followers placed in crucial positions in the various agencies of the Executive Branch."[16] The suggested modifications were a reaffirmation that the president is subject to legal and constitutional restrictions, that safeguards should be imposed to guarantee the historic principle of equal treatment to all and closer congressional scrutiny and control over agencies such as the FBI, CIA, and IRS.

3. *The Attorney General and Department of Justice*
   The report, after criticizing the recently partisan uses of the agency, suggested limiting the number of political appointees, prohibiting the

attorney general from advising the president on political or personal matters, creating a Permanent Special Prosecutor to handle cases involving illegal activities of government officials, and transferring some functions out of the Justice Department. All of the suggested modifications were intended to remove the agency from politics.

4. *Congressional Oversight*

The report comments on the idea that our system is founded on a balance of power between the branches of government, but that a great imbalance exists between the executive and legislative branches. The panel suggested that there is a great need for Congress to hold the executive branch accountable through review and evaluation techniques.

5. *Information, Disclosure, Secrecy, and Executive Privilege*

The panel struggled with how to balance the need for public access to information and the demands of national security, how to insure that executive privilege, which is needed to protect the confidentiality of presidential conversations with advisors, is not used to conceal illegal acts. It arrived at no precise answers but concluded that vigilance by Congress and the public, supplemented by the courts as a last resort, are probably the only safeguards.

6. *The Public Service*

The panel, as well as all other commentators, agree that Watergate damaged the image of the public service and further eroded a declining public confidence in government. The panel recognized that political appointments are the most effective way an incoming president can make an impact on the bureaucracy but made eleven specific suggestions pertaining to the control of political appointments in the executive branch.

The panel was also concerned with the current condition of the merit system. The panel recommended a complete review of the personnel system as well as the Civil Service Commission, and a modified system for appointing senior administrators. The objective would be to remove obsolete regulations and procedures to make the personnel system more responsive to the internal and external demands of our modern society.

7. *Financing Political Campaigns*

The panel felt that campaign finances — amount, sources, number of campaign committees, reporting and control — have an important impact on the public interest. The panel, after concluding that federal funding for all national elections was desirable, discussed other aspects of campaign financing.

8. *The President and the Judiciary*

The panel commented on the sensitive role of the courts and how they stretched their powers to the limit in the Watergate case. In the opinion of the members, the courts not only acted properly but in the future should also be the final arbiter on questions of executive privilege in criminal cases. However, there was agreement that the courts should not consistently abandon their traditional role and interfere in the traditional activities of Congress and the executive or review their actions simply on the basis that the decisions may have been less than optimal.

Conclusions

Administrators, like all other citizens, are covered by the criminal code; any illegal acts on their part are subject to criminal prosecution. Responsibility and ethics, however, are primarily concerned with individual attitudes, values, sensitivities, frames of reference, and other personality characteristics that produce administrative behavior that is not criminal but is less than desirable. This is not a problem for the courts. In the United States, we have passed legislation prescribing administrative procedures and codes of ethical conduct and relied upon internal checks and public opinion to guarantee responsible and ethical administrative conduct. We have not been totally successful. Recent events should not completely distort our view of the ethics of the public servant, because the United States, when compared with most countries, has been fortunate in the ethical level of its employees.

No artificial system of organizational and legal safeguards can prevent unethical behavior. The ultimate control is the internalized value system of individual employees, over which an organization has no control. One suggested guideline for administrators is to ask a question before making decisions: "If this action is held up to public scrutiny, will I still feel that it is what I should have done, and how I should have done it?"[17]

Public administration represents an intersection of many variables, one of which is time. Perhaps more than many other fields of work and study, public administration faces the past, the present, and the future. In the concluding chapter, this dimension of change is explored further.

NOTES

1. Some recent literature on responsibility includes Frederick C. Mosher, *Democracy in the Public Service* (New York: Oxford University Press, 1968); Lewis C. Mainzer, *Political Bureaucracy* (Glenview, Ill.: Scott, Foresman, 1973); Eugene P. Dvorin and Robert H. Simmons, *From Amoral to Humane Bureaucracy* (San Francisco: Canfield Press, 1972); Bruce L. R. Smith and D. C. Hague, eds., *The Dilemma of Accountability in Modern Government* (New York: St. Martin's Press, 1971); and William A. Niskanen, Jr., *Bureaucracy and Representative Government* (New York: Atherton Press, 1971).

2. Mosher, *Democracy in the Public Service*, p. 7. Used by permission.

3. Ibid., p. 8. Used by permission.

4. George A. Graham, "Ethical Guidelines for Public Administrators: Observations on the Rules of the Game," *Public Administration Review* 34, no. 1 (January-February 1974): 91.

5. A draft of some suggested guidelines or rules may be found in the above article, pp. 91–92.

6. For example, the Brownlow Committee on Administrative Management and the Hoover Commission.

7. For staffing implications, see William D. Carey, "Presidential Staffing in the Sixties and Seventies," *Public Administration Review* 29, no. 5 (September-October 1969): 450–58.

8. James L. Sundquist, "Reflections on Watergate," *Public Administration Review* 34, no. 5 (September-October 1974): 455.

9. At the invitation of Senator Sam J. Ervin, Jr., chairman of the Senate Select Committee on Presidential Campaign Activities, the National Academy of Public Administration (NAPA) created a panel to analyze Watergate. The findings were published in Frederick C. Mosher and others, *Watergate: Implications for Responsible Government* (New York: Basic Books, 1974).

10. Sundquist, "Reflections on Watergate," p. 457.

11. Ibid., p. 457.

12. Much of this section was taken from two publications which agree in some cases and disagree in others. One is Sundquist, "Reflections on Watergate," pp. 453–61; and the other is paraphrasing and quotes from *Watergate: Implications for Responsible Government,* by Frederick C. Mosher and others, © 1974 by Basic Books, Inc., Publishers, New York. Used by permission.

13. Mosher, *Watergate,* p. 18. Used by permission.

14. Sundquist, "Reflections on Watergate," p. 460. Used by permission.

15. Mosher, *Watergate,* p. 41. Used by permission.

16. Ibid., pp. 46–47. Used by permission.

17. Harlan Cleveland, "Systems, Purposes, and the Watergate," *Public Administration Review* 34, no. 3 (May-June 1974): 267.

Retrospect and Prospect

In American public administration, as in our national life generally, there is an ambivalence — a nostalgia for the past and a yearning for the future. On the one hand, there is a conservative orientation in public administration — a concern with order, stability, and continuity. On the other hand, there is a sincere belief that public administration is and should be an agent of change. In this final chapter, we examine briefly the challenge which change presents to this field of public administration whose roots are deeply imbedded in the past, but whose imagination is attuned to the future.

Public Administration in a Time of Change

There is nothing new about the challenge which change presents. During the past few years, probably due in part to the great social, political, moral, and other upheavals of the 1960s and early 1970s, much has been written and said about change in the environment of American public administration. In chapter 3, we explored this matter in some detail. Although public administration did not attain identity as a discrete field until well into the twentieth century, it has in fact, long been implicated in the great changes and turbulence of American life. For instance, it was in the American Revolution of the eighteenth century that some of the basic values and attitudes toward governmental power, executive leadership, taxation, and other administrative details were forged. Similarly, it was in the protracted struggle over slavery and in the Civil War that constitutional, organizational, and procedural issues involving public administration were resolved. The settling of the American West, the rise of corporate business, the Spanish-American War, World Wars I and II, great waves of immigration, the Great Depression of the 1930s, the Cold War and the anti-Communist obsession of the 1950s and 1960s, and assassinations of presidents — all have been part of this changing and turbulent environment in which American public administration has evolved for 200 years.

From the elitist influences of the founding fathers after 1789, to the democratizing effects of Jacksonian government by the "common man" after 1829, to the moralistic and politically neutralist tendencies of the civil-service and government-reform movements after 1883, to the preoccupation with efficiency associated with the scientific management movement after 1906, to the emphasis on executive leadership and administrative centralization after 1937, to the rise of the behavioral persuasion since the early 1960s, public administration in the United States has been in transaction with a continuously dynamic environment.

It is a temptation to look about at the great social, economic, political, and technological changes that are occurring and to speculate about the impacts which these changes will have on the art and science of governance. But there should be no great surprise in this, especially for the public administrator, for the essence of public administration is the recognition of changes in society and the exercise of initiative and leadership in responding to those changes. Herein lies the essence of public administration as change agentry.

No Final Solutions; No One Best Way

This spirit of restless change that characterizes American public administration is reflected in the American resistance to faith in final solutions to public problems and to any one best way of coping with those problems. In comparative and development administration, for instance, we have seen that methods employed successfully in one country or region may fail miserably in another. In the administration of American cities, the council-manager form of municipal government has been widely adopted, but not as a panacea; the form has not replaced other municipal forms in many major cities. Also, to escape the difficulties of a very complex constitutional system, no final solution has been found, no one best way has been developed to improve the relationships among the various levels of government. Rather, diversity rules.

Among the American states, there have been similarities and common features in state constitutions, governmental structures, public policies, and administrative details, but there have been no final solutions and no one best way. To a remarkable degree, the states continue to innovate and to go their own ways.

The spirit of restless change also prevails in the internal features of American public administration generally. As we have seen in this book, diversity, flexibility, and sensitivity to change have ruled the making of public policies and decisions, the exercise of leadership, the conduct of communication, the establishment and maintenance of organizations, the management of public personnel, and the raising of public revenues and expenditure of public funds. As has been shown in the previous chapter on ethics in the public service, no final solution has been found to the problem of assuring ethical behavior in the public service, and no one best way has been proferred.

Public Administration in the Future

Perhaps it is a yearning to escape from contemporary problems and dilemmas that seem to defy resolution, or maybe it is the millennial mystique of the approaching twenty-first century; or, perhaps it is the existence of computers and certain future-related analytical methods, such as the "Delphi," which permit more educated guessing about future possibilities; for whatever reasons, there is growing preoccupation with the shape of things to come.

For example, in 1964, the Carnegie Corporation and the American Academy of Arts and Sciences created The Commission on the Year 2000, which assembled a group of distinguished social scientists, natural scientists, government officials, and other specialists to study future trends in politics, government, the economy, education, and other fields. In 1966, the World Future Society was founded in Washington, D.C., and since that time has grown to be a major professional association of scientists, business people, scholars, engineers, communication specialists, and others, with local chapters in major cities in the United States and abroad. In France, Bertrand de Jouvenal has directed the *Futuribles* project in Paris. In England, the English Social Science Research Council has created the Committee on the Next Thirty Years. In the United States, the American Institute of Planners has organized systematic study on "The Next Fifty Years." A flood of books, professional articles, and films have been unleashed, and on academic campuses, "futurology" is becoming a major specialization for courses, institutes, and conferences.[1]

Crystal-ball gazing is probably no closer to becoming an exact science than it was when the ancients read tea leaves and studied the entrails of chickens for clues to the shape of things to come. Nevertheless, the study of the future is one of the more popular and provocative preoccupations of the 1970s. Public administration will surely be implicated in the trends that are being projected in this futures movement.

To catalogue the prognostications that will affect public administration would be a large and risky task, but certain scenarios for the future are illustrative. For instance, in 1967, Kahn and Weiner predicted that 100 technical innovations were likely in the remaining years of the twentieth century. Many of these would have important impacts on public administration. These included: revolutionary new technologies in communication and transportation; automated recordkeeping and information retrieval; behavior modification; new and more effective "educational" and "propaganda" methods of persuasion; and new and more effective methods of control, investigation, and monitoring of individual citizens and organizations.[2]

In 1969, in an address at the Federal Executive Institute, in Charlottesville, Virginia, Elmer B. Staats, comptroller general of the United States, sketched the portrait of public administration in the year 2000. His predictions included the following: virtually all Americans would be covered by Social Security and Medicare; citizen demands on government for services will be much greater; there will be even greater reliance on the national government for financial support, planning, and administrative leadership; the distinction between public and private sectors of society will be more blurred, as will be the line between public administration and private participation; and there will be more freedom for executives to move between governmental and nongovernmental positions.[3]

In 1973, Dwight Waldo edited a symposium in the *Public Administration Review* on "Organizations for the Future." Following are some of the prophecies that were offered: there will be greater diversity of interests and participants in public decision making of the future; very large public organizations will continue to grow in size, complexity, and influence, and sweep into their vortex other satellite organizations; popular complaints and disenchantment with large-scale government will continue; leaders in public administration will more consciously and systematically try to improve their intellectual and skill competencies, so as better to achieve their personal and organizational purposes; there will be a growth of a "third sector," between government and business, which will include such organizations and institutions as the American Red Cross, the League of Women Voters, the Ford Foundation and other nonprofit corporations, and the United States Postal Service; and greater speed and skill will be developed by governments in mobilizing and deploying administrative resources and powers to cope with unexpected and far-flung situations.[4]

The efforts of the National Academy of Public Administration, in 1971, to promote the professionalization of public administration included research on trends in public administration that were likely to prevail during the 1970's. Their findings suggested the following possibilities: hierarchical authority, based on official position, could be expected to decline; routine public employees would attain higher levels of education; public employees could be expected to enjoy greater power and influence in their relations with their supervisors; unionization would increase among public employees, and this could be expected to encourage more and better consultation between these employees and the heads of public agencies; public administration generally could be expected to experience stronger political pressures; there would be more detailed and intense legislative interest in and overseeing of public administration; and there would be greater breadth, complexity, and interdependence of public policies.[5]

Similarly, in a Delphi conducted in 1972 by Emanual Wald at Syracuse University, as part of a doctoral dissertation in public administration, the following trends were found to be expected to characterize the study of public administration from 1973 to about 1990:

1. A "softened" normatism, with greater balance between value preferences and theory building
2. Fluctuating boundaries, with movement toward greater interdisciplinary orientation in public administration and the study of public administration as part of the general field of management science

3. Movement toward social technology, with less emphasis on strict discipline-building in public administration and more emphasis on public administration as an applied field
4. Greater emphasis on the making and analysis of public policy, as an important part of the field of public administration
5. Abandonment of the traditional POSDCORB categories of dividing the work of public administration, with development of new and more complex specializations[6]

Perils and Pitfalls in the Future of Public Administration

Futurists may very well be improving their powers of innovation and prediction, and the futures movement might be strengthening the rationality of future-building, but there are serious perils and pitfalls lying ahead for a responsible and democratic public administration. For instance, in 1965 Robert Boguslaw, characterizing systems analysts and other future-oriented "econologicians" as "the new utopians," warned that democracy can be subverted or eroded not only by political despotism, but also by "technical obfuscation." Similarly, in 1969, Victor A. Thompson warned against the power implicit in allowing management scientists to dictate value choices. In 1972, Ida R. Hoos warned against "the self-fulfilling prophetic propensities" of systems analysis and its contribution to futurology. There can be no denying that the trends at work in public administration do challenge some of the democratic and humanist principles of American government.[7]

Public administration, based on the enormously powerful attraction of efficiency as an underlying principle, strengthened by sophisticated technology, buffered from effective citizen intervention, and legitimized by the argument that these future trends are all part of the "wave of the future," can help to convert the American dream into a national nightmare. Watergate, and the charges and allegations involving the CIA, the FBI, and other public agencies, suggest that expressions of alarm are not merely academic mouthings. The nightmare of a highly efficient but amoral system of public administration can be avoided if public administration's love affair with efficiency and productivity can be moderated by greater sensitivity to humane values. What is needed, perhaps, is more of what William G. Scott and David K. Hart have called "metaphysical speculation" — a conception of the "good life" and how public administration can contribute to it.[8]

NOTES

1. Arthur C. Clarke, *Profiles of the Future: An Inquiry into the Limits of the Possible* (New York: Bantam, 1963); Daniel Bell and others, *Toward the Year 2000: Work in Progress, Daedalus*, special issue 96 (Summer 1967): 639–1002; Mark R. Hillegas, *The Future as Nightmare: H.G. Wells and the Anti-Utopians* (New York: Oxford University Press, 1967); Bertrand de Jouvenal, *The Art of Conjecture* (New York: Basic Books, 1967); Herman Kahn and Anthony J. Wiener, *The Year 2000: A Framework for Speculation on the Next Thirty-Three Years* (New York: Macmillan, 1967); Donald N. Michael, ed., *The Future Society* (Chicago: Aldine, 1970); Harvey S. Perloff, ed., *The Future of the U.S. Government: Toward the Year 2000* (New York: Braziller, 1971); Robert Theobald and

J.M. Scott, *TEG's 1994* (Chicago: Swallow, 1972); Alvin Toffler, *Future Shock* (New York: Bantam, 1970); and Marvin E. Wolfgang, "The Future Society: Aspects of America in the Year 2000,'" *The Annals of the American Academy of Political Science* 408 (July 1973): 1–102.

2. Herman Kahn and Anthony J. Wiener, "The Next Thirty-Three Years: A Framework for Speculation," in Bell, *Toward the Year 2000,* pp. 711–16.

3. Elmer B. Staats, "Manager of Tomorrow," *Civil Service Journal* 10 (January–March 1970): 4–6.

4. Dwight Waldo, editor, "Organizations for the Future," Symposium, *Public Administration Review* 33, no. 4 (July–August 1973): 299–335.

5. Richard L. Chapman and Frederic N. Cleaveland, "The Changing Character of the Public Service and the Administrator of the 1980's," *Public Administration Review* 33, no. 4 (July–August 1973): 358–66. See also, Chapman and Cleaveland, eds., *Meeting the Needs of Tomorrow's Public Service: Guidelines for Professional Education in Public Administration* (Washington, D.C.: National Academy of Public Administration, 1972), pp. 235–47.

6. Emanuel Wald, "Toward a Paradigm of Future Public Administration," *Public Administration Review* 33, no. 4 (July–August 1973): 366–72.

7. Robert Boguslaw, *The New Utopians: A Study of System Design and Social Change* (Englewood Cliffs, N.J.: Prentice-Hall, 1965), pp. 187–204; Victor A. Thompson, *Bureaucracy and Innovation* (University: University of Alabama Press, 1969), pp. 52–60; Ida R. Hoos, *Systems Analysis in Public Policy* (Berkeley: University of California Press, 1972), pp. 235–47.

8. William G. Scott and David K. Hart, "Administrative Crisis: The Neglect of Metaphysical Speculation," *Public Administration Review* 33, no. 5 (September–October 1973): 415–22.

BIBLIOGRAPHY

The literature of public administration is plentiful and diverse. Following is a small sample of books that are informative, insightful, and provocative. Students whose interest and curiosity may have been whetted by this book are invited to explore some of these:

Altshuler, Alan A., ed. *Politics of the Federal Bureaucracy.* New York: Dodd, Mead, 1968.

Banovetz, James M. *Managing the Modern City.* Washington, D.C.: The International City Management Association, 1971.

Barnard, Chester I. *The Functions of the Executive.* Cambridge, Mass.: Harvard University Press, 1968.

Bell, Gerald D., ed. *Organization and Human Behavior.* Englewood Cliffs, N.J.: Prentice-Hall, 1967.

Bennis, Warren. *Beyond Bureaucracy: Essays on the Development and Evolution of Human Organizations.* New York: McGraw-Hill, 1973.

Bennis, Warren G., and Philip E. Slater. *The Temporary Society.* New York: Harper & Row, 1968.

Benton, John B. *Managing the Organizational Decision Process.* Lexington, Mass.: D. C. Heath, 1973.

Blau, Peter M. *Bureaucracy in Modern Society.* New York: Random House, 1956.

———. *The Dynamics of Bureaucracy.* Rev. ed. Chicago: University of Chicago Press, 1962.

Blau, Peter M., and Richard W. Scott. *Formal Organizations.* San Francisco: Chandler, 1962.

Blechman, Barry M., Edward M. Gramlich, and R. Bert W. Hartman. *Setting National Priorities: The 1976 Budget.* Washington, D.C.: The Brookings Institution, 1975.

Blindner, Alan S., and Robert M. Solow, George F. Break, Peter O. Steiner, and Dick Netzer. *The Economics of Public Finance.* Washington, D.C.: The Brookings Institution, 1974.

Bocchino, William A. *Management Information Systems: Tools and Techniques.* Englewood Cliffs, N.J.: Prentice-Hall, 1972.

Brewer, Garry D. *Politicians, Bureaucrats, and the Consultant: A Critique of Urban Problem Solving.* New York: Basic Books, 1973.

Burns, Tom, and G. M. Stalker. *The Management of Innovation.* London: Tavistock Publications Ltd., 1961.

Caiden, Gerald. *The Dynamics of Public Administration: Guidelines to Current Transformations in Theory and Practice.* New York: Holt, Rinehart & Winston, 1971.

Chapman, Brian. *The Profession of Government.* London: George Allen & Unwin, Ltd., 1959.

Chapman, Richard L., and Frederick N. Cleaveland. *Meeting the Needs of Tomorrow's Public Service: Guidelines for Professional Education in Public Administration.* Washington, D.C.: National Academy of Public Administration, 1973.

Charlesworth, James C., ed. *Theory and Practice of Public Administration: Scope, Objectives, and Methods,* Monograph 8. Philadelphia: American Academy of Political and Social Science, 1968.

Churchman, C. West. *Challenge to Reason.* New York: McGraw-Hill, 1968.

Clark, Terry N., ed. *Community Structure and Decision-Making: Comparative Analysis.* San Francisco: Chandler, 1968.

Cleveland, Harlan. *The Future Executive: A Guide for Tomorrow's Managers.* New York: Harper & Row, 1972.

Cyert, Richard M., and James G. March. *A Behavioral Theory of the Firm.* Englewood Cliffs, N.J.: Prentice-Hall, 1963.

Davis, Kenneth Culp. *Administrative Law: Cases, Text Problems.* 5th ed. St. Paul, Minn.: West Publishing Co., 1973.

————. *Discretionary Justice*. Baton Rouge: Louisiana State University Press, 1969.

Derthick, Martha, with assistance of Garry Bumbardier. *Between State and Nation: Regional Organizations of the United States*. Washington, D.C.: The Brookings Institution, 1974.

Donahue, Mary, and James L. Spates. *Action Research Handbook for Social Change in Urban America*. New York: Harper & Row, 1972.

Downs, Anthony. *Inside Bureaucracy*. Boston: Little, Brown, 1967.

Dror, Yehezkel. *Public Policymaking Reexamined*. San Francisco: Chandler, 1968.

Dunsire, A. *Administration: The Word and the Science*. New York: John Wiley, 1973.

Dvorin, Eugene, and Robert H. Simmons. *From Amoral to Humane Bureaucracy*. San Francisco: Canfield Press, 1972.

Dye, Thomas R. *Understanding Public Policy*. 2d ed. Englewood Cliffs, N.J.: Prentice-Hall, 1975.

Eimicke, William B. *Public Administration in a Democratic Context: Theory and Practice*. Beverly Hills, Calif.: Sage Publications, 1974.

Elazar, Daniel J. *American Federalism: A View from the States*. New York: Crowell, 1966.

Ermer, Virginia B., and John H. Strange. *Blacks and Bureaucracy: Readings in the Problems and Politics of Change*. New York: Crowell, 1972.

Etzioni, Amitai. *Modern Organization*. Englewood Cliffs, N.J.: Prentice-Hall, 1964.

Feld, Richard D., and Carl Grafton, eds. *The Uneasy Partnership: The Dynamics of Federal, State and Urban Relations*. Palo Alto: National Press Books, 1973.

Fowler, Floyd J., Jr. *Citizen Attitudes Toward Local Government, Services, and Taxes*. Cambridge, Mass.: Ballinger, 1974.

Gawthrop, Louis C. *Administrative Politics and Social Change*. New York: St. Martin's Press, 1971.

————. *The Administrative Process and Democratic Theory*. Boston: Houghton Mifflin, 1970.

————. *Bureaucratic Behavior in the Executive Branch, An Analysis of Organizational Change*. New York: Free Press, 1969.

Gellhorn, Walter. *When Americans Complain, Governmental Grievance Procedures*. Cambridge, Mass.: Harvard University Press, 1966.

Gellhorn, Walter, and Clark Byse. *Administrative Law: Cases and Comments*. 6th ed. Mineola, N.Y.: Foundation Press, 1974.

Gilroy, Thomas P., and Anthony V. Sincrop. *Dispute Settlement in the Public Sector: The State of the Art*. Washington, D.C.: Government Printing Office, 1972.

Gladden, E.N. *A History of Public Administration* (Vol. 1, From the Earliest Times to the Eleventh Century; Vol. II, From the Eleventh Century to the Present Day). London: Frank Cass, 1972.

Golembiewski, Robert. *Men, Management and Morality: Toward a New Organizational Ethic*. New York: McGraw-Hill, 1965.

Golembiewski, Robert T., and Michael Cohen, eds. *People in Public Service: A Reader in Public Personnel Administration*. Itasca, Ill.: Peacock, 1970.

Golembiewski, Robert T., and Michael White, eds. *Cases in Public Management*. Chicago: Rand McNally, 1973.

Goodall, Leonard E., and Donald P. Sprengel. *The American Metropolis*. 2nd ed. Columbus, Ohio: Charles E. Merrill, 1975.

Gore, William J. *Administrative Decision-Making: A Heuristic Model*. New York: John Wiley, 1964.

Gross, Bertram M. *Organizations and Their Managing*. New York: Free Press, 1964.

Heady, Ferrell. *Public Administration: A Comparative Perspective*. Englewood Cliffs, N.J.: Prentice-Hall, 1966.

Henry, Nicholas. *Public Administration and Public Affairs*. Englewood Cliffs, N.J.: Prentice-Hall, 1975.

Henry, William V. *Communication and Organizational Behavior: Text and Cases*. Homewood, Ill.: Richard D. Irwin, 1972.

Hoos, Ida R. *Systems Analysis in Public Policy, A Critique*. Berkeley: University of California Press, 1972.

Kaufman, Herbert. *Administrative Feedback: Monitoring Subordinates' Behavior*. Washington, D.C.: The Brookings Institution, 1973.

———. *Evolution of Federal Agencies*. Washington, D.C.: The Brookings Institution, forthcoming.

Kotler, Milton. *Neighborhood Government: The Local Foundations of Political Life*. Indianapolis, Ind.: Bobbs-Merrill, 1969.

Kramer, Fred A., ed. *Perspectives on Public Bureaucracy*. Cambridge, Mass.: Winthrop Publishers, 1973.

Krislov, Samuel. *Representative Bureaucracy*. Englewood Cliffs, N.J.: Prentice-Hall, 1974.

Lassey, William R., ed. *Leadership and Social Change*. Iowa City, Ia.: University Associates Press, 1971.

Lee, Robert D., Jr., and Ronald W. Johnson. *Public Budgeting System*. Baltimore: University Park Press, 1973.

Lewis, Eugene. *The Urban Political System*. Hinsdale, Ill.: The Dryden Press, 1973.

Lindbloom, Charles E. *The Policy-Making Process*. Englewood Cliffs, N.J.: Prentice-Hall, 1968.

McCurdy, Howard E. *Public Administration: A Bibliography*. Washington, D.C.: American University, 1972.

McGregor, Douglas. *The Human Side of Enterprise*. New York: McGraw-Hill, 1960.

Mailick, Sidney, and Edward H. Van Ness, eds. *Concepts and Issues in Administrative Behavior*. Englewood Cliffs, N.J.: Prentice-Hall, 1962.

Mainzer, Lewis C. *Political Bureaucracy*. Glenview, Ill.: Scott, Foresman, 1973.

March, James G., ed. *Handbook of Organizations*. Chicago: Rand McNally, 1965.

March, James G., and Herbert A. Simon. *Organizations*. New York: John Wiley, 1958.

Marini, Frank, ed. *Toward a New Public Administration: The Minnowbrook Perspective*. Scranton, Pa.: Chandler, 1971.

Millett, John D. *Organization for the Public Service*. New York: D. Van Nostrand, 1966.

Mosher, Frederick C. *Democracy and the Public Service*. New York: Oxford University Press, 1968.

Mosher, Frederick C., and others. *Watergate: Implications for Responsible Government*. New York: Basic Books, 1974.

Mouzelis, Nicos P. *Organisation and Bureaucracy: An Analysis of Modern Theories*. Chicago: Aldine, 1969.

Murphy, Thomas P., and Charles R. Warren. *Organizing Public Services in Metropolitan America*. Lexington, Mass.: Lexington Books, 1974.

Nathan, Richard P., Allen D. Manuel, Susannah E. Calkins, and Associates. *Monitoring Revenue Sharing*. Washington, D.C.: The Brookings Institution, 1975.

Neustadt, Richard. *Presidential Power: The Politics of Leadership*. New York: John Wiley, 1960.

Ostrom, Vincent. *The Intellectual Crisis in American Public Administration*. Rev. ed. University: University of Alabama Press, 1974.

Peabody, Robert L. *Organizational Authority*. New York: Atherton Press, 1964.

Perry, David C. *Police in the Metropolis*. Columbus, Ohio: Charles E. Merrill, 1975.

Peter, Lawrence J., and Raymond Hull. *The Peter Principle: Why Things Always Go Wrong*. New York: Bantam Books, 1969.

Pfiffner, John M., and Frank P. Sherwood. *Administrative Organization.* Englewood Cliffs, N.J.: Prentice-Hall, 1960.

Powers, Stanley P., F. Gerald Brown, and David S. Arnold. *Developing the Municipal Organization.* Washington, D.C.: International City Management Association, 1974.

Pressman, Jeffrey L., and Aaron Wildavsky. *Implementation.* Berkeley: University of California Press, 1974.

Presthus, Robert. *Behavioral Approaches to Public Administration.* University: University of Alabama Press, 1965.

Reagan, Michael D. *The New Federalism.* New York: Oxford University Press, 1972.

Redford, Emmette S. *Democracy in the Administrative State.* New York: Oxford University Press, 1969.

Riggs, Fred W. *Administration in Developing Countries: The Theory of Prismatic Society.* Boston: Houghton Mifflin, 1964.

———. *The Ecology of Public Administration.* New York: Asia Publishing House, 1961.

Rothman, Jack. *Planning and Organizing for Social Change, Action Principles From Social Science Research.* New York: Columbia University Press, 1974.

Rourke, Francis E. *Bureaucracy, Politics, and Public Policy.* Boston: Little, Brown, 1969.

Sayles, Leonard R., and Margaret K. Chandler. *Managing Large Systems, Organizations for the Future.* New York: Harper & Row, 1971.

Seidman, Harold. *Politics, Position, and Power.* 2d ed. New York: Oxford University Press, 1975.

Sharkansky, Ira, ed. *Policy Analysis in Political Science.* Chicago: Markham, 1970.

Simon, Herbert A. *Administrative Behavior.* New York: Crowell Collier & Macmillan, 1947.

———. *The New Science of Management Decision.* New York: Harper & Row, 1960.

Sofer, Cyril. *Organization in Theory and Practice.* New York: Basic Books, 1972.

Stanley, David T. *Managing Local Government Under Union Pressure.* Washington, D.C.: The Brookings Institution, 1972.

Stieber, Jack. *Public Employee Unionism, Structure, Growth, Policy.* Washington, D.C.: The Brookings Institution, 1973.

Stogdill, Ralph M. *Handbook of Leadership: A Survey of Theory and Research.* New York: Free Press, 1974.

Strouse, James C. *The Mass Media, Public Opinion, and Public Policy Analysis: Linkage Explorations.* Columbus, Ohio: Charles E. Merrill, 1975.

Sundquist, James L. *Making Federalism Work.* Washington, D.C.: The Brookings Institution, 1969.

Telch, Albert H., ed. *Technology and Man's Future.* New York: St. Martin's Press, 1972.

Van Riper, Paul T. *History of the United States Civil Service.* Evanston, Ill.: Row, Peterson, 1958.

Vickers, Geoffrey. *Making Institutions Work.* New York: John Wiley, 1973.

Vollmer, Howard M., and Donald L. Mills. *Professionalization.* Englewood Cliffs, N.J.: Prentice-Hall, 1966.

Waldo, Dwight. *Ideas and Issues in Public Administration.* New York: McGraw-Hill, 1953.

———. *Public Administration in a Time of Turbulence.* Scranton, Pa.: Chandler, 1971.

Wamsley, Gary L., and Mayer N. Zald. *The Poltical Economy of Public Organizations.* Lexington, Mass.: D.C. Heath, 1973.

Whyte, William H. *The Organization Man.* New York: Simon & Schuster, 1956.

Wildavsky, Aaron. *The Politics of the Budgetary Process.* Boston: Little, Brown, 1964.

Index